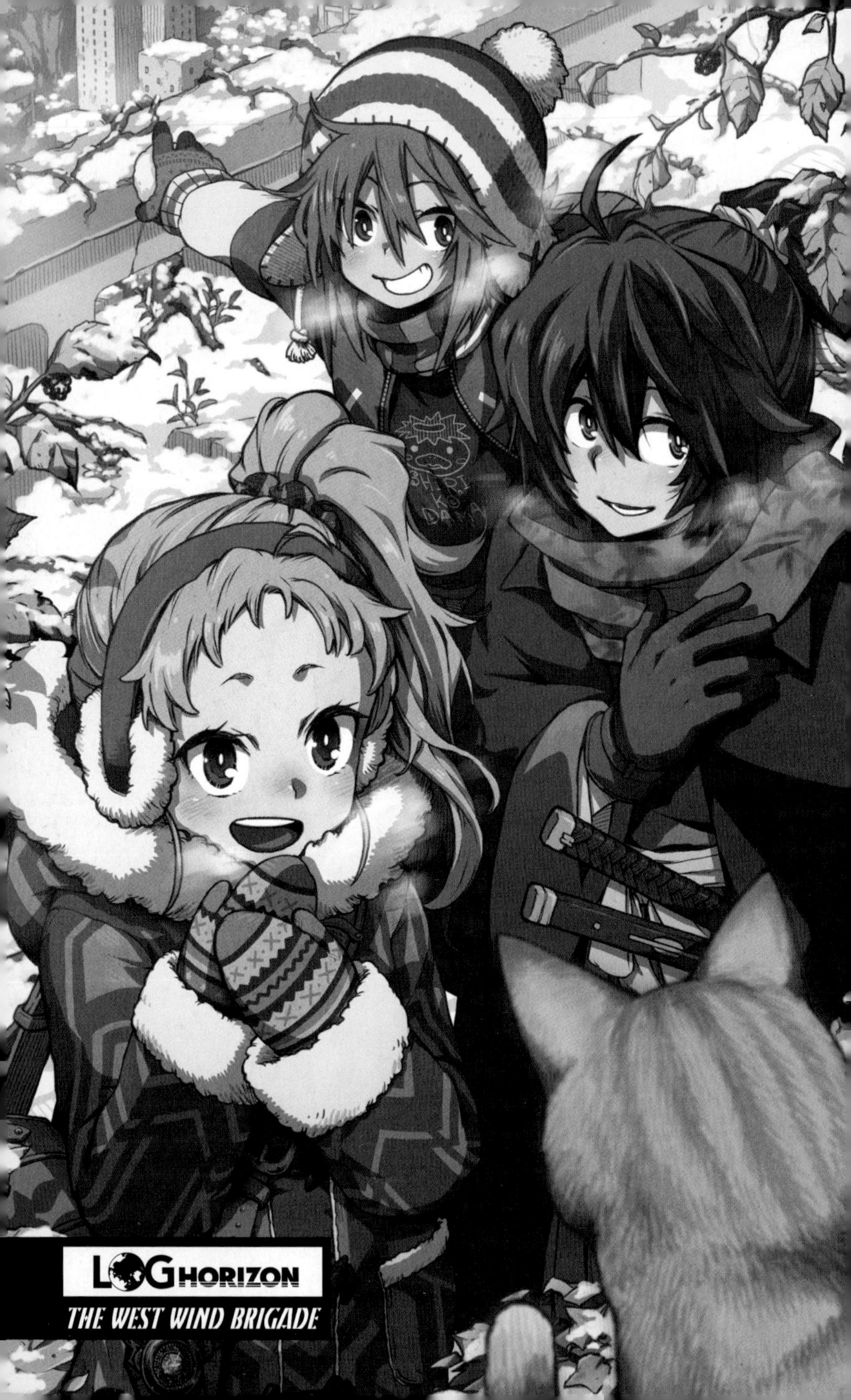
LOG HORIZON
THE WEST WIND BRIGADE

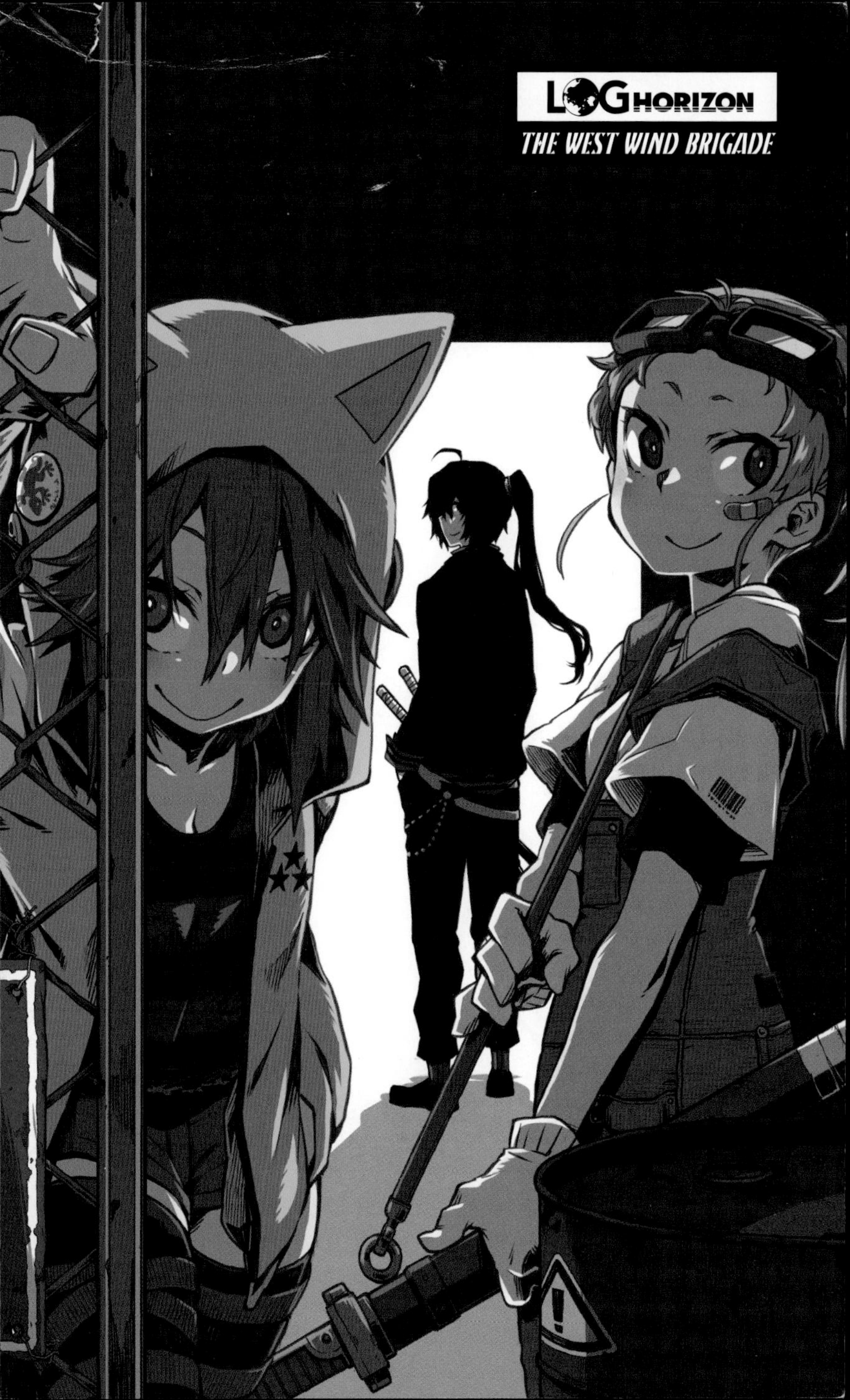
LOG HORIZON
THE WEST WIND BRIGADE

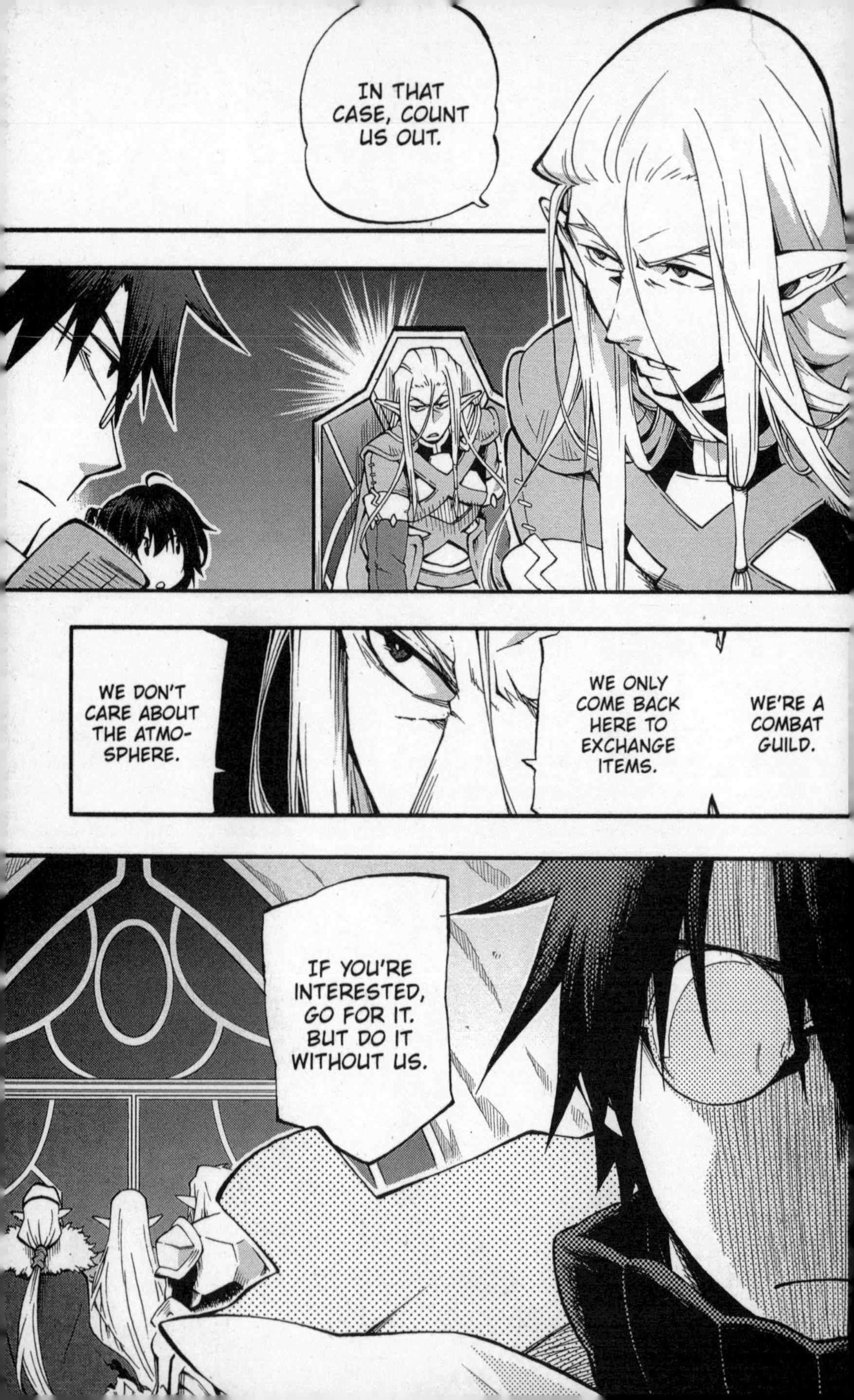
IN THAT CASE, COUNT US OUT.
WE'RE A COMBAT GUILD.
WE ONLY COME BACK HERE TO EXCHANGE ITEMS.
WE DON'T CARE ABOUT THE ATMO-SPHERE.
IF YOU'RE INTERESTED, GO FOR IT. BUT DO IT WITHOUT US.

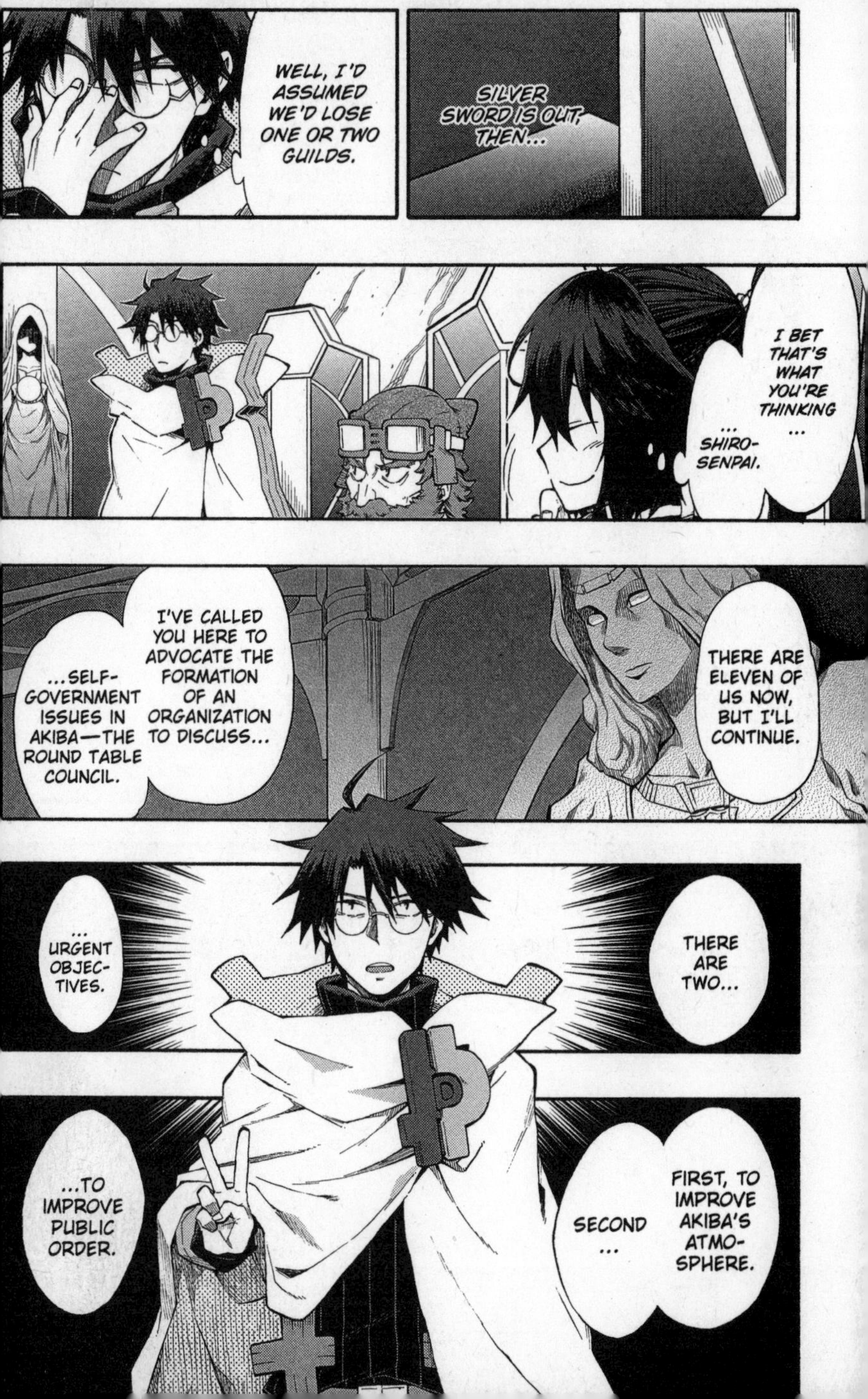
SILVER SWORD IS OUT, THEN...
WELL, I'D ASSUMED WE'D LOSE ONE OR TWO GUILDS.
I BET THAT'S WHAT YOU'RE THINKING ...
... SHIRO-SENPAI.
THERE ARE ELEVEN OF US NOW, BUT I'LL CONTINUE.
I'VE CALLED YOU HERE TO ADVOCATE THE FORMATION OF AN ORGANIZATION TO DISCUSS...
...SELF-GOVERNMENT ISSUES IN AKIBA—THE ROUND TABLE COUNCIL.
THERE ARE TWO...
... URGENT OBJECTIVES.
FIRST, TO IMPROVE AKIBA'S ATMOSPHERE.
SECOND ...
...TO IMPROVE PUBLIC ORDER.

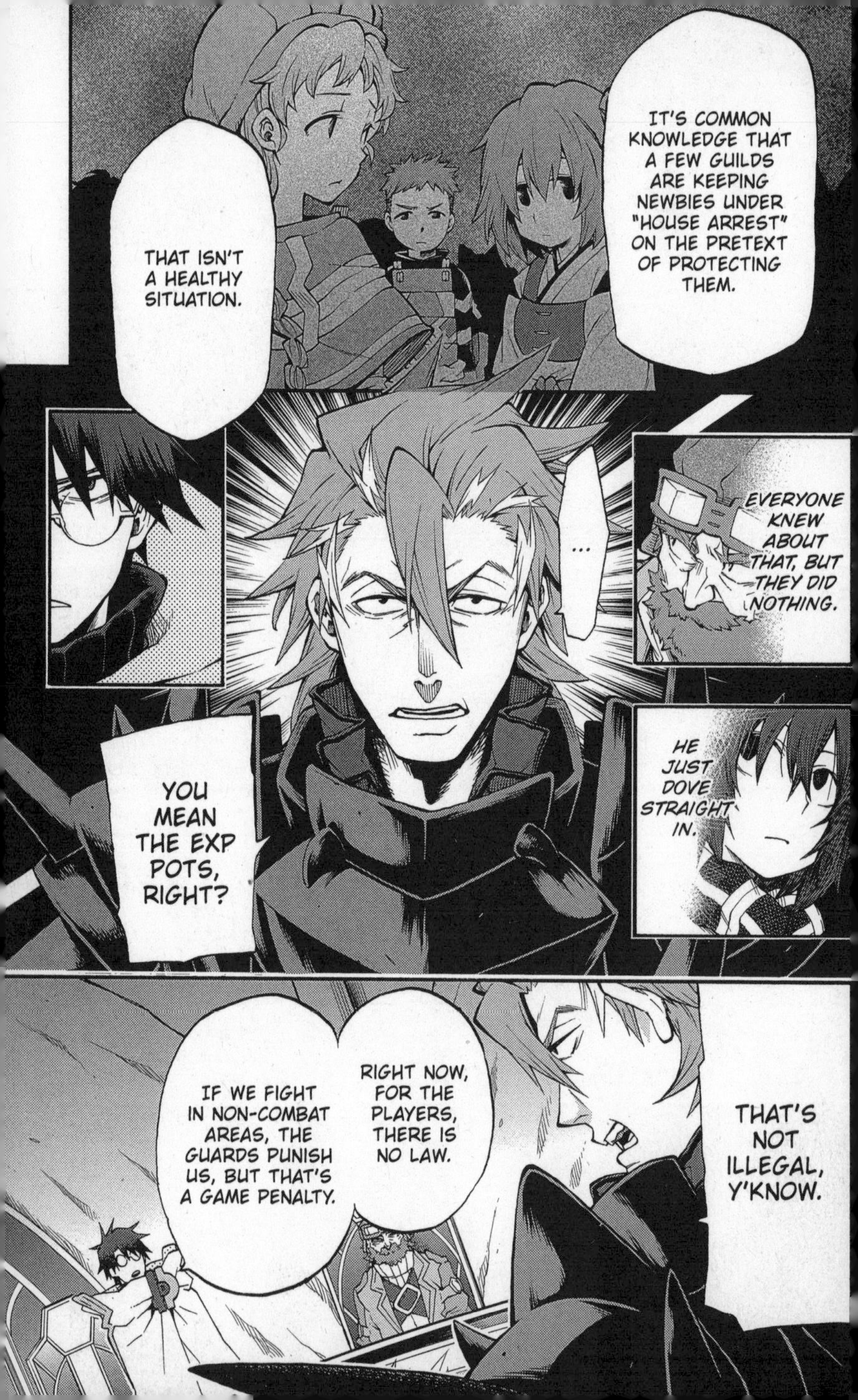
IT'S COMMON KNOWLEDGE THAT A FEW GUILDS ARE KEEPING NEWBIES UNDER "HOUSE ARREST" ON THE PRETEXT OF PROTECTING THEM.
THAT ISN'T A HEALTHY SITUATION.
EVERYONE KNEW ABOUT THAT, BUT THEY DID NOTHING.
HE JUST DOVE STRAIGHT IN.
...
YOU MEAN THE EXP POTS, RIGHT?
THAT'S NOT ILLEGAL, Y'KNOW.
RIGHT NOW, FOR THE PLAYERS, THERE IS NO LAW.
IF WE FIGHT IN NON-COMBAT AREAS, THE GUARDS PUNISH US, BUT THAT'S A GAME PENALTY.

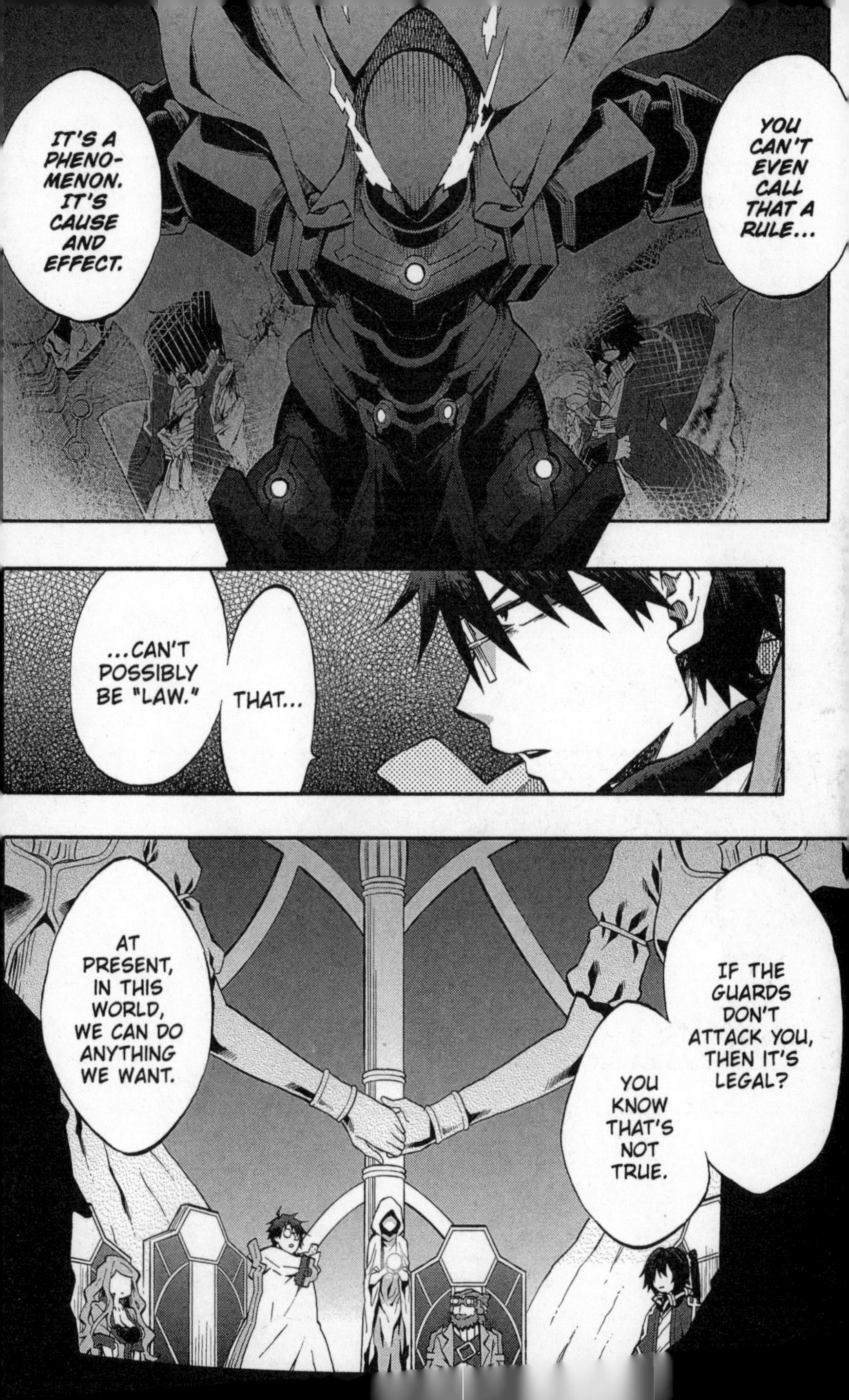
YOU CAN'T EVEN CALL THAT A RULE...
IT'S A PHENO-MENON. IT'S CAUSE AND EFFECT.
THAT...
...CAN'T POSSIBLY BE "LAW."
IF THE GUARDS DON'T ATTACK YOU, THEN IT'S LEGAL?
YOU KNOW THAT'S NOT TRUE.
AT PRESENT, IN THIS WORLD, WE CAN DO ANYTHING WE WANT.

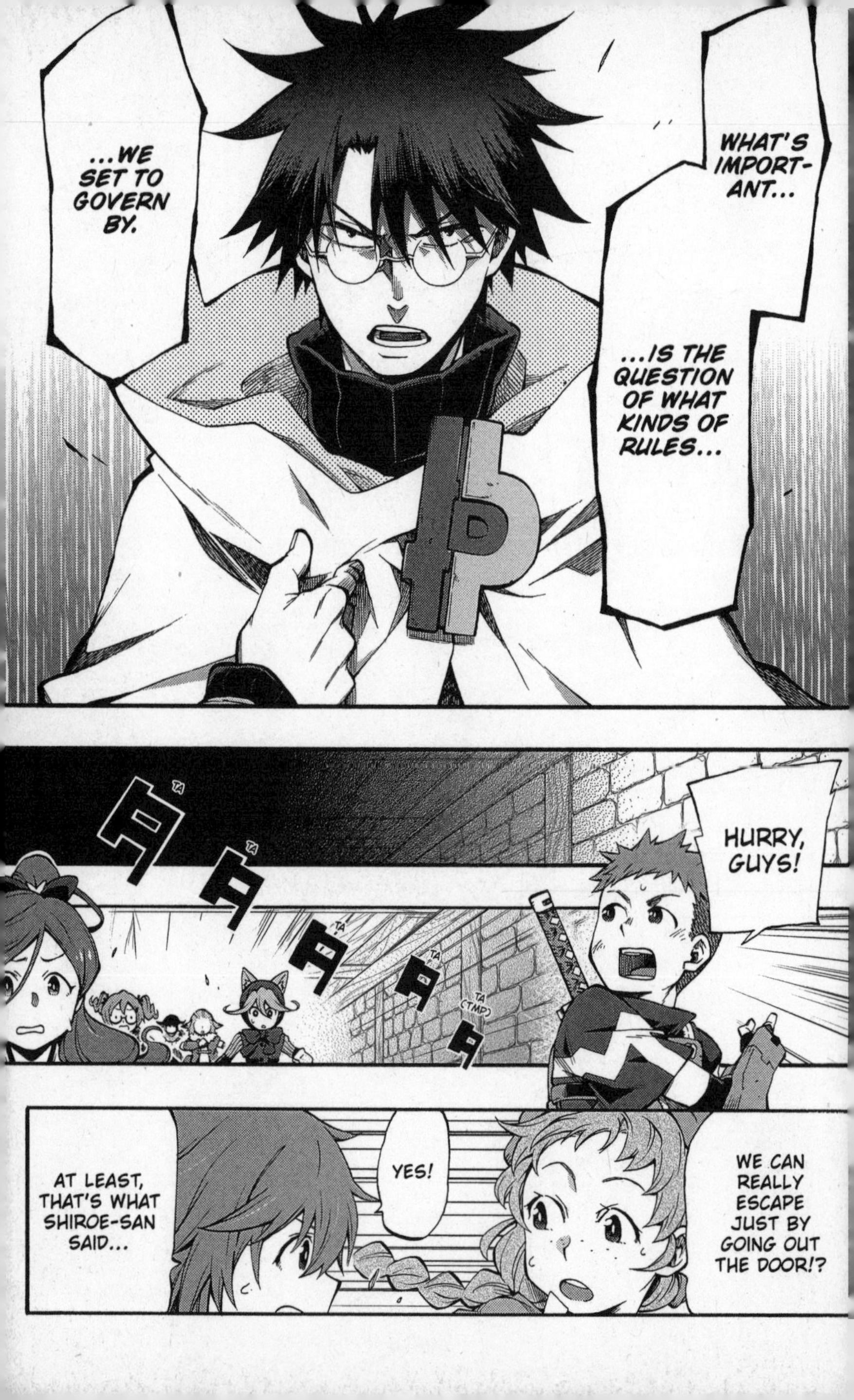
WHAT'S IMPORTANT...
...IS THE QUESTION OF WHAT KINDS OF RULES...
...WE SET TO GOVERN BY.
HURRY, GUYS!
TA (TMP)
TA
TA
TA
TA
WE CAN REALLY ESCAPE JUST BY GOING OUT THE DOOR!?
YES!
AT LEAST, THAT'S WHAT SHIROE-SAN SAID...

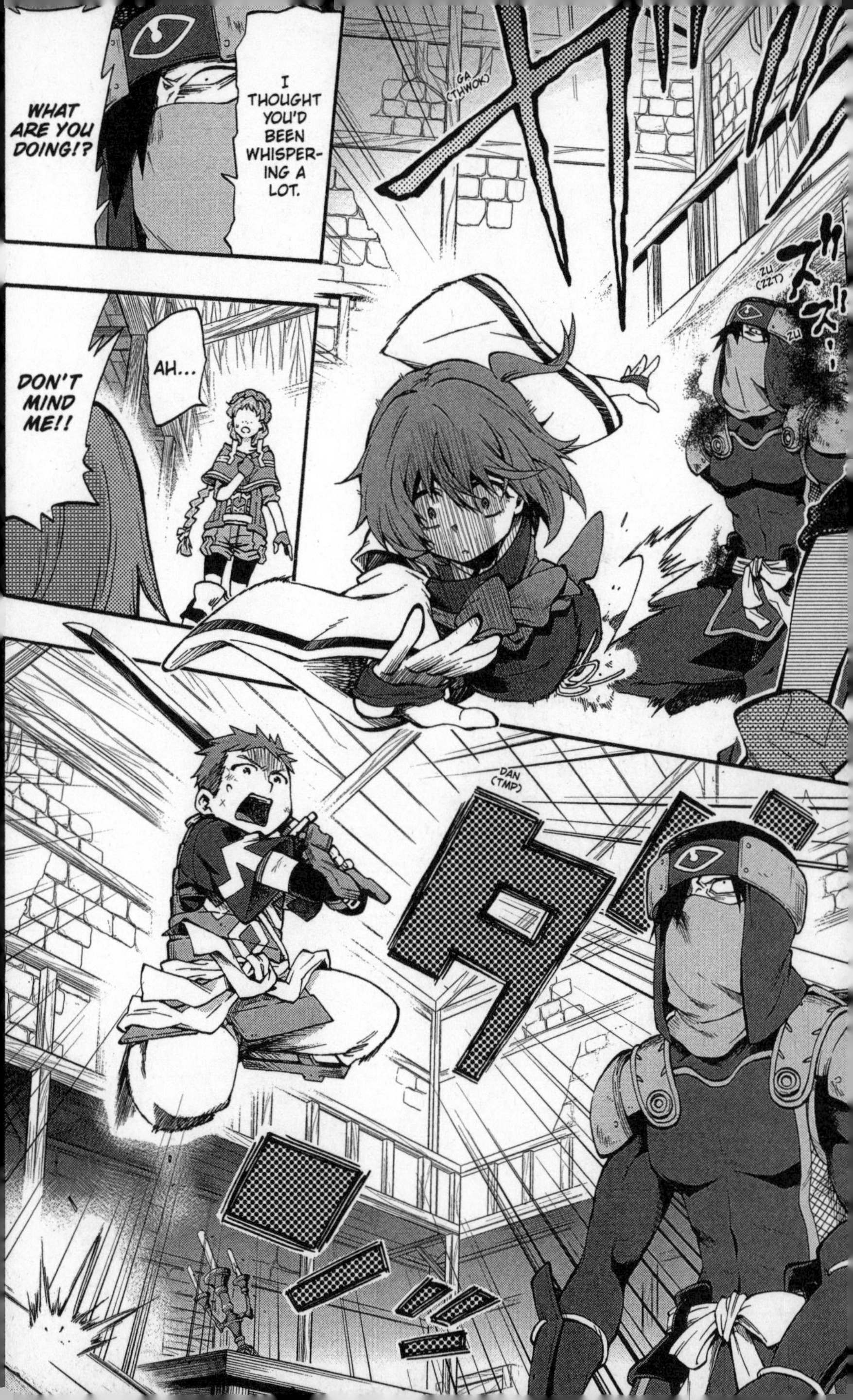
GA (THWOK)
ZU (ZZT)
ZU
I THOUGHT YOU'D BEEN WHISPER-ING A LOT.
WHAT ARE YOU DOING!?
AH...
DON'T MIND ME!!
DAN (TMP)

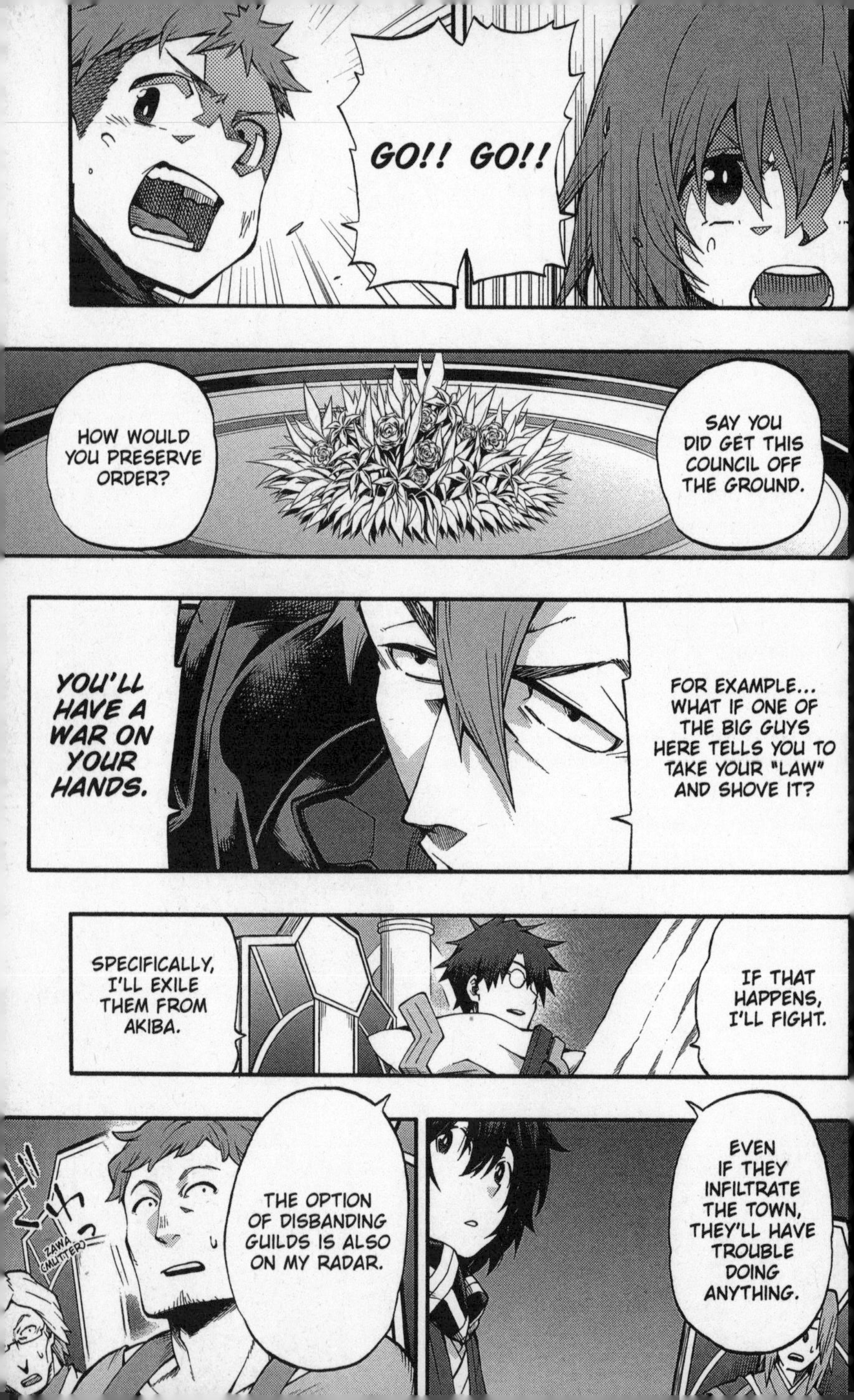
GO!! GO!!
SAY YOU DID GET THIS COUNCIL OFF THE GROUND.
HOW WOULD YOU PRESERVE ORDER?
FOR EXAMPLE... WHAT IF ONE OF THE BIG GUYS HERE TELLS YOU TO TAKE YOUR "LAW" AND SHOVE IT?
YOU'LL HAVE A WAR ON YOUR HANDS.
IF THAT HAPPENS, I'LL FIGHT.
SPECIFICALLY, I'LL EXILE THEM FROM AKIBA.
EVEN IF THEY INFILTRATE THE TOWN, THEY'LL HAVE TROUBLE DOING ANYTHING.
THE OPTION OF DISBANDING GUILDS IS ALSO ON MY RADAR.
ZAWA (MUTTER)

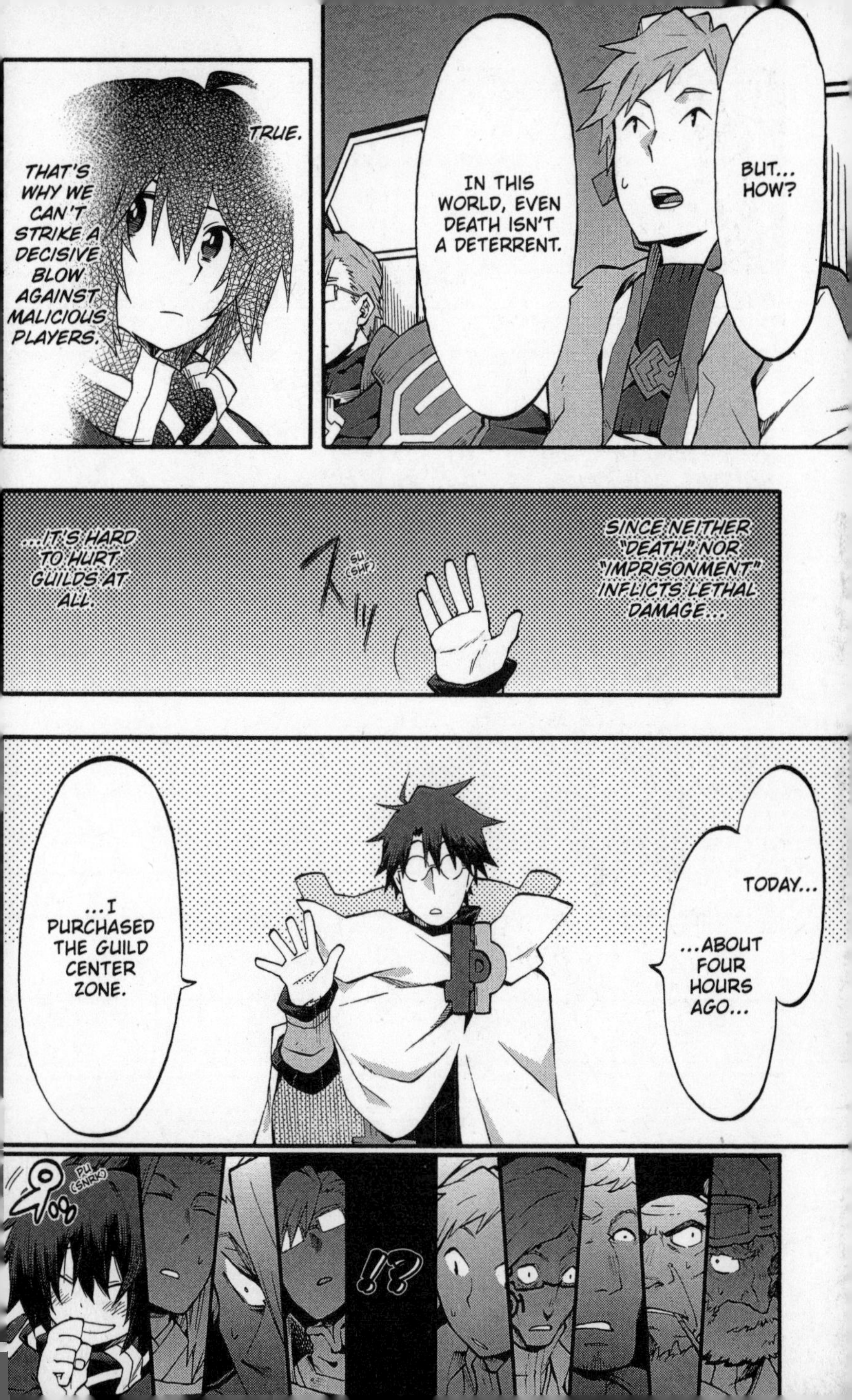
BUT... HOW?
IN THIS WORLD, EVEN DEATH ISN'T A DETERRENT.
TRUE.
THAT'S WHY WE CAN'T STRIKE A DECISIVE BLOW AGAINST MALICIOUS PLAYERS.
SINCE NEITHER "DEATH" NOR "IMPRISONMENT" INFLICTS LETHAL DAMAGE...
SU (SHF)
...IT'S HARD TO HURT GUILDS AT ALL.
TODAY...
...ABOUT FOUR HOURS AGO...
...I PURCHASED THE GUILD CENTER ZONE.
!?
PU (SNRK)

NOTE: SHIRO MEANS WHITE, KURO MEANS BLACK

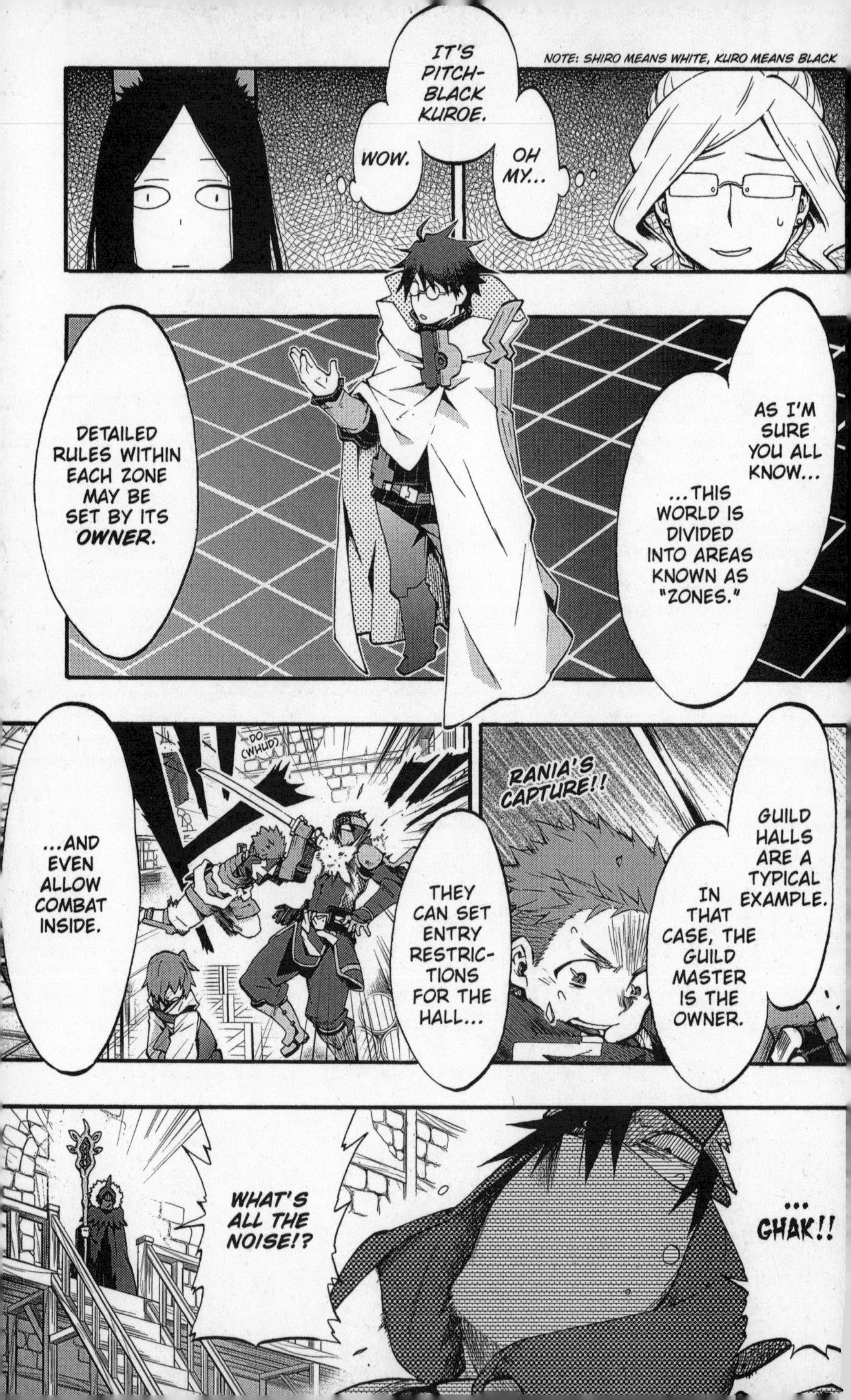
IT'S PITCH-BLACK KUROE.
OH MY...
WOW.
AS I'M SURE YOU ALL KNOW...
...THIS WORLD IS DIVIDED INTO AREAS KNOWN AS "ZONES."
DETAILED RULES WITHIN EACH ZONE MAY BE SET BY ITS OWNER.
GUILD HALLS ARE A TYPICAL EXAMPLE.
IN THAT CASE, THE GUILD MASTER IS THE OWNER.
RANIA'S CAPTURE!!
THEY CAN SET ENTRY RESTRICTIONS FOR THE HALL...
DO (WHUD)
...AND EVEN ALLOW COMBAT INSIDE.
...GHAK!!
WHAT'S ALL THE NOISE!?

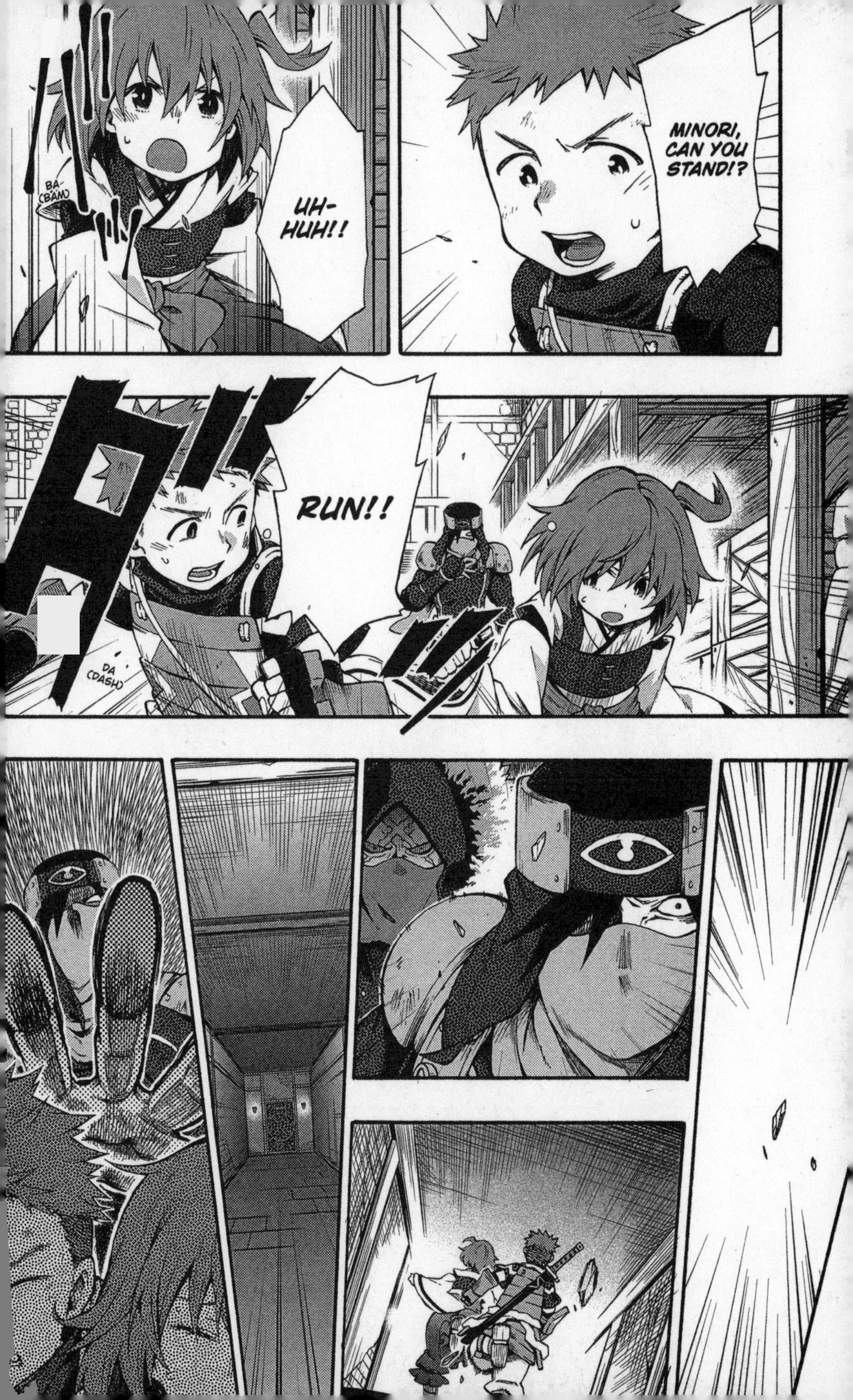
MINORI, CAN YOU STAND!?
UH-HUH!!
BA- (BAM)
RUN!!
DA (DASH)

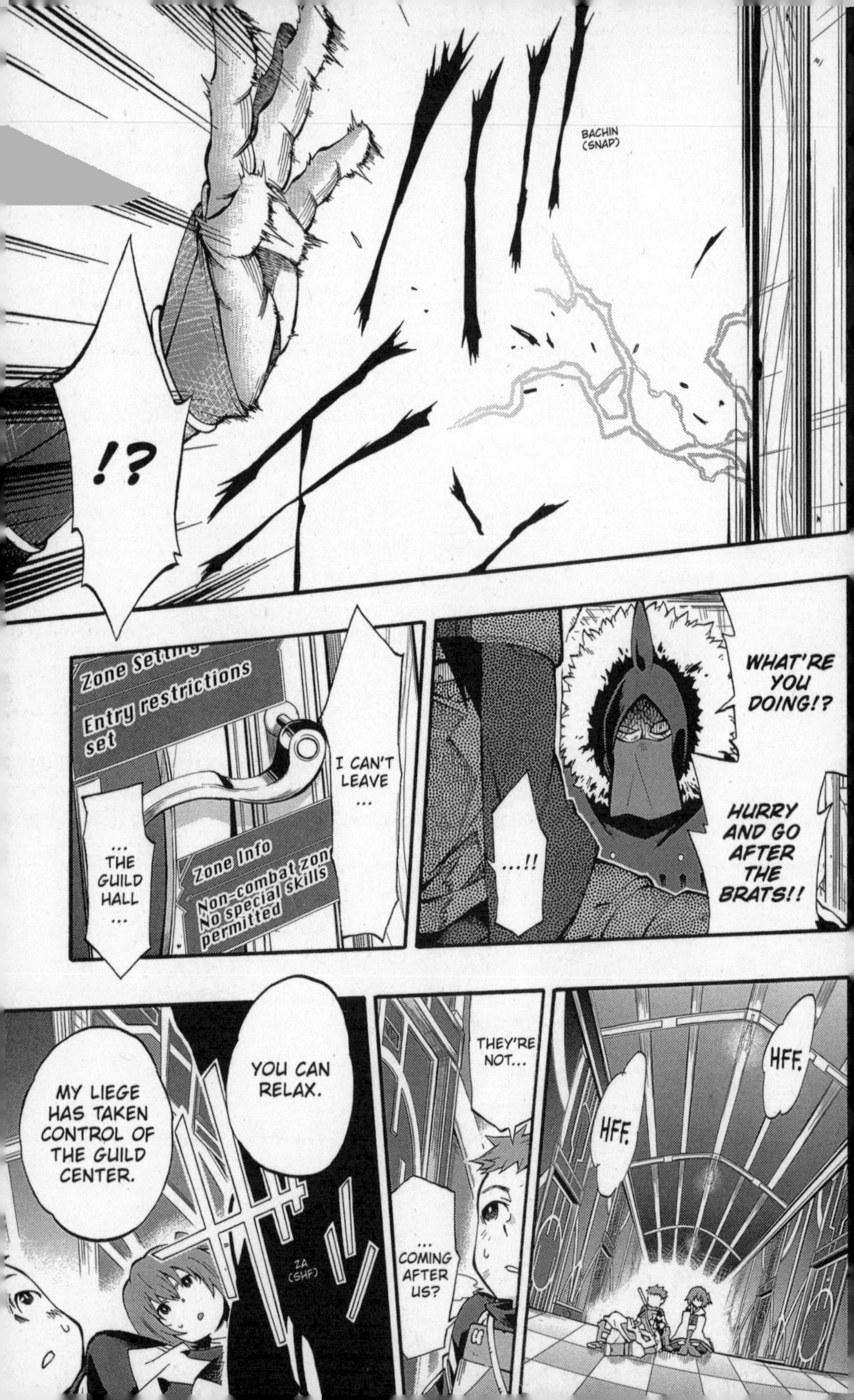
BACHIN (SNAP)
!?
WHAT'RE YOU DOING!?
HURRY AND GO AFTER THE BRATS!!
...!!
I CAN'T LEAVE ...
... THE GUILD HALL ...
Zone Setting
Entry restrictions set
Zone Info
Non-combat zon
No special skills permitted
HFF.
HFF.
THEY'RE NOT...
... COMING AFTER US?
YOU CAN RELAX.
MY LIEGE HAS TAKEN CONTROL OF THE GUILD CENTER.
ZA (SHF)

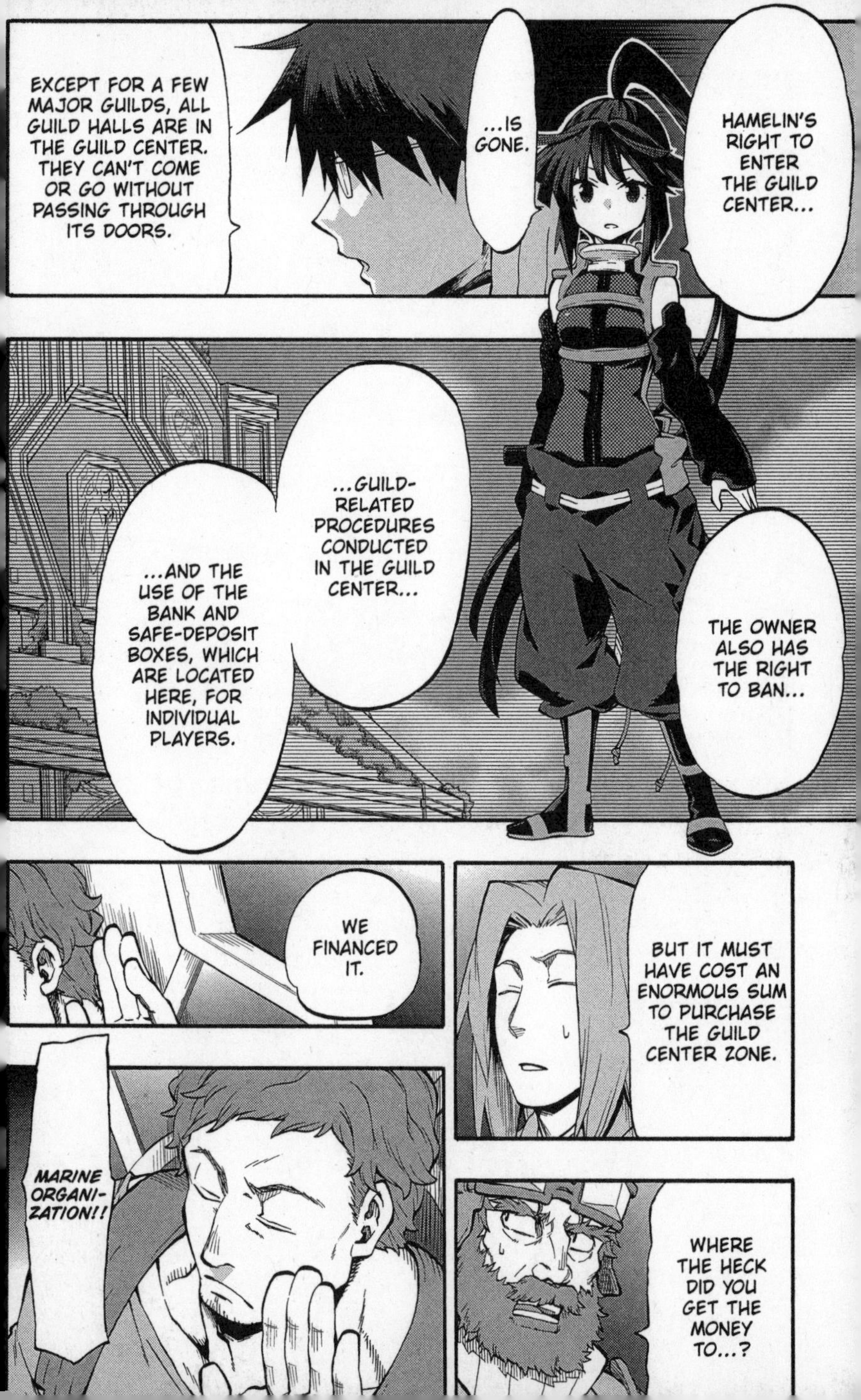
HAMELIN'S RIGHT TO ENTER THE GUILD CENTER...
...IS GONE.
EXCEPT FOR A FEW MAJOR GUILDS, ALL GUILD HALLS ARE IN THE GUILD CENTER. THEY CAN'T COME OR GO WITHOUT PASSING THROUGH ITS DOORS.
THE OWNER ALSO HAS THE RIGHT TO BAN...
...GUILD-RELATED PROCEDURES CONDUCTED IN THE GUILD CENTER...
...AND THE USE OF THE BANK AND SAFE-DEPOSIT BOXES, WHICH ARE LOCATED HERE, FOR INDIVIDUAL PLAYERS.
BUT IT MUST HAVE COST AN ENORMOUS SUM TO PURCHASE THE GUILD CENTER ZONE.
WE FINANCED IT.
WHERE THE HECK DID YOU GET THE MONEY TO...?
MARINE ORGANI-ZATION!!

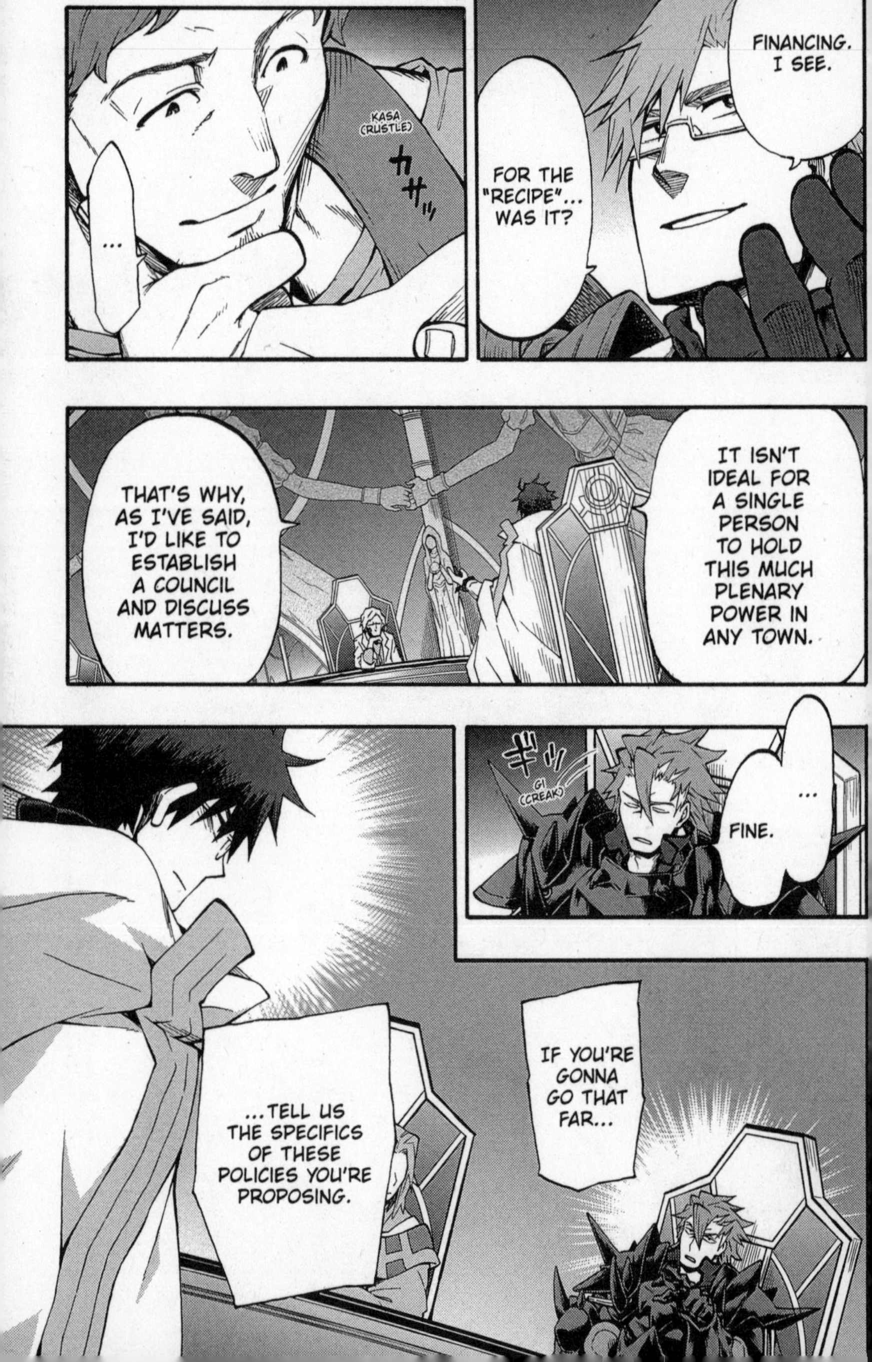
FINANCING. I SEE.
FOR THE "RECIPE"... WAS IT?
KASA (RUSTLE)
カサッ
...
IT ISN'T IDEAL FOR A SINGLE PERSON TO HOLD THIS MUCH PLENARY POWER IN ANY TOWN.
THAT'S WHY, AS I'VE SAID, I'D LIKE TO ESTABLISH A COUNCIL AND DISCUSS MATTERS.
ギッ
GI (CREAK)
... FINE.
IF YOU'RE GONNA GO THAT FAR...
...TELL US THE SPECIFICS OF THESE POLICIES YOU'RE PROPOSING.

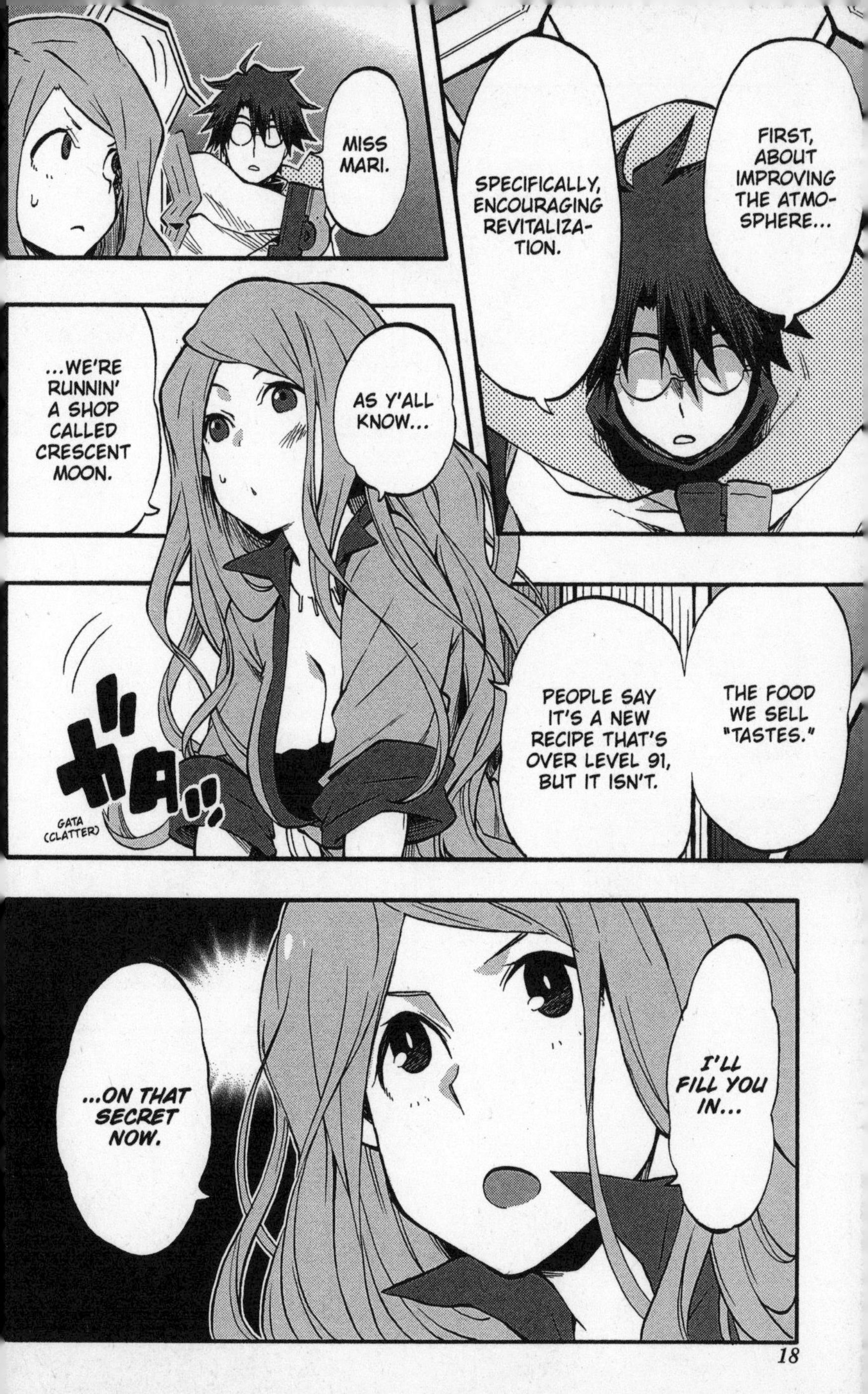
FIRST, ABOUT IMPROVING THE ATMOSPHERE...
SPECIFICALLY, ENCOURAGING REVITALIZATION.
MISS MARI.
AS Y'ALL KNOW...
...WE'RE RUNNIN' A SHOP CALLED CRESCENT MOON.
THE FOOD WE SELL "TASTES."
PEOPLE SAY IT'S A NEW RECIPE THAT'S OVER LEVEL 91, BUT IT ISN'T.
ガタッ
GATA (CLATTER)
I'LL FILL YOU IN...
...ON THAT SECRET NOW.

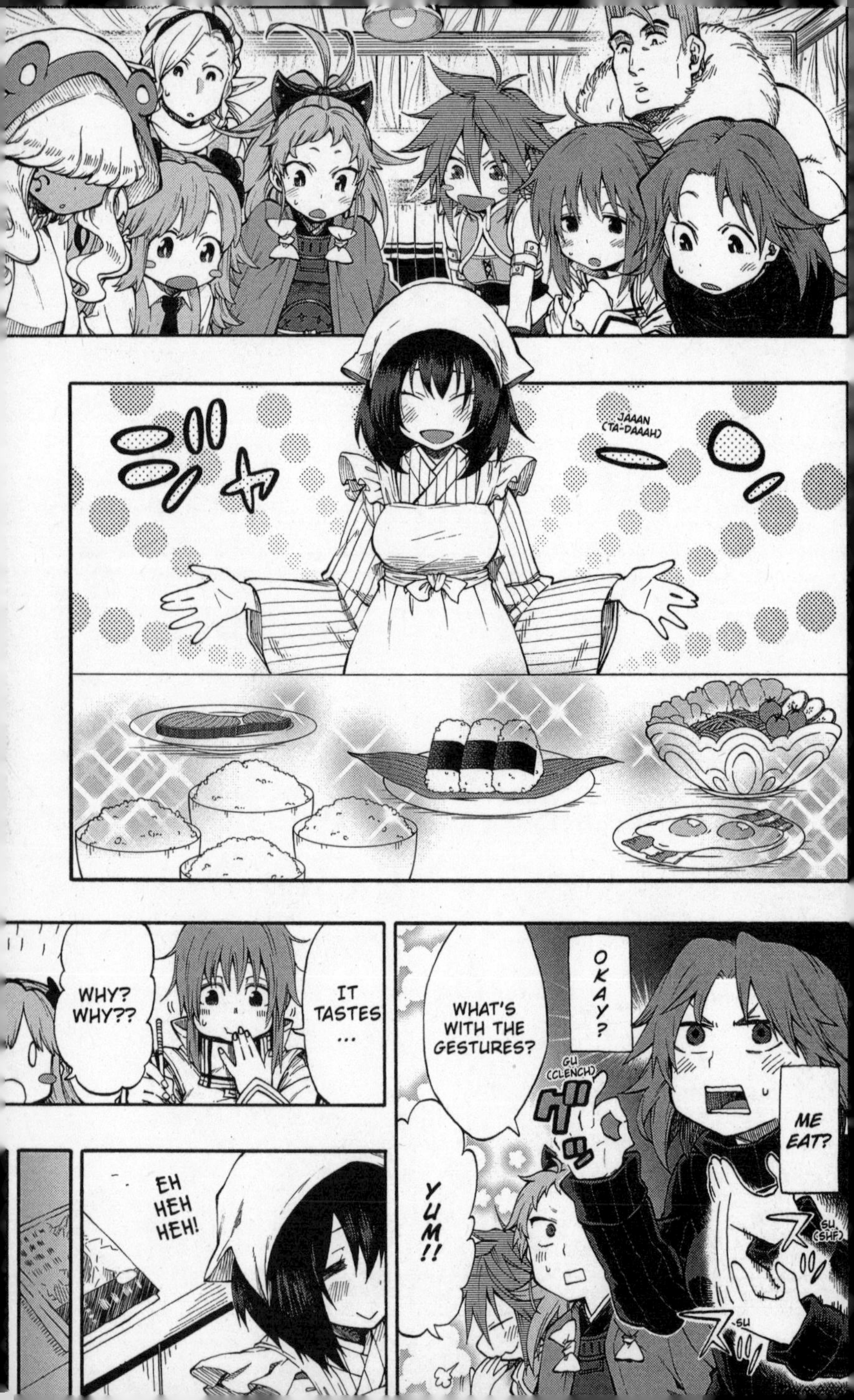
JAAAN
(TA-DAAAH)
ME EAT?
OKAY?
GU
(CLENCH)
WHAT'S WITH THE GESTURES?
SU
(SHF)
YUM!!
SU
IT TASTES...
WHY? WHY??
EH HEH HEH!

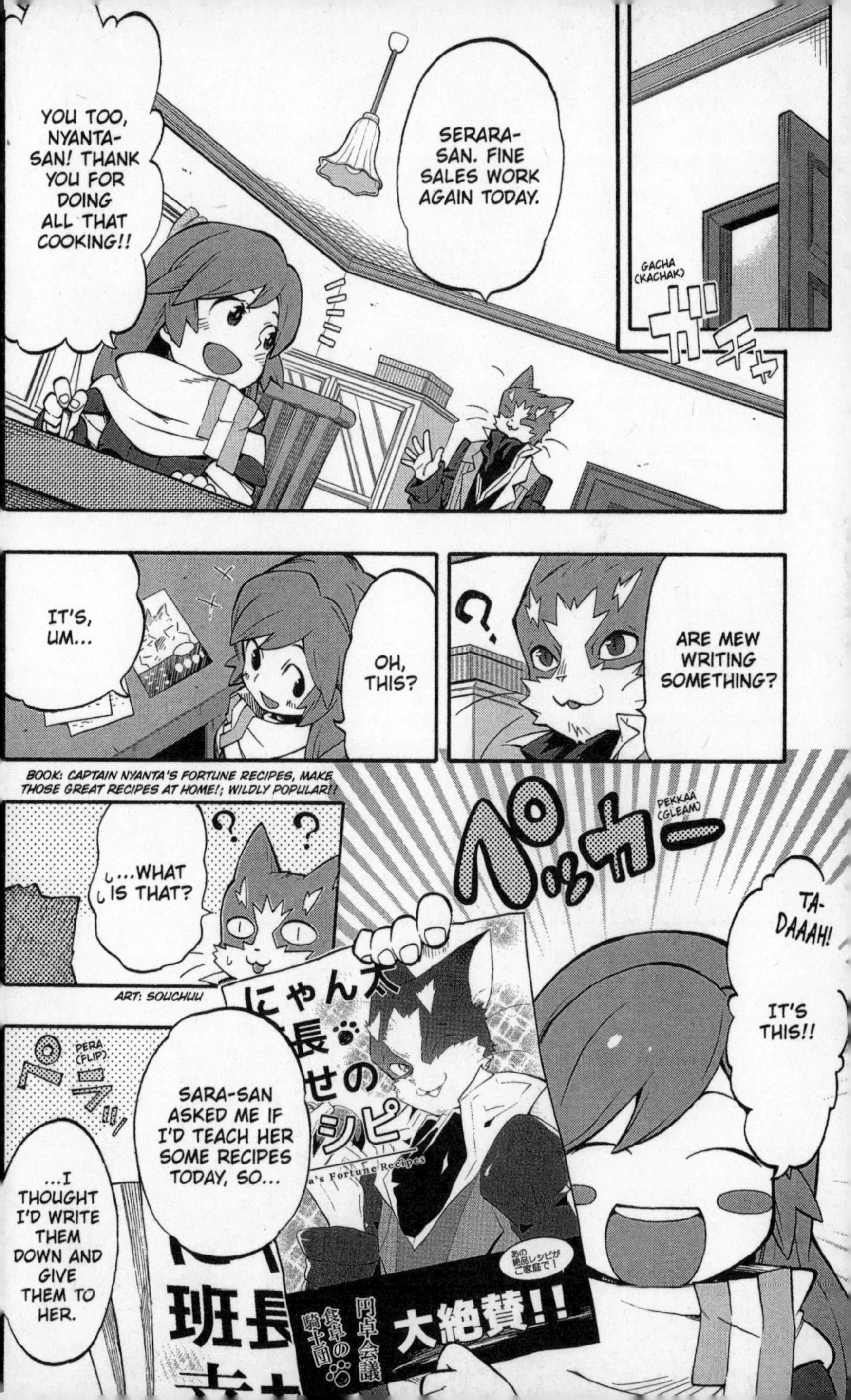
GACHA (KACHAK)
ガチャ
SERARA-SAN. FINE SALES WORK AGAIN TODAY.
YOU TOO, NYANTA-SAN! THANK YOU FOR DOING ALL THAT COOKING!!
ARE MEW WRITING SOMETHING?
OH, THIS?
IT'S, UM...
PEKKAA (GLEAM)
ペッカー
TA-DAAAH!
IT'S THIS!!
BOOK: CAPTAIN NYANTA'S FORTUNE RECIPES, MAKE THOSE GREAT RECIPES AT HOME!; WILDLY POPULAR!!
あの絶品レシピがご家庭で！
円卓会議
食卓の騎士団
大絶賛!!
...WHAT IS THAT?
ART: SOUCHUU
SARA-SAN ASKED ME IF I'D TEACH HER SOME RECIPES TODAY, SO...
PERA (FLIP)
ペラッ
...I THOUGHT I'D WRITE THEM DOWN AND GIVE THEM TO HER.

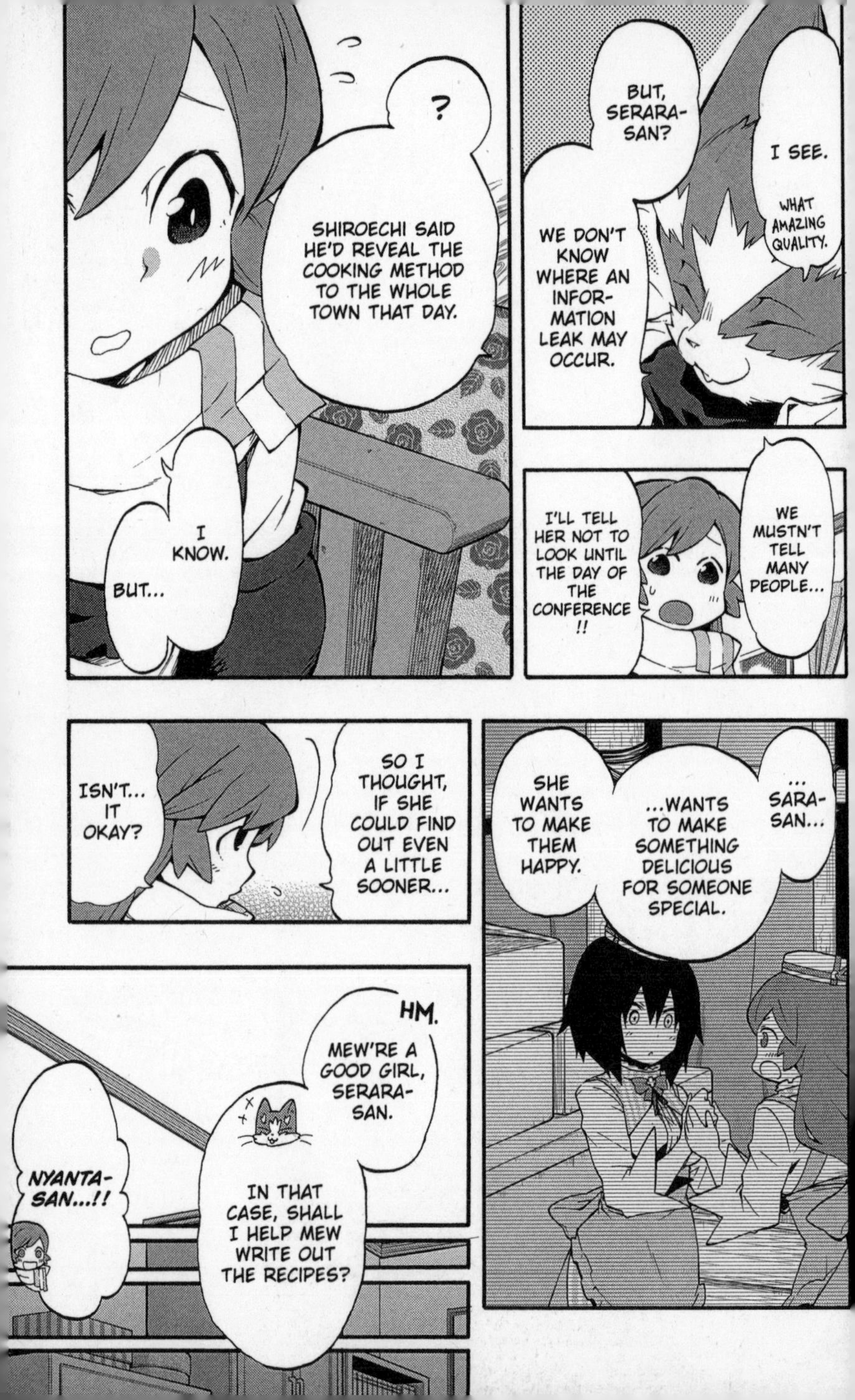
I SEE.
WHAT AMAZING QUALITY.
BUT, SERARA-SAN?
WE DON'T KNOW WHERE AN INFORMATION LEAK MAY OCCUR.
WE MUSTN'T TELL MANY PEOPLE...
I'LL TELL HER NOT TO LOOK UNTIL THE DAY OF THE CONFERENCE !!
?
SHIROECHI SAID HE'D REVEAL THE COOKING METHOD TO THE WHOLE TOWN THAT DAY.
I KNOW.
BUT...
... SARA-SAN...
...WANTS TO MAKE SOMETHING DELICIOUS FOR SOMEONE SPECIAL.
SHE WANTS TO MAKE THEM HAPPY.
SO I THOUGHT, IF SHE COULD FIND OUT EVEN A LITTLE SOONER...
ISN'T... IT OKAY?
HM.
MEW'RE A GOOD GIRL, SERARA-SAN.
IN THAT CASE, SHALL I HELP MEW WRITE OUT THE RECIPES?
NYANTA-SAN...!!

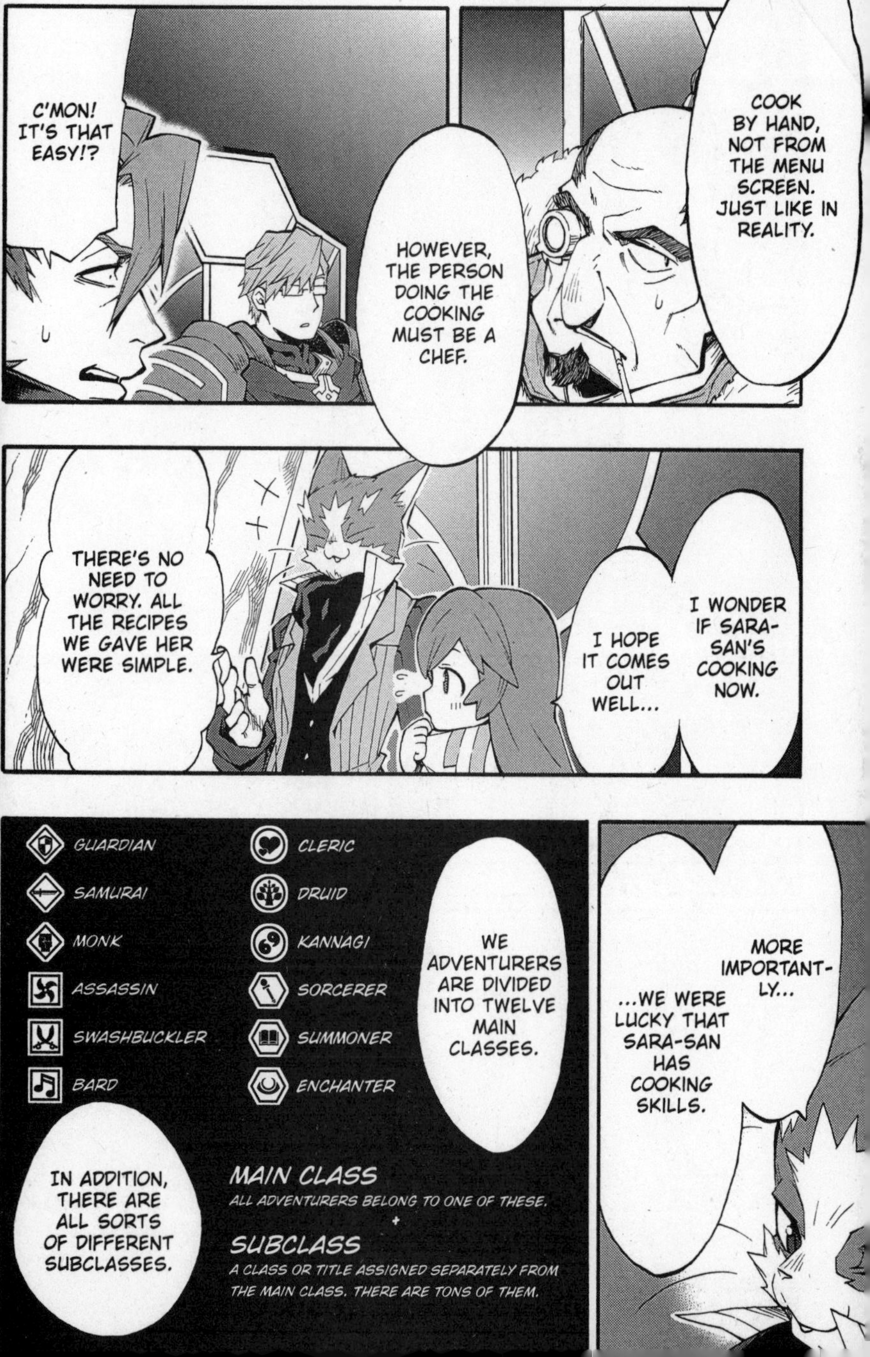
COOK BY HAND, NOT FROM THE MENU SCREEN. JUST LIKE IN REALITY.
HOWEVER, THE PERSON DOING THE COOKING MUST BE A CHEF.
C'MON! IT'S THAT EASY!?
I WONDER IF SARA-SAN'S COOKING NOW.
I HOPE IT COMES OUT WELL...
THERE'S NO NEED TO WORRY. ALL THE RECIPES WE GAVE HER WERE SIMPLE.
MORE IMPORTANT-LY...
...WE WERE LUCKY THAT SARA-SAN HAS COOKING SKILLS.
WE ADVENTURERS ARE DIVIDED INTO TWELVE MAIN CLASSES.
GUARDIAN
SAMURAI
MONK
ASSASSIN
SWASHBUCKLER
BARD
CLERIC
DRUID
KANNAGI
SORCERER
SUMMONER
ENCHANTER
IN ADDITION, THERE ARE ALL SORTS OF DIFFERENT SUBCLASSES.
MAIN CLASS
ALL ADVENTURERS BELONG TO ONE OF THESE.
+
SUBCLASS
A CLASS OR TITLE ASSIGNED SEPARATELY FROM THE MAIN CLASS. THERE ARE TONS OF THEM.

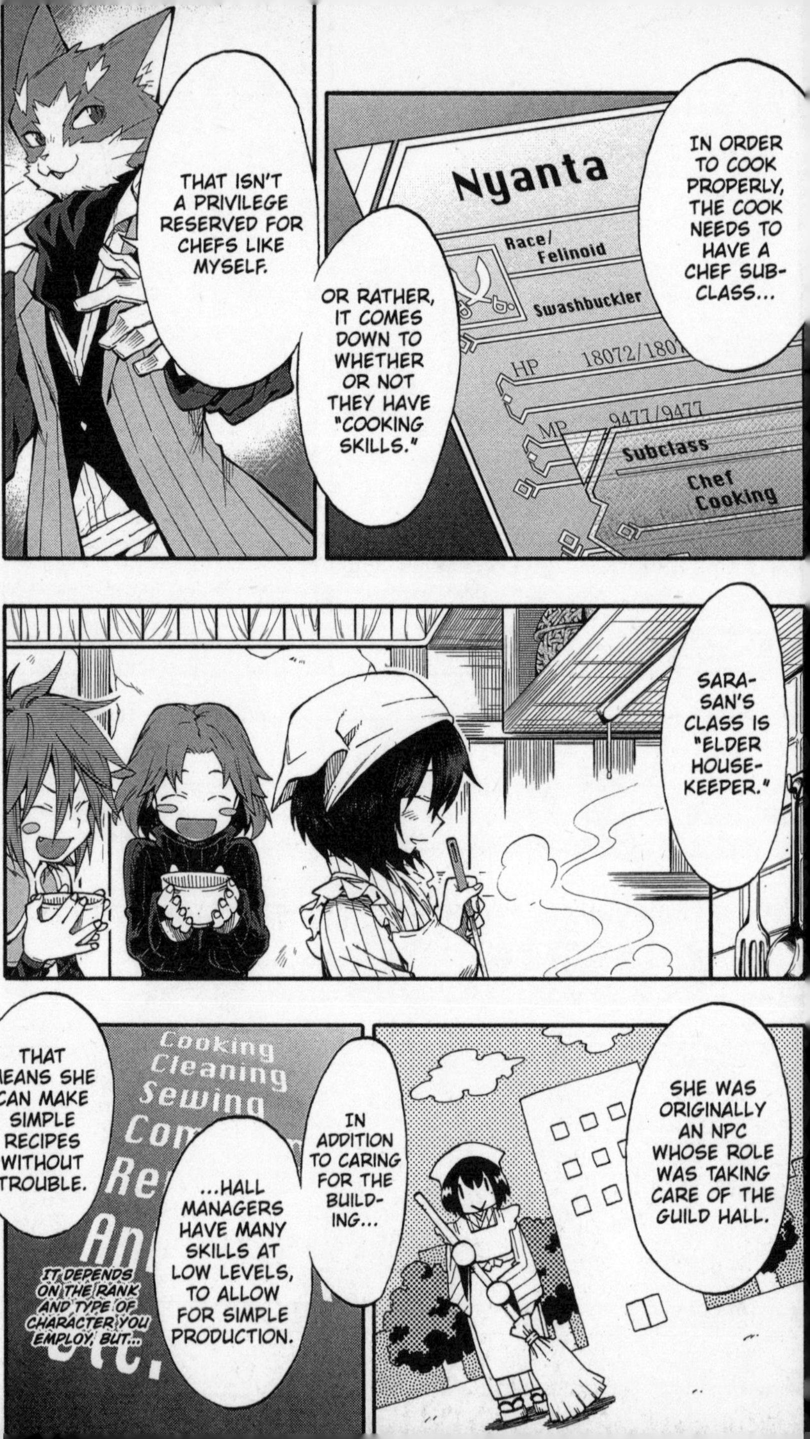
Nyanta
Race/
Felinoid
Swashbuckler
HP 18072/1807
MP 9477/9477
Subclass
Chef
Cooking
IN ORDER TO COOK PROPERLY, THE COOK NEEDS TO HAVE A CHEF SUB-CLASS...
THAT ISN'T A PRIVILEGE RESERVED FOR CHEFS LIKE MYSELF.
OR RATHER, IT COMES DOWN TO WHETHER OR NOT THEY HAVE "COOKING SKILLS."
SARA-SAN'S CLASS IS "ELDER HOUSE-KEEPER."
SHE WAS ORIGINALLY AN NPC WHOSE ROLE WAS TAKING CARE OF THE GUILD HALL.
IN ADDITION TO CARING FOR THE BUILD-ING...
...HALL MANAGERS HAVE MANY SKILLS AT LOW LEVELS, TO ALLOW FOR SIMPLE PRODUCTION.
Cooking
Cleaning
Sewing
THAT MEANS SHE CAN MAKE SIMPLE RECIPES WITHOUT TROUBLE.
IT DEPENDS ON THE RANK AND TYPE OF CHARACTER YOU EMPLOY, BUT...

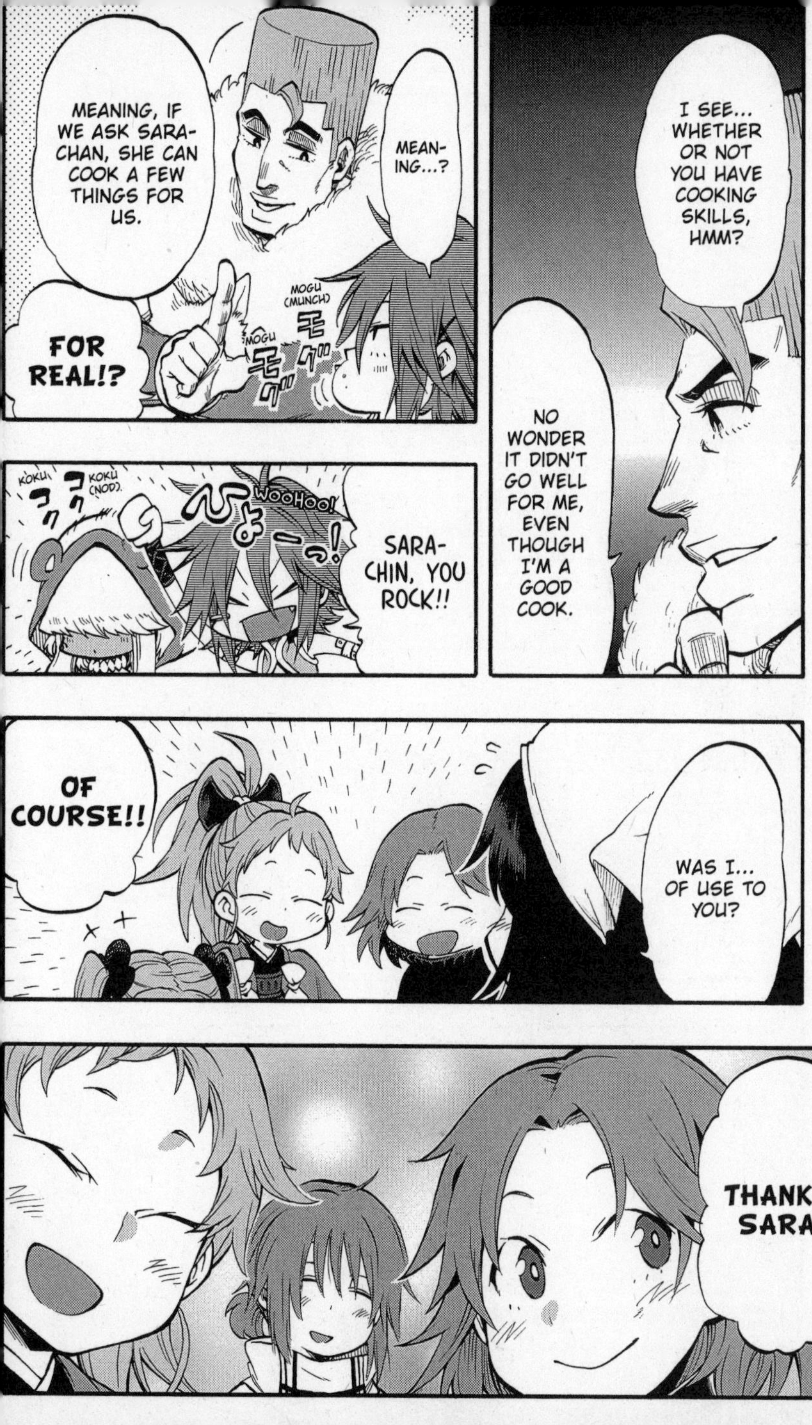
I SEE... WHETHER OR NOT YOU HAVE COOKING SKILLS, HMM?
NO WONDER IT DIDN'T GO WELL FOR ME, EVEN THOUGH I'M A GOOD COOK.
MEAN-ING...?
MEANING, IF WE ASK SARA-CHAN, SHE CAN COOK A FEW THINGS FOR US.
MOGU (MUNCH)
MOGU
FOR REAL!?
SARA-CHIN, YOU ROCK!!
WOOHOO!
KOKU (NOD)
KOKU
WAS I... OF USE TO YOU?
OF COURSE!!
THANKS, SARA!

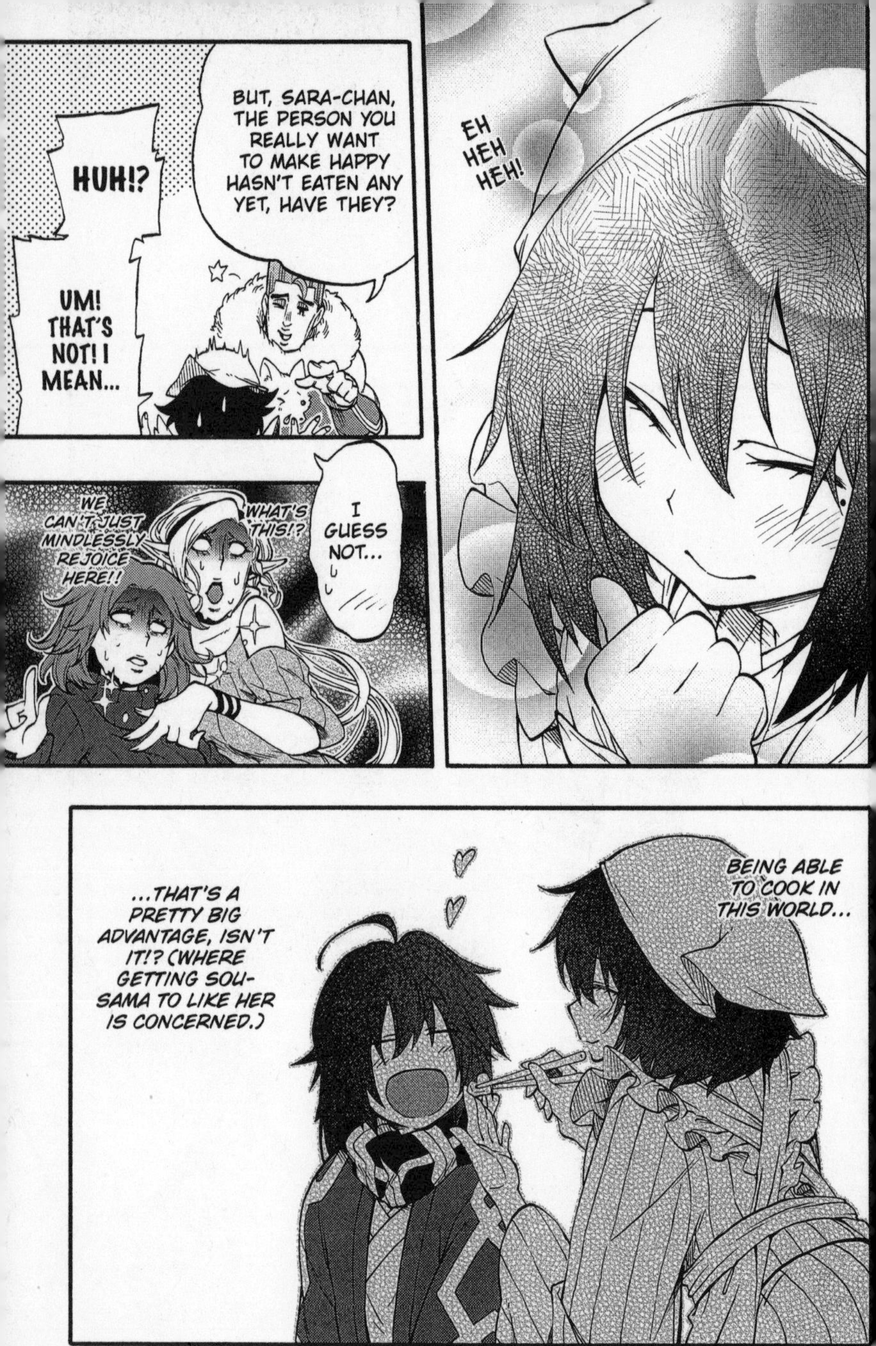
EH HEH HEH!
BUT, SARA-CHAN, THE PERSON YOU REALLY WANT TO MAKE HAPPY HASN'T EATEN ANY YET, HAVE THEY?
HUH!?
UM! THAT'S NOT! I MEAN...
I GUESS NOT...
WHAT'S THIS!?
WE CAN'T JUST MINDLESSLY REJOICE HERE!!
BEING ABLE TO COOK IN THIS WORLD...
...THAT'S A PRETTY BIG ADVANTAGE, ISN'T IT!? (WHERE GETTING SOU-SAMA TO LIKE HER IS CONCERNED.)

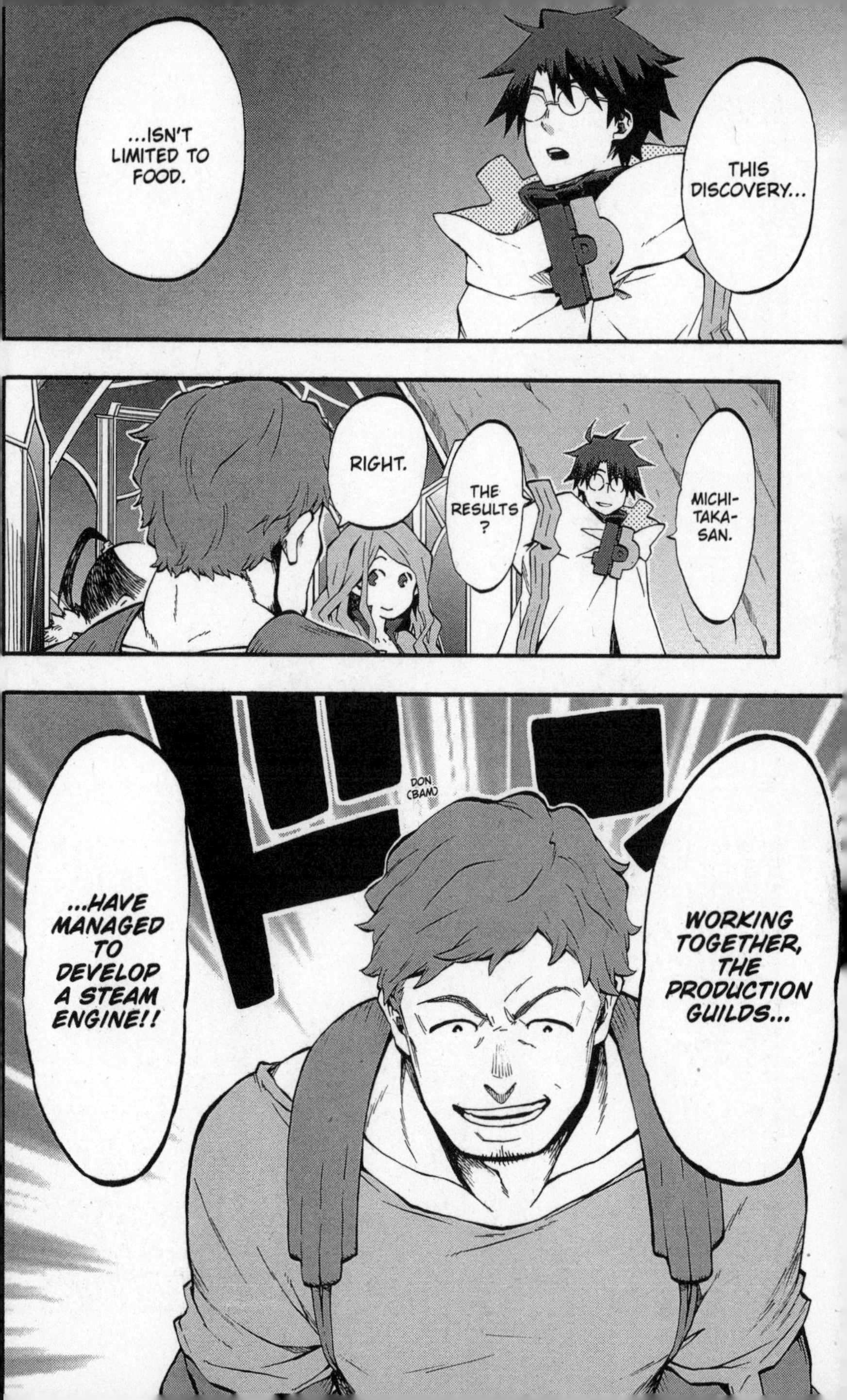
THIS DISCOVERY...
...ISN'T LIMITED TO FOOD.
MICHI-TAKA-SAN.
THE RESULTS?
RIGHT.
WORKING TOGETHER, THE PRODUCTION GUILDS...
DON (BAM)
...HAVE MANAGED TO DEVELOP A STEAM ENGINE!!

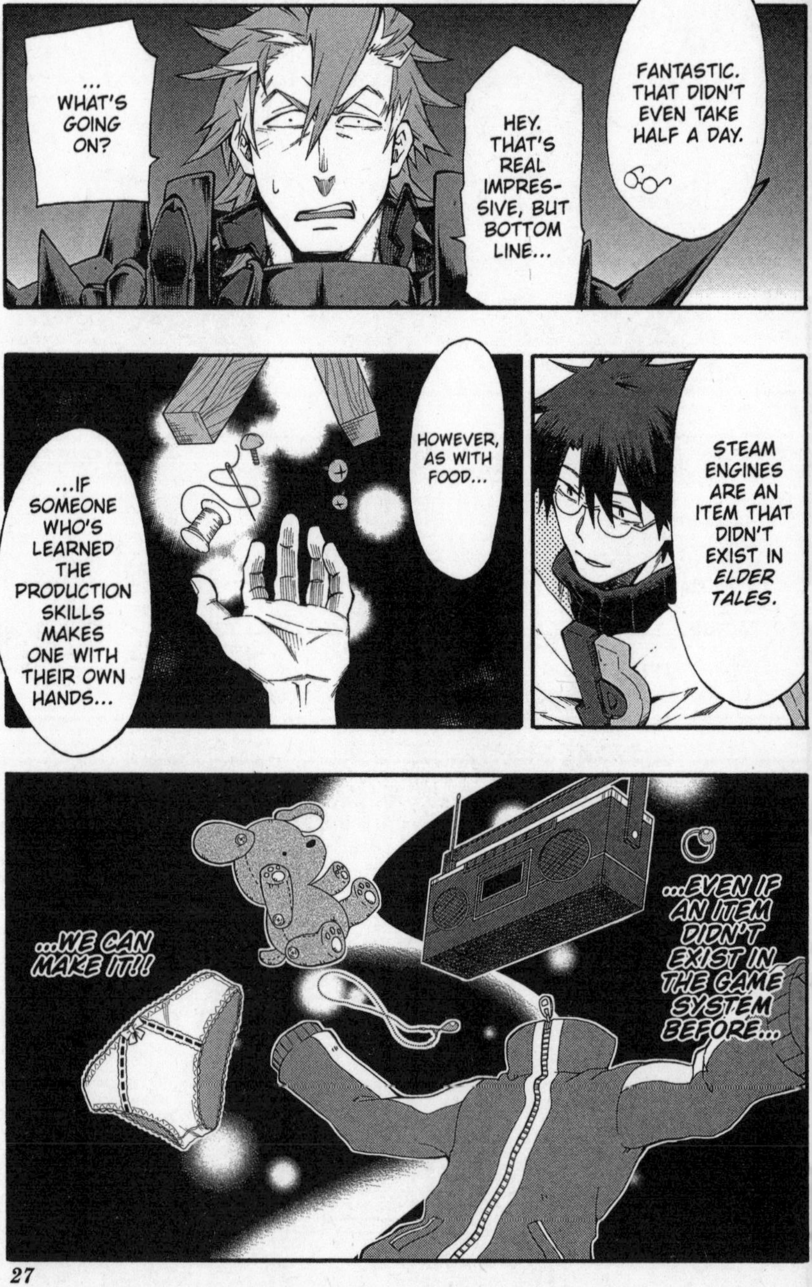
FANTASTIC. THAT DIDN'T EVEN TAKE HALF A DAY.
HEY. THAT'S REAL IMPRES-SIVE, BUT BOTTOM LINE...
...WHAT'S GOING ON?
STEAM ENGINES ARE AN ITEM THAT DIDN'T EXIST IN *ELDER TALES*.
HOWEVER, AS WITH FOOD...
...IF SOMEONE WHO'S LEARNED THE PRODUCTION SKILLS MAKES ONE WITH THEIR OWN HANDS...
...EVEN IF AN ITEM DIDN'T EXIST IN THE GAME SYSTEM BEFORE...
...WE CAN MAKE IT!!

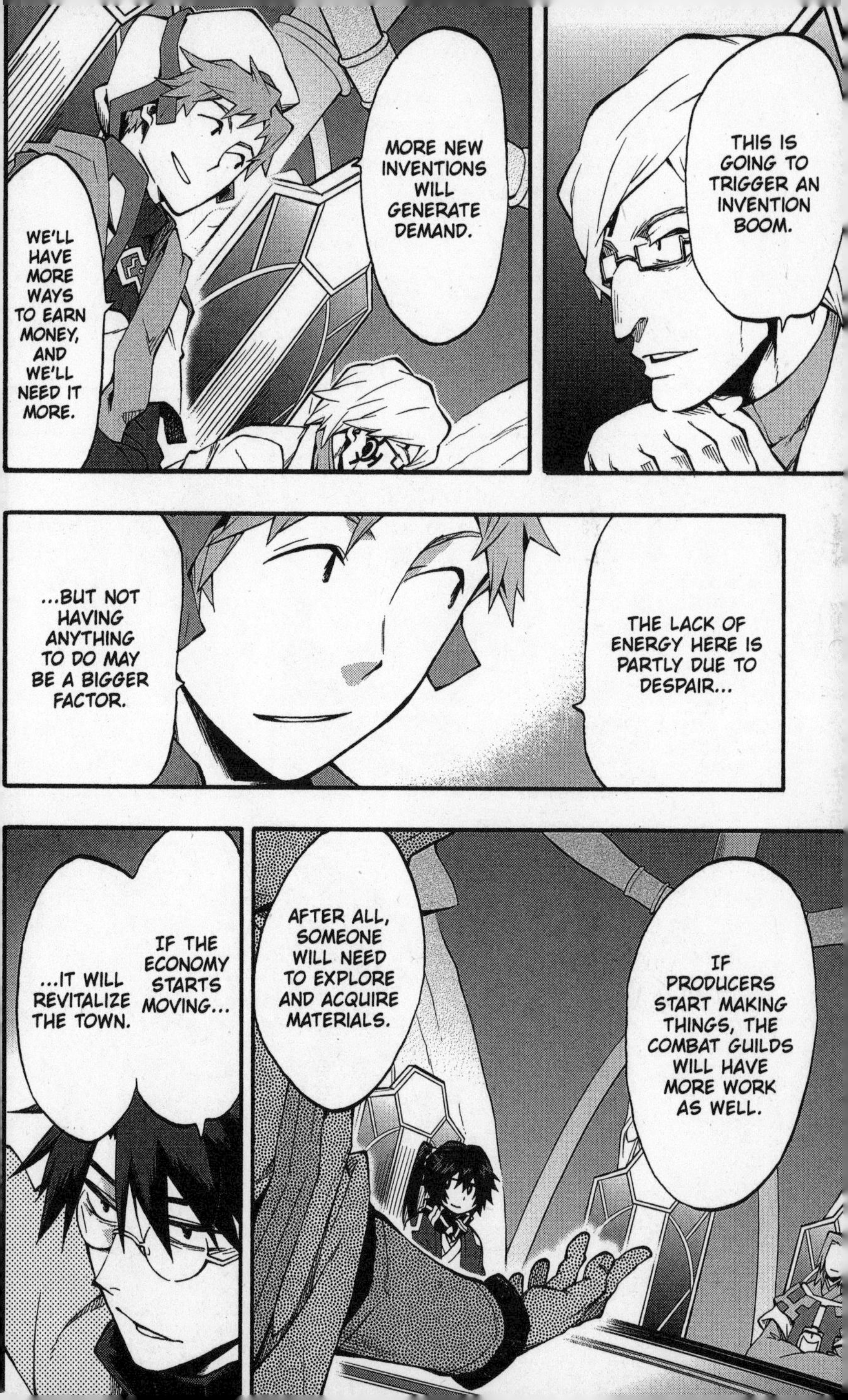
THIS IS GOING TO TRIGGER AN INVENTION BOOM.
MORE NEW INVENTIONS WILL GENERATE DEMAND.
WE'LL HAVE MORE WAYS TO EARN MONEY, AND WE'LL NEED IT MORE.
THE LACK OF ENERGY HERE IS PARTLY DUE TO DESPAIR...
...BUT NOT HAVING ANYTHING TO DO MAY BE A BIGGER FACTOR.
IF PRODUCERS START MAKING THINGS, THE COMBAT GUILDS WILL HAVE MORE WORK AS WELL.
AFTER ALL, SOMEONE WILL NEED TO EXPLORE AND ACQUIRE MATERIALS.
IF THE ECONOMY STARTS MOVING...
...IT WILL REVITALIZE THE TOWN.

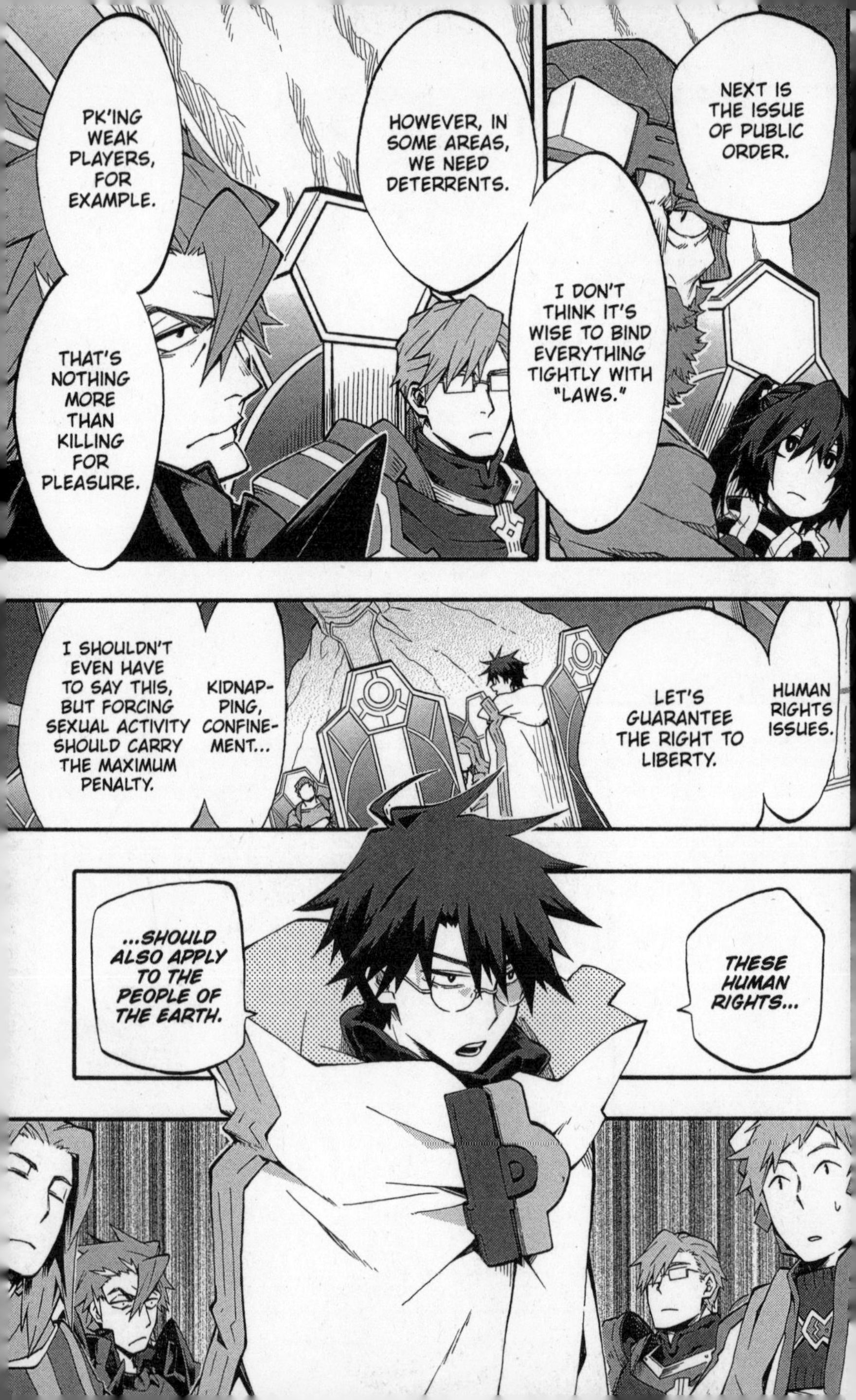
NEXT IS THE ISSUE OF PUBLIC ORDER.
I DON'T THINK IT'S WISE TO BIND EVERYTHING TIGHTLY WITH "LAWS."
HOWEVER, IN SOME AREAS, WE NEED DETERRENTS.
PK'ING WEAK PLAYERS, FOR EXAMPLE.
THAT'S NOTHING MORE THAN KILLING FOR PLEASURE.
HUMAN RIGHTS ISSUES.
LET'S GUARANTEE THE RIGHT TO LIBERTY.
KIDNAPPING, CONFINEMENT...
I SHOULDN'T EVEN HAVE TO SAY THIS, BUT FORCING SEXUAL ACTIVITY SHOULD CARRY THE MAXIMUM PENALTY.
THESE HUMAN RIGHTS...
...SHOULD ALSO APPLY TO THE PEOPLE OF THE EARTH.

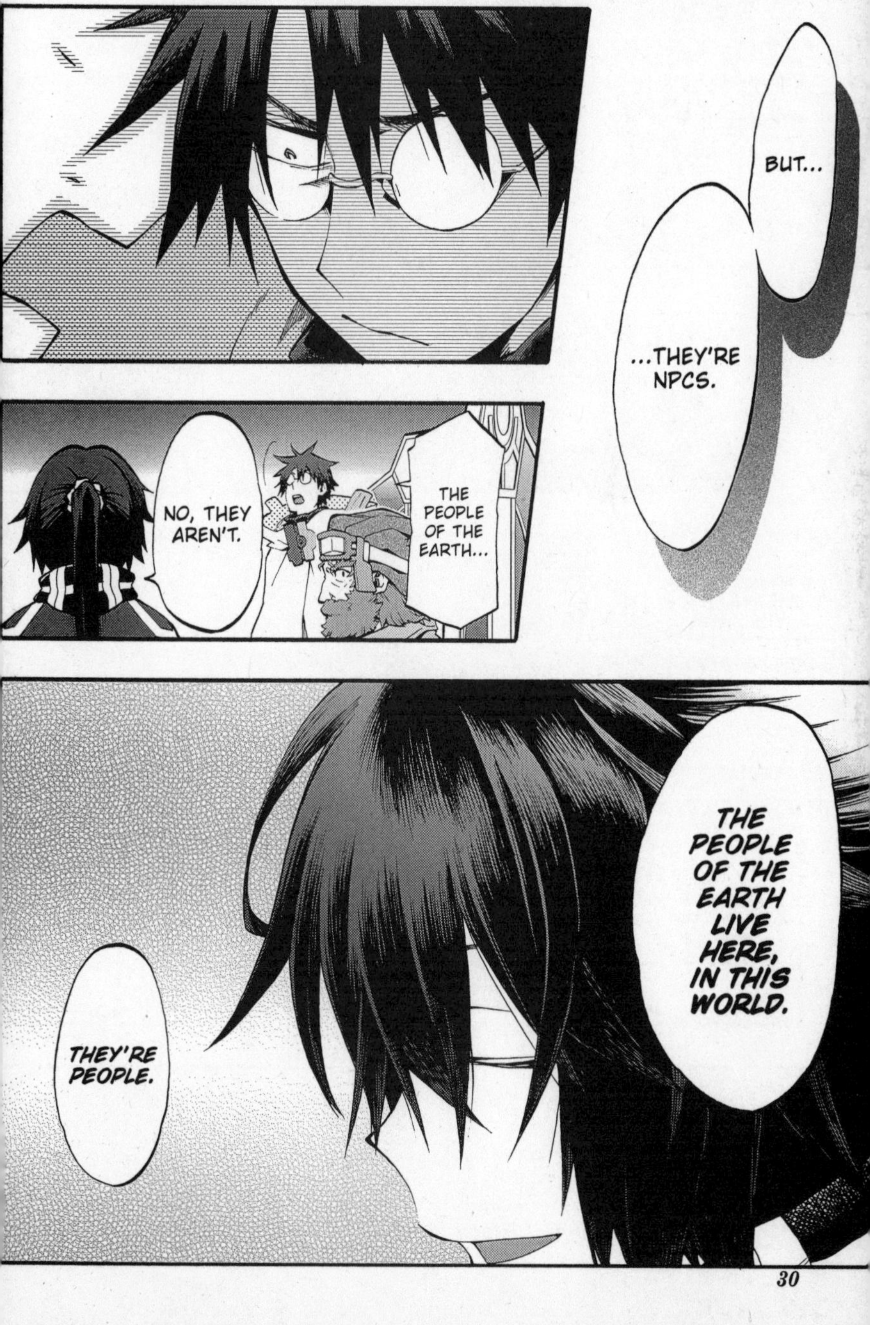
BUT...
...THEY'RE NPCS.
THE PEOPLE OF THE EARTH...
NO, THEY AREN'T.
THE PEOPLE OF THE EARTH LIVE HERE, IN THIS WORLD.
THEY'RE PEOPLE.

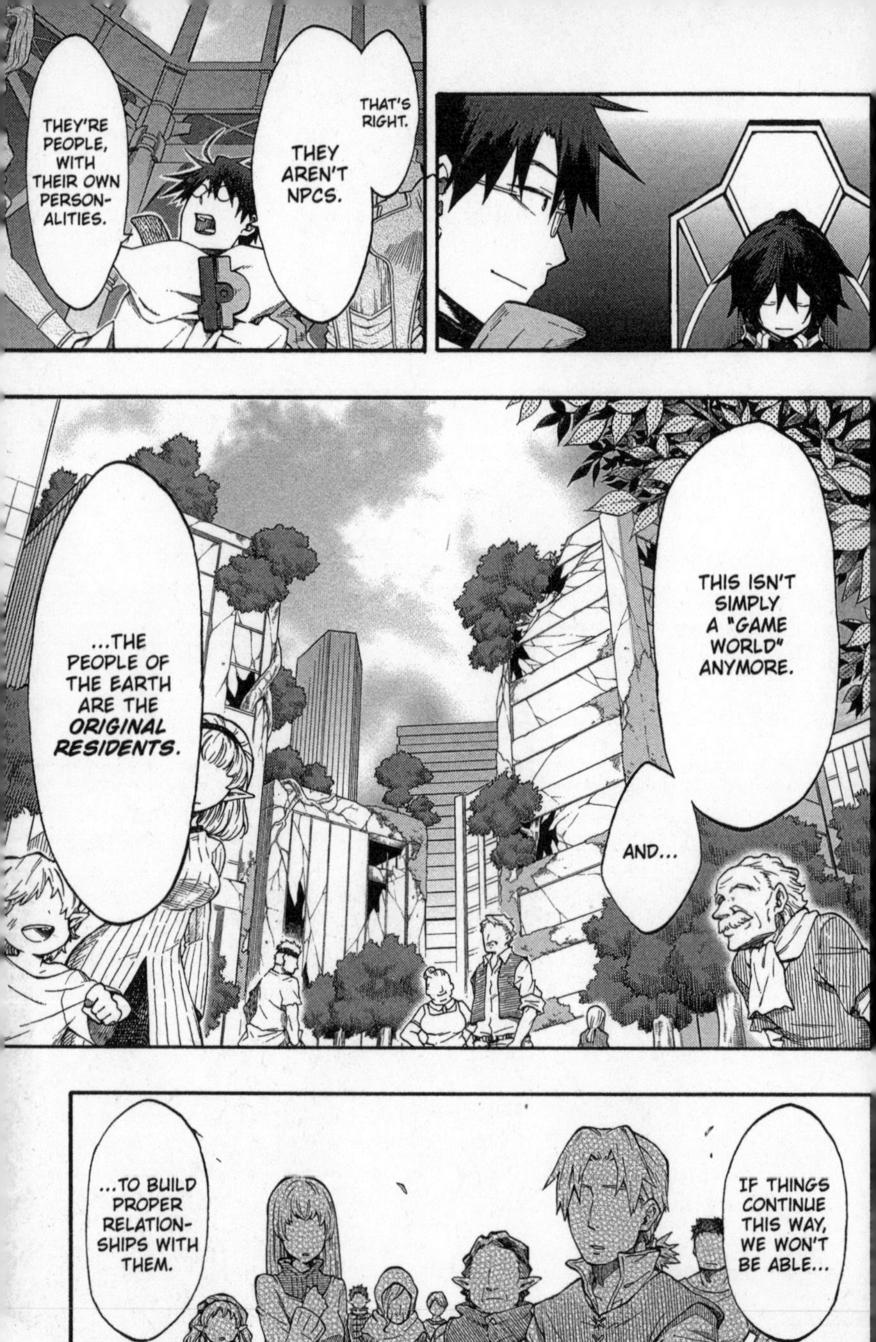
THAT'S RIGHT.
THEY AREN'T NPCS.
THEY'RE PEOPLE, WITH THEIR OWN PERSON-ALITIES.
THIS ISN'T SIMPLY A "GAME WORLD" ANYMORE.
...THE PEOPLE OF THE EARTH ARE THE ORIGINAL RESIDENTS.
AND...
IF THINGS CONTINUE THIS WAY, WE WON'T BE ABLE...
...TO BUILD PROPER RELATION-SHIPS WITH THEM.

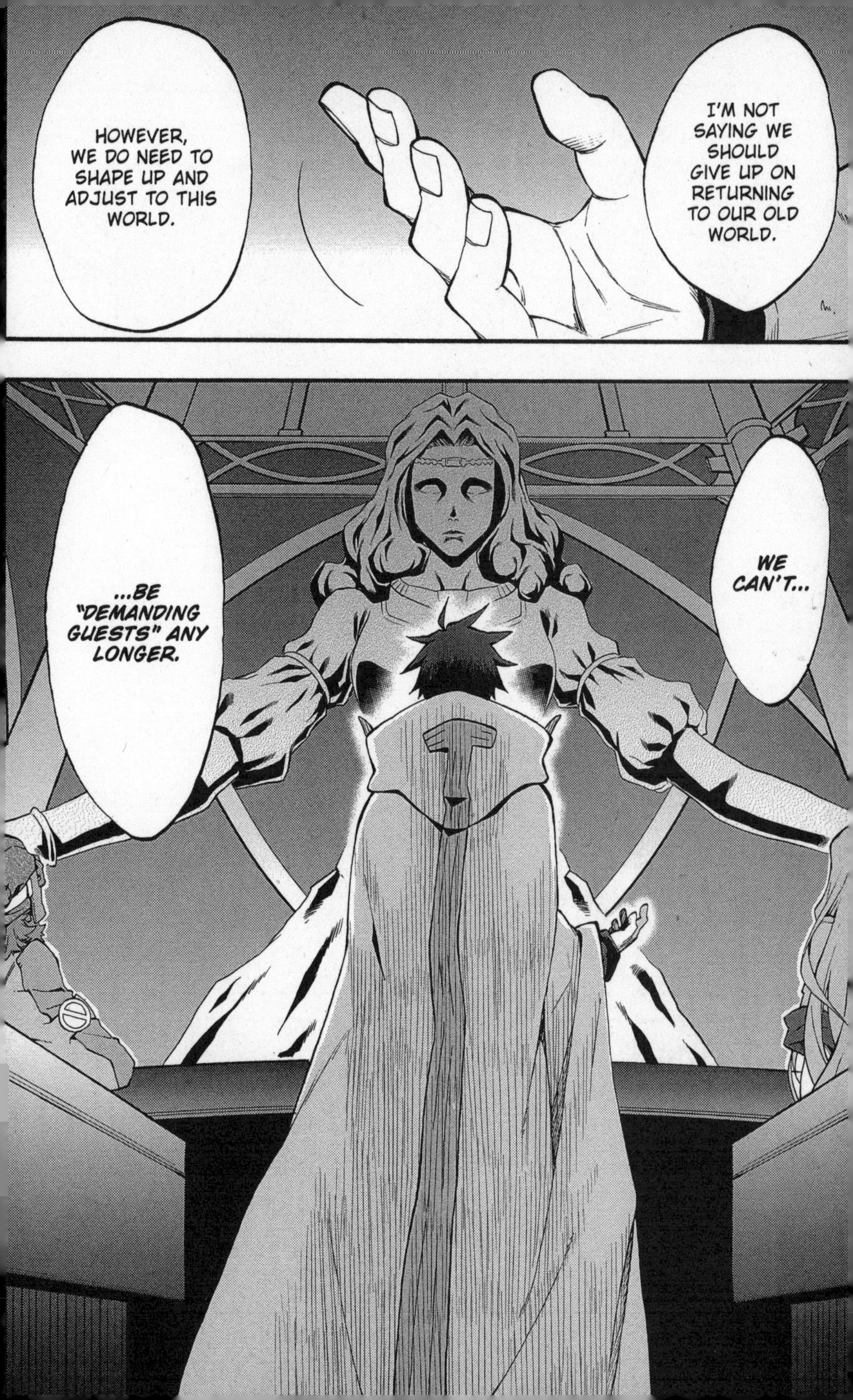
I'M NOT SAYING WE SHOULD GIVE UP ON RETURNING TO OUR OLD WORLD.
HOWEVER, WE DO NEED TO SHAPE UP AND ADJUST TO THIS WORLD.
WE CAN'T...
...BE "DEMANDING GUESTS" ANY LONGER.

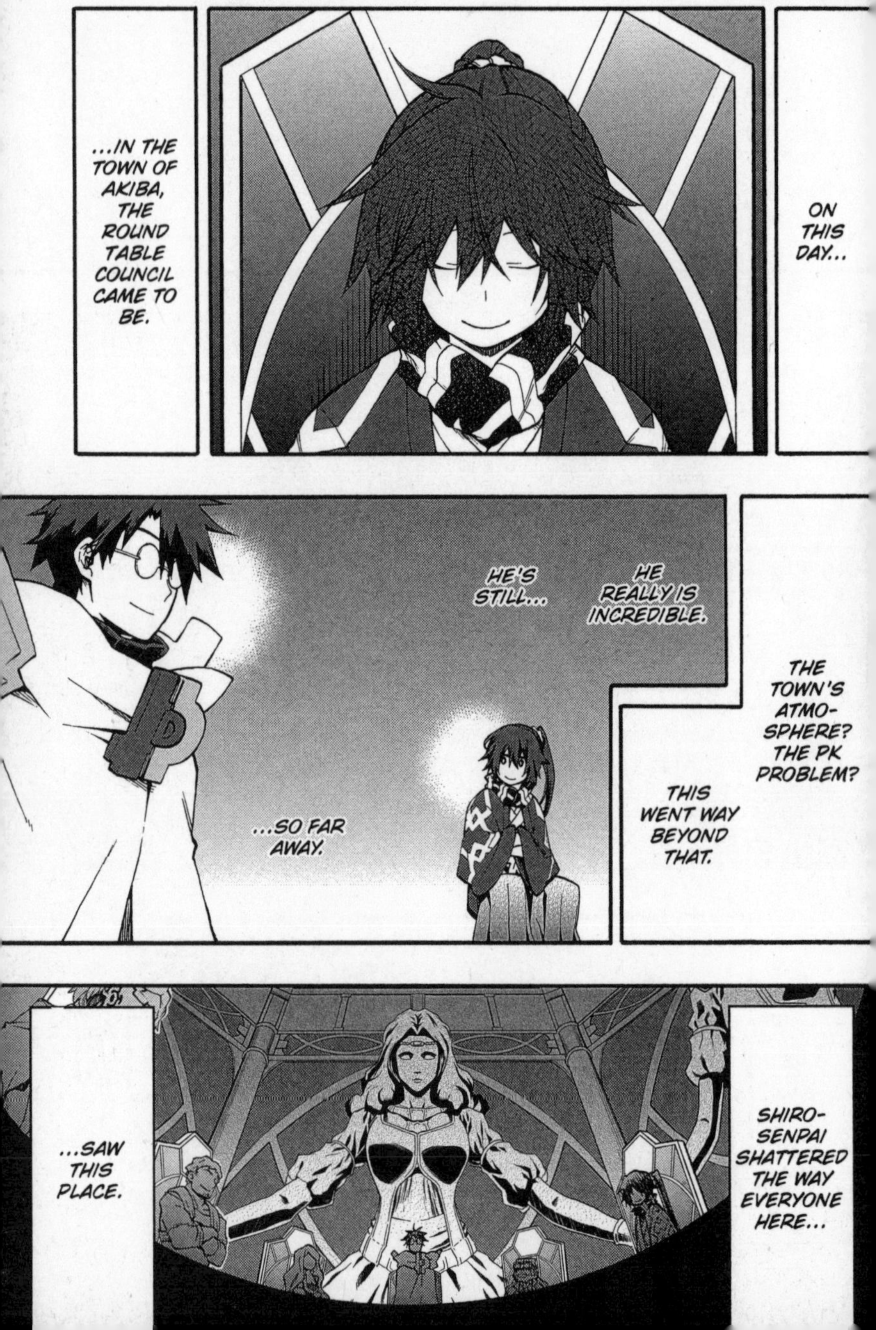
ON THIS DAY...
...IN THE TOWN OF AKIBA, THE ROUND TABLE COUNCIL CAME TO BE.
THE TOWN'S ATMO-SPHERE? THE PK PROBLEM?
THIS WENT WAY BEYOND THAT.
HE REALLY IS INCREDIBLE.
HE'S STILL...
...SO FAR AWAY.
SHIRO-SENPAI SHATTERED THE WAY EVERYONE HERE...
...SAW THIS PLACE.

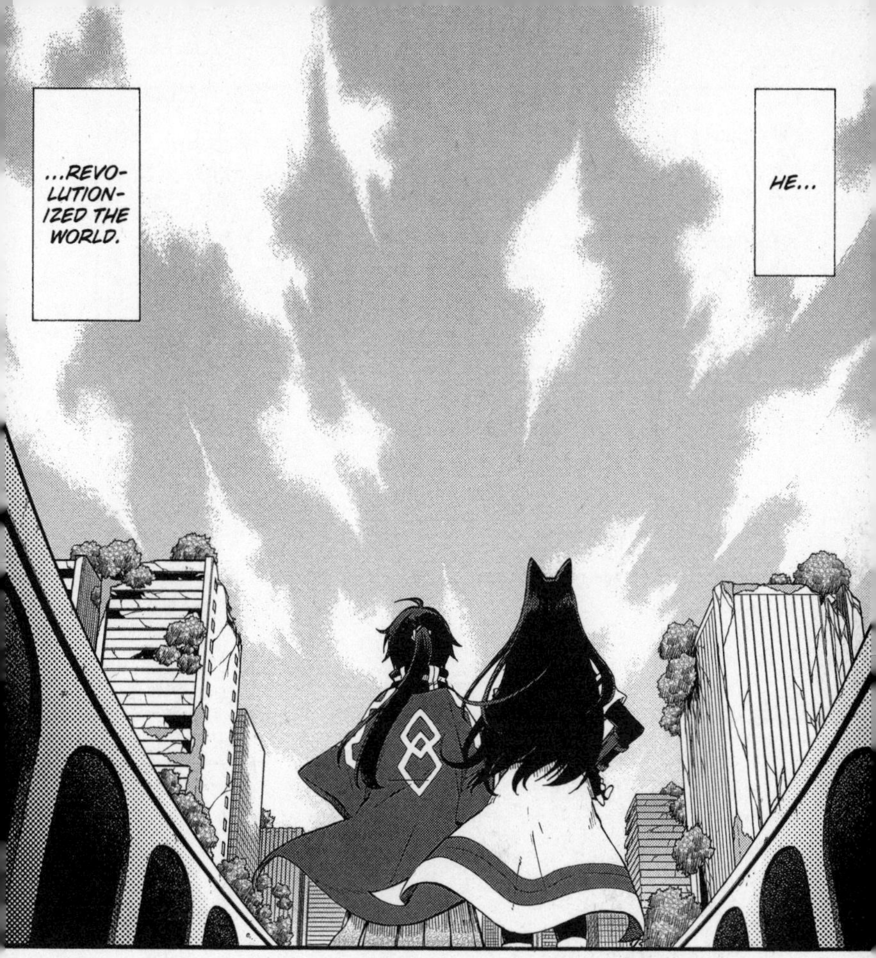
HE...
...REVOLUTIONIZED THE WORLD.

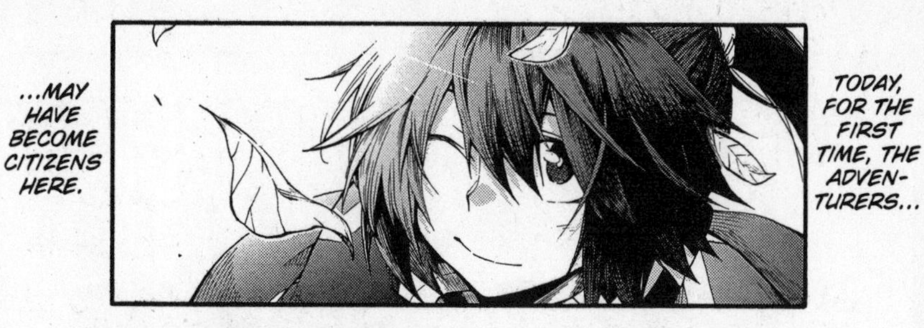
TODAY, FOR THE FIRST TIME, THE ADVENTURERS...
...MAY HAVE BECOME CITIZENS HERE.

[CHAPTER : 24 Game's End]

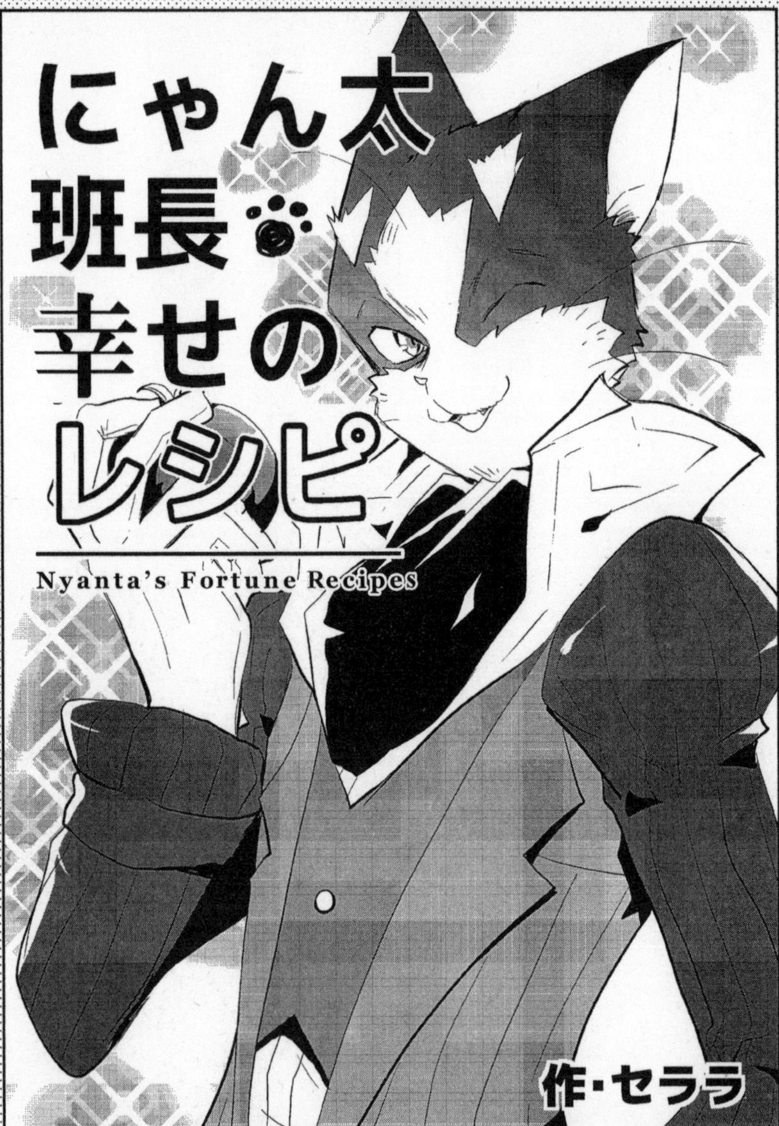
にゃん太班長幸せのレシピ
Nyanta's Fortune Recipes
作・セララ

THE COVER OF THE RECIPE NOTEBOOK THAT APPEARS IN CHAPTER 24, THE ONE SERARA GIVES TO SARA, WAS DRAWN BY SOUCHUU-SENSEI OF "LOG HORIZON - CAPTAIN NYANTA'S FORTUNE RECIPES"! EVEN THOUGH IT WAS A SMALL PART OF A SMALL PANEL, SOUCHUU-SENSEI DREW VERSIONS WITH AND WITHOUT OBI STRIPS, RIGHT DOWN TO THE DETAILS...! THANK YOU VERY MUCH!

LOG HORIZON

THE WEST WIND BRIGADE

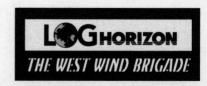

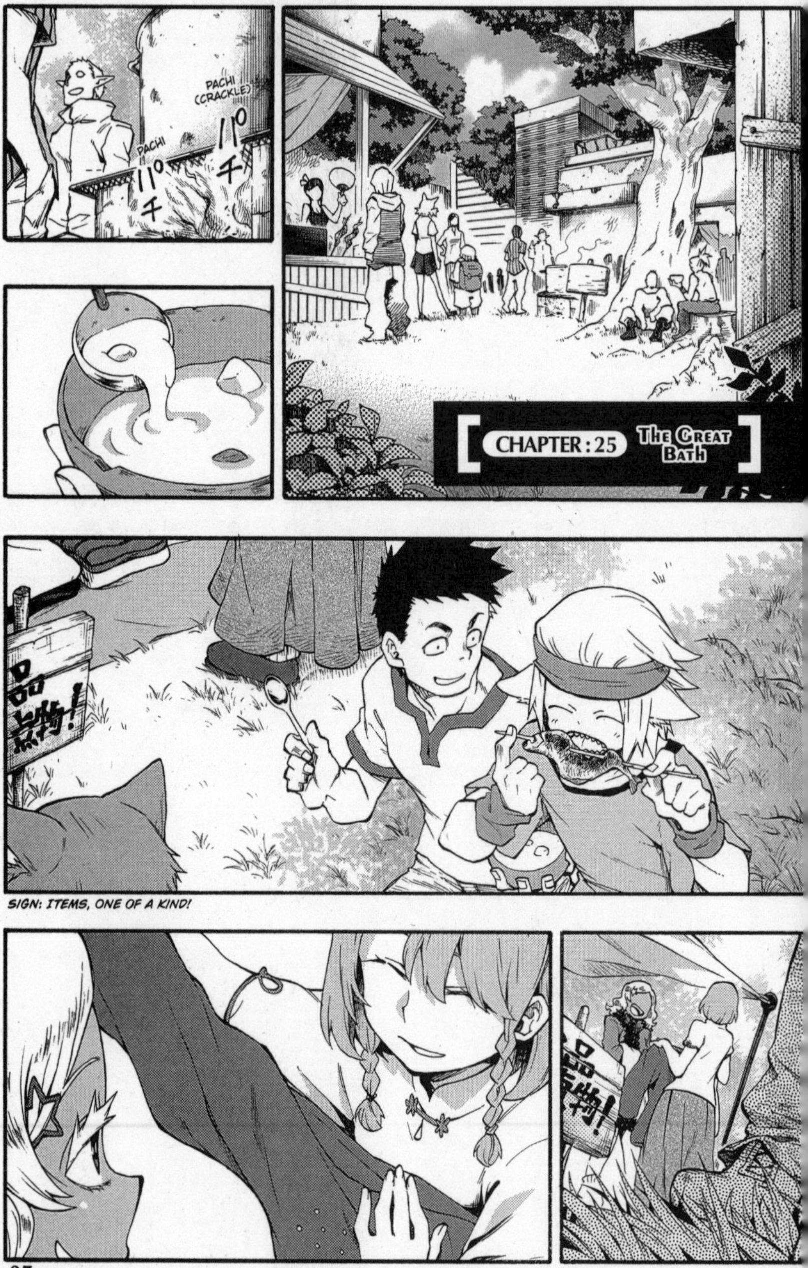
CHAPTER : 25
The Great Bath
PACHI (CRACKLE)
パチ
PACHI
パチ
SIGN: ITEMS, ONE OF A KIND!

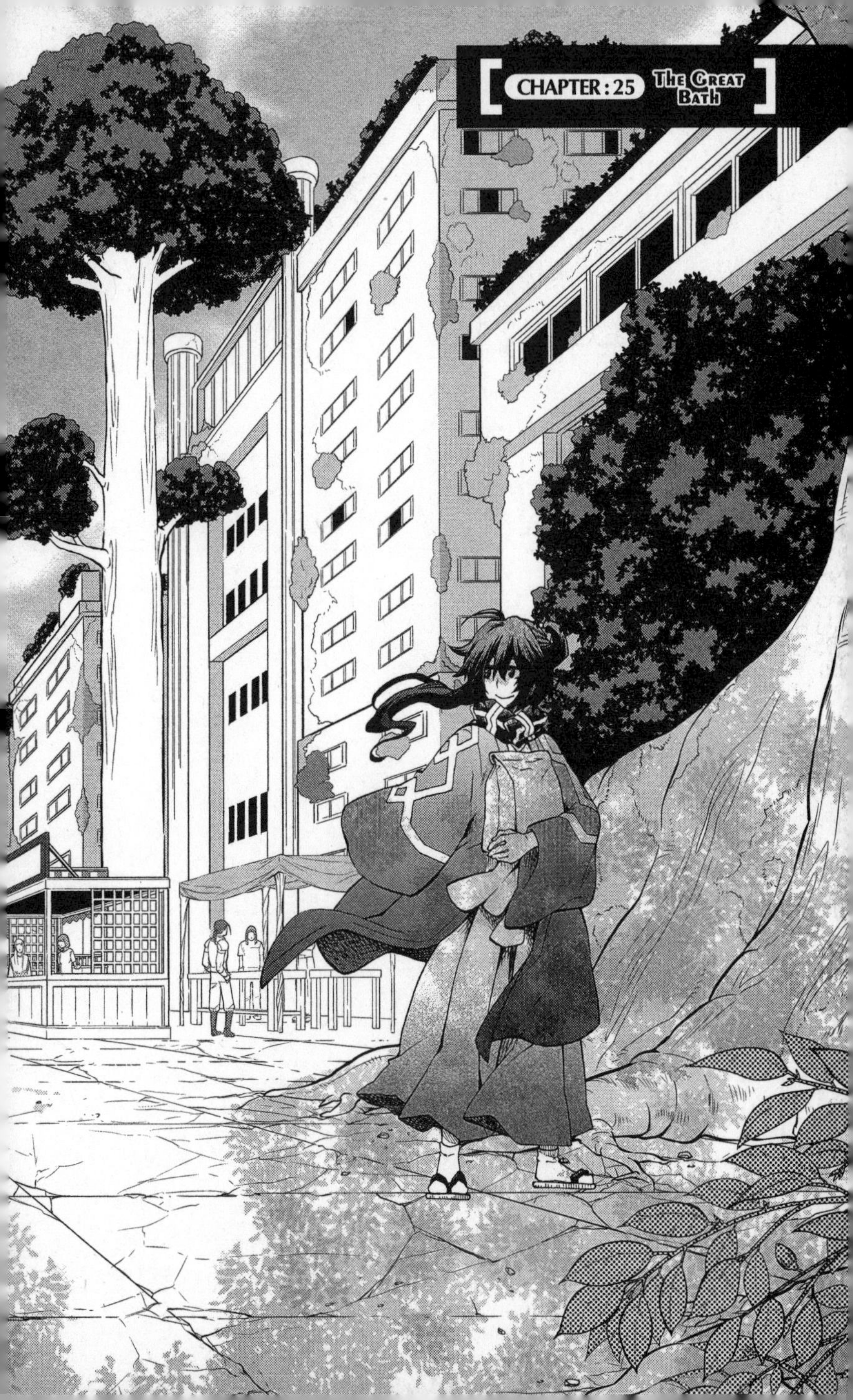
CHAPTER : 25
The Great Bath

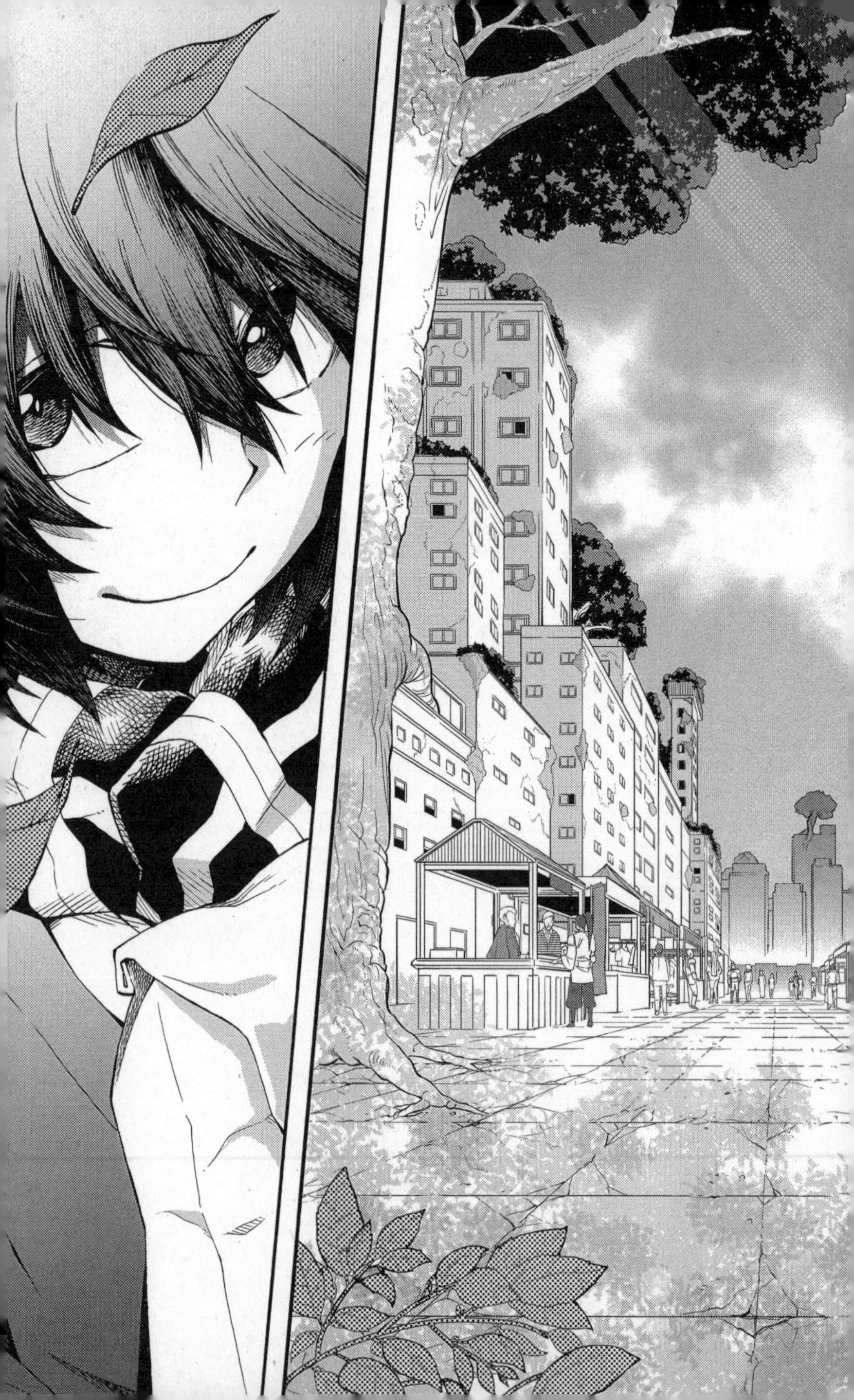

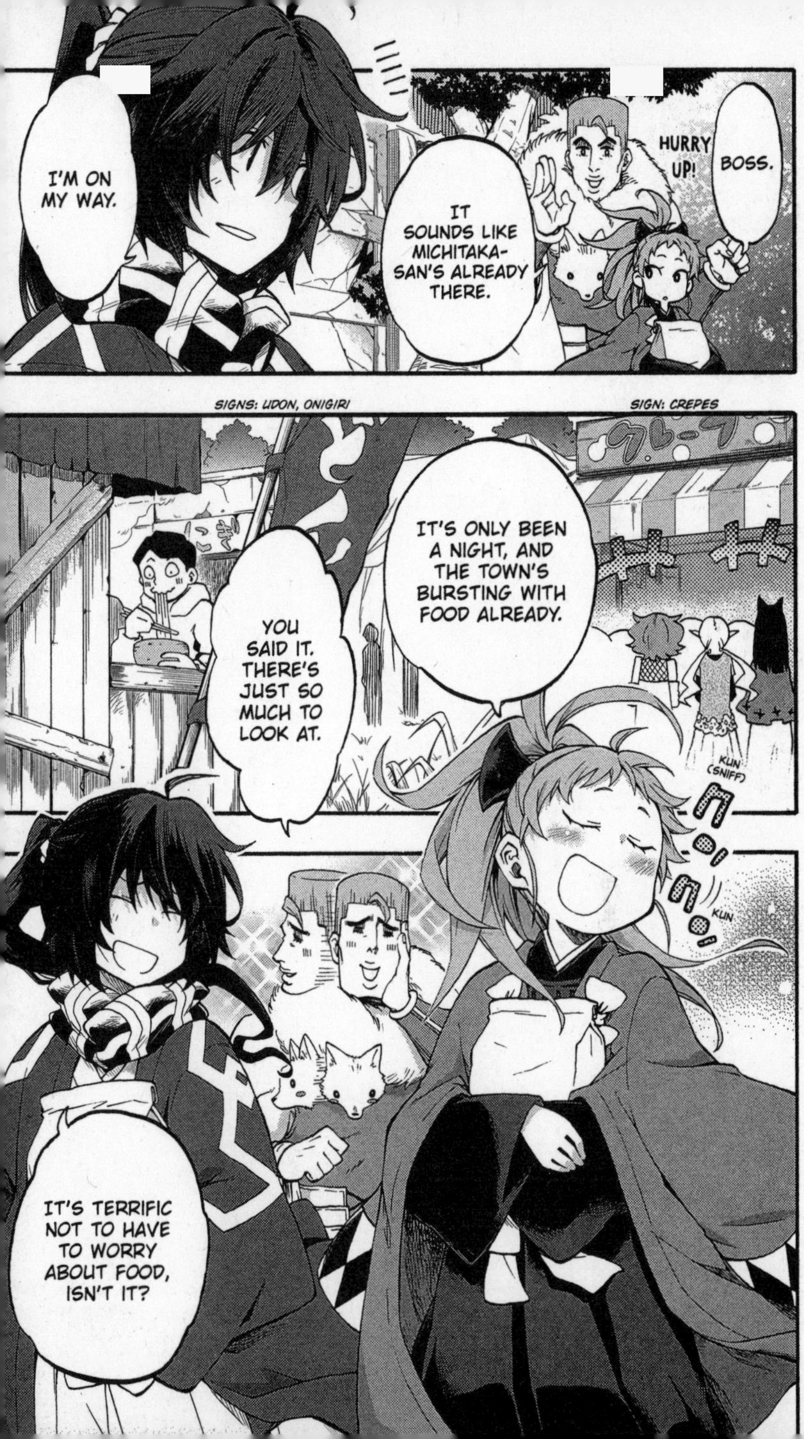

BOSS.
HURRY UP!
IT SOUNDS LIKE MICHITAKA-SAN'S ALREADY THERE.
I'M ON MY WAY.
SIGN: CREPES
SIGNS: UDON, ONIGIRI
IT'S ONLY BEEN A NIGHT, AND THE TOWN'S BURSTING WITH FOOD ALREADY.
YOU SAID IT. THERE'S JUST SO MUCH TO LOOK AT.
KUN (SNIFF)
KUN
IT'S TERRIFIC NOT TO HAVE TO WORRY ABOUT FOOD, ISN'T IT?

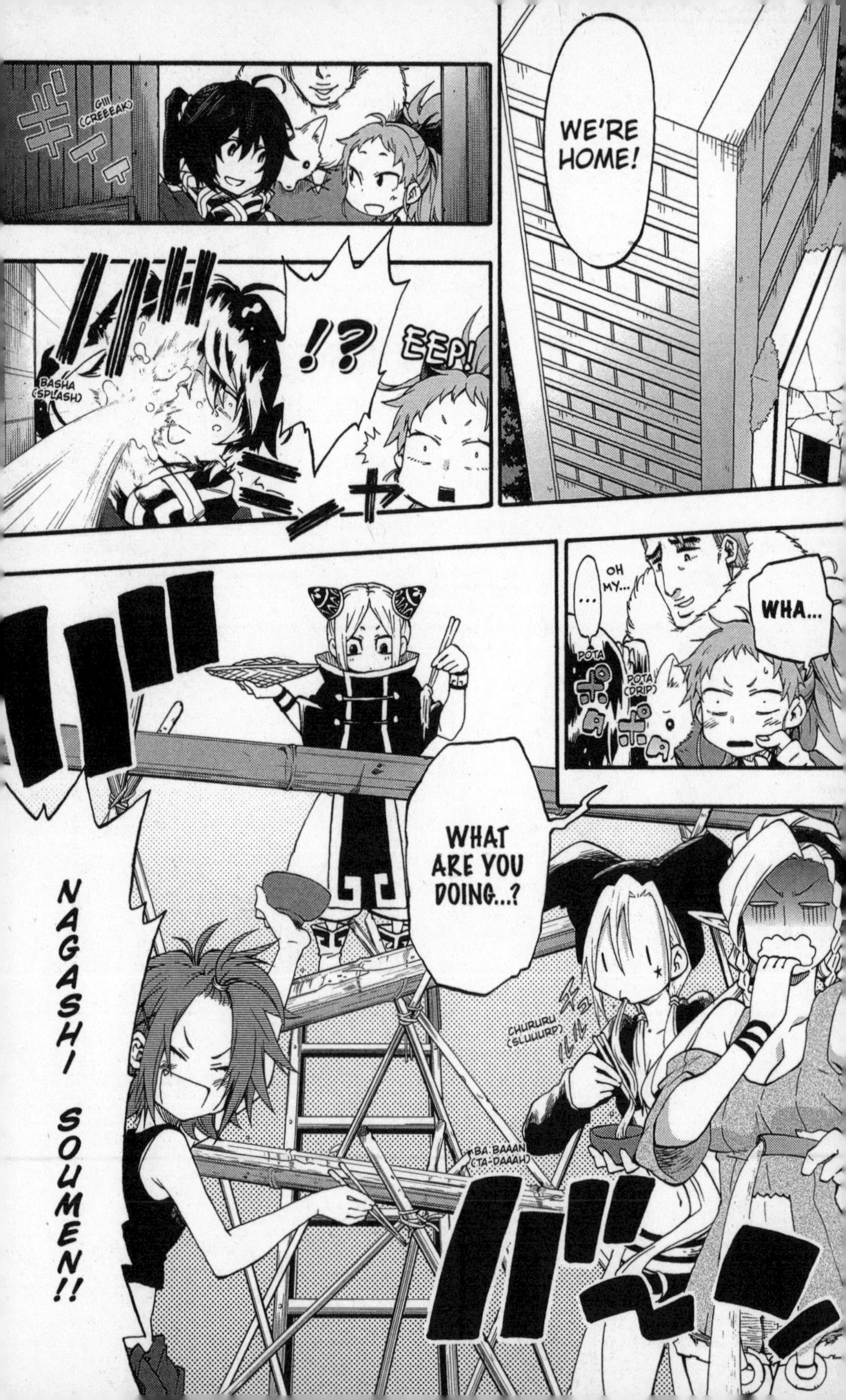
WE'RE HOME!
GIII (CREEEAK)
EEP!
!?
BASHA (SPLASH)
WHA...
OH MY...
...
POTA POTA (DRIP)
WHAT ARE YOU DOING...?
NAGASHI SOUMEN!!
CHURURU (SLUUURP)
BA BAAAN (TA-DAAAH)

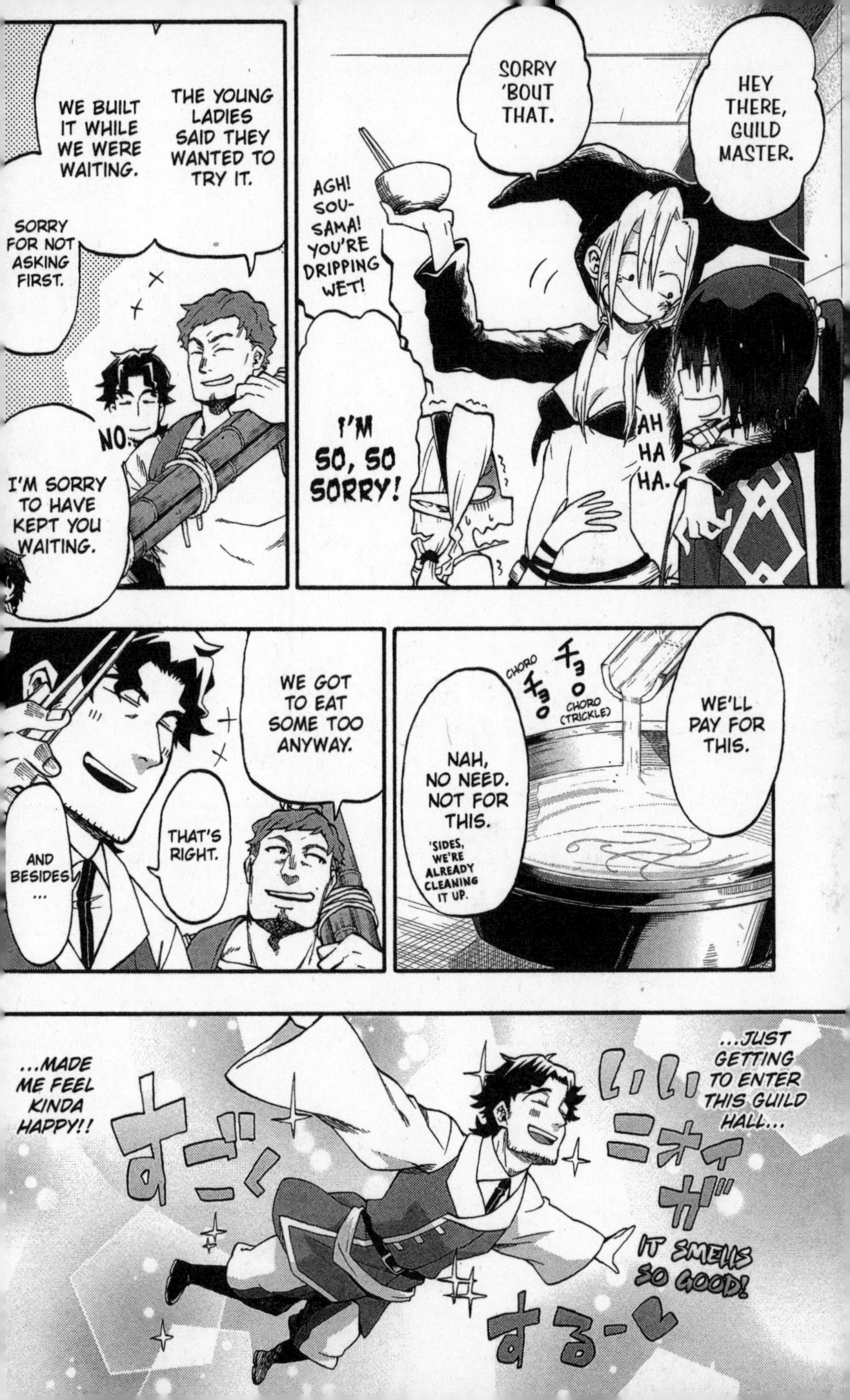
HEY THERE, GUILD MASTER.
SORRY 'BOUT THAT.
AGH! SOU-SAMA! YOU'RE DRIPPING WET!
I'M SO, SO SORRY!
AH HA HA.
THE YOUNG LADIES SAID THEY WANTED TO TRY IT.
WE BUILT IT WHILE WE WERE WAITING.
SORRY FOR NOT ASKING FIRST.
NO.
I'M SORRY TO HAVE KEPT YOU WAITING.
WE'LL PAY FOR THIS.
チョロ
CHORO (TRICKLE)
チョロ
CHORO
NAH, NO NEED. NOT FOR THIS.
'SIDES, WE'RE ALREADY CLEANING IT UP.
WE GOT TO EAT SOME TOO ANYWAY.
THAT'S RIGHT.
AND BESIDES...
...JUST GETTING TO ENTER THIS GUILD HALL...
いいニオイが
IT SMELLS SO GOOD!
すごく
...MADE ME FEEL KINDA HAPPY!!
するー

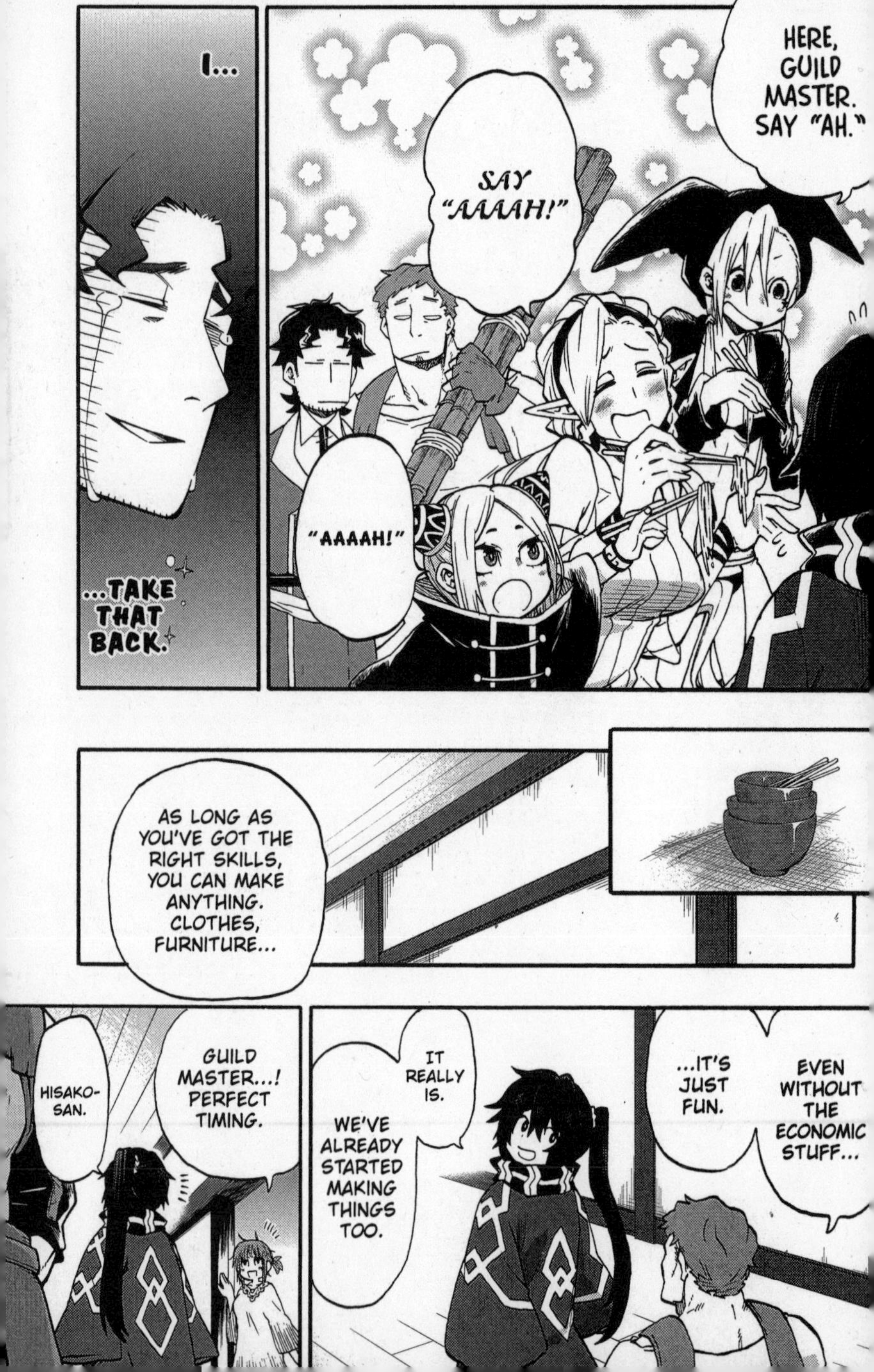
HERE, GUILD MASTER. SAY "AH."
SAY "AAAAH!"
"AAAAH!"
I...
...TAKE THAT BACK.
AS LONG AS YOU'VE GOT THE RIGHT SKILLS, YOU CAN MAKE ANYTHING. CLOTHES, FURNITURE...
EVEN WITHOUT THE ECONOMIC STUFF...
...IT'S JUST FUN.
IT REALLY IS.
WE'VE ALREADY STARTED MAKING THINGS TOO.
GUILD MASTER...! PERFECT TIMING.
HISAKO-SAN.

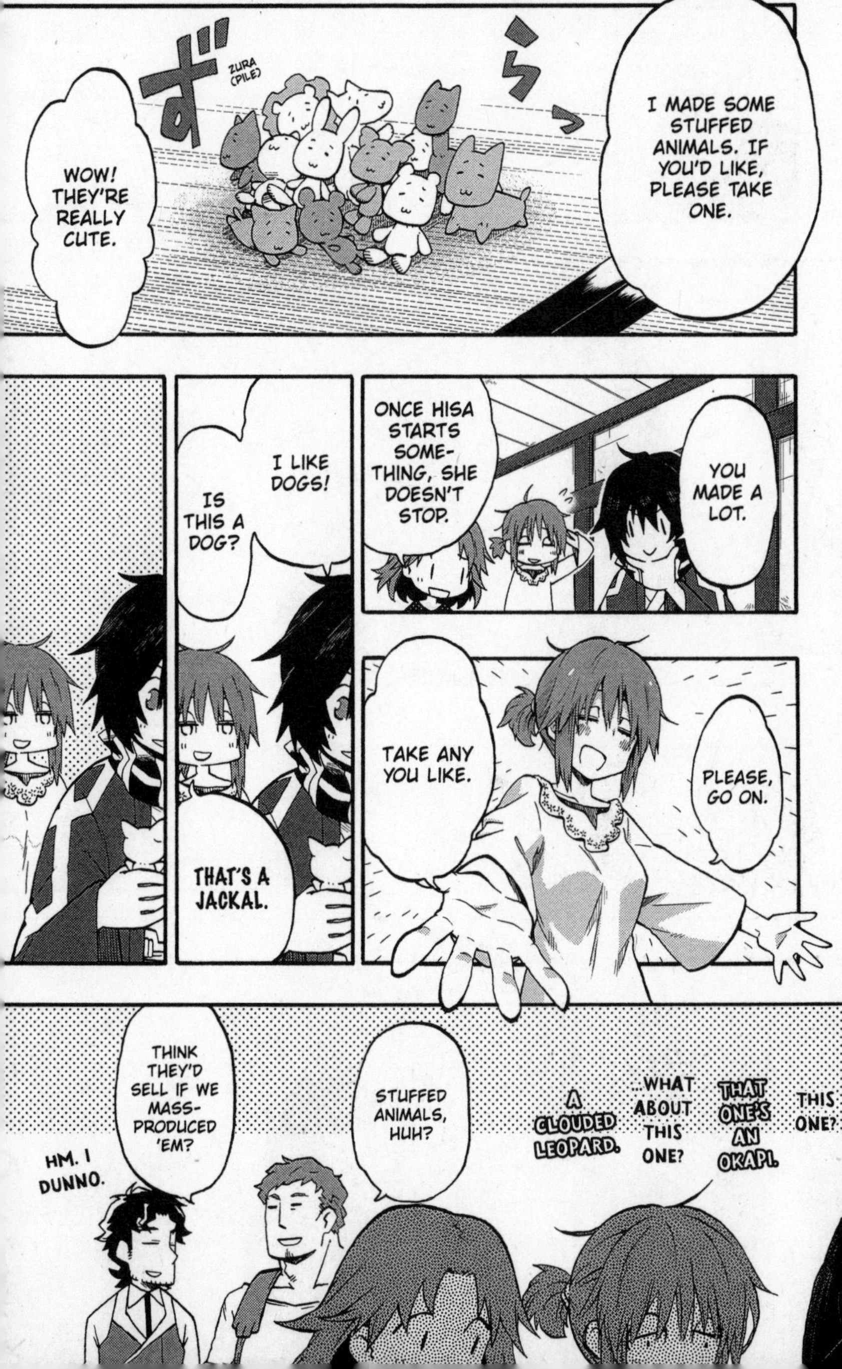
I MADE SOME STUFFED ANIMALS. IF YOU'D LIKE, PLEASE TAKE ONE.
ずらっ
ZURA (PILE)
WOW! THEY'RE REALLY CUTE.
YOU MADE A LOT.
ONCE HISA STARTS SOME-THING, SHE DOESN'T STOP.
PLEASE, GO ON.
TAKE ANY YOU LIKE.
I LIKE DOGS!
IS THIS A DOG?
THAT'S A JACKAL.
THIS ONE?
THAT ONE'S AN OKAPI.
...WHAT ABOUT THIS ONE?
A CLOUDED LEOPARD.
STUFFED ANIMALS, HUH?
THINK THEY'D SELL IF WE MASS-PRODUCED 'EM?
HM. I DUNNO.

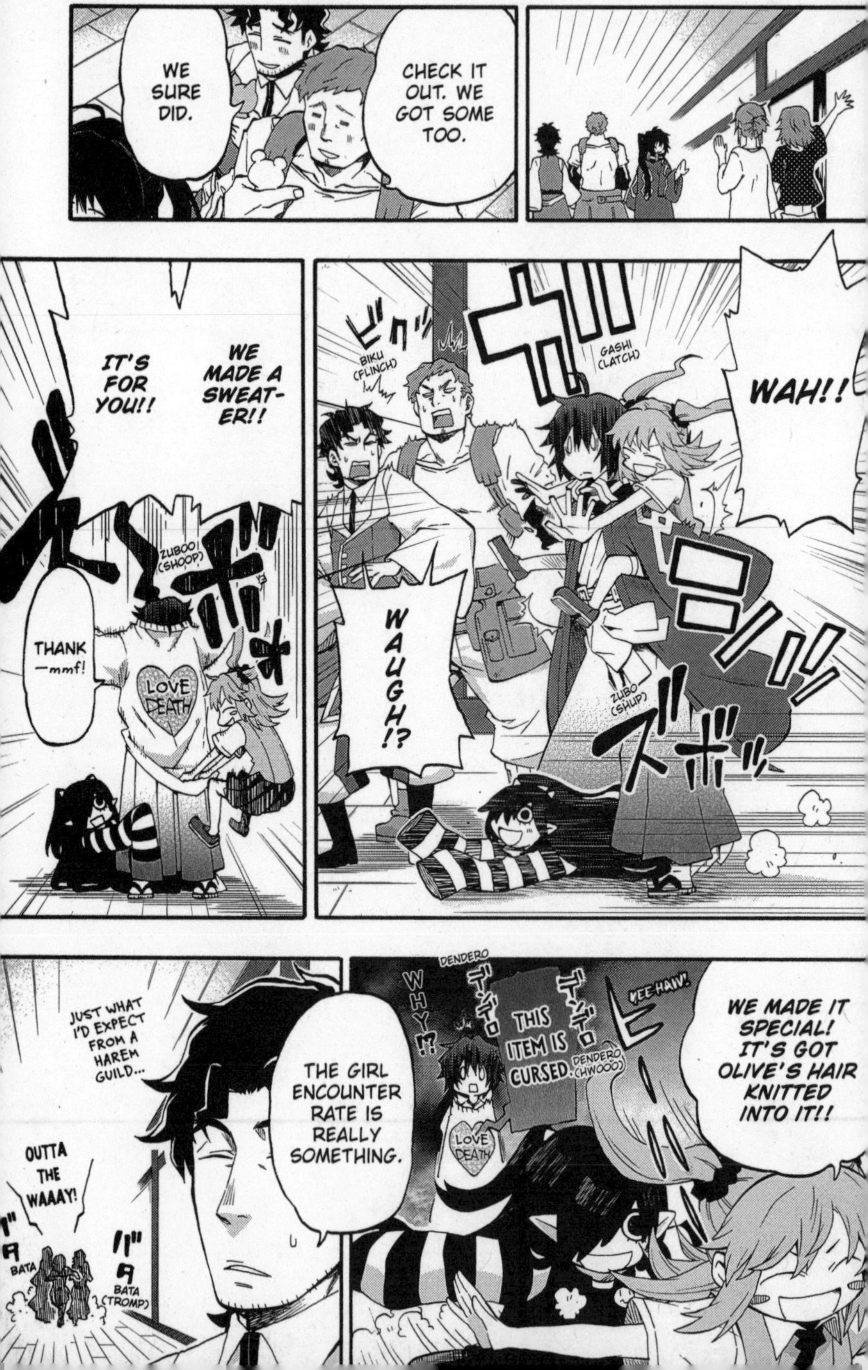
CHECK IT OUT. WE GOT SOME TOO.
WE SURE DID.
WAH!!
GASHI (LATCH)
BIKU (FLINCH)
WAUGH!?
ZUBO (SHUP)
WE MADE A SWEATER!!
IT'S FOR YOU!!
ZUBOO (SHOOP)
THANK—mmf!
LOVE DEATH
WE MADE IT SPECIAL! IT'S GOT OLIVE'S HAIR KNITTED INTO IT!!
YEE-HAW!
DENDERO (HWOOO)
THIS ITEM IS CURSED.
DENDERO
WHY!?
LOVE DEATH
THE GIRL ENCOUNTER RATE IS REALLY SOMETHING.
JUST WHAT I'D EXPECT FROM A HAREM GUILD...
OUTTA THE WAAAY!
BATA
BATA (TROMP)

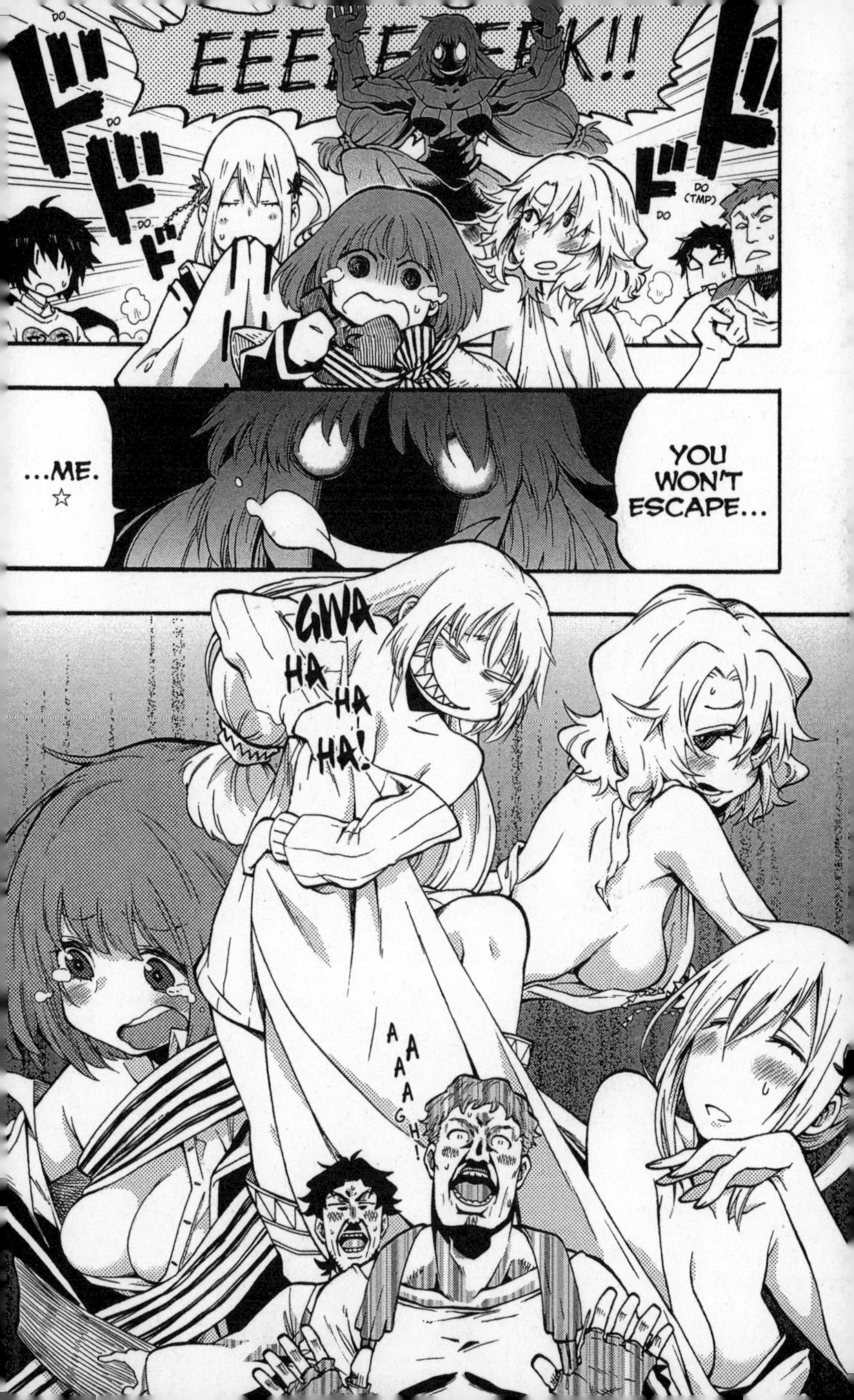
ド
DO (TMP)
DO
EEEEEEEEK!!
ドドド
DO
DO
DO
YOU WON'T ESCAPE...
...ME. ☆
GWA HA HA HA!
AAAAAGH!

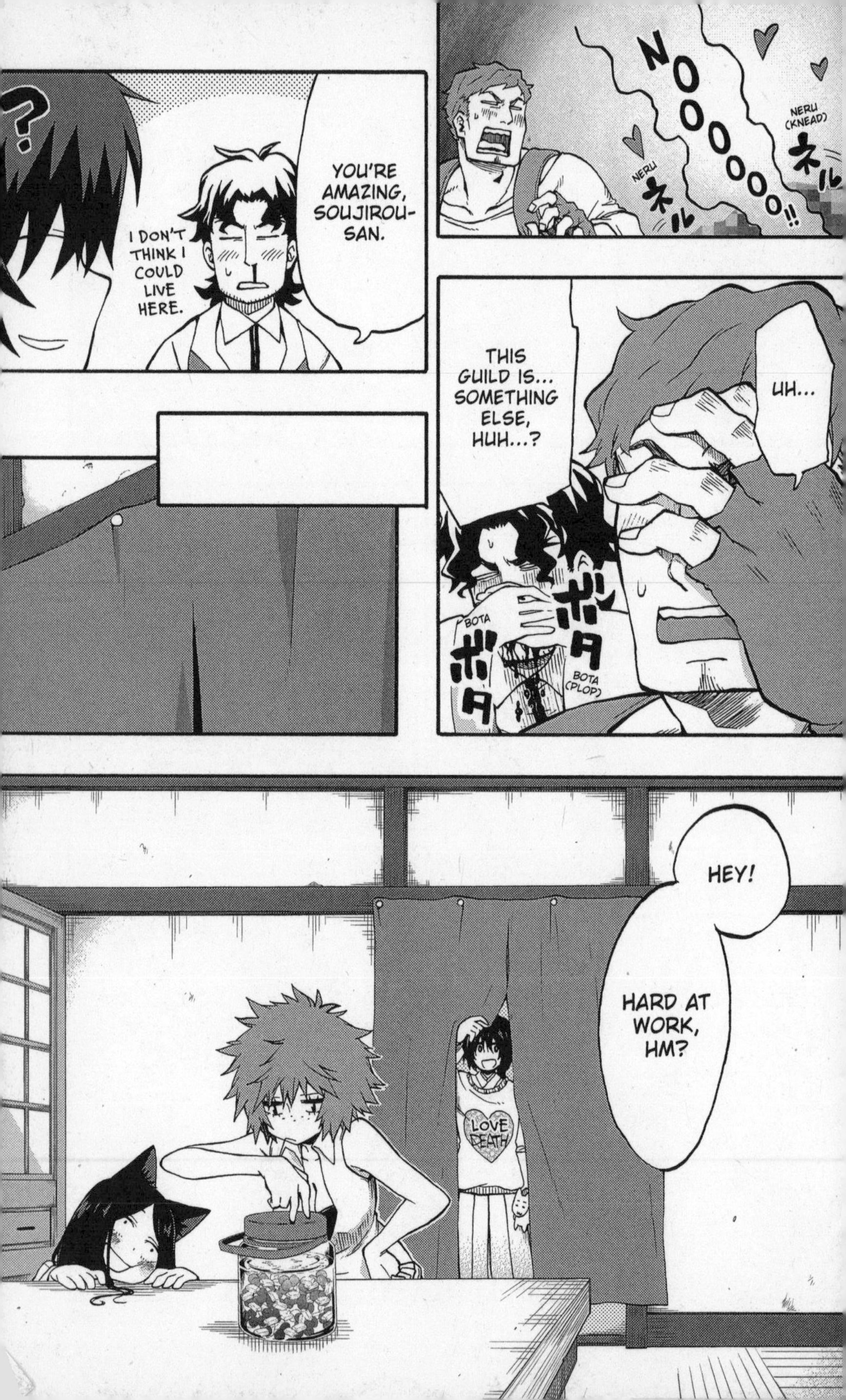
NOOOOOO!!
NERU (KNEAD)
ネル
NERU
ネル
YOU'RE AMAZING, SOUJIROU-SAN.
I DON'T THINK I COULD LIVE HERE.
UH...
THIS GUILD IS... SOMETHING ELSE, HUH...?
ボタ
BOTA (PLOP)
ボタ
BOTA
HEY!
HARD AT WORK, HM?
LOVE DEATH

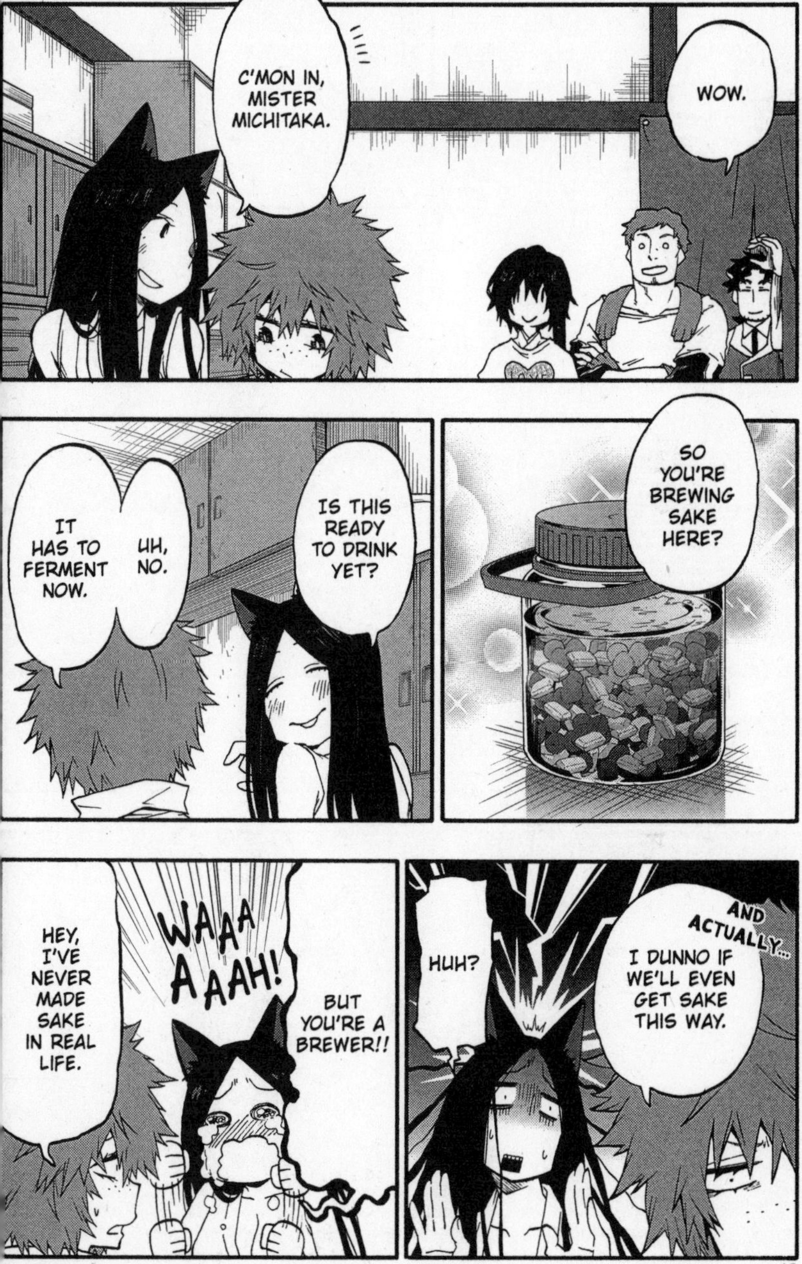
WOW.
C'MON IN, MISTER MICHITAKA.
SO YOU'RE BREWING SAKE HERE?
IS THIS READY TO DRINK YET?
UH, NO.
IT HAS TO FERMENT NOW.
AND ACTUALLY...
I DUNNO IF WE'LL EVEN GET SAKE THIS WAY.
HUH?
...
BUT YOU'RE A BREWER!!
WAAAAAAH!
HEY, I'VE NEVER MADE SAKE IN REAL LIFE.

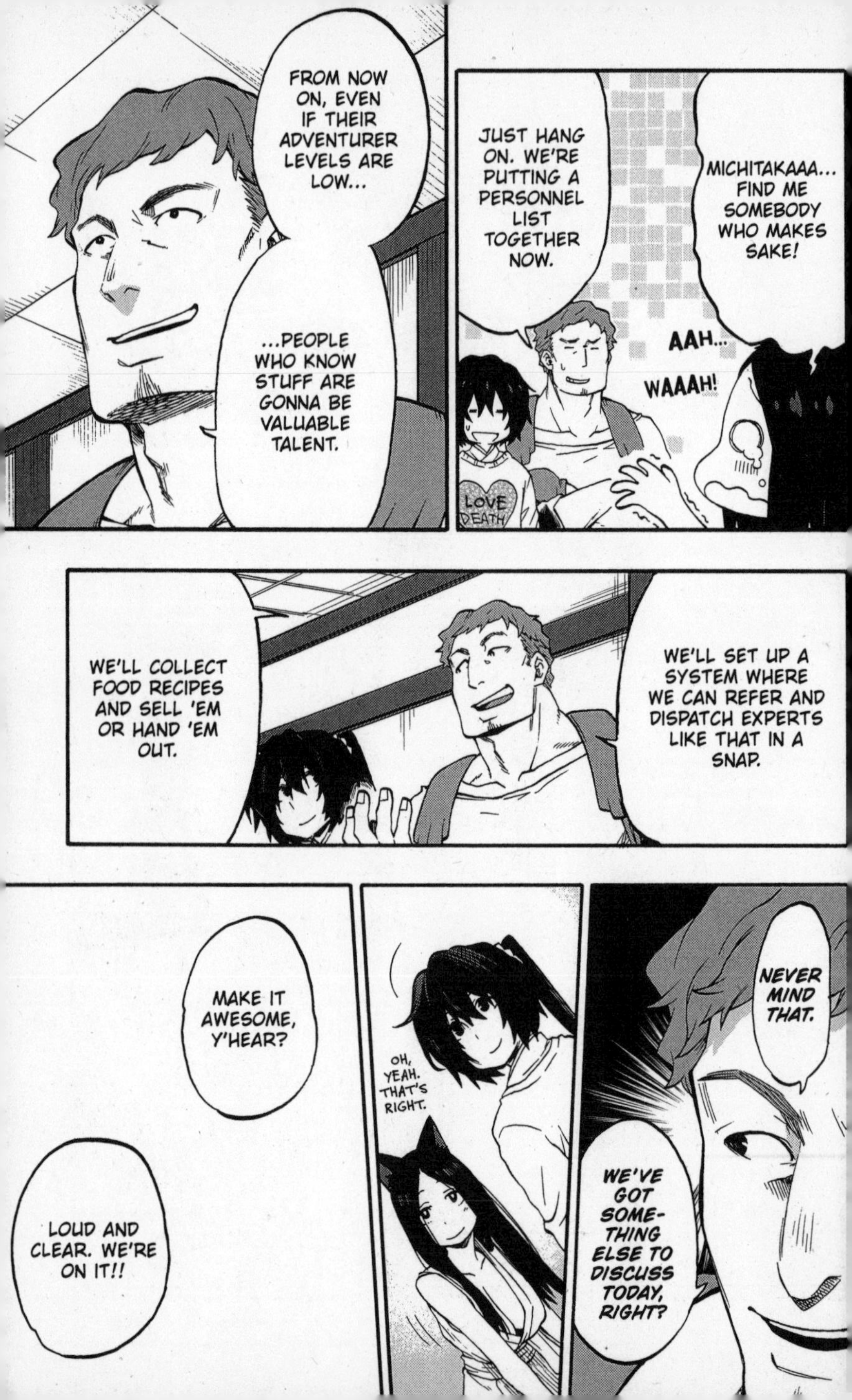
MICHITAKAAA... FIND ME SOMEBODY WHO MAKES SAKE!
AAH...
WAAAH!
JUST HANG ON. WE'RE PUTTING A PERSONNEL LIST TOGETHER NOW.
LOVE DEATH
FROM NOW ON, EVEN IF THEIR ADVENTURER LEVELS ARE LOW...
...PEOPLE WHO KNOW STUFF ARE GONNA BE VALUABLE TALENT.
WE'LL SET UP A SYSTEM WHERE WE CAN REFER AND DISPATCH EXPERTS LIKE THAT IN A SNAP.
WE'LL COLLECT FOOD RECIPES AND SELL 'EM OR HAND 'EM OUT.
NEVER MIND THAT.
WE'VE GOT SOME-THING ELSE TO DISCUSS TODAY, RIGHT?
OH, YEAH. THAT'S RIGHT.
MAKE IT AWESOME, Y'HEAR?
LOUD AND CLEAR. WE'RE ON IT!!

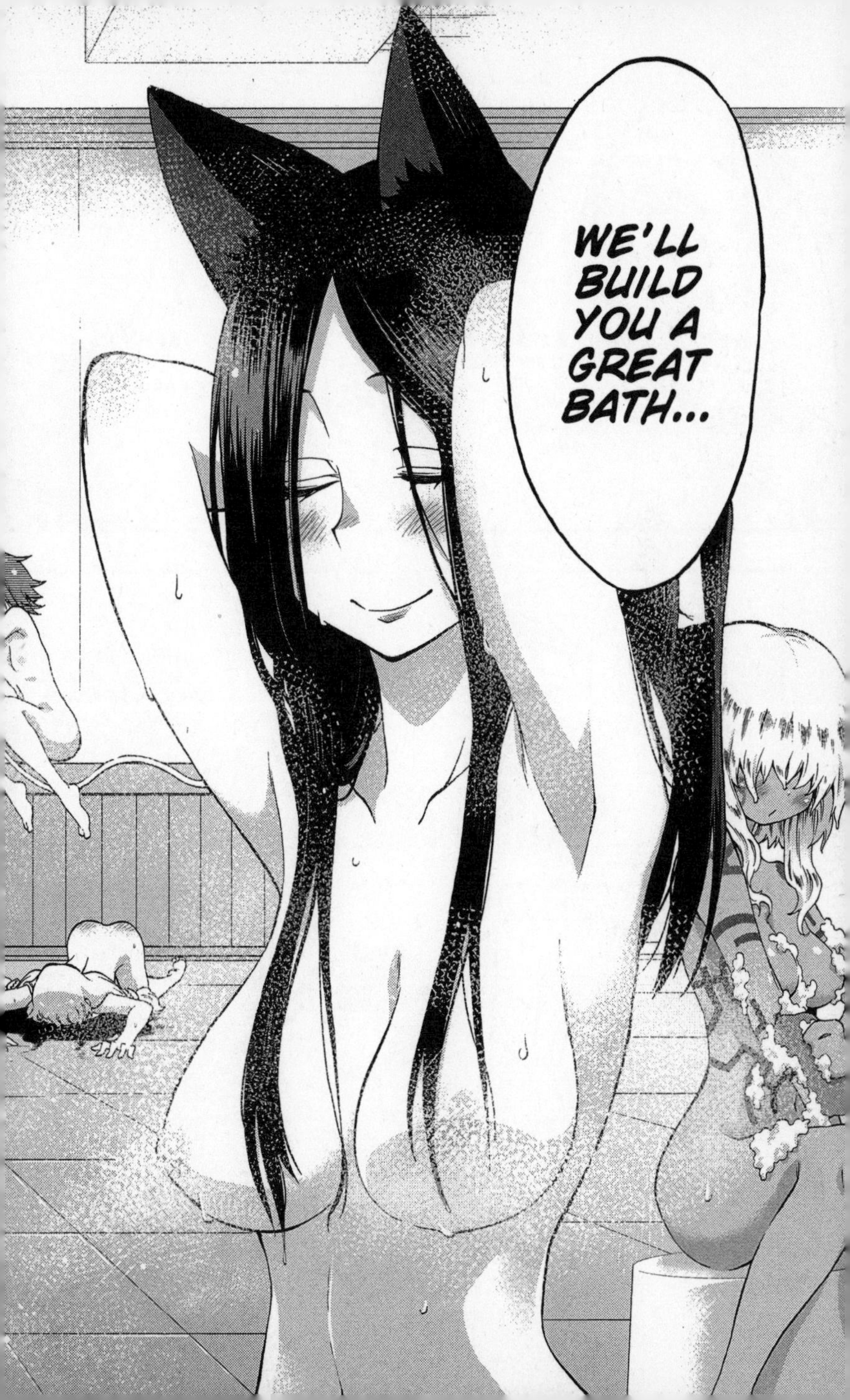
WE'LL BUILD YOU A GREAT BATH...

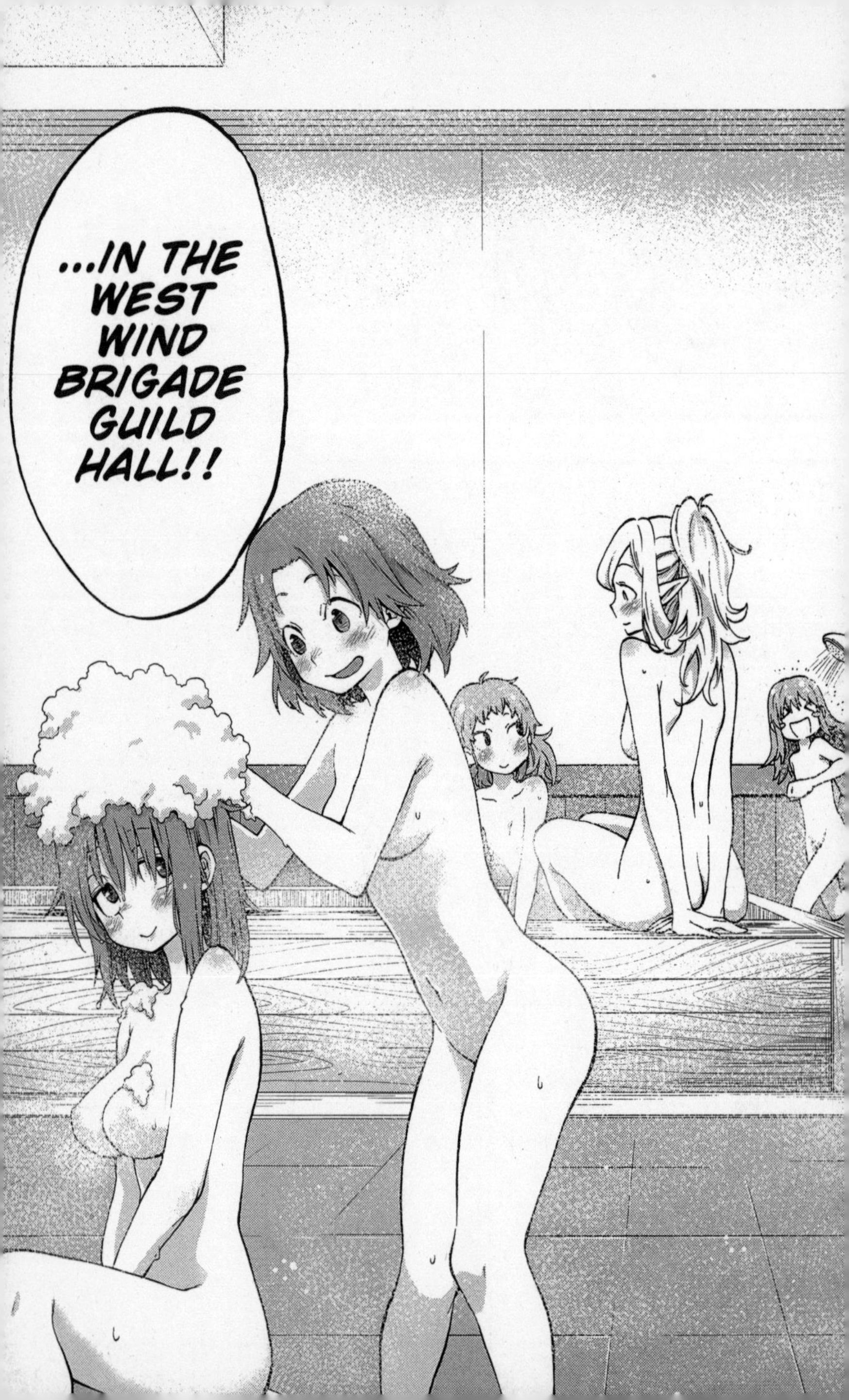
...IN THE WEST WIND BRIGADE GUILD HALL!!

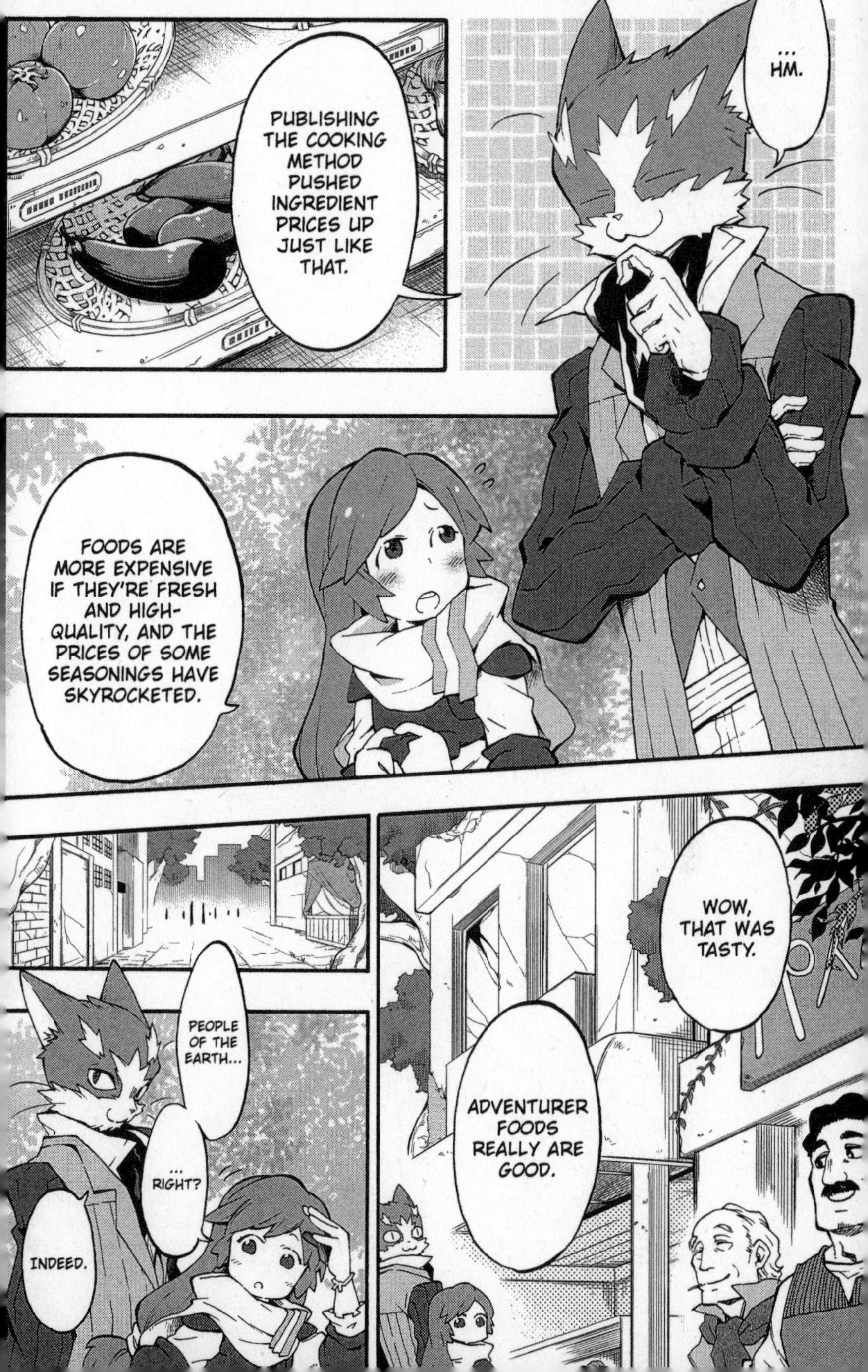
... HM.
PUBLISHING THE COOKING METHOD PUSHED INGREDIENT PRICES UP JUST LIKE THAT.
FOODS ARE MORE EXPENSIVE IF THEY'RE FRESH AND HIGH-QUALITY, AND THE PRICES OF SOME SEASONINGS HAVE SKYROCKETED.
WOW, THAT WAS TASTY.
ADVENTURER FOODS REALLY ARE GOOD.
PEOPLE OF THE EARTH...
... RIGHT?
INDEED.

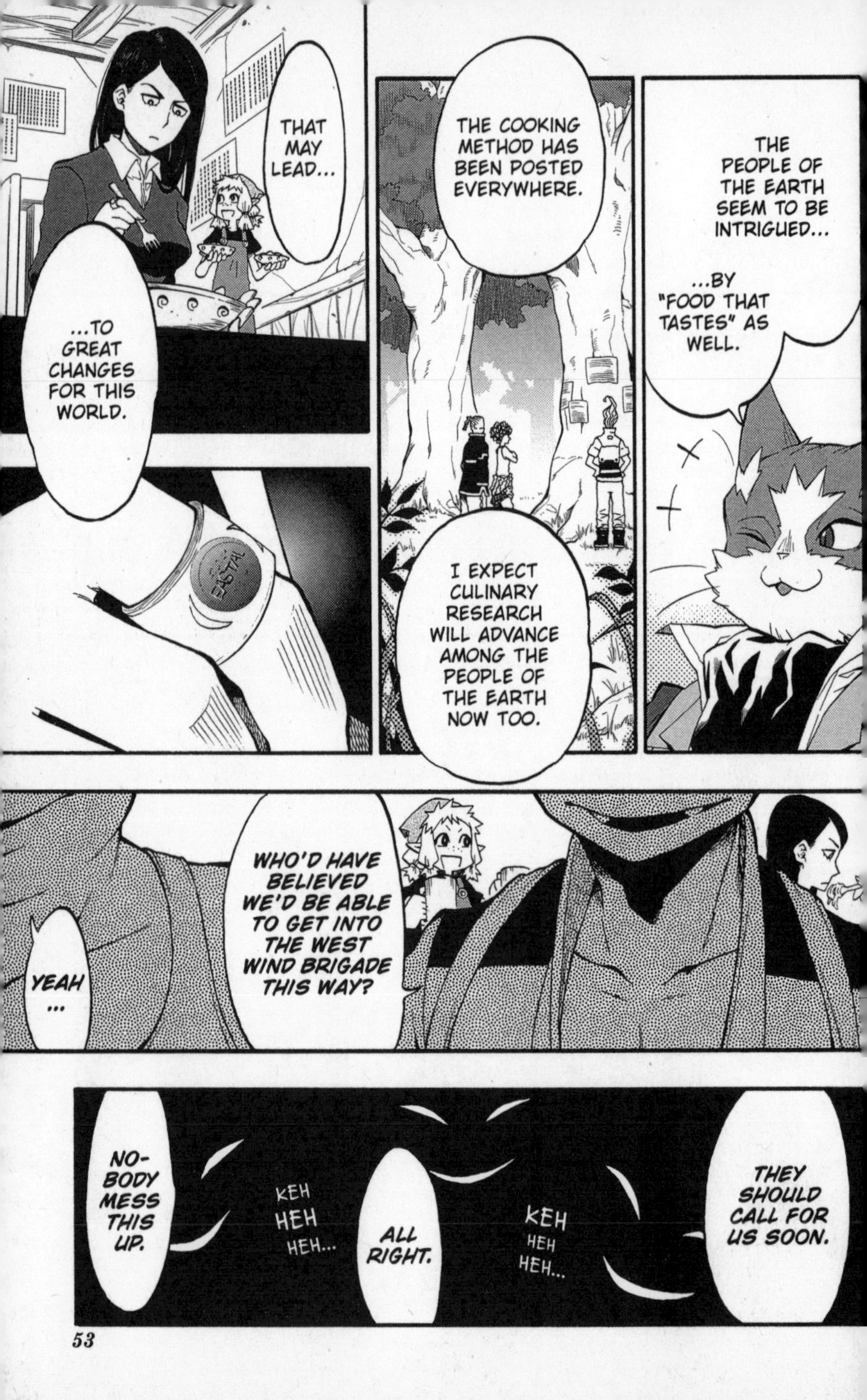
THE PEOPLE OF THE EARTH SEEM TO BE INTRIGUED...
...BY "FOOD THAT TASTES" AS WELL.
THE COOKING METHOD HAS BEEN POSTED EVERYWHERE.
I EXPECT CULINARY RESEARCH WILL ADVANCE AMONG THE PEOPLE OF THE EARTH NOW TOO.
THAT MAY LEAD...
...TO GREAT CHANGES FOR THIS WORLD.
PASTA
WHO'D HAVE BELIEVED WE'D BE ABLE TO GET INTO THE WEST WIND BRIGADE THIS WAY?
YEAH...
THEY SHOULD CALL FOR US SOON.
KEH HEH HEH...
ALL RIGHT.
KEH HEH HEH...
NO-BODY MESS THIS UP.

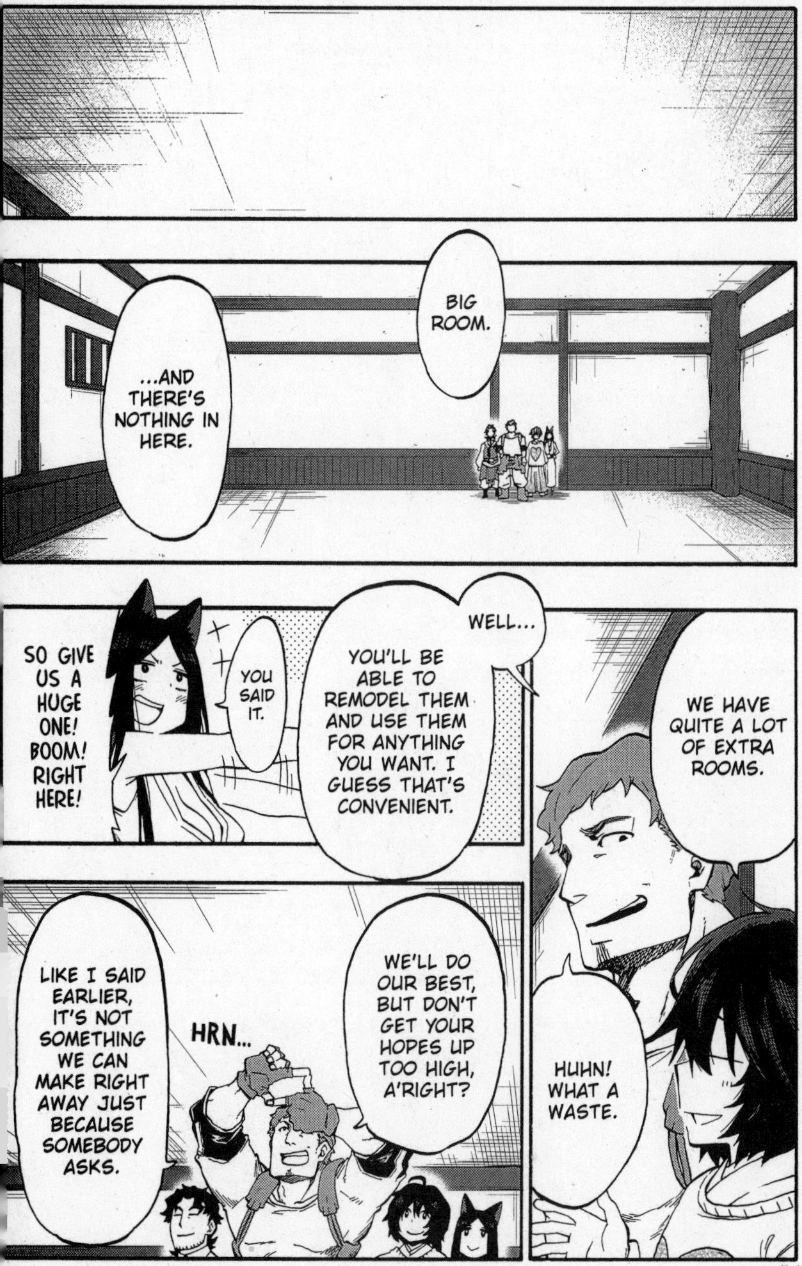
BIG ROOM.
...AND THERE'S NOTHING IN HERE.
WE HAVE QUITE A LOT OF EXTRA ROOMS.
HUHN! WHAT A WASTE.
WELL...
YOU'LL BE ABLE TO REMODEL THEM AND USE THEM FOR ANYTHING YOU WANT. I GUESS THAT'S CONVENIENT.
YOU SAID IT.
SO GIVE US A HUGE ONE! BOOM! RIGHT HERE!
WE'LL DO OUR BEST, BUT DON'T GET YOUR HOPES UP TOO HIGH, A'RIGHT?
HRN...
LIKE I SAID EARLIER, IT'S NOT SOMETHING WE CAN MAKE RIGHT AWAY JUST BECAUSE SOMEBODY ASKS.

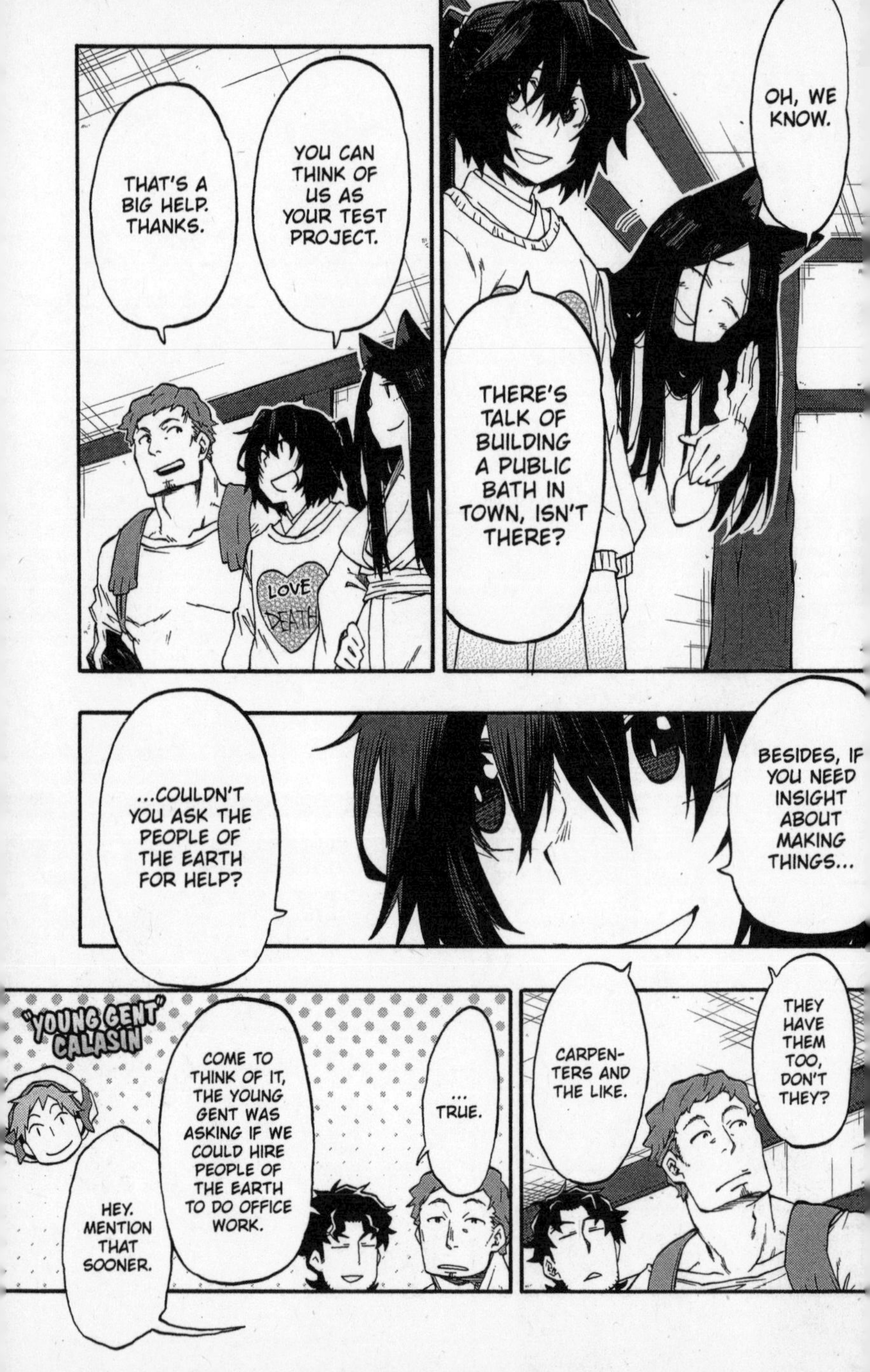
OH, WE KNOW.
THERE'S TALK OF BUILDING A PUBLIC BATH IN TOWN, ISN'T THERE?
YOU CAN THINK OF US AS YOUR TEST PROJECT.
THAT'S A BIG HELP. THANKS.
LOVE DEATH
BESIDES, IF YOU NEED INSIGHT ABOUT MAKING THINGS...
...COULDN'T YOU ASK THE PEOPLE OF THE EARTH FOR HELP?
THEY HAVE THEM TOO, DON'T THEY?
CARPEN-TERS AND THE LIKE.
... TRUE.
COME TO THINK OF IT, THE YOUNG GENT WAS ASKING IF WE COULD HIRE PEOPLE OF THE EARTH TO DO OFFICE WORK.
"YOUNG GENT" CALASIN
HEY. MENTION THAT SOONER.

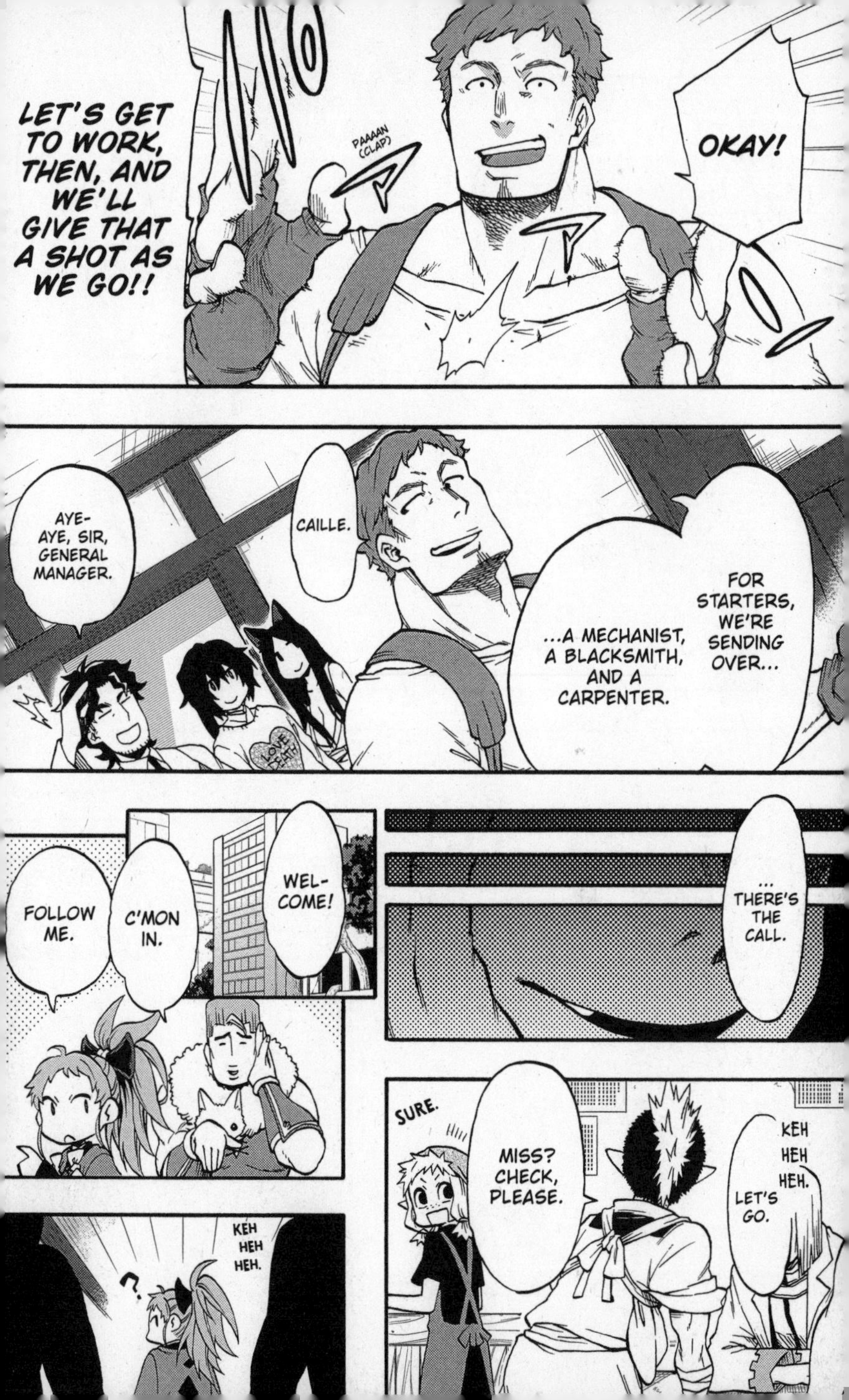
OKAY!
PAAAAN (CLAP)
LET'S GET TO WORK, THEN, AND WE'LL GIVE THAT A SHOT AS WE GO!!
FOR STARTERS, WE'RE SENDING OVER...
...A MECHANIST, A BLACKSMITH, AND A CARPENTER.
CAILLE.
AYE-AYE, SIR, GENERAL MANAGER.
...THERE'S THE CALL.
WEL-COME!
C'MON IN.
FOLLOW ME.
KEH HEH HEH.
LET'S GO.
MISS? CHECK, PLEASE.
SURE.
KEH HEH HEH.

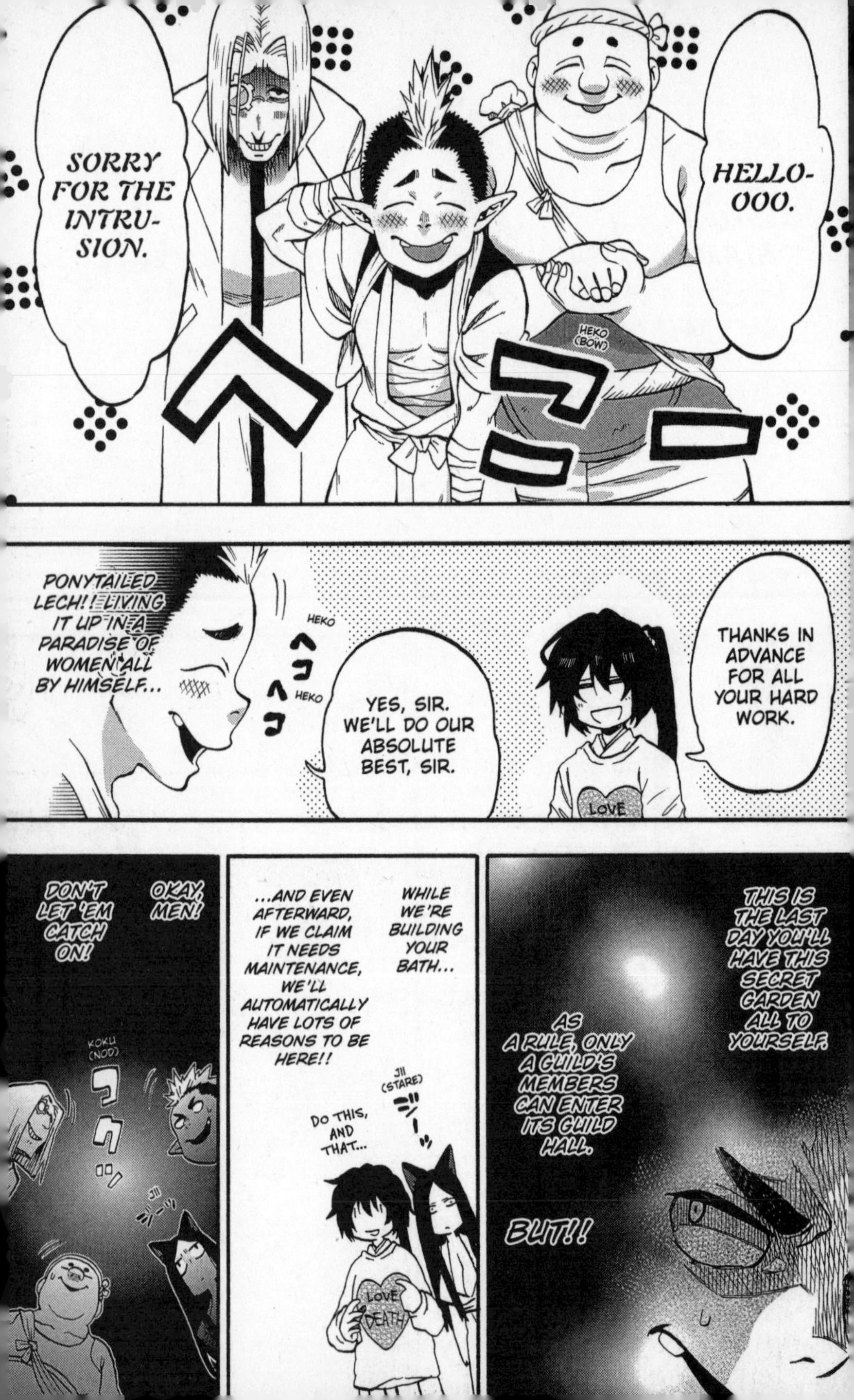
HELLO-OOO.
HEKO (BOW)
SORRY FOR THE INTRU-SION.
THANKS IN ADVANCE FOR ALL YOUR HARD WORK.
LOVE
YES, SIR. WE'LL DO OUR ABSOLUTE BEST, SIR.
HEKO
HEKO
PONYTAILED LECH!! LIVING IT UP IN A PARADISE OF WOMEN ALL BY HIMSELF...
THIS IS THE LAST DAY YOU'LL HAVE THIS SECRET GARDEN ALL TO YOURSELF.
AS A RULE, ONLY A GUILD'S MEMBERS CAN ENTER ITS GUILD HALL.
BUT!!
WHILE WE'RE BUILDING YOUR BATH...
...AND EVEN AFTERWARD, IF WE CLAIM IT NEEDS MAINTENANCE, WE'LL AUTOMATICALLY HAVE LOTS OF REASONS TO BE HERE!!
JII (STARE)
DO THIS, AND THAT...
LOVE DEATH
OKAY, MEN!
DON'T LET 'EM CATCH ON!
KOKU (NOD)
JII

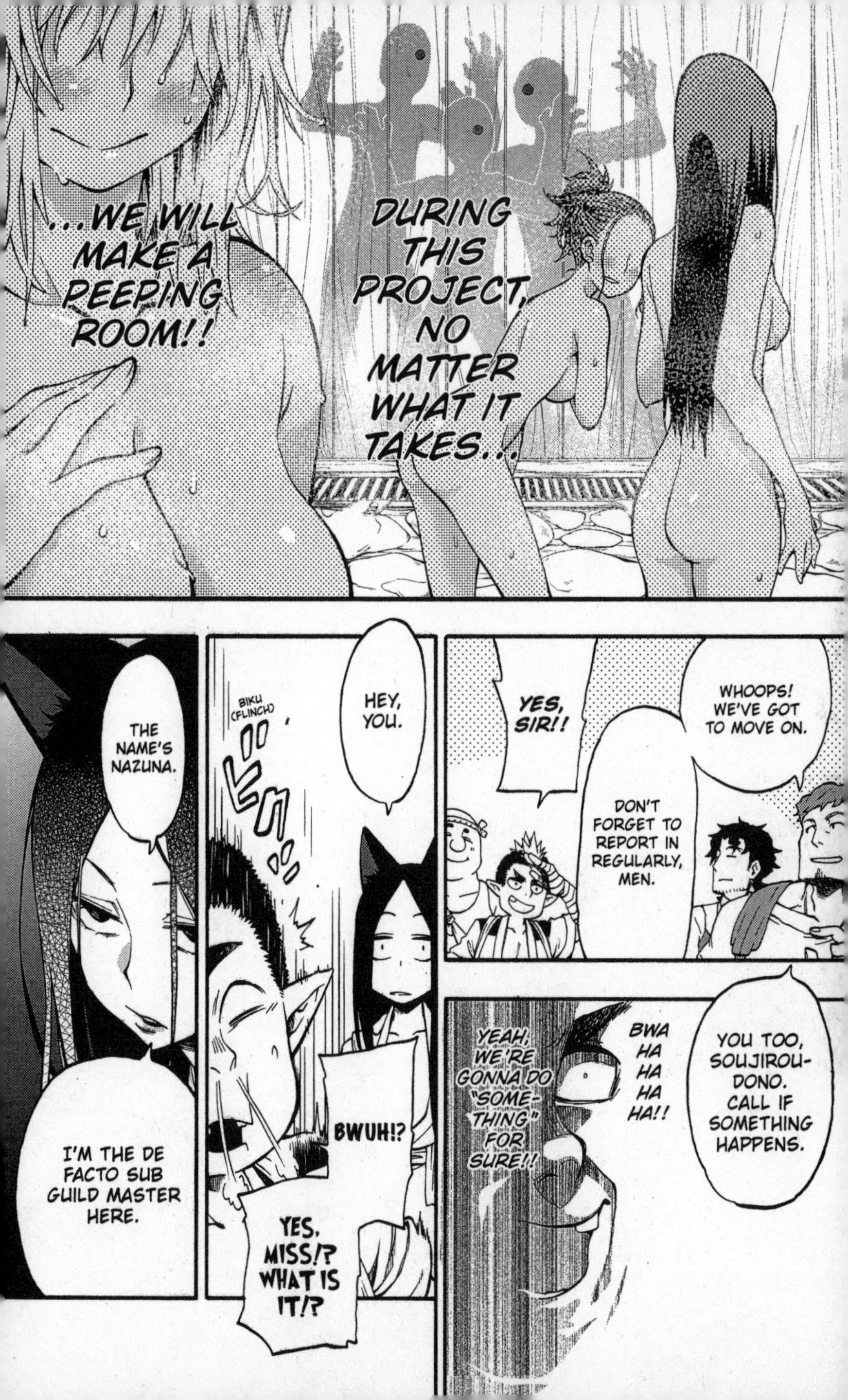
DURING THIS PROJECT, NO MATTER WHAT IT TAKES...
...WE WILL MAKE A PEEPING ROOM!!
WHOOPS! WE'VE GOT TO MOVE ON.
YES, SIR!!
DON'T FORGET TO REPORT IN REGULARLY, MEN.
YOU TOO, SOUJIROU-DONO. CALL IF SOMETHING HAPPENS.
BWA HA HA HA HA!!
YEAH, WE'RE GONNA DO "SOMETHING" FOR SURE!!
HEY, YOU.
BIKU (FLINCH)
BWUH!?
YES, MISS!? WHAT IS IT!?
THE NAME'S NAZUNA.
I'M THE DE FACTO SUB GUILD MASTER HERE.

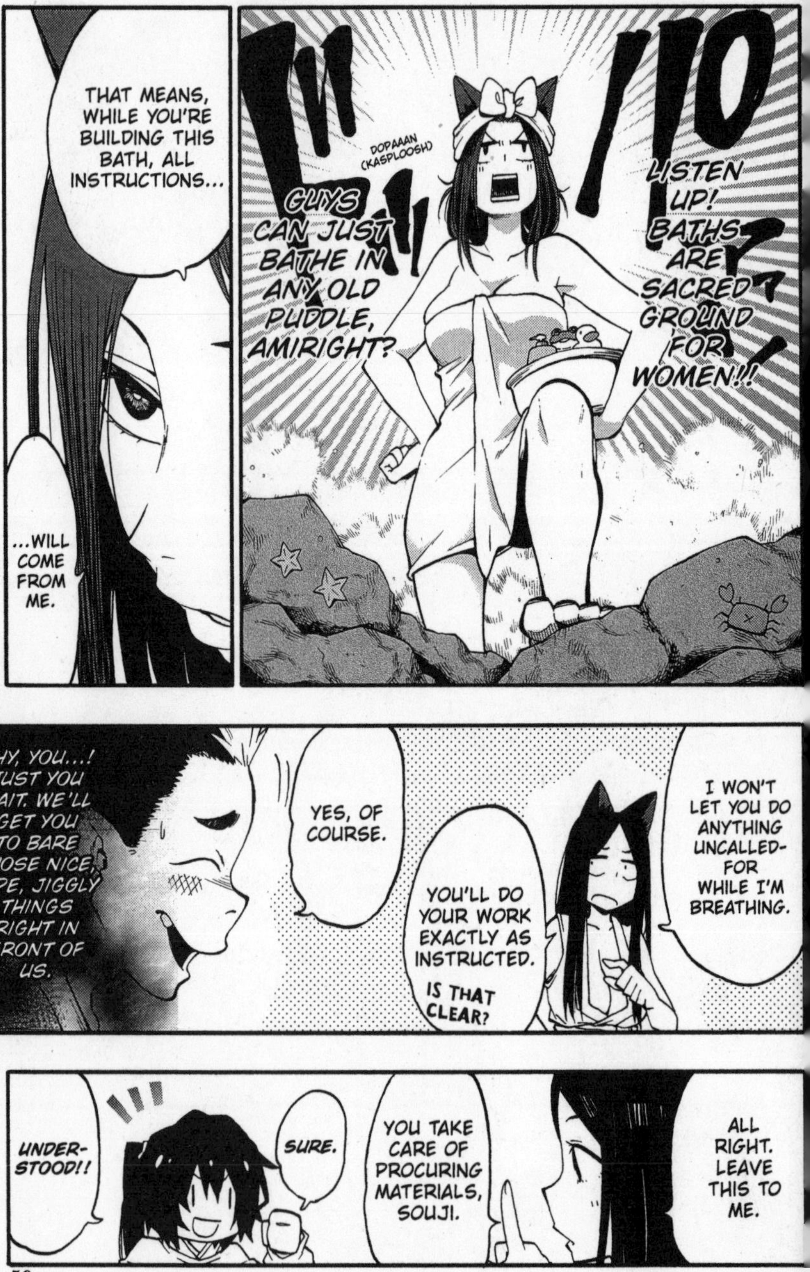
DOPAAAN (KASPLOOSH)
LISTEN UP! BATHS ARE SACRED GROUND FOR WOMEN!!
GUYS CAN JUST BATHE IN ANY OLD PUDDLE, AMIRIGHT?
THAT MEANS, WHILE YOU'RE BUILDING THIS BATH, ALL INSTRUCTIONS...
...WILL COME FROM ME.
I WON'T LET YOU DO ANYTHING UNCALLED-FOR WHILE I'M BREATHING.
YOU'LL DO YOUR WORK EXACTLY AS INSTRUCTED.
IS THAT CLEAR?
YES, OF COURSE.
WHY, YOU...! JUST YOU WAIT. WE'LL GET YOU TO BARE THOSE NICE, RIPE, JIGGLY THINGS RIGHT IN FRONT OF US.
ALL RIGHT. LEAVE THIS TO ME.
YOU TAKE CARE OF PROCURING MATERIALS, SOUJI.
SURE.
UNDER-STOOD!!

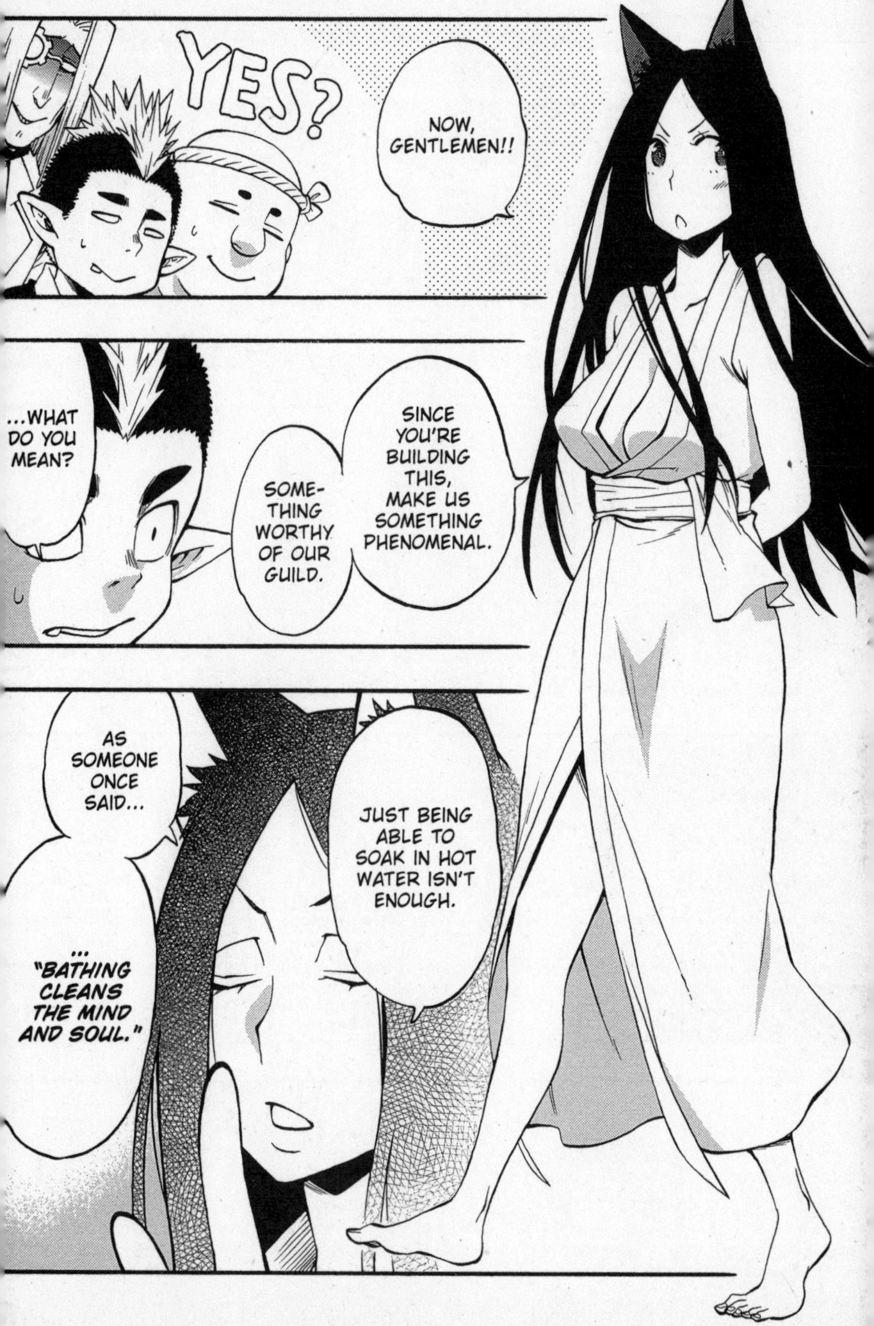
NOW, GENTLEMEN!!
YES?
SINCE YOU'RE BUILDING THIS, MAKE US SOMETHING PHENOMENAL.
SOME-THING WORTHY OF OUR GUILD.
...WHAT DO YOU MEAN?
JUST BEING ABLE TO SOAK IN HOT WATER ISN'T ENOUGH.
AS SOMEONE ONCE SAID...
..."BATHING CLEANS THE MIND AND SOUL."

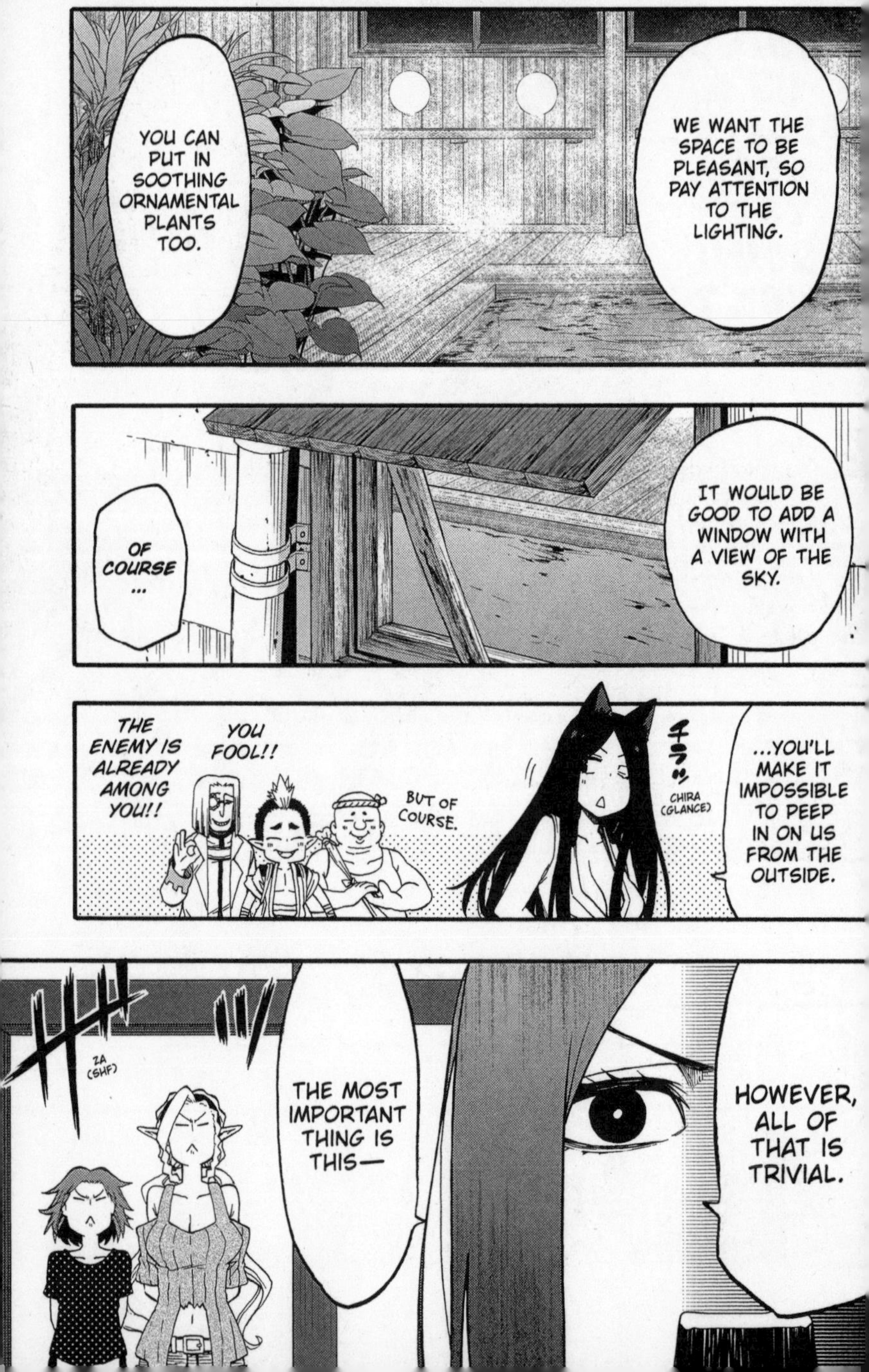
WE WANT THE SPACE TO BE PLEASANT, SO PAY ATTENTION TO THE LIGHTING.
YOU CAN PUT IN SOOTHING ORNAMENTAL PLANTS TOO.
IT WOULD BE GOOD TO ADD A WINDOW WITH A VIEW OF THE SKY.
OF COURSE...
...YOU'LL MAKE IT IMPOSSIBLE TO PEEP IN ON US FROM THE OUTSIDE.
チラッ
CHIRA (GLANCE)
BUT OF COURSE.
YOU FOOL!!
THE ENEMY IS ALREADY AMONG YOU!!
HOWEVER, ALL OF THAT IS TRIVIAL.
THE MOST IMPORTANT THING IS THIS—
ZA (SHF)

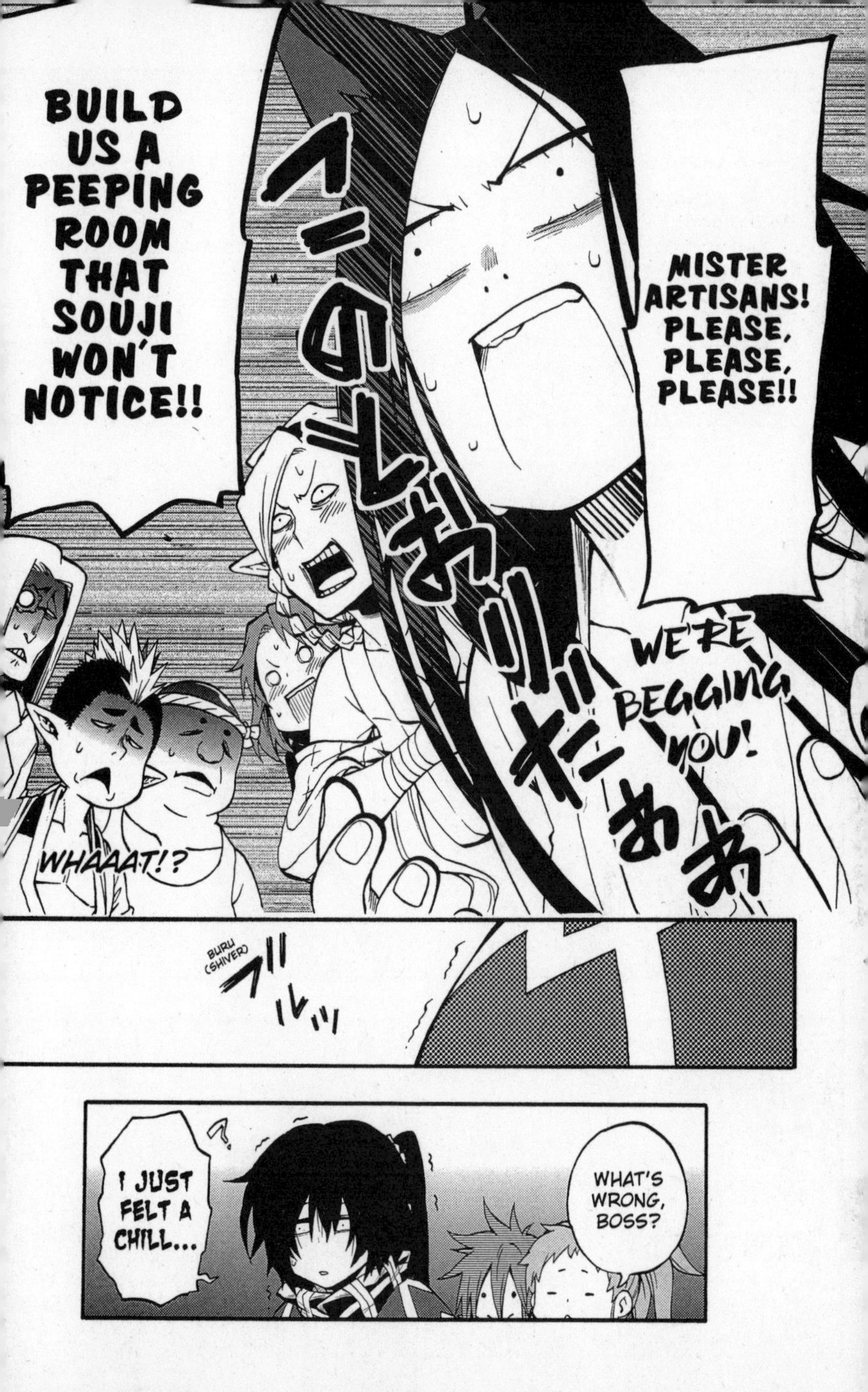
MISTER ARTISANS! PLEASE, PLEASE, PLEASE!!
WE'RE BEGGING YOU!
BUILD US A PEEPING ROOM THAT SOUJI WON'T NOTICE!!
WHAAAT!?
BURU (SHIVER)
ブルッ
WHAT'S WRONG, BOSS?
I JUST FELT A CHILL...

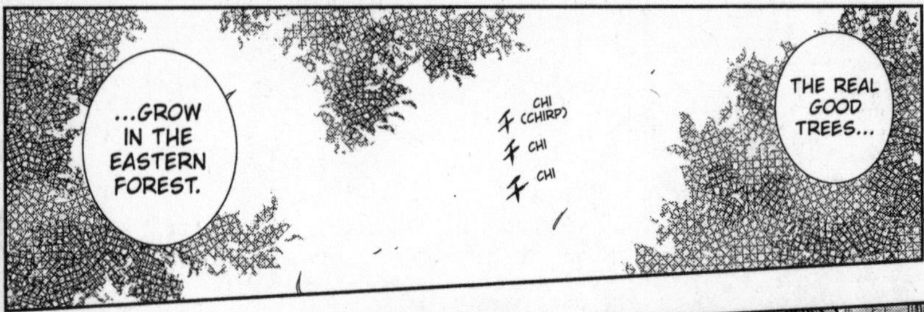
THE REAL GOOD TREES...
チ CHI (CHIRP)
チ CHI
チ CHI
...GROW IN THE EASTERN FOREST.

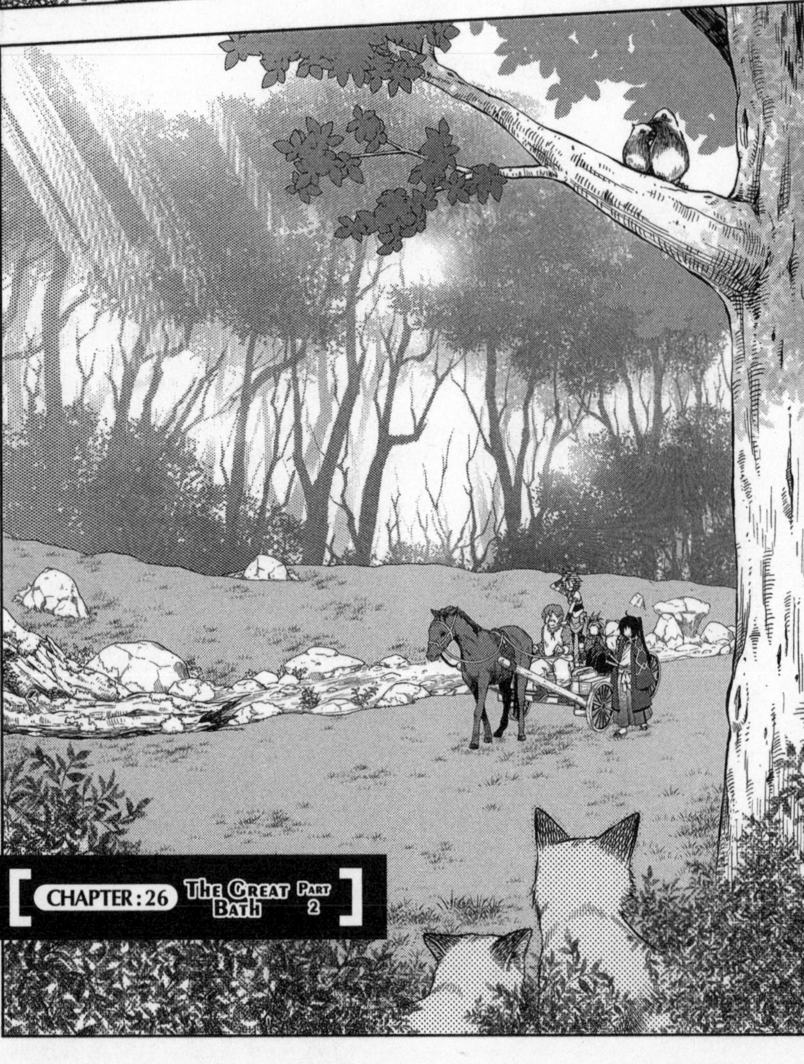

CHAPTER : 26 The Great Bath Part 2

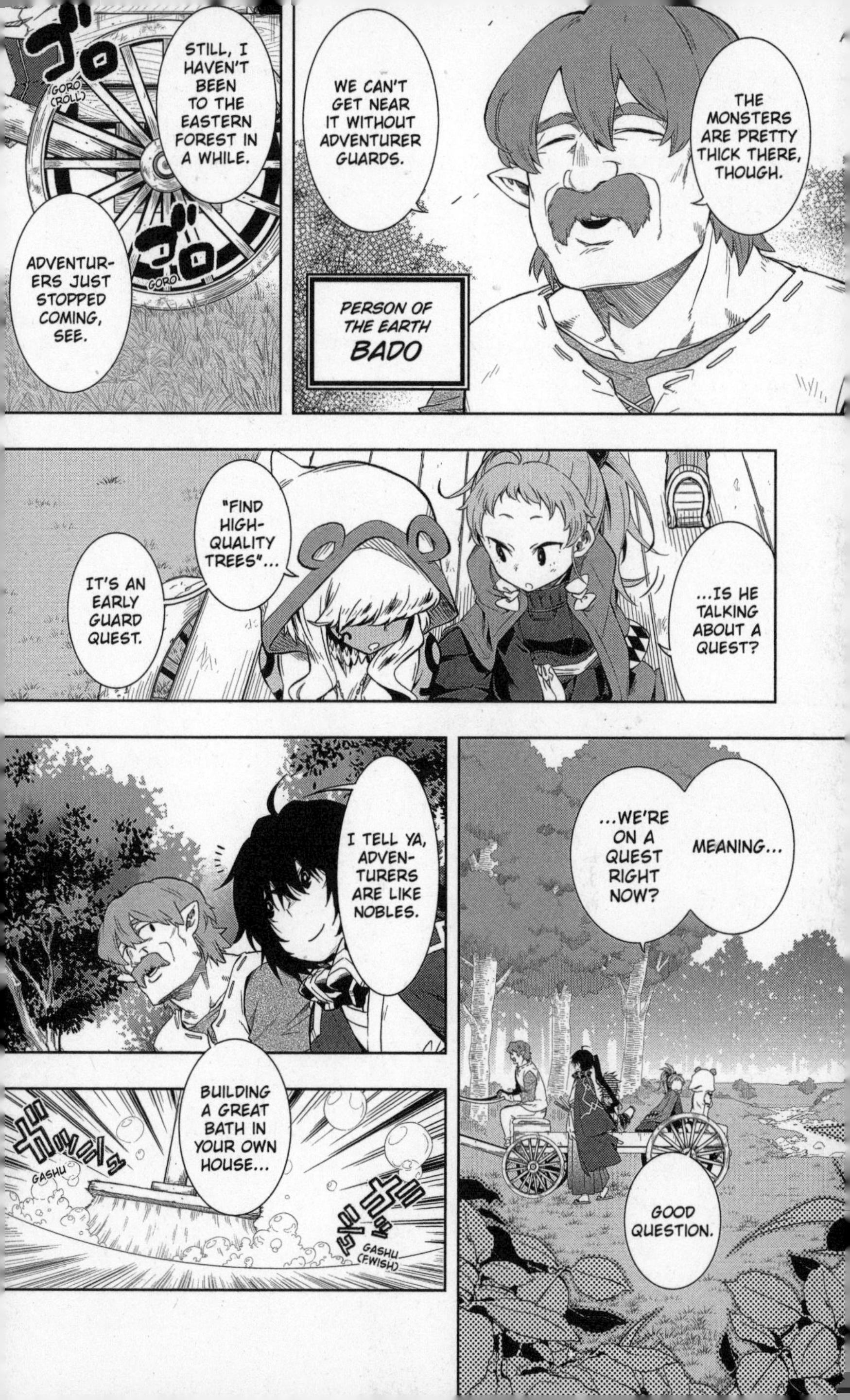
THE MONSTERS ARE PRETTY THICK THERE, THOUGH.
WE CAN'T GET NEAR IT WITHOUT ADVENTURER GUARDS.
PERSON OF THE EARTH BADO
ゴロ
GORO (ROLL)
STILL, I HAVEN'T BEEN TO THE EASTERN FOREST IN A WHILE.
ゴロ
GORO
ADVENTURERS JUST STOPPED COMING, SEE.
...IS HE TALKING ABOUT A QUEST?
"FIND HIGH-QUALITY TREES"...
IT'S AN EARLY GUARD QUEST.
MEANING...
...WE'RE ON A QUEST RIGHT NOW?
GOOD QUESTION.
I TELL YA, ADVENTURERS ARE LIKE NOBLES.
BUILDING A GREAT BATH IN YOUR OWN HOUSE...
GASHU
GASHU (FWISH)

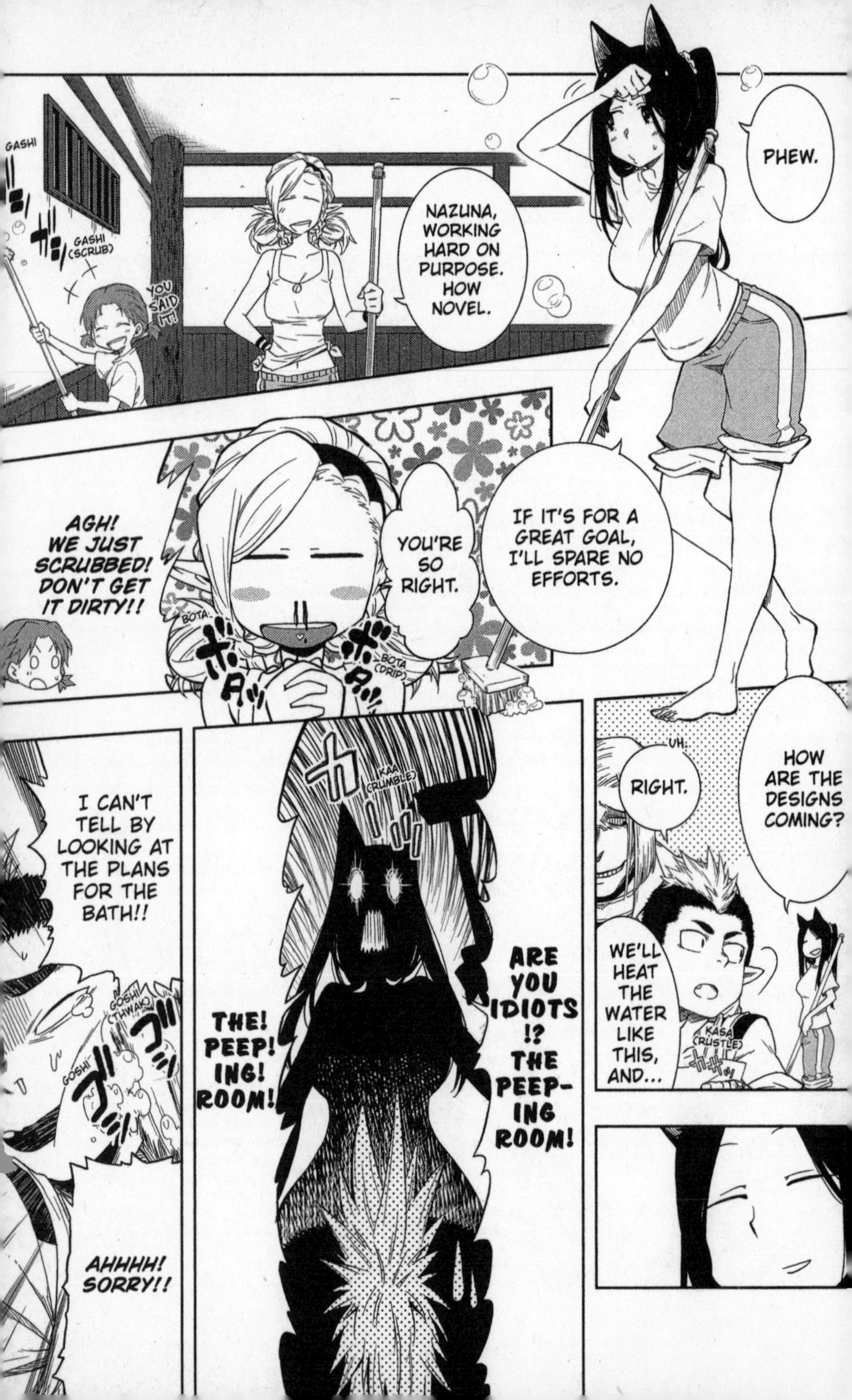
PHEW.
IF IT'S FOR A GREAT GOAL, I'LL SPARE NO EFFORTS.
NAZUNA, WORKING HARD ON PURPOSE. HOW NOVEL.
YOU SAID IT!
GASHI
GASHI (SCRUB)
YOU'RE SO RIGHT.
BOTA
BOTA (DRIP)
AGH! WE JUST SCRUBBED! DON'T GET IT DIRTY!!
HOW ARE THE DESIGNS COMING?
UH:
RIGHT.
WE'LL HEAT THE WATER LIKE THIS, AND...
KASA (RUSTLE)
KAA (RUMBLE)
ARE YOU IDIOTS!? THE PEEP-ING ROOM!
THE! PEEP! ING! ROOM!
I CAN'T TELL BY LOOKING AT THE PLANS FOR THE BATH!!
GOSHI (THWAK)
GOSHI
AHHHH! SORRY!!

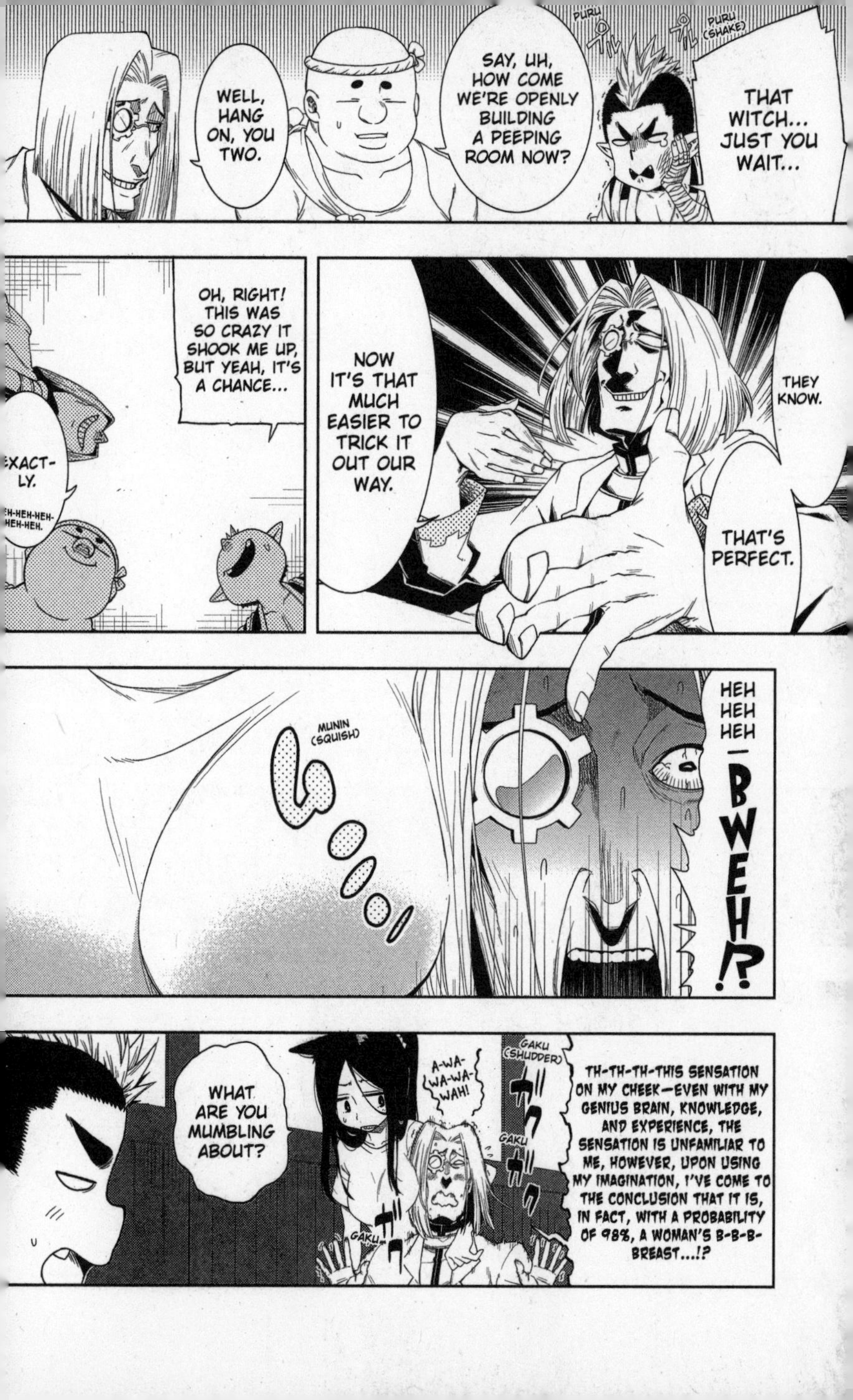
PURU PURU (SHAKE)
THAT WITCH... JUST YOU WAIT...
SAY, UH, HOW COME WE'RE OPENLY BUILDING A PEEPING ROOM NOW?
WELL, HANG ON, YOU TWO.
THEY KNOW.
THAT'S PERFECT.
NOW IT'S THAT MUCH EASIER TO TRICK IT OUT OUR WAY.
OH, RIGHT! THIS WAS SO CRAZY IT SHOOK ME UP, BUT YEAH, IT'S A CHANCE...
XACT-LY.
EH-HEH-HEH-HEH-HEH.
HEH HEH HEH—BWEH!?
MUNIN (SQUISH)
TH-TH-TH-THIS SENSATION ON MY CHEEK—EVEN WITH MY GENIUS BRAIN, KNOWLEDGE, AND EXPERIENCE, THE SENSATION IS UNFAMILIAR TO ME, HOWEVER, UPON USING MY IMAGINATION, I'VE COME TO THE CONCLUSION THAT IT IS, IN FACT, WITH A PROBABILITY OF 98%, A WOMAN'S B-B-B-BREAST...!?
GAKU (SHUDDER)
A-WA-WA-WA-WAH!
GAKU
GAKU
WHAT ARE YOU MUMBLING ABOUT?

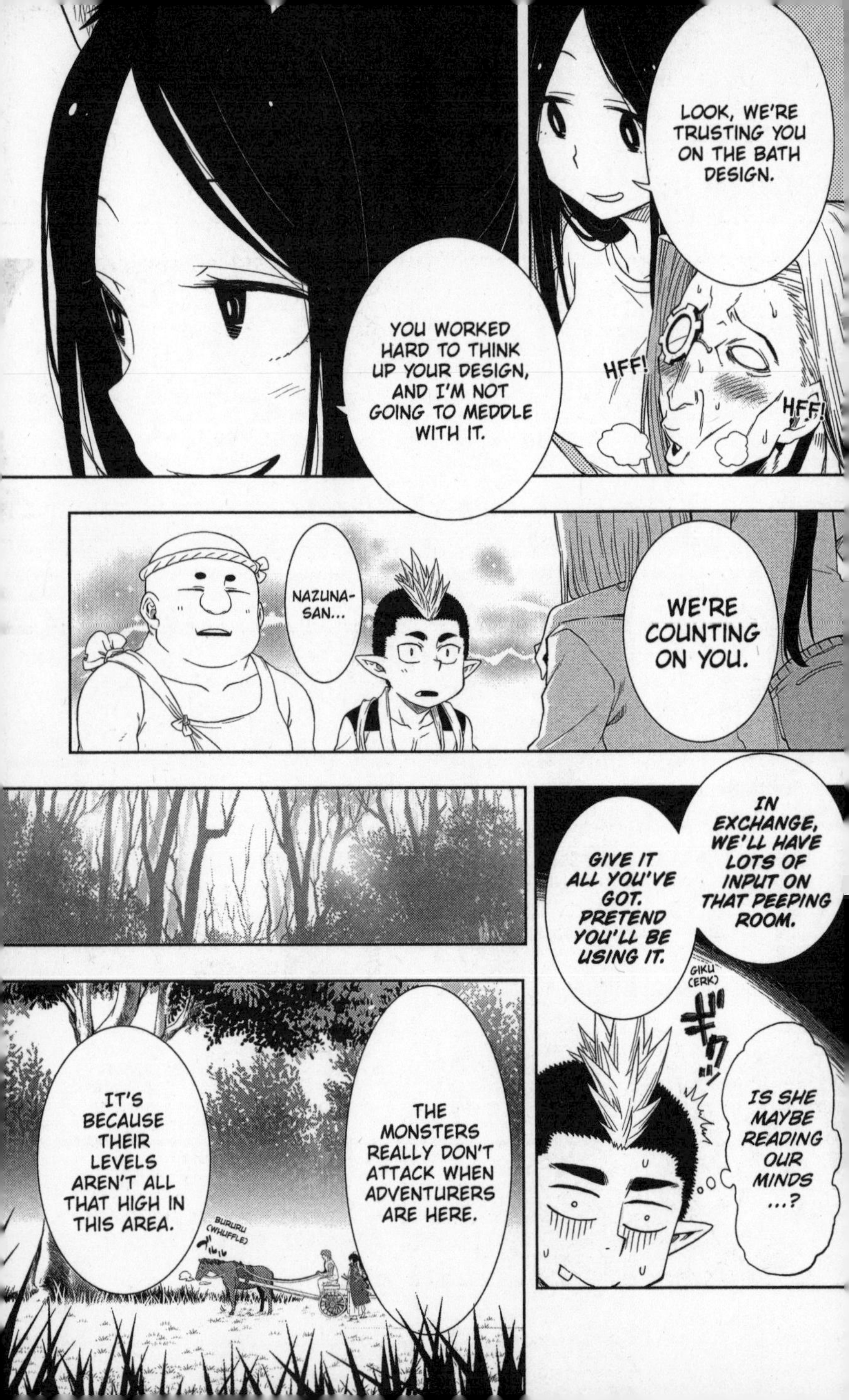
LOOK, WE'RE TRUSTING YOU ON THE BATH DESIGN.
HFF!
HFF!
YOU WORKED HARD TO THINK UP YOUR DESIGN, AND I'M NOT GOING TO MEDDLE WITH IT.
WE'RE COUNTING ON YOU.
NAZUNA-SAN...
IN EXCHANGE, WE'LL HAVE LOTS OF INPUT ON THAT PEEPING ROOM.
GIVE IT ALL YOU'VE GOT. PRETEND YOU'LL BE USING IT.
GIKU (ERK)
IS SHE MAYBE READING OUR MINDS ...?
THE MONSTERS REALLY DON'T ATTACK WHEN ADVENTURERS ARE HERE.
IT'S BECAUSE THEIR LEVELS AREN'T ALL THAT HIGH IN THIS AREA.
BURURU (WHUFFLE)

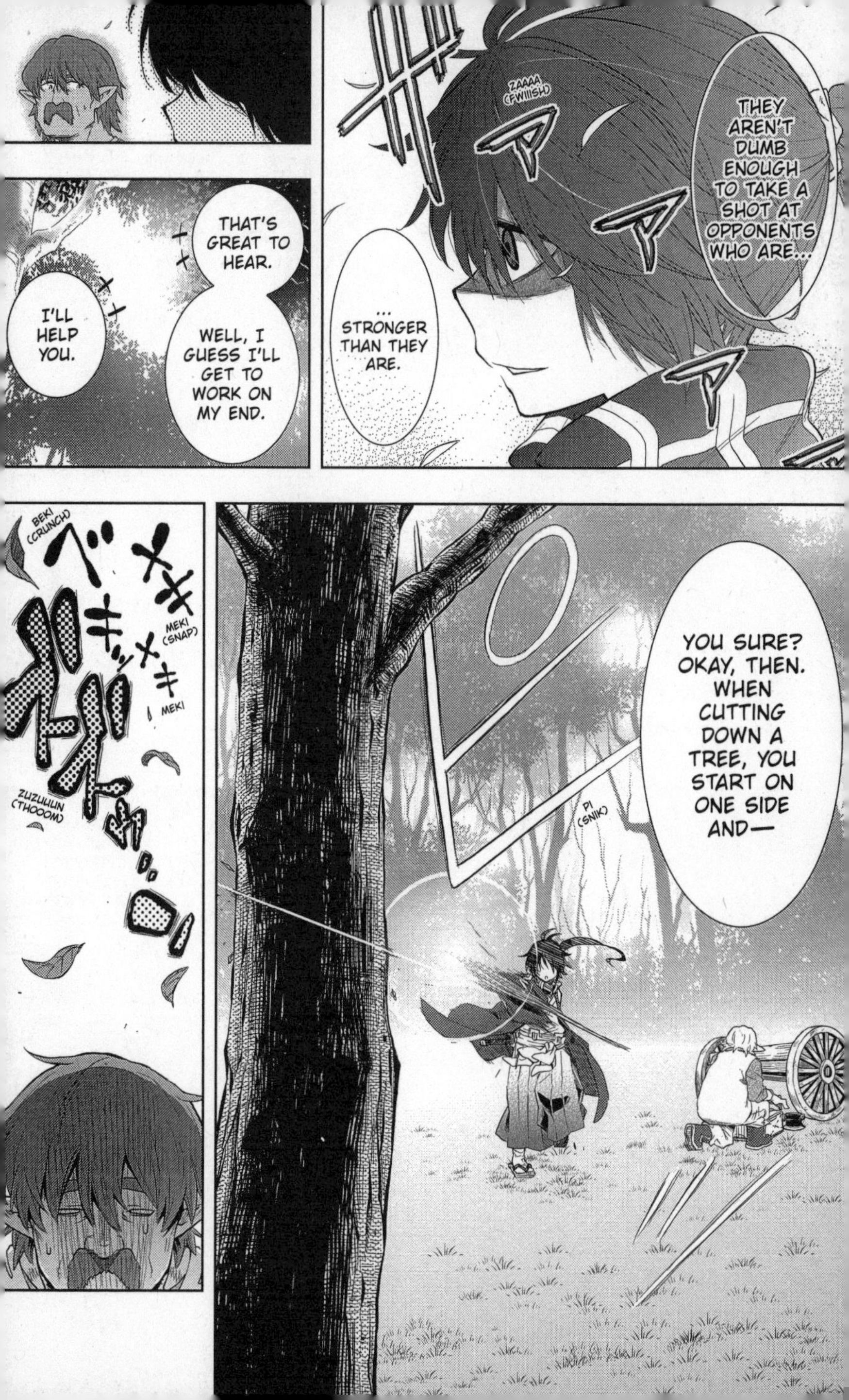
ZAAAA (FWIIISH)
THEY AREN'T DUMB ENOUGH TO TAKE A SHOT AT OPPONENTS WHO ARE...
... STRONGER THAN THEY ARE.
THAT'S GREAT TO HEAR.
WELL, I GUESS I'LL GET TO WORK ON MY END.
I'LL HELP YOU.
YOU SURE? OKAY, THEN. WHEN CUTTING DOWN A TREE, YOU START ON ONE SIDE AND—
PI (SNIK)
BEKI (CRUNCH)
MEKI (SNAP)
MEKI
ZUZUUUN (THOOOM)

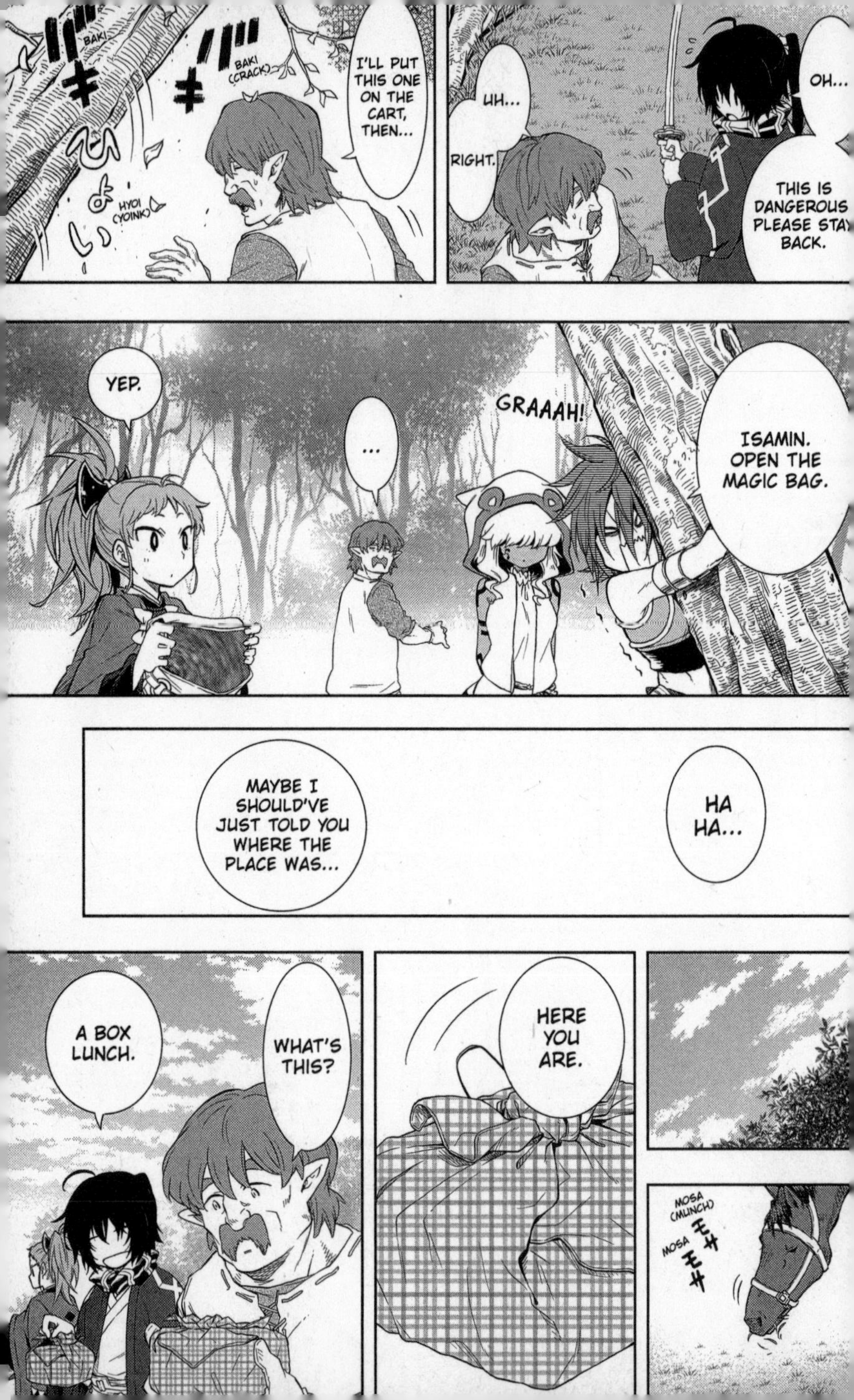
OH...
THIS IS DANGEROUS PLEASE STAY BACK.
UH...
RIGHT.
I'LL PUT THIS ONE ON THE CART, THEN...
BAKI (CRACK)
BAKI
HYOI (YOINK)
ISAMIN. OPEN THE MAGIC BAG.
GRAAAH!
...
YEP.
HA HA...
MAYBE I SHOULD'VE JUST TOLD YOU WHERE THE PLACE WAS...
MOSA (MUNCH)
MOSA
HERE YOU ARE.
WHAT'S THIS?
A BOX LUNCH.

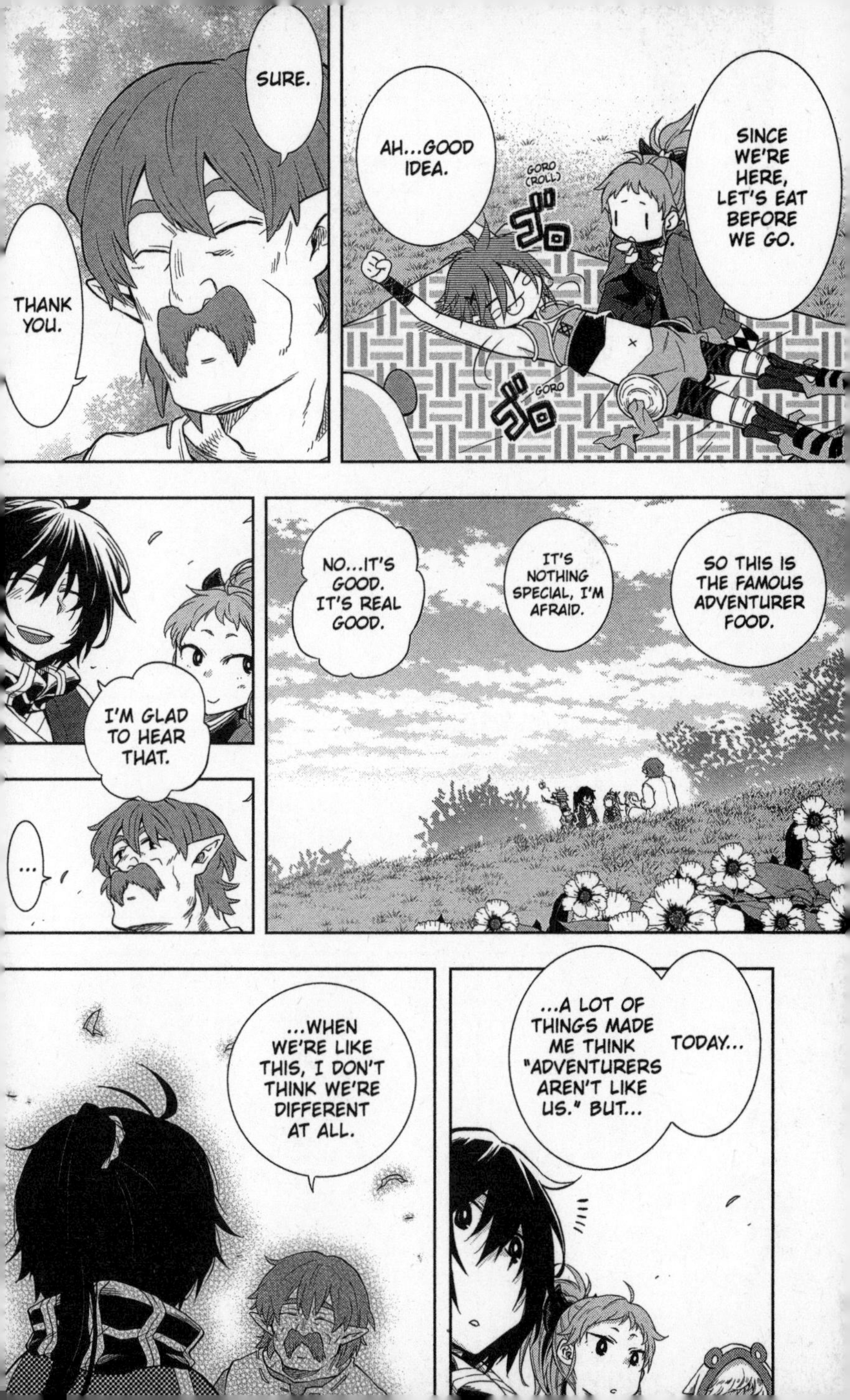
SINCE WE'RE HERE, LET'S EAT BEFORE WE GO.
AH...GOOD IDEA.
GORO (ROLL)
GORO
SURE.
THANK YOU.
SO THIS IS THE FAMOUS ADVENTURER FOOD.
IT'S NOTHING SPECIAL, I'M AFRAID.
NO...IT'S GOOD. IT'S REAL GOOD.
I'M GLAD TO HEAR THAT.
...
TODAY...
...A LOT OF THINGS MADE ME THINK "ADVENTURERS AREN'T LIKE US." BUT...
...WHEN WE'RE LIKE THIS, I DON'T THINK WE'RE DIFFERENT AT ALL.

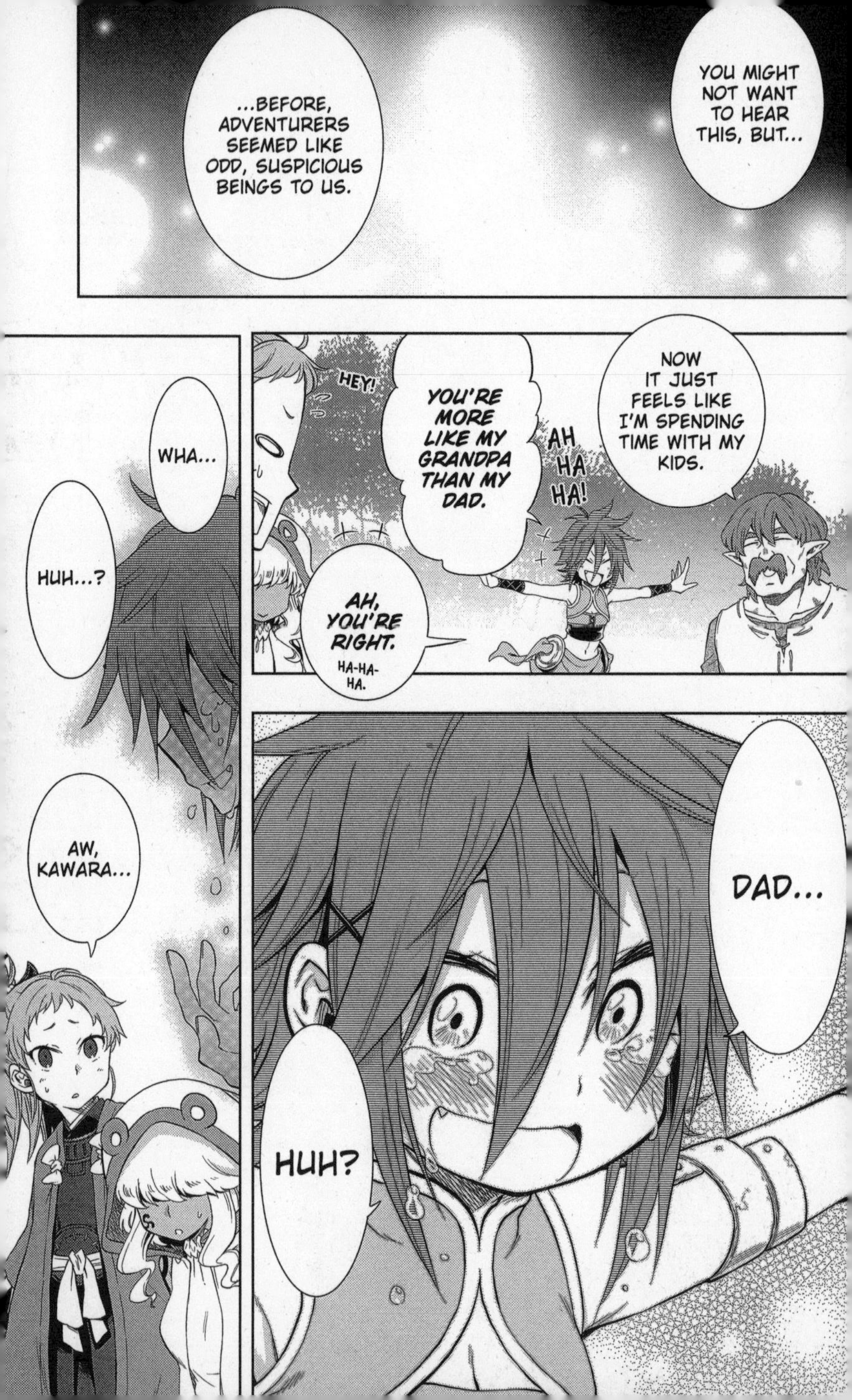
YOU MIGHT NOT WANT TO HEAR THIS, BUT...
...BEFORE, ADVENTURERS SEEMED LIKE ODD, SUSPICIOUS BEINGS TO US.
NOW IT JUST FEELS LIKE I'M SPENDING TIME WITH MY KIDS.
AH HA HA!
YOU'RE MORE LIKE MY GRANDPA THAN MY DAD.
HEY!
AH, YOU'RE RIGHT.
HA-HA-HA.
DAD...
HUH?
WHA...
HUH...?
AW, KAWARA...

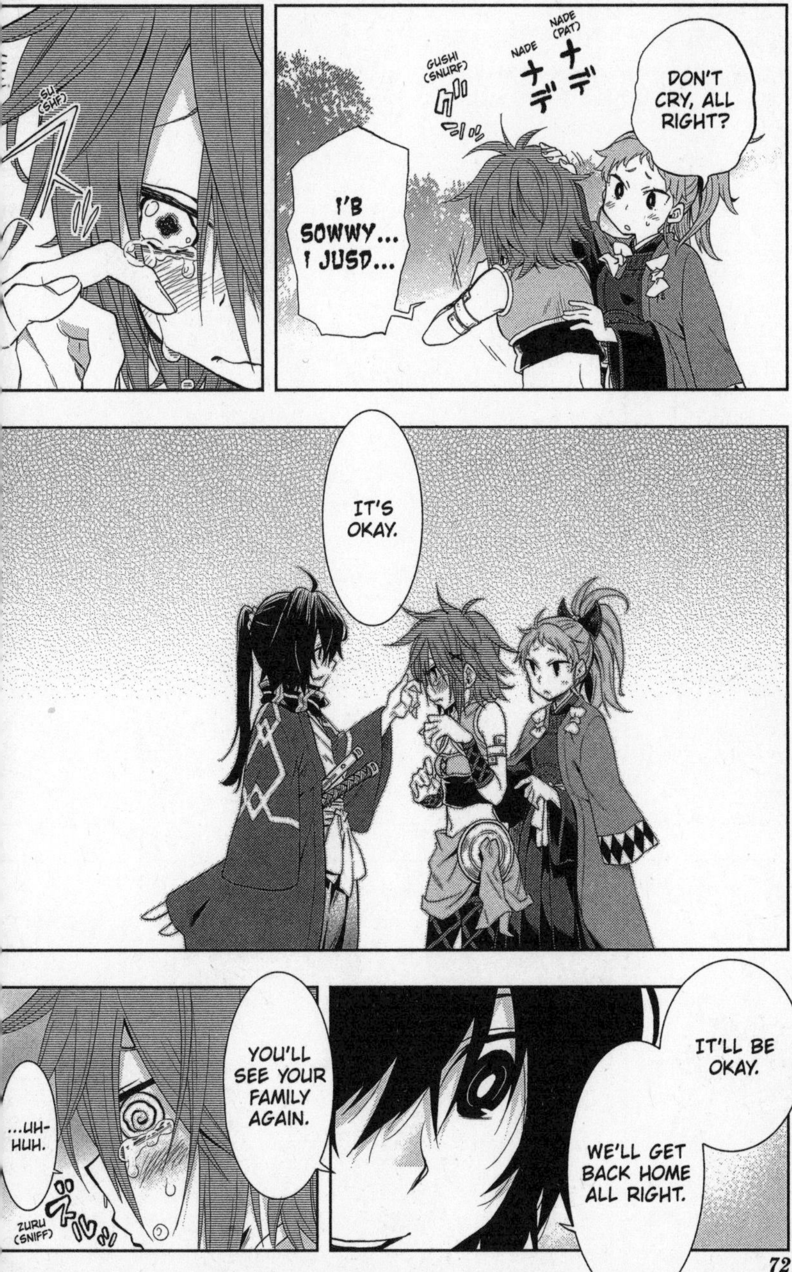
DON'T CRY, ALL RIGHT?
NADE (PAT)
ナデ
NADE
ナデ
GUSHI (SNURF)
I'B SOWWY... I JUSD...
SU (SHF)
IT'S OKAY.
IT'LL BE OKAY.
WE'LL GET BACK HOME ALL RIGHT.
YOU'LL SEE YOUR FAMILY AGAIN.
...UH-HUH.
ZURU (SNIFF)

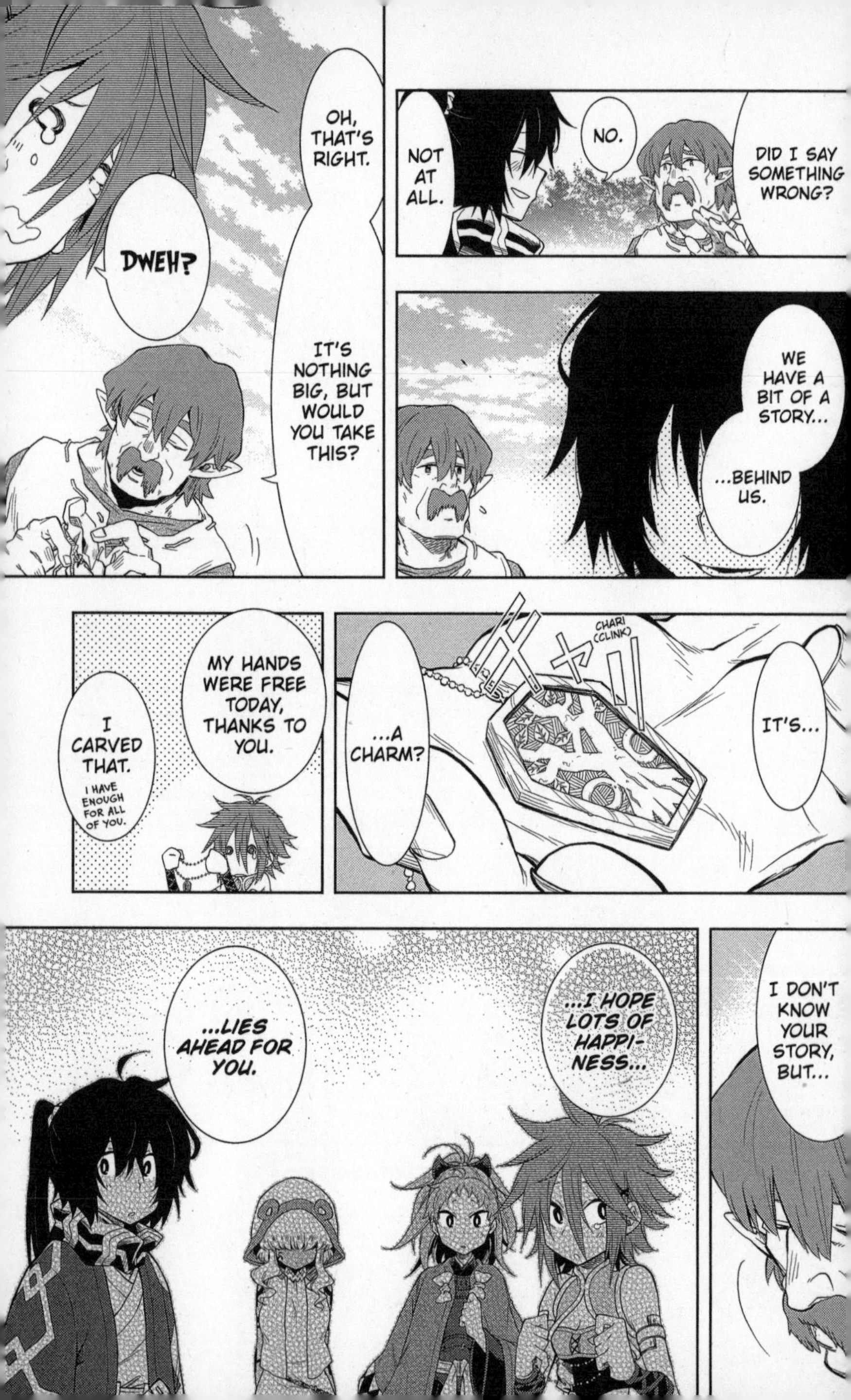
DID I SAY SOMETHING WRONG?
NO.
NOT AT ALL.
WE HAVE A BIT OF A STORY...
...BEHIND US.
OH, THAT'S RIGHT.
DWEH?
IT'S NOTHING BIG, BUT WOULD YOU TAKE THIS?
IT'S...
CHARI (CLINK)
...A CHARM?
MY HANDS WERE FREE TODAY, THANKS TO YOU.
I CARVED THAT.
I HAVE ENOUGH FOR ALL OF YOU.
I DON'T KNOW YOUR STORY, BUT...
...I HOPE LOTS OF HAPPI-NESS...
...LIES AHEAD FOR YOU.

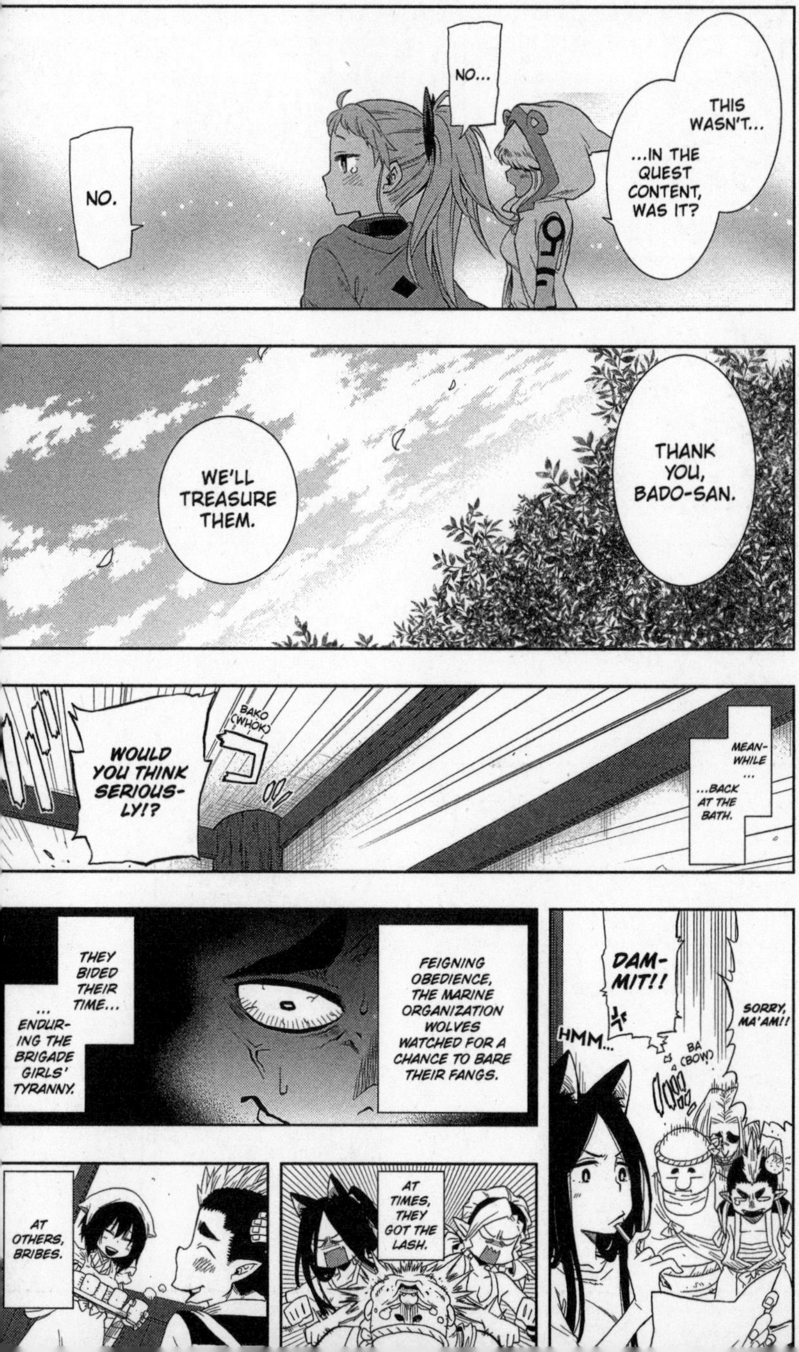
THIS WASN'T...
...IN THE QUEST CONTENT, WAS IT?
NO...
NO.
THANK YOU, BADO-SAN.
WE'LL TREASURE THEM.
MEAN-WHILE...
...BACK AT THE BATH.
BAKO (WHOK)
WOULD YOU THINK SERIOUS-LY!?
DAM-MIT!!
SORRY, MA'AM!!
HMM...
BA (BOW)
FEIGNING OBEDIENCE, THE MARINE ORGANIZATION WOLVES WATCHED FOR A CHANCE TO BARE THEIR FANGS.
THEY BIDED THEIR TIME...
...ENDUR-ING THE BRIGADE GIRLS' TYRANNY.
AT TIMES, THEY GOT THE LASH.
AT OTHERS, BRIBES.

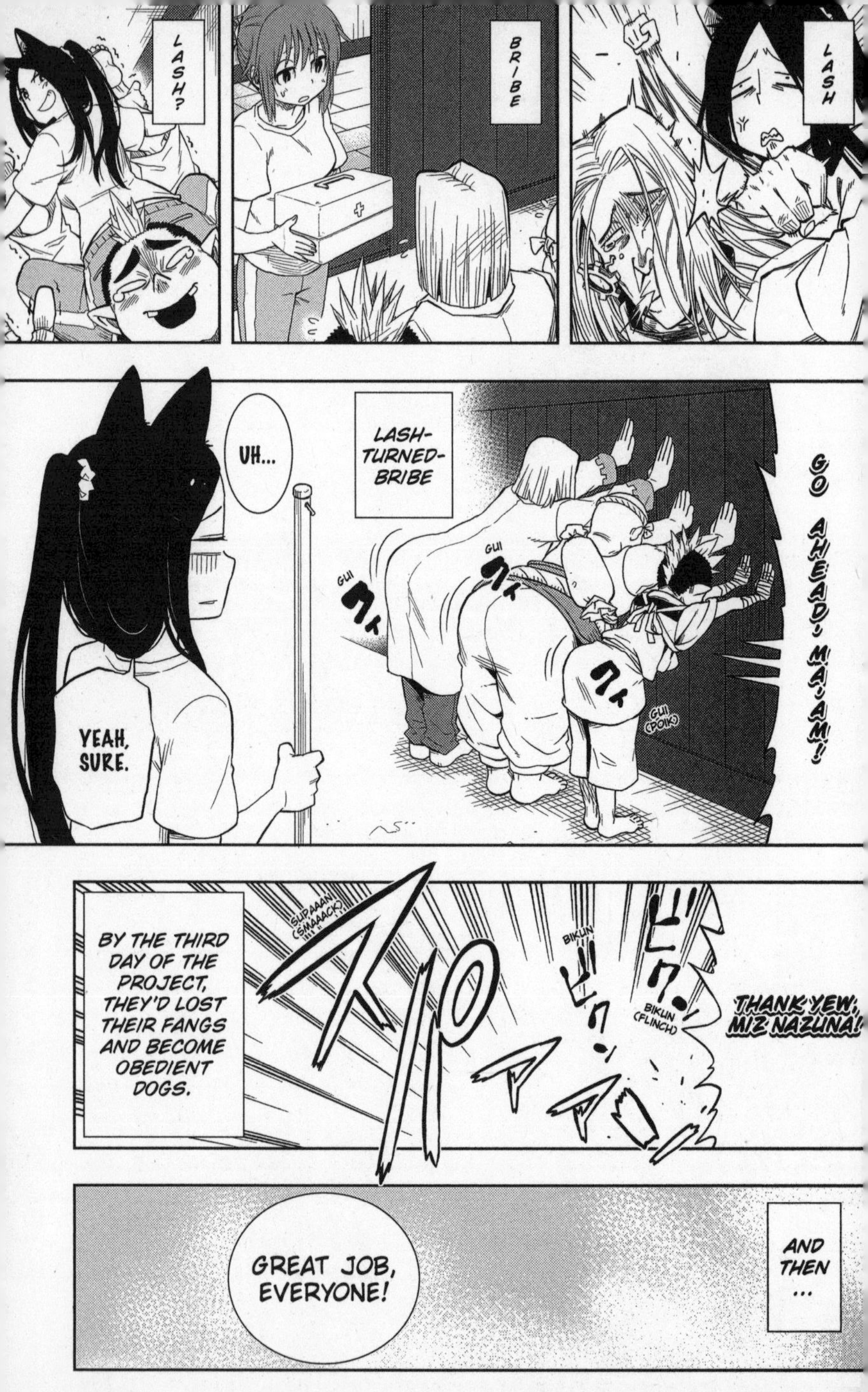
LASH
BRIBE
LASH?
GO AHEAD, MA'AM!
LASH-TURNED-BRIBE
GUI
GUI
GUI (POIK)
UH...
YEAH, SURE.
THANK YEW, MIZ NAZUNA!
BIKUN (FLINCH)
BIKUN
SUPAAAN (SNAAACK)
BY THE THIRD DAY OF THE PROJECT, THEY'D LOST THEIR FANGS AND BECOME OBEDIENT DOGS.
AND THEN ...
GREAT JOB, EVERYONE!

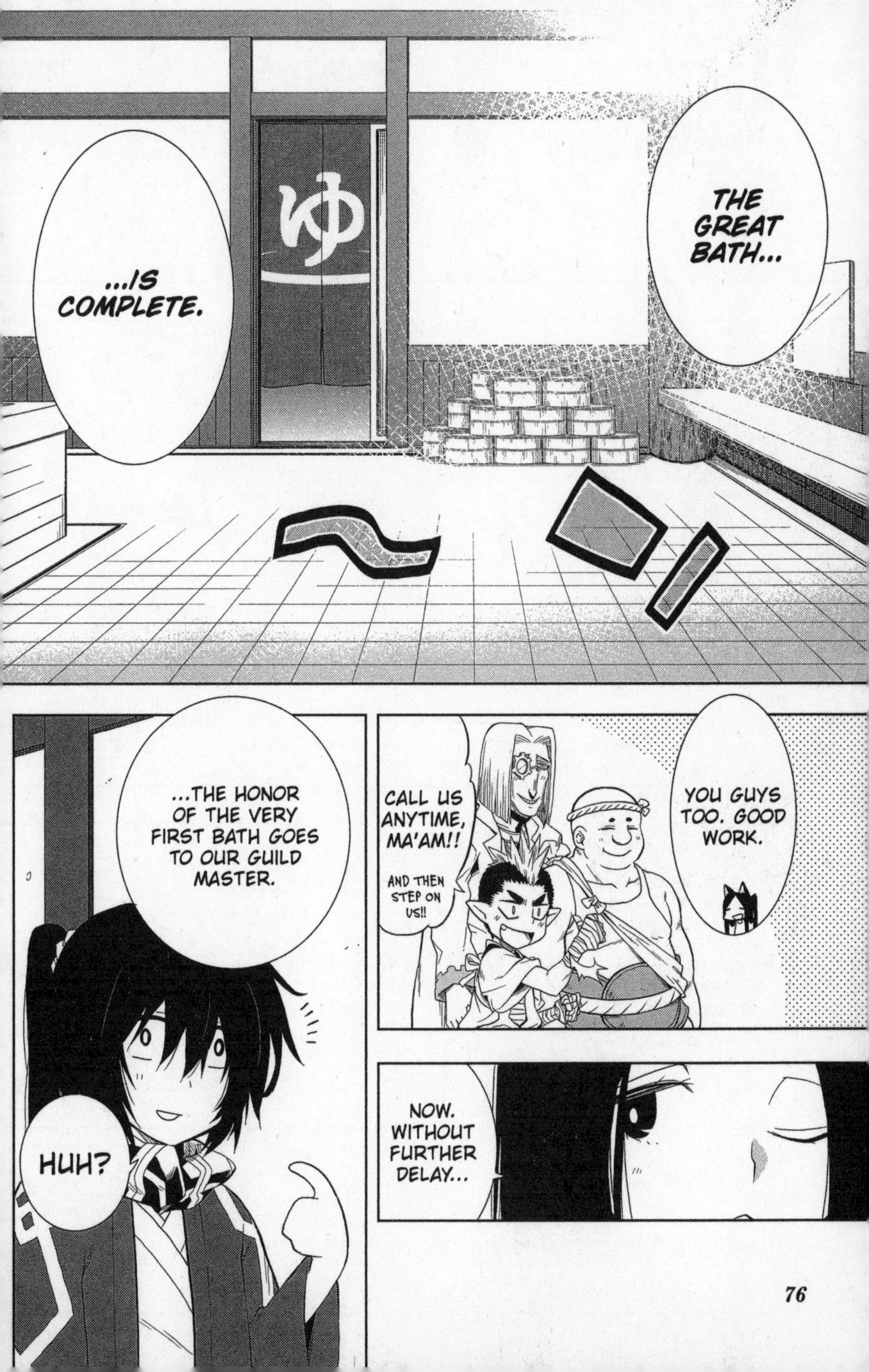
THE GREAT BATH...
...IS COMPLETE.
YOU GUYS TOO. GOOD WORK.
CALL US ANYTIME, MA'AM!!
AND THEN STEP ON US!!
NOW. WITHOUT FURTHER DELAY...
...THE HONOR OF THE VERY FIRST BATH GOES TO OUR GUILD MASTER.
HUH?

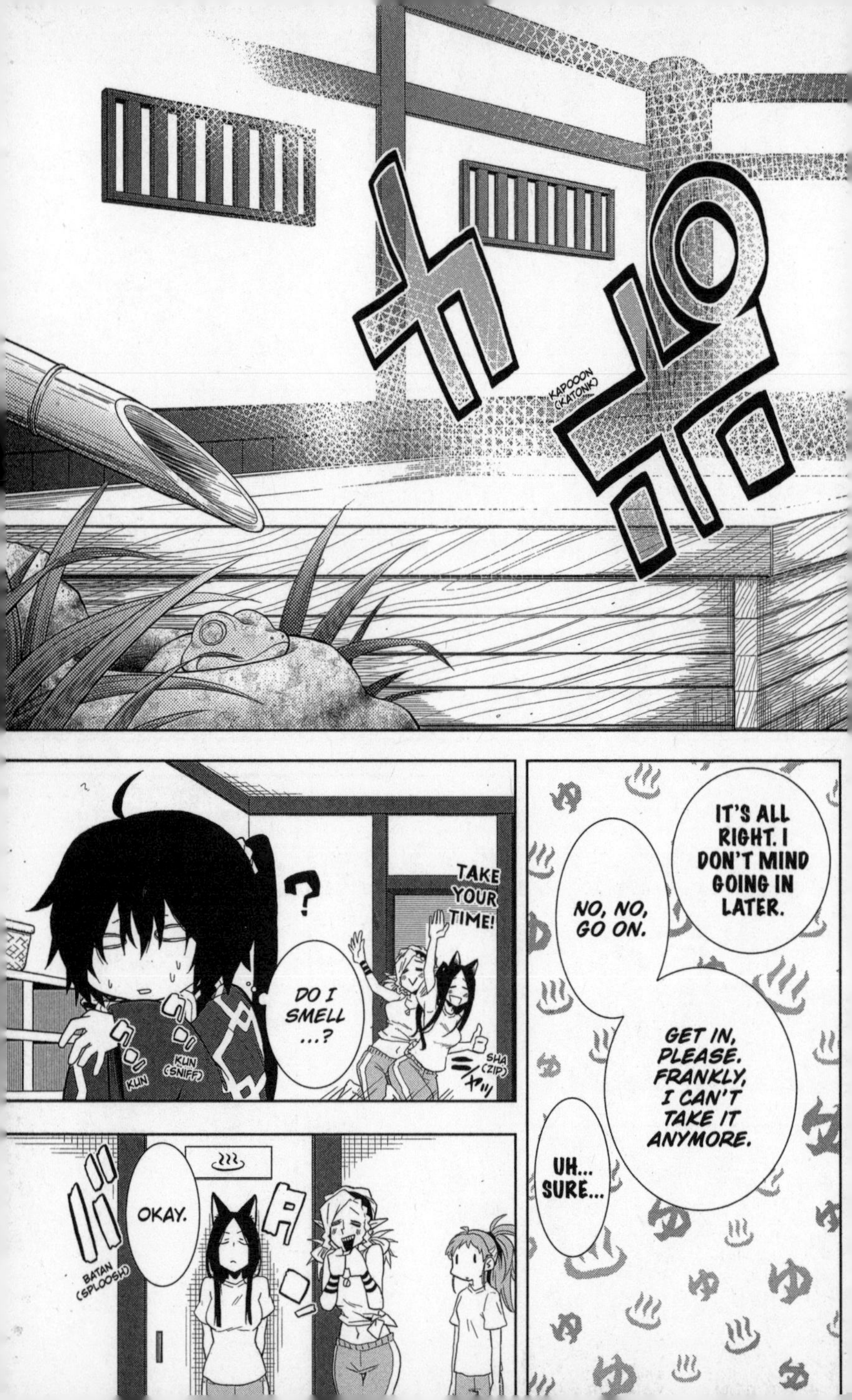
KAPOOON (KATONK)
IT'S ALL RIGHT. I DON'T MIND GOING IN LATER.
NO, NO, GO ON.
GET IN, PLEASE. FRANKLY, I CAN'T TAKE IT ANYMORE.
UH... SURE...
TAKE YOUR TIME!
SHA (ZIP)
DO I SMELL ...?
KUN (SNIFF)
KUN
OKAY.
BATAN (SPLOOSH)

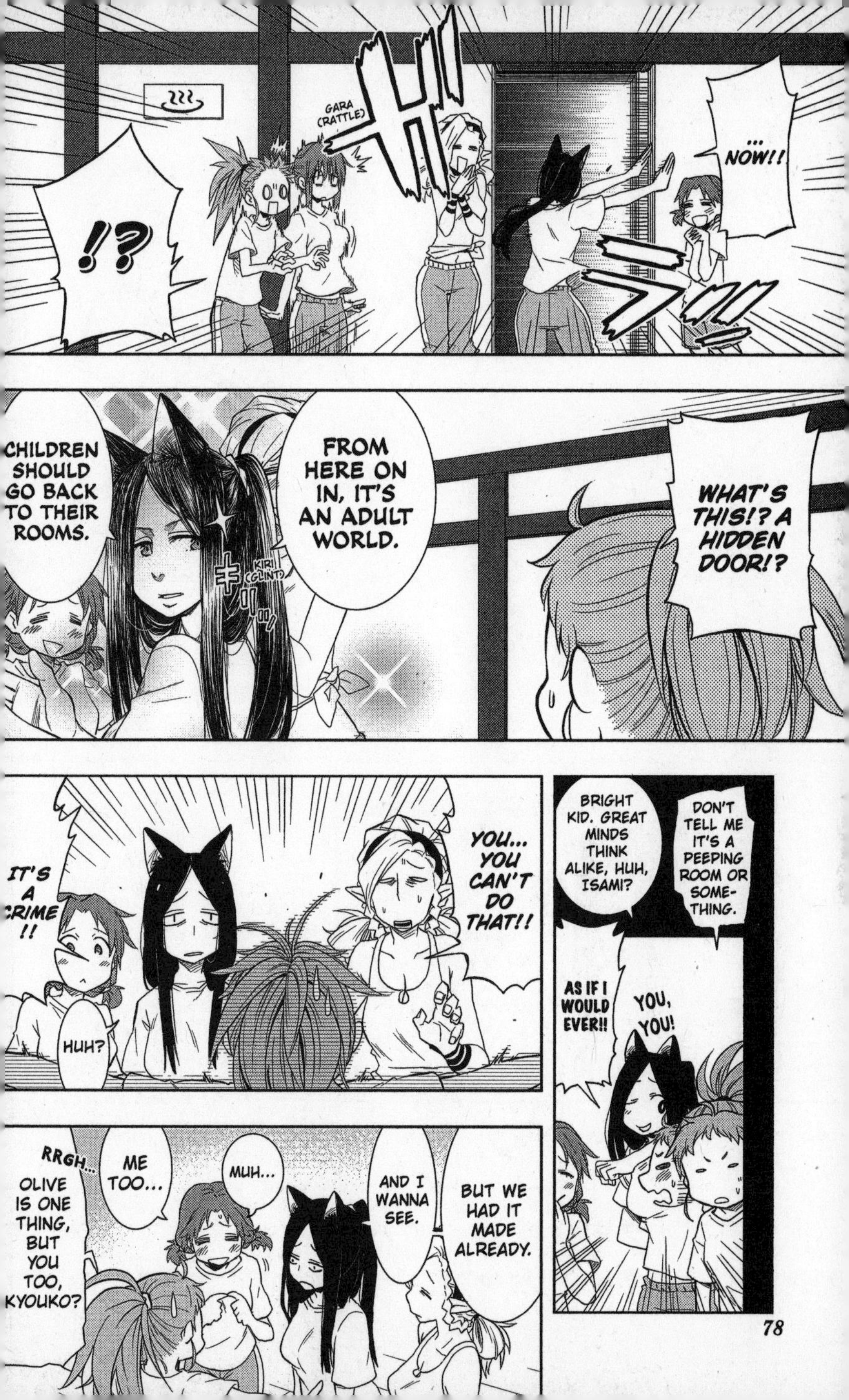
...NOW!!
GARA (RATTLE)
!?
WHAT'S THIS!? A HIDDEN DOOR!?
FROM HERE ON IN, IT'S AN ADULT WORLD.
KIRI (GLINT)
CHILDREN SHOULD GO BACK TO THEIR ROOMS.
DON'T TELL ME IT'S A PEEPING ROOM OR SOME-THING.
BRIGHT KID. GREAT MINDS THINK ALIKE, HUH, ISAMI?
YOU, YOU!
AS IF I WOULD EVER!!
YOU... YOU CAN'T DO THAT!!
IT'S A CRIME!!
HUH?
BUT WE HAD IT MADE ALREADY.
AND I WANNA SEE.
MUH...
ME TOO...
RRGH...
OLIVE IS ONE THING, BUT YOU TOO, KYOUKO?

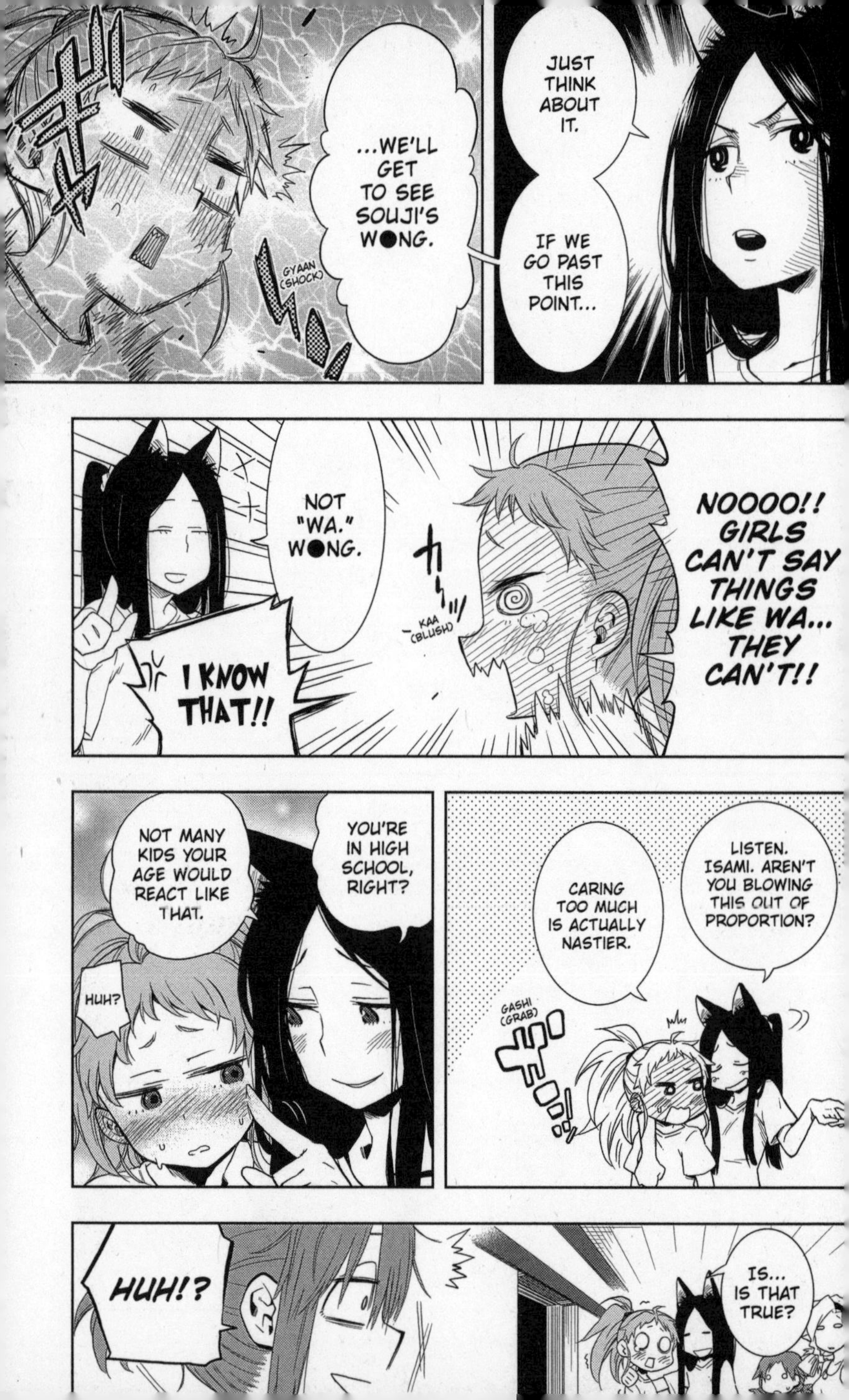
JUST THINK ABOUT IT.
IF WE GO PAST THIS POINT...
...WE'LL GET TO SEE SOUJI'S W●NG.
GYAAN (SHOCK)
NOOOO!! GIRLS CAN'T SAY THINGS LIKE WA... THEY CAN'T!!
KAA (BLUSH)
NOT "WA." W●NG.
I KNOW THAT!!
LISTEN. ISAMI. AREN'T YOU BLOWING THIS OUT OF PROPORTION?
CARING TOO MUCH IS ACTUALLY NASTIER.
GASHI (GRAB)
YOU'RE IN HIGH SCHOOL, RIGHT?
NOT MANY KIDS YOUR AGE WOULD REACT LIKE THAT.
HUH?
IS... IS THAT TRUE?
HUH!?

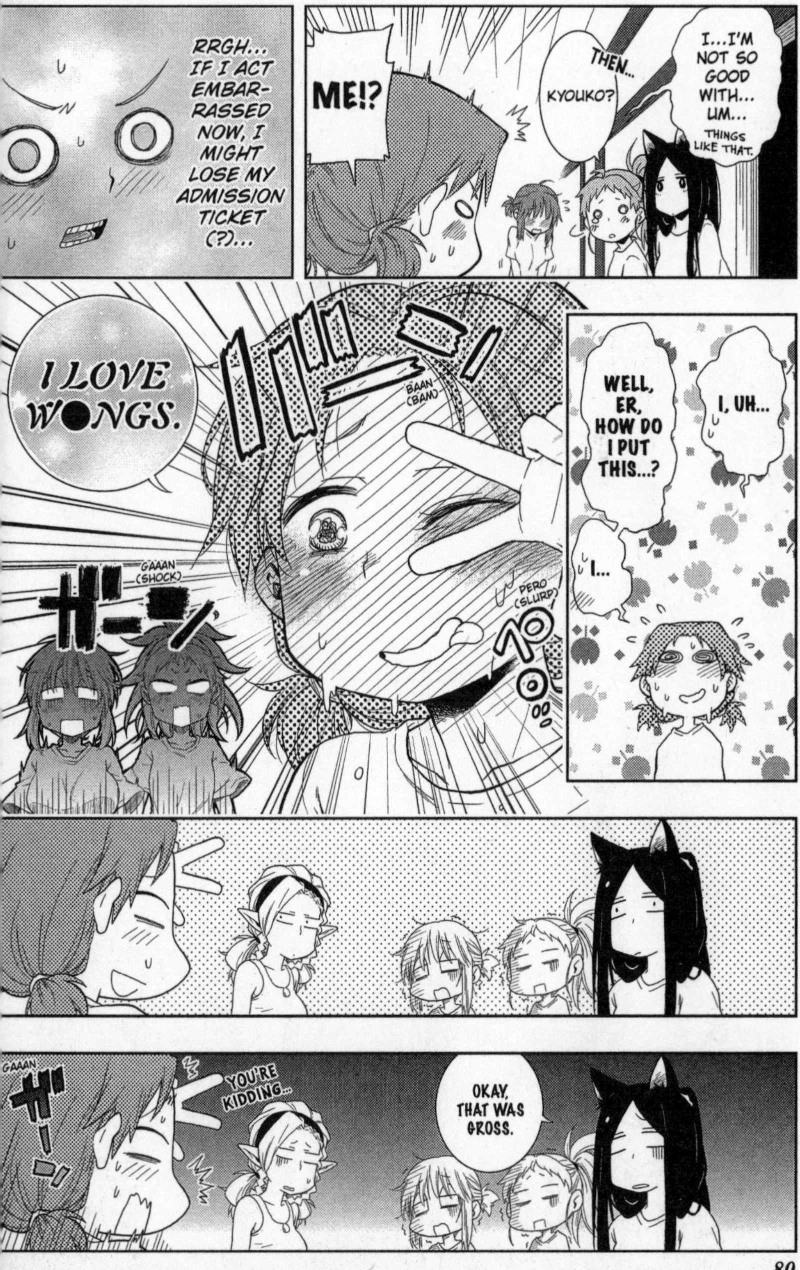
I...I'M NOT SO GOOD WITH... UM... THINGS LIKE THAT.
THEN... KYOUKO?
ME!?
RRGH... IF I ACT EMBAR-RASSED NOW, I MIGHT LOSE MY ADMISSION TICKET (?)...
I, UH...
WELL, ER, HOW DO I PUT THIS...?
I...
BAAN (BAM)
PERO (SLURP)
I LOVE W●NGS.
GAAAN (SHOCK)
OKAY, THAT WAS GROSS.
YOU'RE KIDDING...
GAAAN

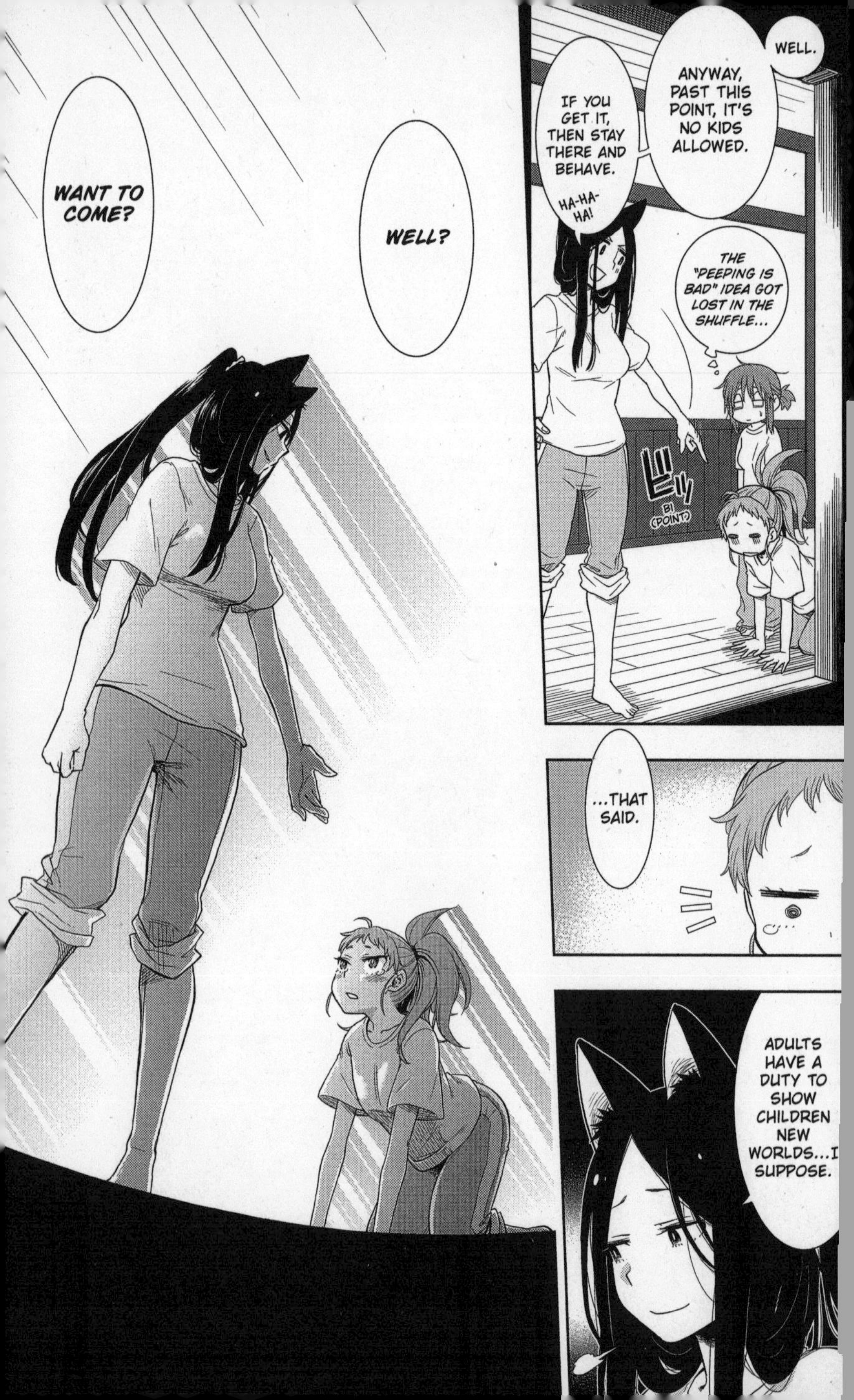
WELL.
ANYWAY, PAST THIS POINT, IT'S NO KIDS ALLOWED.
IF YOU GET IT, THEN STAY THERE AND BEHAVE.
HA-HA-HA!
THE "PEEPING IS BAD" IDEA GOT LOST IN THE SHUFFLE...
ビッ
BI (POINT)
...THAT SAID.
ADULTS HAVE A DUTY TO SHOW CHILDREN NEW WORLDS...I SUPPOSE.
WELL?
WANT TO COME?

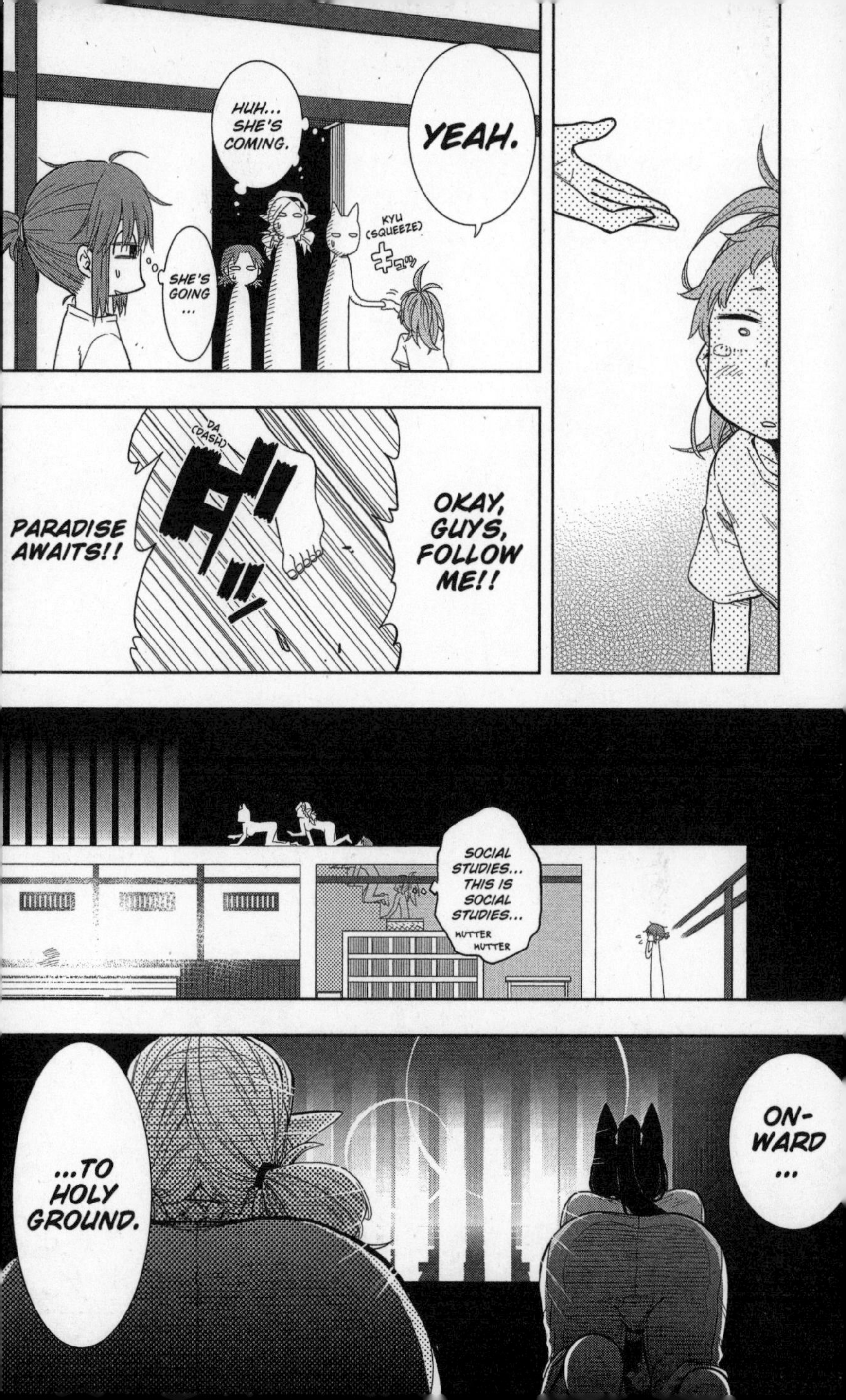
YEAH.
KYU (SQUEEZE)
HUH... SHE'S COMING.
SHE'S GOING...
OKAY, GUYS, FOLLOW ME!!
DA (DASH)
PARADISE AWAITS!!
SOCIAL STUDIES... THIS IS SOCIAL STUDIES...
MUTTER MUTTER
ON-WARD...
...TO HOLY GROUND.

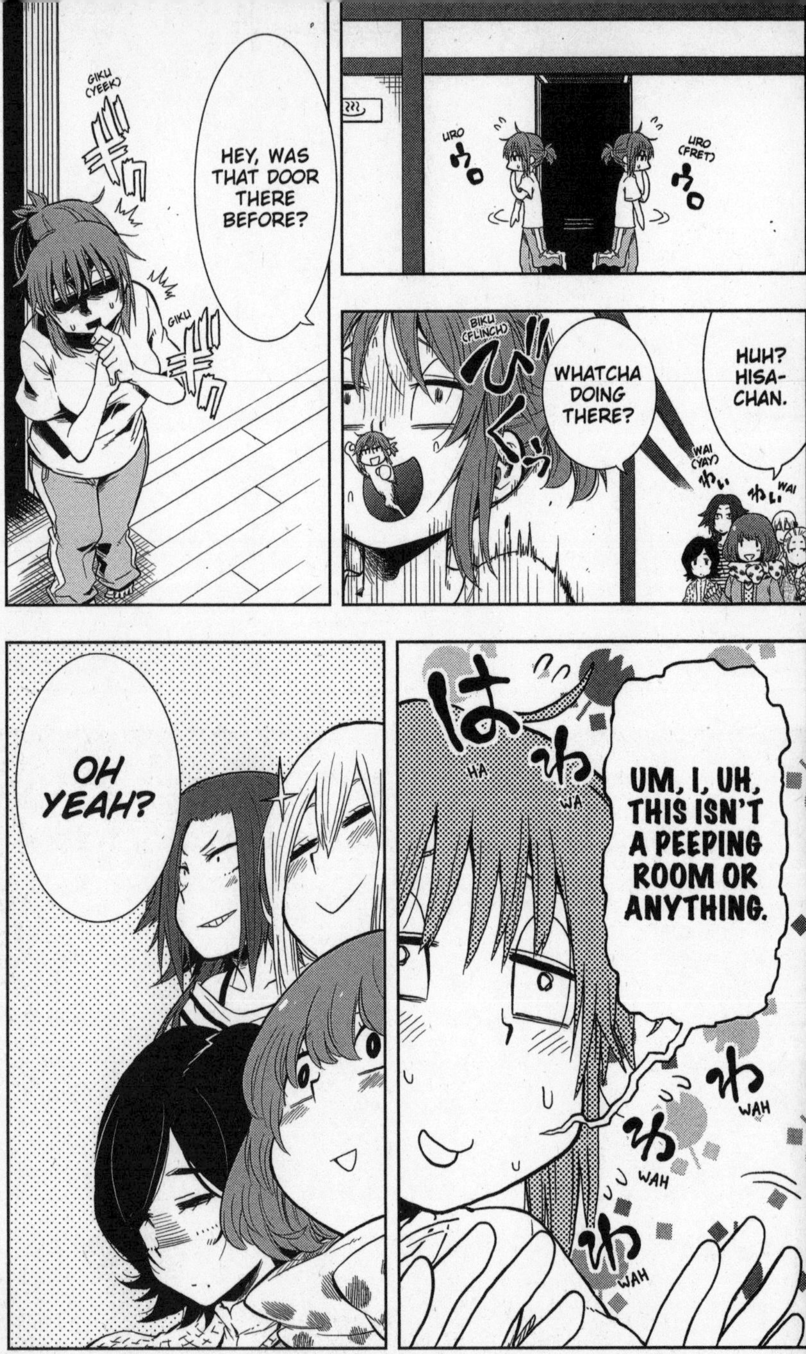
URO (FRET)
URO
HUH? HISA-CHAN.
WAI (YAY)
WAI
WHATCHA DOING THERE?
BIKU (FLINCH)
HEY, WAS THAT DOOR THERE BEFORE?
GIKU (YEEK)
GIKU
UM, I, UH, THIS ISN'T A PEEPING ROOM OR ANYTHING.
HA
WA
WAH
WAH
WAH
OH YEAH?

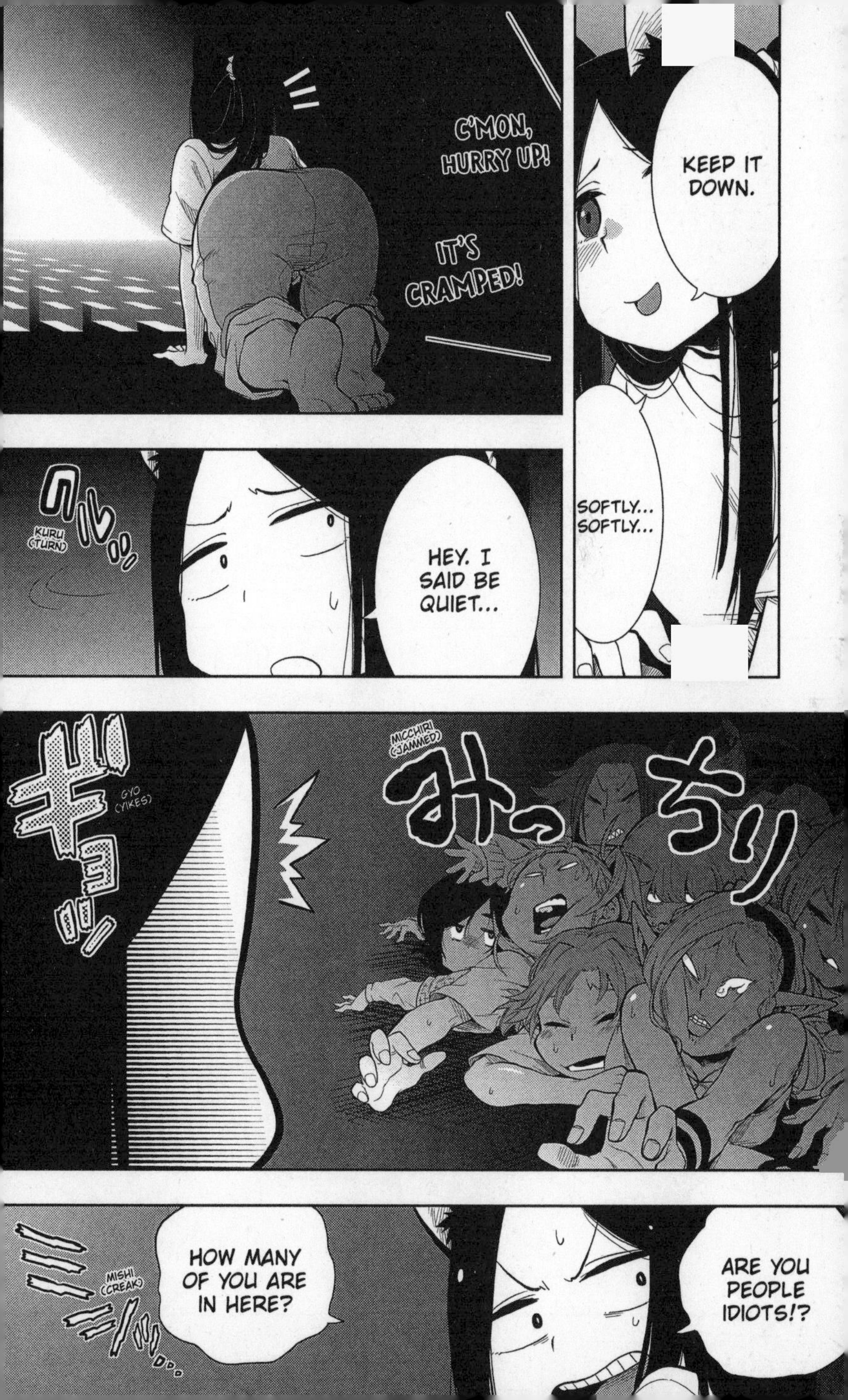
KEEP IT DOWN.
SOFTLY... SOFTLY...
C'MON, HURRY UP!
IT'S CRAMPED!
KURU (TURN)
HEY. I SAID BE QUIET...
MICCHIRI (JAMMED)
みっちり
GYO (YIKES)
ARE YOU PEOPLE IDIOTS!?
HOW MANY OF YOU ARE IN HERE?
MISHI (CREAK)

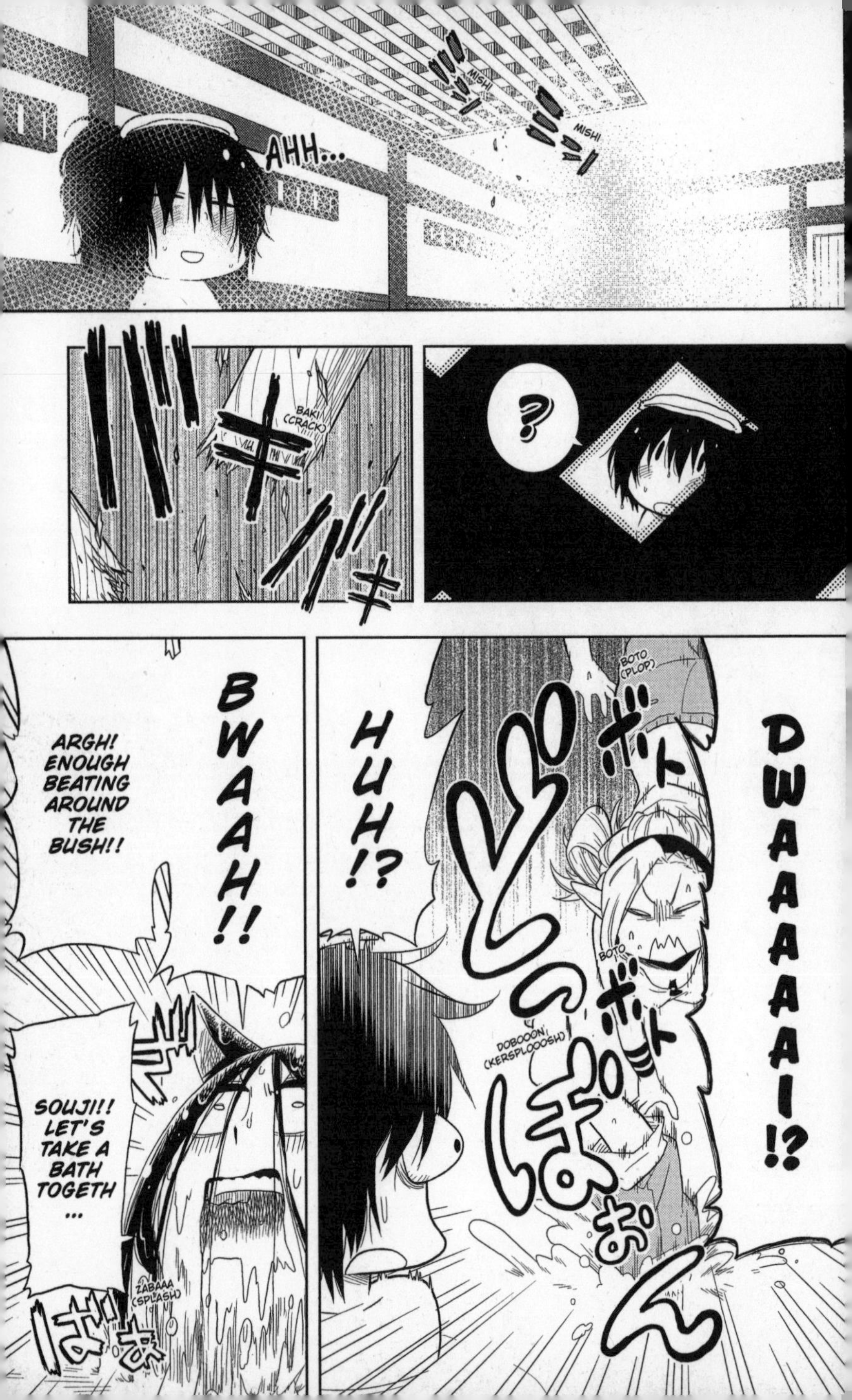
MISHI
MISHI
AHH...
?
BAKI (CRACK)
DWAAAAAAI!?
BOTO (PLOP)
BOTO
DOBOOON (KERSPLOOOSH)
HUH!?
BWAAAH!!
ARGH! ENOUGH BEATING AROUND THE BUSH!!
SOUJI!! LET'S TAKE A BATH TOGETH...
ZABAAA (SPLASH)

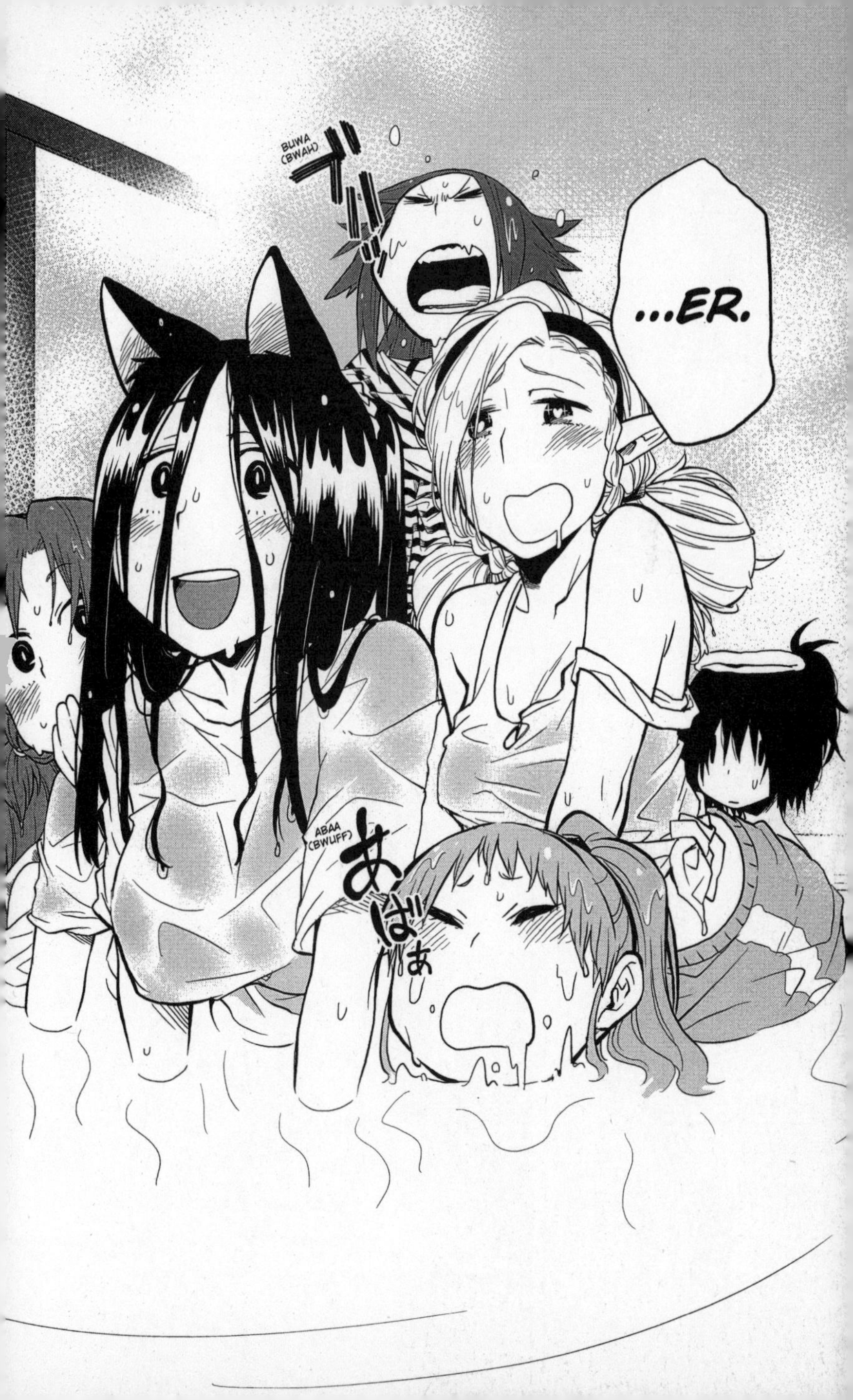
…ER.
BUWA (BWAH)
ABAA (BWUFF)
あばぁ

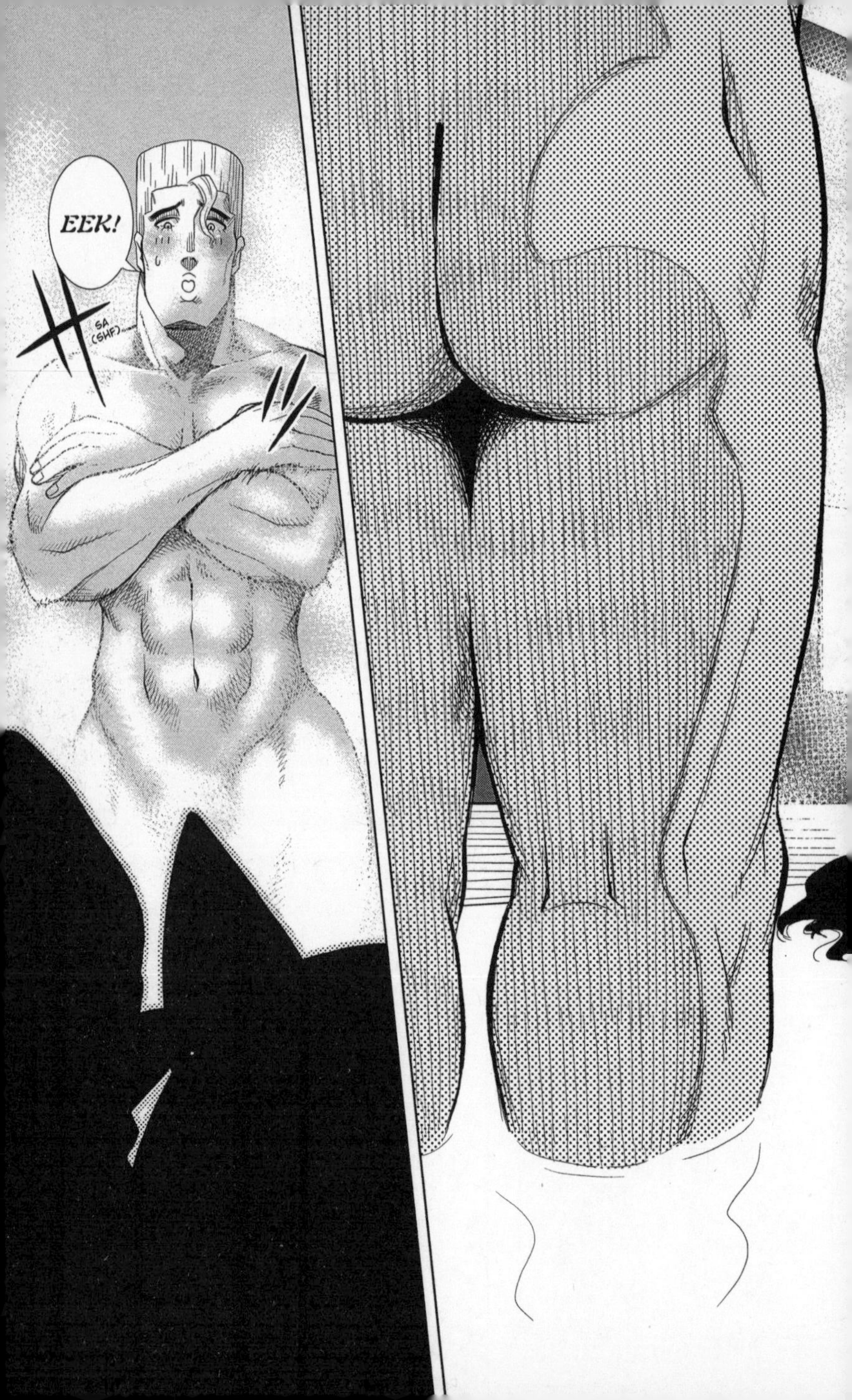
EEK!
SA (SHF)

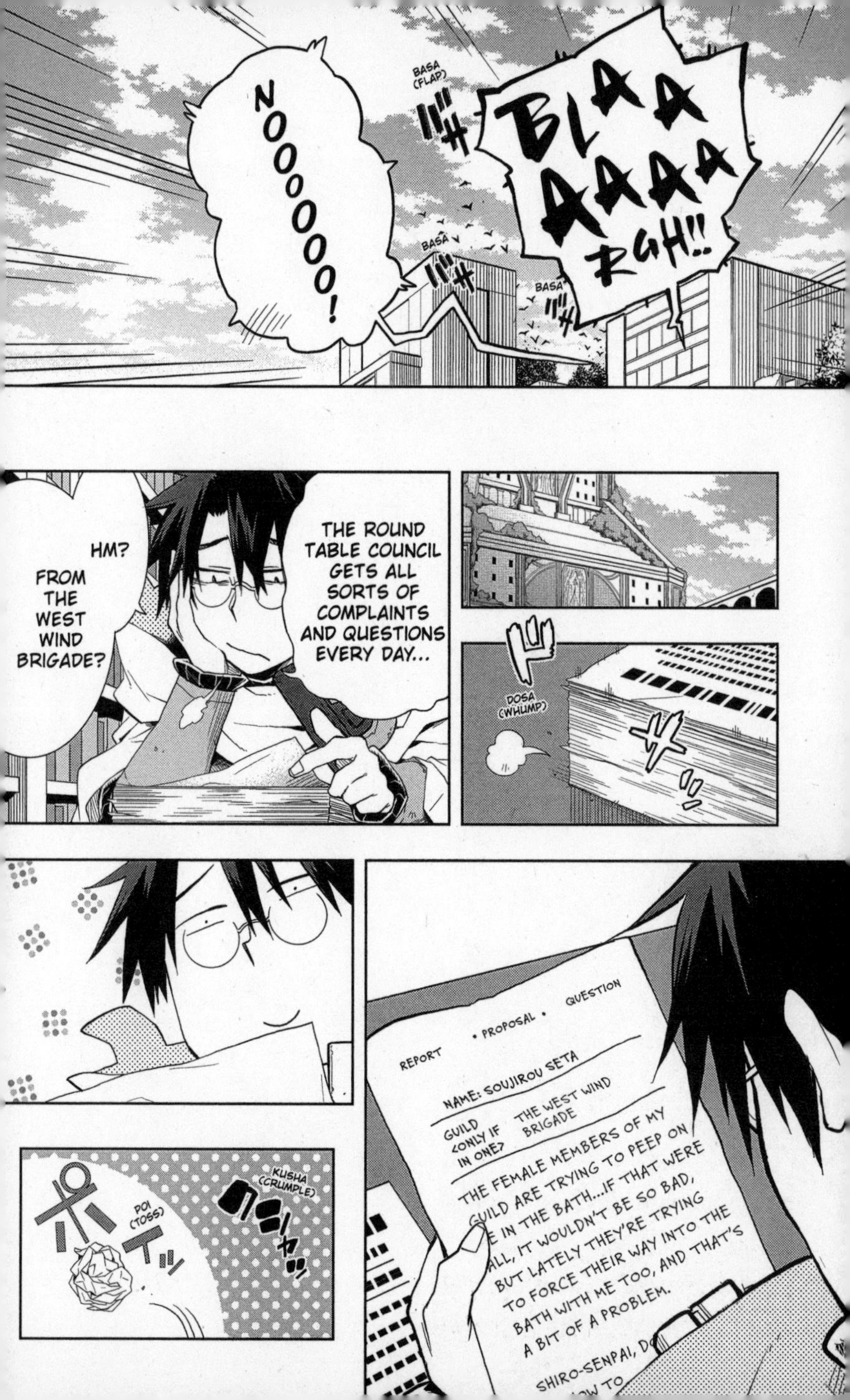
BLAAAAAARGH!!
NOOOOOOO!
BASA (FLAP)
BASA
BASA
DOSA (WHUMP)
THE ROUND TABLE COUNCIL GETS ALL SORTS OF COMPLAINTS AND QUESTIONS EVERY DAY...
HM? FROM THE WEST WIND BRIGADE?
REPORT • PROPOSAL • QUESTION
NAME: SOUJIROU SETA
GUILD <ONLY IF IN ONE> THE WEST WIND BRIGADE
THE FEMALE MEMBERS OF MY GUILD ARE TRYING TO PEEP ON ME IN THE BATH...IF THAT WERE ALL, IT WOULDN'T BE SO BAD, BUT LATELY THEY'RE TRYING TO FORCE THEIR WAY INTO THE BATH WITH ME TOO, AND THAT'S A BIT OF A PROBLEM.
SHIRO-SENPAI, D
KUSHA (CRUMPLE)
POI (TOSS)

LOG HORIZON

THE WEST WIND BRIGADE

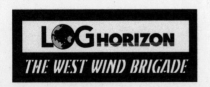

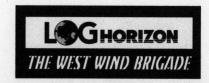

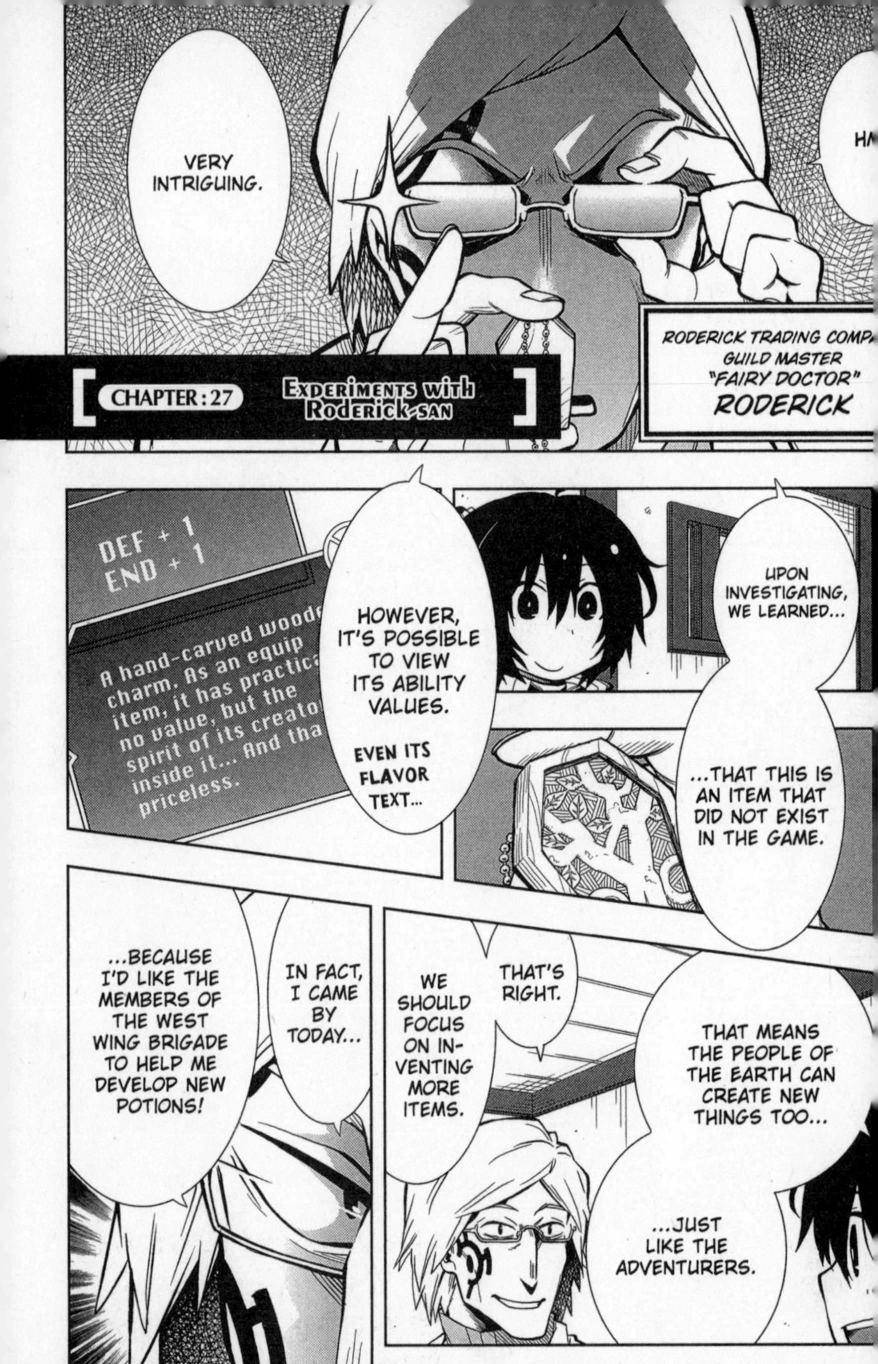
HM
VERY INTRIGUING.
RODERICK TRADING COMP GUILD MASTER "FAIRY DOCTOR" RODERICK
CHAPTER : 27 Experiments with Roderick-san
UPON INVESTIGATING, WE LEARNED...
...THAT THIS IS AN ITEM THAT DID NOT EXIST IN THE GAME.
DEF + 1
END + 1
A hand-carved wood charm. As an equip item, it has practica no value, but the spirit of its creato inside it... And tha priceless.
HOWEVER, IT'S POSSIBLE TO VIEW ITS ABILITY VALUES.
EVEN ITS FLAVOR TEXT...
THAT MEANS THE PEOPLE OF THE EARTH CAN CREATE NEW THINGS TOO...
...JUST LIKE THE ADVENTURERS.
THAT'S RIGHT.
WE SHOULD FOCUS ON IN-VENTING MORE ITEMS.
IN FACT, I CAME BY TODAY...
...BECAUSE I'D LIKE THE MEMBERS OF THE WEST WING BRIGADE TO HELP ME DEVELOP NEW POTIONS!

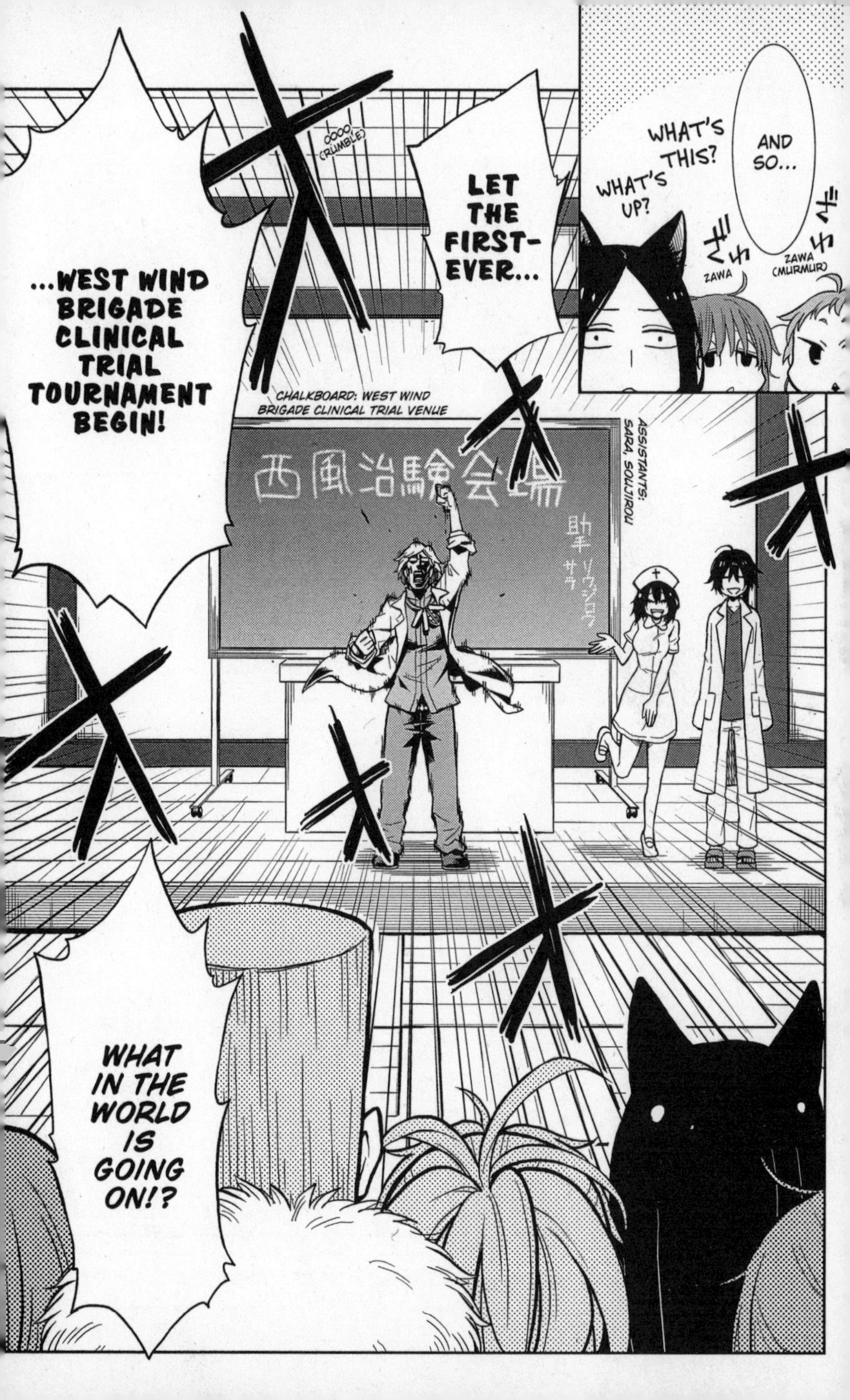
AND SO...
WHAT'S THIS?
WHAT'S UP?
ZAWA
ZAWA (MURMUR)
LET THE FIRST-EVER...
OOOO! (RUMBLE)
...WEST WIND BRIGADE CLINICAL TRIAL TOURNAMENT BEGIN!
CHALKBOARD: WEST WIND BRIGADE CLINICAL TRIAL VENUE
ASSISTANTS: SARA, SOUJIROU
WHAT IN THE WORLD IS GOING ON!?

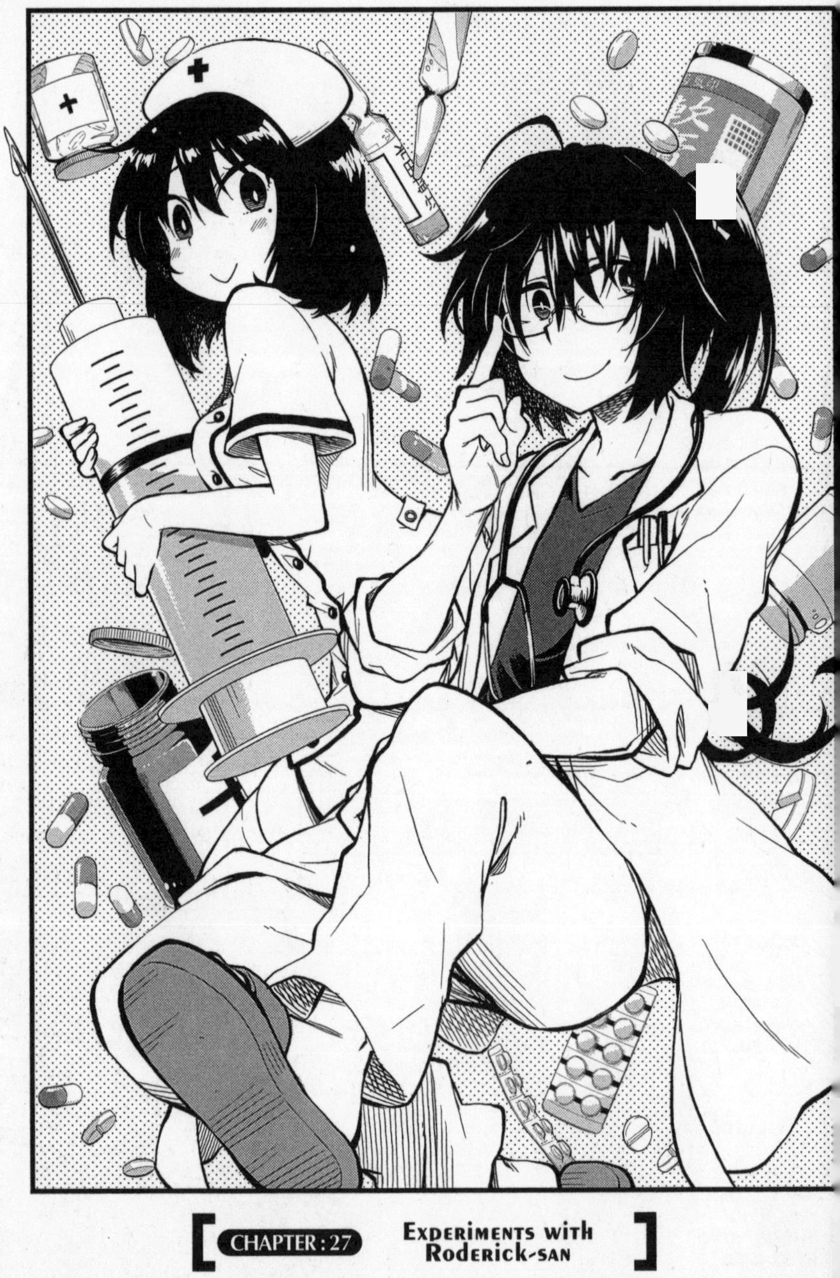

CHAPTER : 27 Experiments with Roderick-san

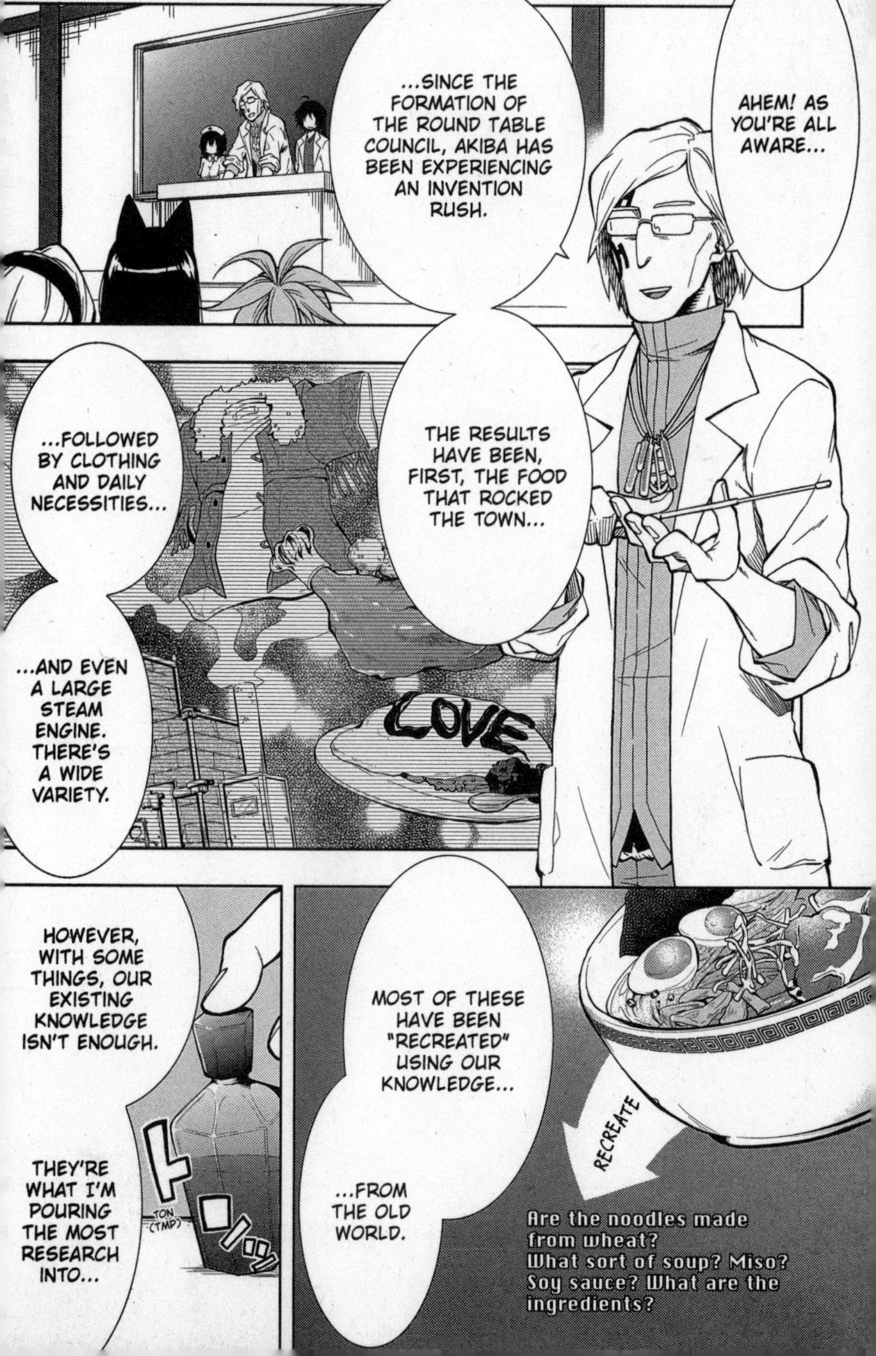
AHEM! AS YOU'RE ALL AWARE...
...SINCE THE FORMATION OF THE ROUND TABLE COUNCIL, AKIBA HAS BEEN EXPERIENCING AN INVENTION RUSH.
THE RESULTS HAVE BEEN, FIRST, THE FOOD THAT ROCKED THE TOWN...
LOVE
...FOLLOWED BY CLOTHING AND DAILY NECESSITIES...
...AND EVEN A LARGE STEAM ENGINE. THERE'S A WIDE VARIETY.
MOST OF THESE HAVE BEEN "RECREATED" USING OUR KNOWLEDGE...
...FROM THE OLD WORLD.
RECREATE
Are the noodles made from wheat?
What sort of soup? Miso? Soy sauce? What are the ingredients?
HOWEVER, WITH SOME THINGS, OUR EXISTING KNOWLEDGE ISN'T ENOUGH.
TON (TMP)
THEY'RE WHAT I'M POURING THE MOST RESEARCH INTO...

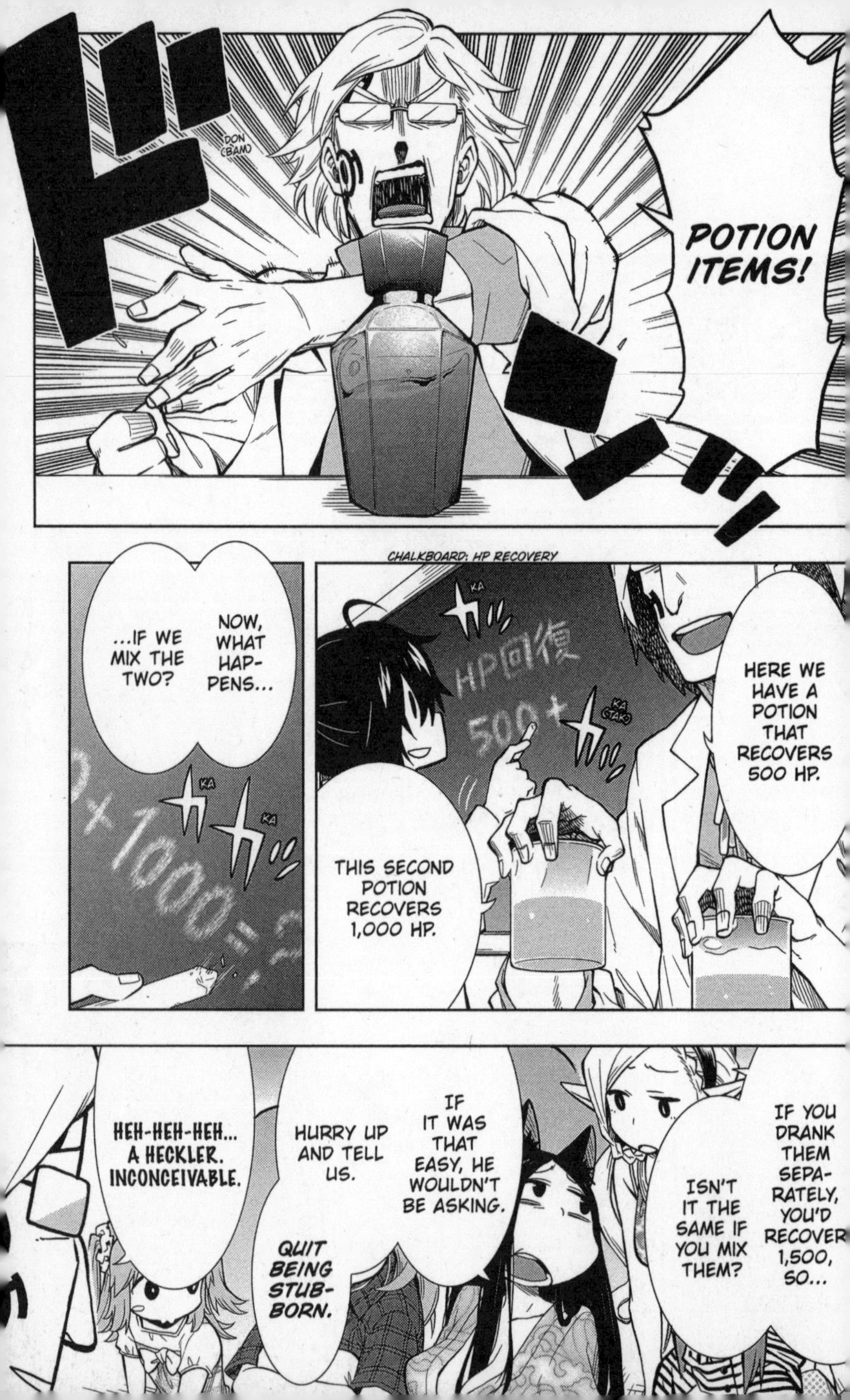
POTION ITEMS!
DON (BAM)
CHALKBOARD: HP RECOVERY
HERE WE HAVE A POTION THAT RECOVERS 500 HP.
HP回復
500+
KA
KA (TAK)
THIS SECOND POTION RECOVERS 1,000 HP.
NOW, WHAT HAP-PENS...
...IF WE MIX THE TWO?
KA
KA
IF YOU DRANK THEM SEPA-RATELY, YOU'D RECOVER 1,500, SO...
ISN'T IT THE SAME IF YOU MIX THEM?
IF IT WAS THAT EASY, HE WOULDN'T BE ASKING.
HURRY UP AND TELL US.
QUIT BEING STUB-BORN.
HEH-HEH-HEH... A HECKLER. INCONCEIVABLE.

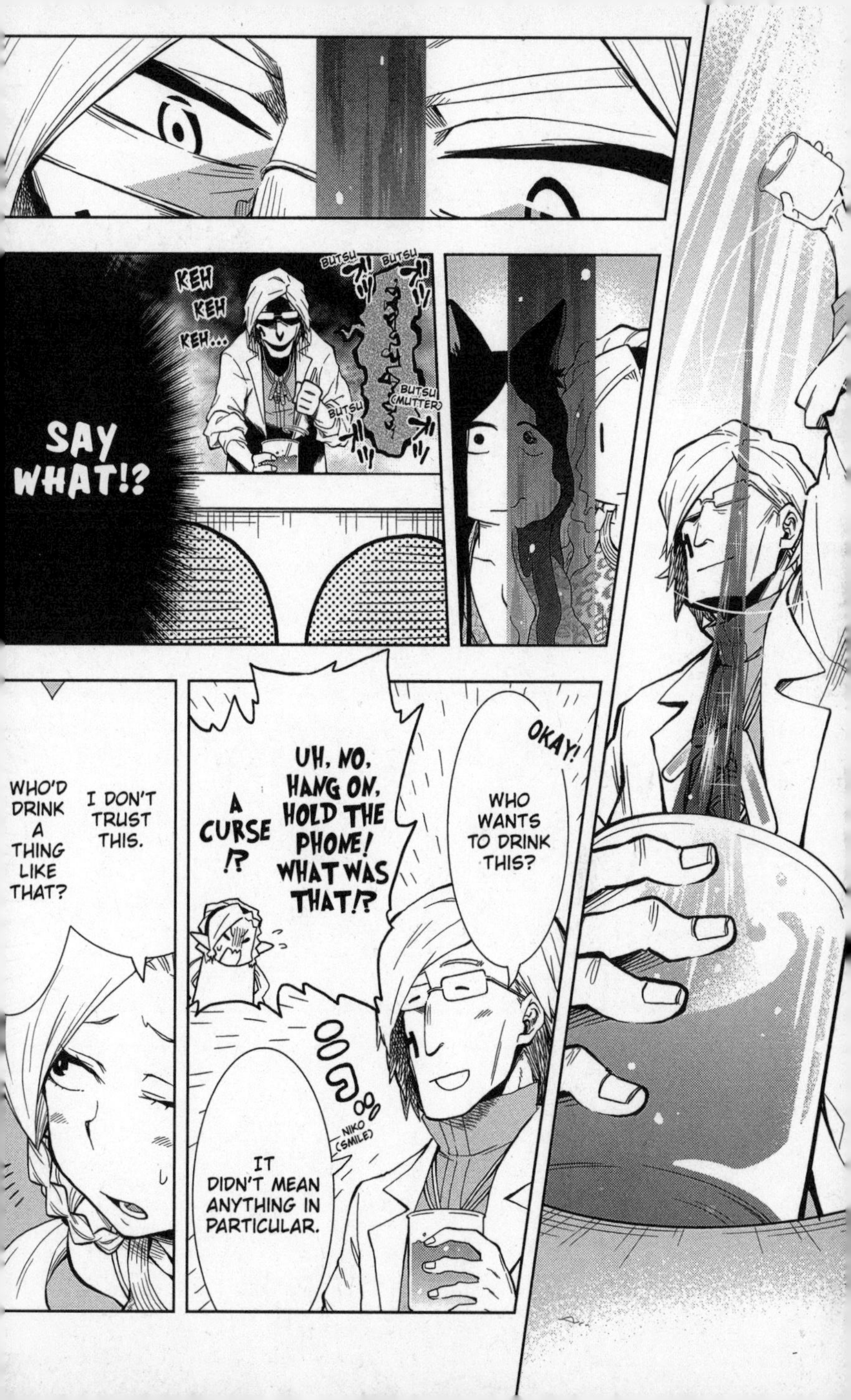
KEH KEH KEH...
BUTSU BUTSU
BUTSU BUTSU (MUTTER)
SAY WHAT!?
UH, NO, HANG ON, HOLD THE PHONE! WHAT WAS THAT!?
A CURSE!?
NIKO (SMILE)
IT DIDN'T MEAN ANYTHING IN PARTICULAR.
OKAY!
WHO WANTS TO DRINK THIS?
I DON'T TRUST THIS.
WHO'D DRINK A THING LIKE THAT?

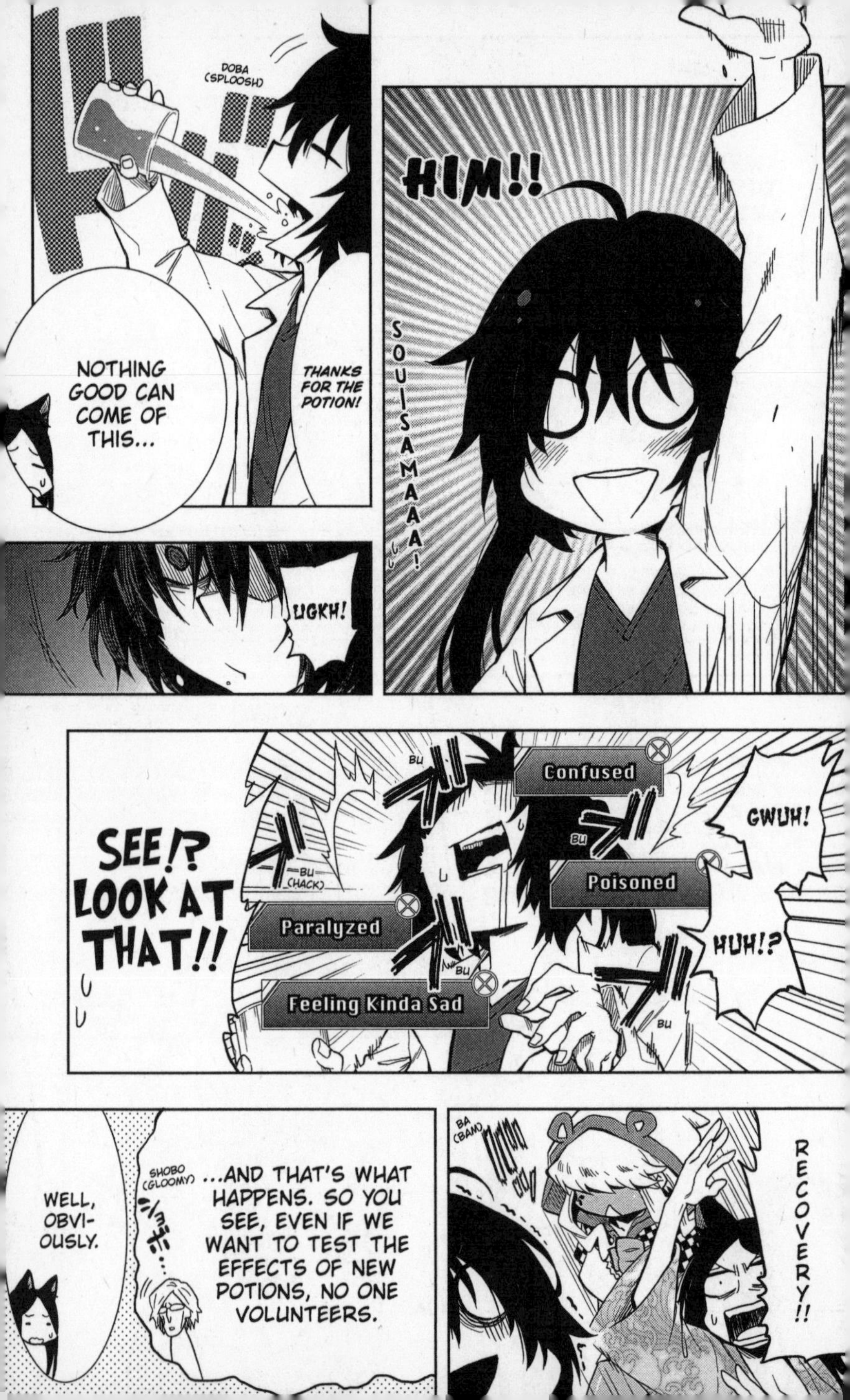
HIM!!
SOUISAMAAAA!
DOBA (SPLOOSH)
THANKS FOR THE POTION!
NOTHING GOOD CAN COME OF THIS...
UGKH!
GWUH!
BU
Confused
BU
Poisoned
HUH!?
BU (HACK)
Paralyzed
BU
Feeling Kinda Sad
BU
SEE!? LOOK AT THAT!!
BA (BAM)
RECOVERY!!
SHOBO (GLOOMY)
...AND THAT'S WHAT HAPPENS. SO YOU SEE, EVEN IF WE WANT TO TEST THE EFFECTS OF NEW POTIONS, NO ONE VOLUNTEERS.
WELL, OBVI-OUSLY.

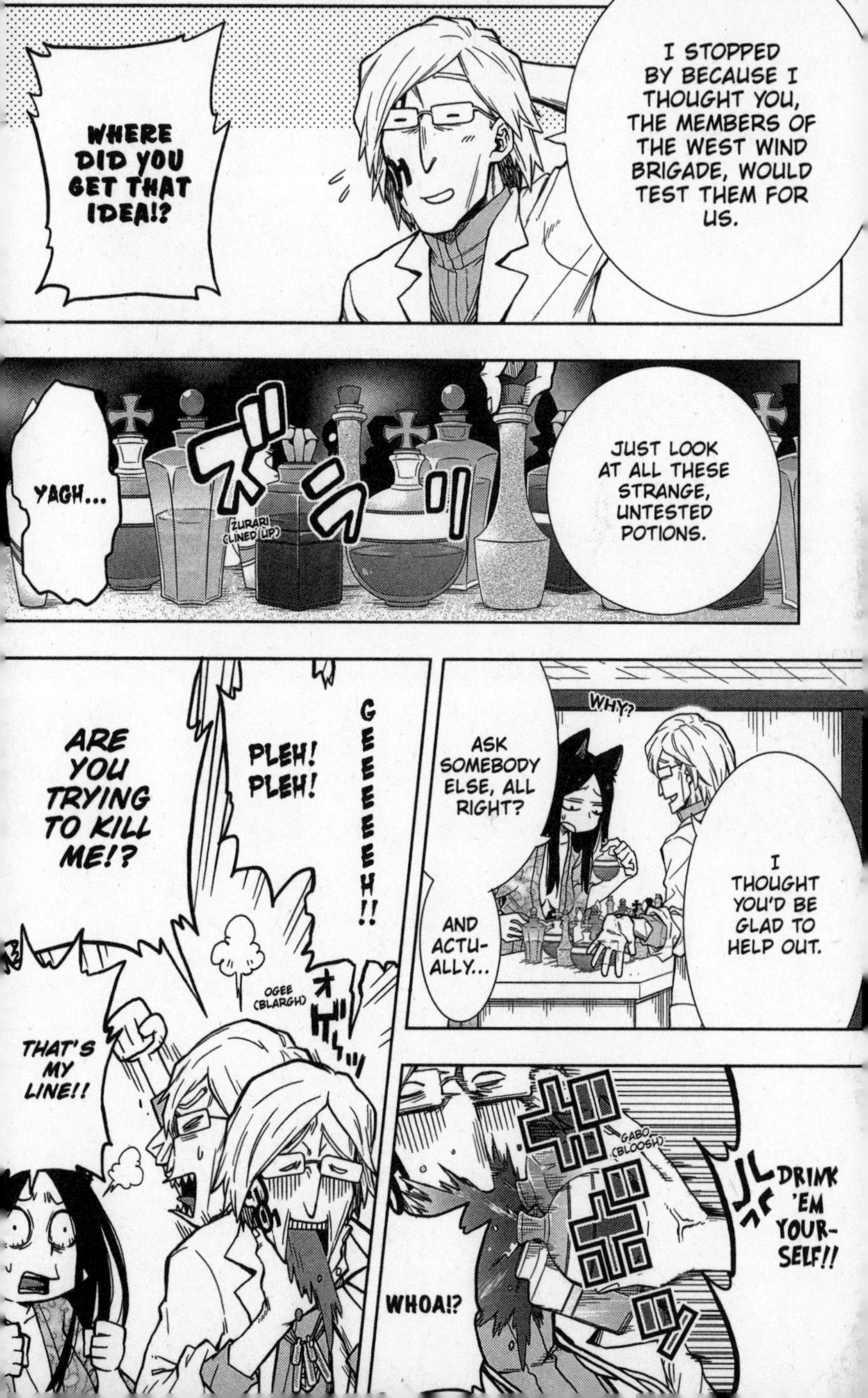
I STOPPED BY BECAUSE I THOUGHT YOU, THE MEMBERS OF THE WEST WIND BRIGADE, WOULD TEST THEM FOR US.
WHERE DID YOU GET THAT IDEA!?
JUST LOOK AT ALL THESE STRANGE, UNTESTED POTIONS.
ZURARI (LINED UP)
YAGH...
I THOUGHT YOU'D BE GLAD TO HELP OUT.
WHY?
ASK SOMEBODY ELSE, ALL RIGHT?
AND ACTU-ALLY...
DRINK 'EM YOUR-SELF!!
GABO (BLOOSH)
WHOA!?
GEEEEEEH!!
PLEH! PLEH!
ARE YOU TRYING TO KILL ME!?
OGEE (BLARGH)
THAT'S MY LINE!!

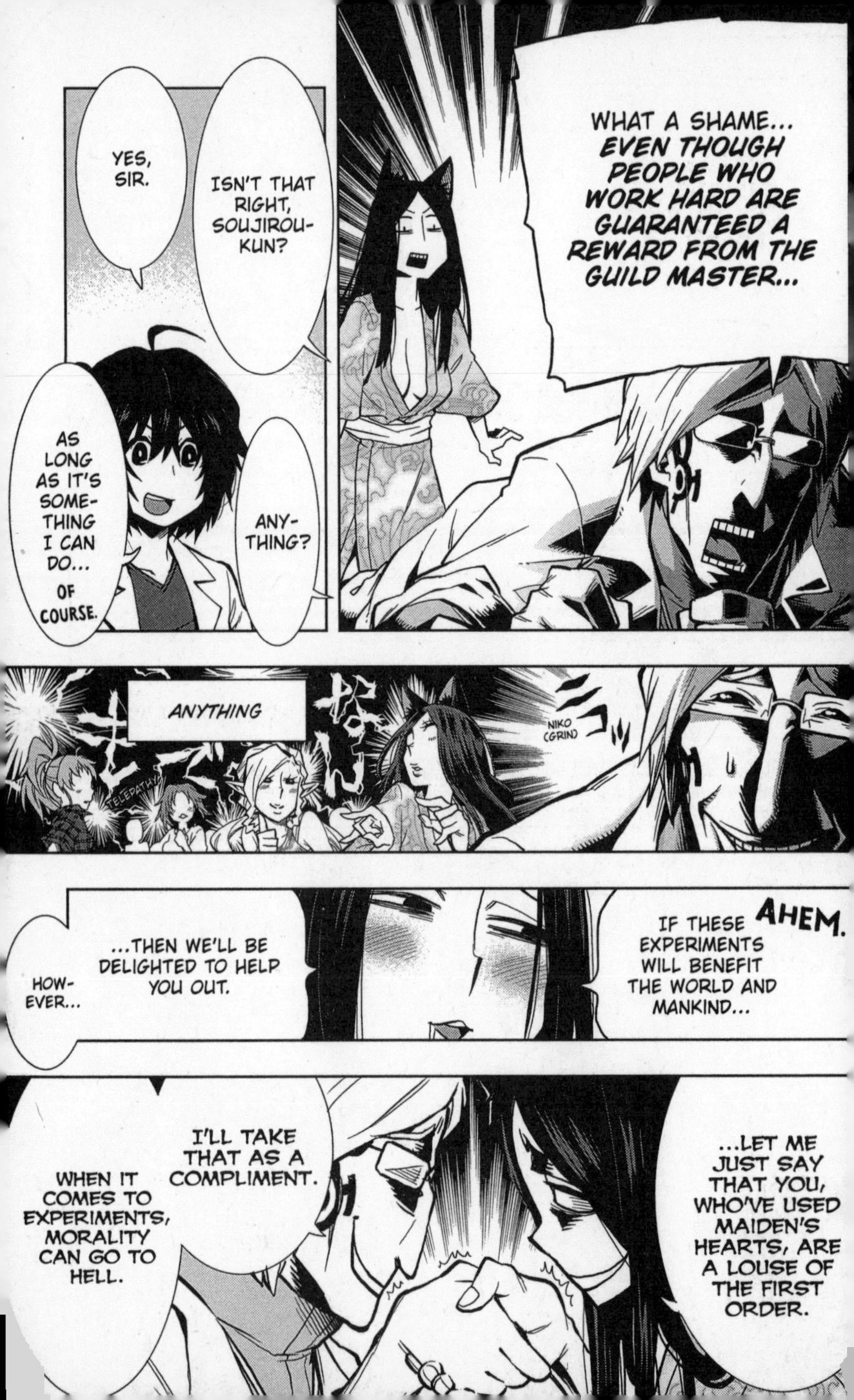
WHAT A SHAME... EVEN THOUGH PEOPLE WHO WORK HARD ARE GUARANTEED A REWARD FROM THE GUILD MASTER...
ISN'T THAT RIGHT, SOUJIROU-KUN?
YES, SIR.
ANYTHING?
AS LONG AS IT'S SOMETHING I CAN DO... OF COURSE.
NIKO (GRIN)
ANYTHING
AHEM.
IF THESE EXPERIMENTS WILL BENEFIT THE WORLD AND MANKIND...
...THEN WE'LL BE DELIGHTED TO HELP YOU OUT.
HOWEVER...
...LET ME JUST SAY THAT YOU, WHO'VE USED MAIDEN'S HEARTS, ARE A LOUSE OF THE FIRST ORDER.
I'LL TAKE THAT AS A COMPLIMENT.
WHEN IT COMES TO EXPERIMENTS, MORALITY CAN GO TO HELL.

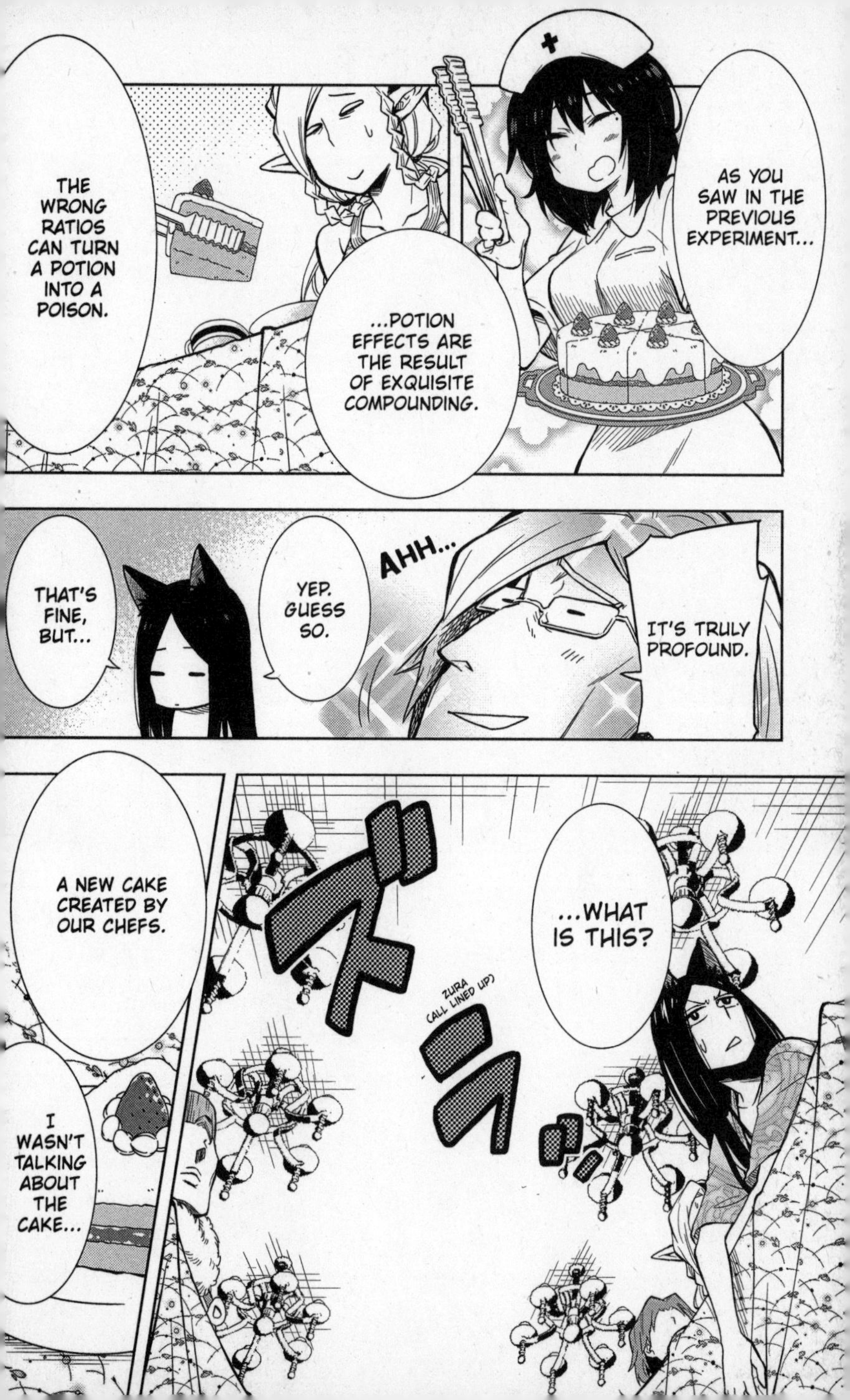
AS YOU SAW IN THE PREVIOUS EXPERIMENT...
...POTION EFFECTS ARE THE RESULT OF EXQUISITE COMPOUNDING.
THE WRONG RATIOS CAN TURN A POTION INTO A POISON.
IT'S TRULY PROFOUND.
AHH...
YEP. GUESS SO.
THAT'S FINE, BUT...
...WHAT IS THIS?
ZURA (ALL LINED UP)
A NEW CAKE CREATED BY OUR CHEFS.
I WASN'T TALKING ABOUT THE CAKE...

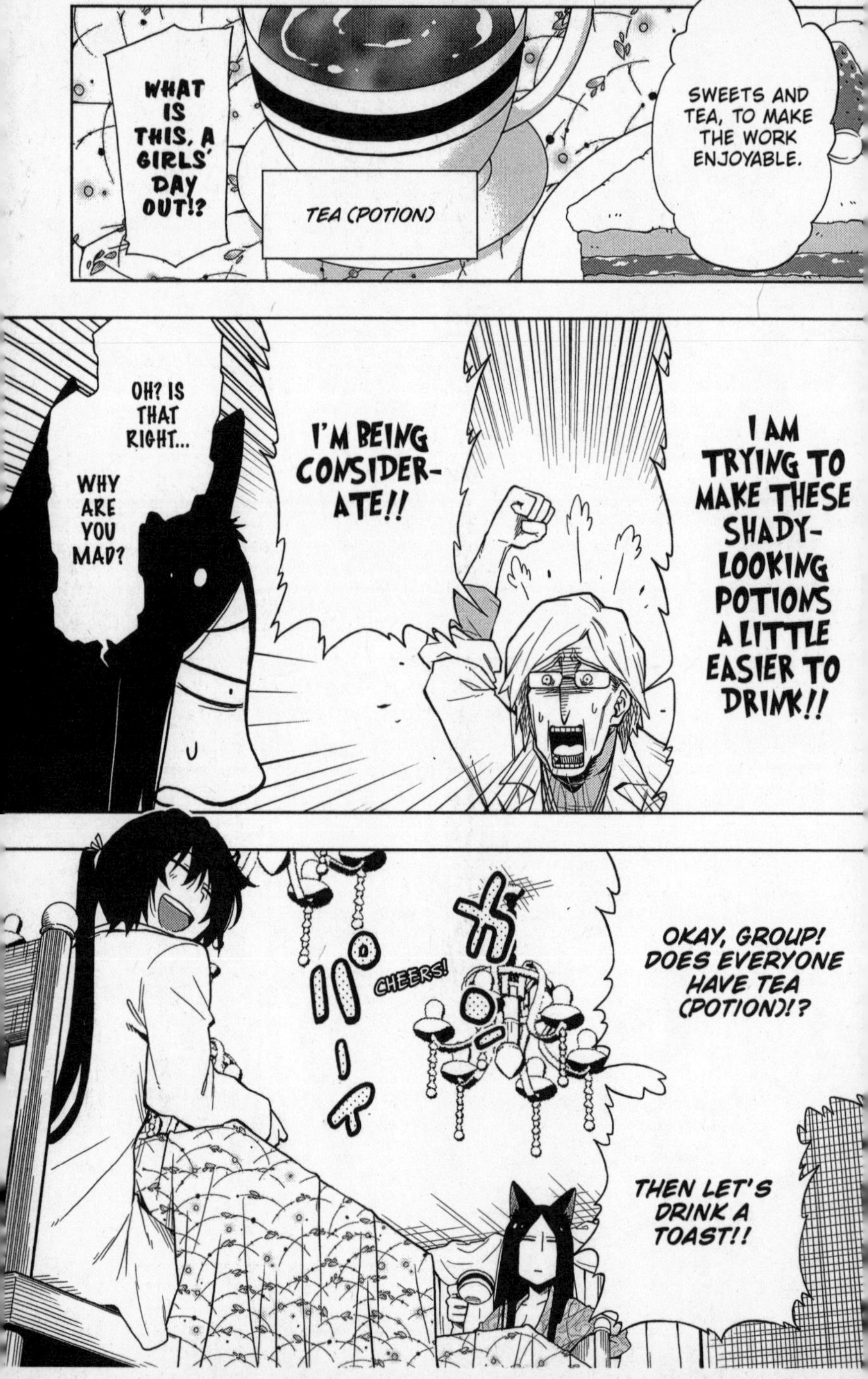
SWEETS AND TEA, TO MAKE THE WORK ENJOYABLE.
TEA (POTION)
WHAT IS THIS, A GIRLS' DAY OUT!?
I AM TRYING TO MAKE THESE SHADY-LOOKING POTIONS A LITTLE EASIER TO DRINK!!
I'M BEING CONSIDER-ATE!!
OH? IS THAT RIGHT...
WHY ARE YOU MAD?
OKAY, GROUP! DOES EVERYONE HAVE TEA (POTION)!?
CHEERS!
THEN LET'S DRINK A TOAST!!

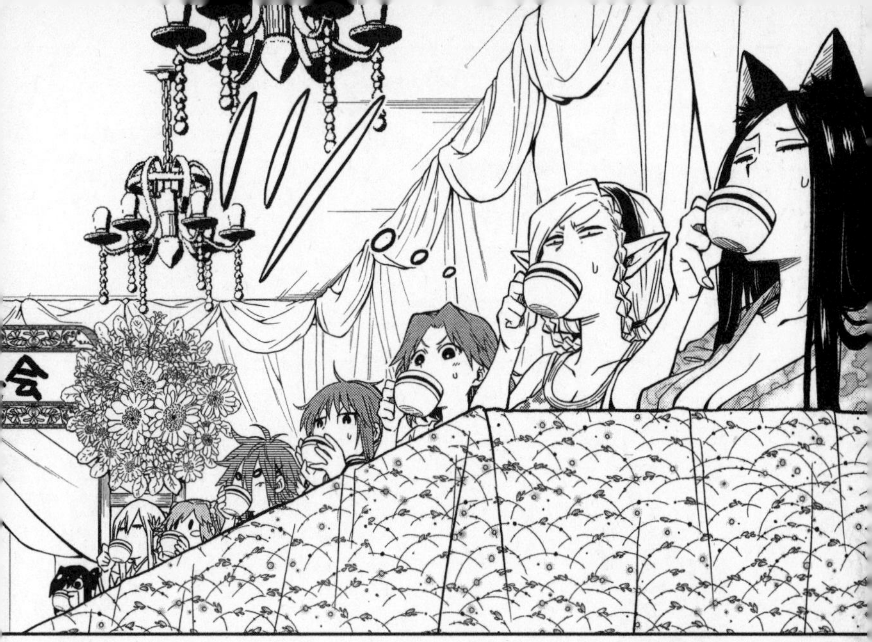

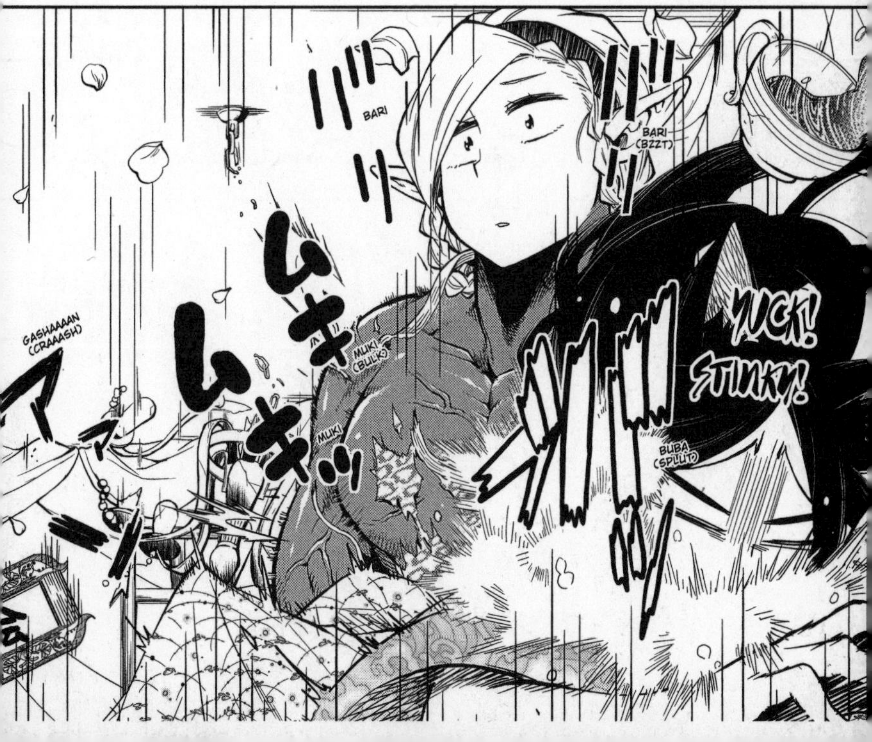
BARI
(BZZT)
BARI
YUCK!
STINKY!
MUKI
(BULK)
BUBA
(SPLUT)
MUKI
GASHAAAAN
(CRAAASH)

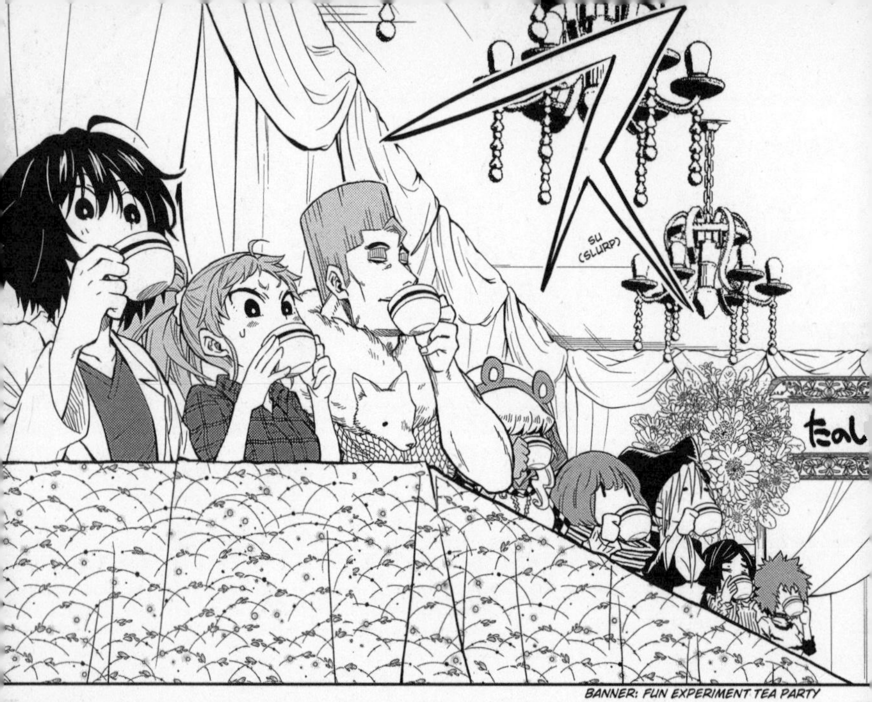
SU (SLURP)
たのし

BANNER: FUN EXPERIMENT TEA PARTY

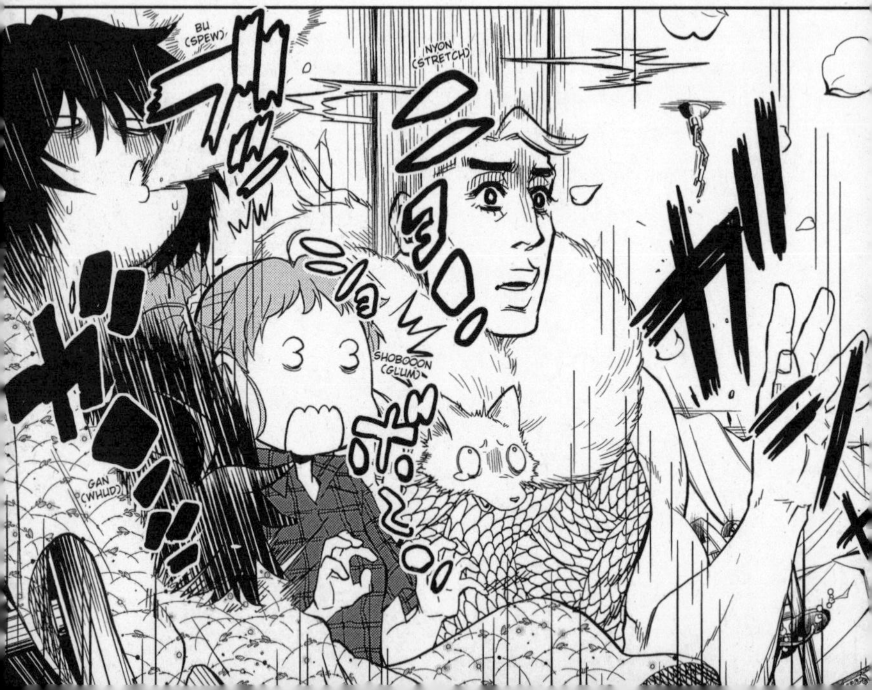
NYON (STRETCH)
BU (SPEW)
SHOBOOON (GLUM)
GAN (WHUD)

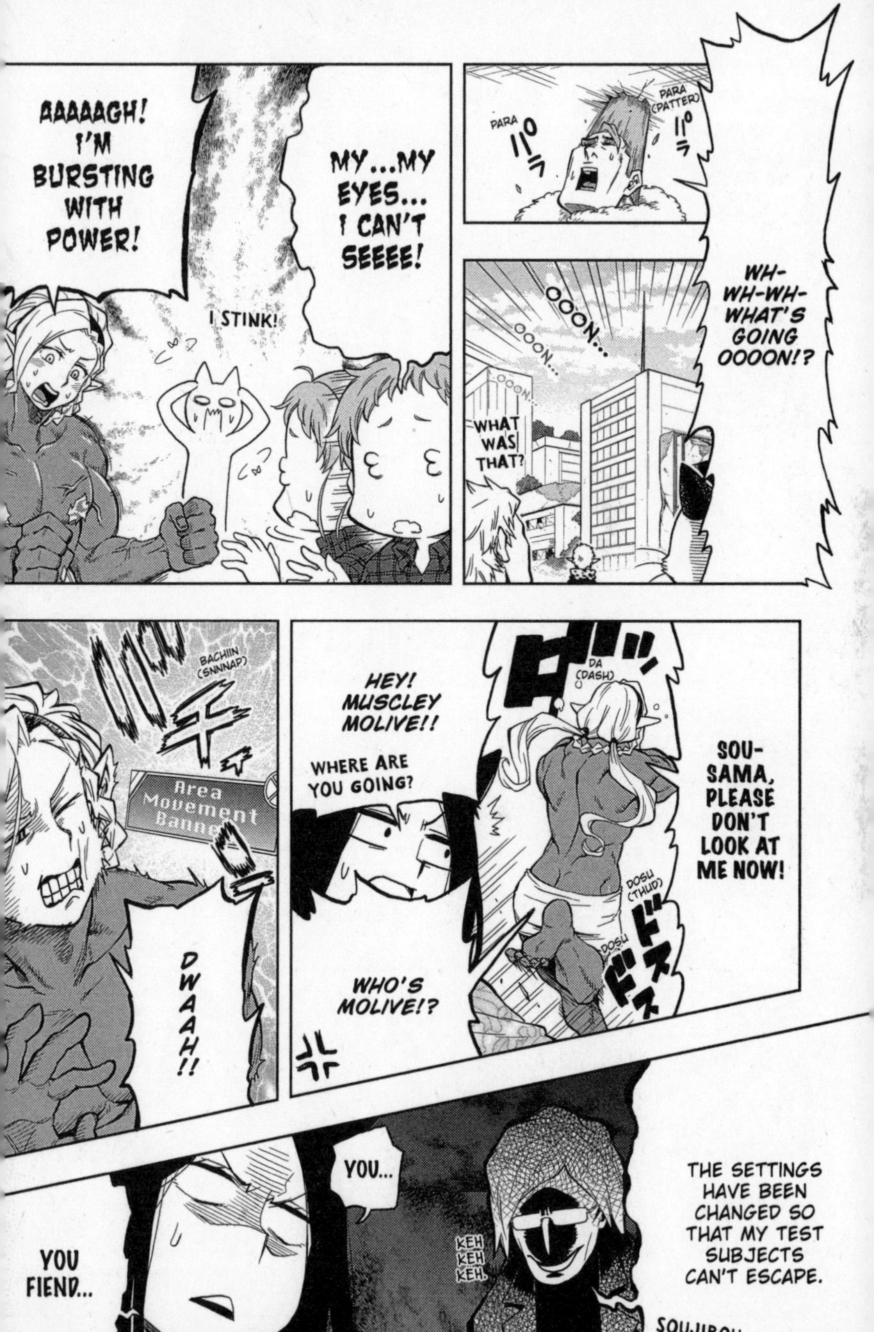
PARA (PATTER)
PARA
WH-WH-WH-WHAT'S GOING OOOON!?
OOON...
OOON...
OOON...
WHAT WAS THAT?
MY...MY EYES... I CAN'T SEEEE!
AAAAAGH! I'M BURSTING WITH POWER!
I STINK!
DA (DASH)
SOU-SAMA, PLEASE DON'T LOOK AT ME NOW!
HEY! MUSCLEY MOLIVE!!
WHERE ARE YOU GOING?
DOSU (THUD)
DOSU
WHO'S MOLIVE!?
BACHIIN (SNNNAP)
Area Movement Banne
DWAAAH!!
THE SETTINGS HAVE BEEN CHANGED SO THAT MY TEST SUBJECTS CAN'T ESCAPE.
SOUJIROU-KUN DID IT.
KEH KEH KEH.
YOU...
YOU FIEND...

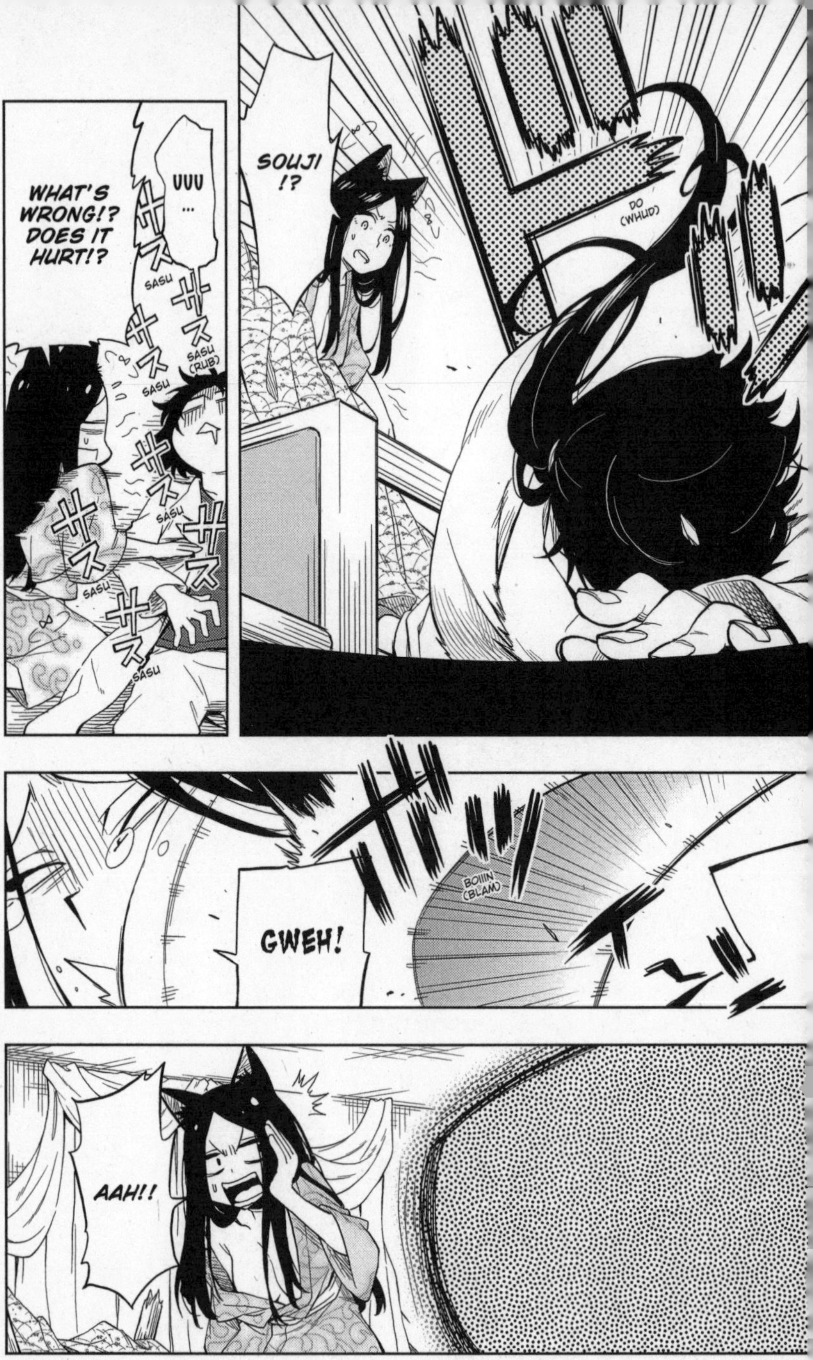
DO (WHUD)
SOUJI !?
UUU ...
WHAT'S WRONG!? DOES IT HURT!?
SASU SASU (RUB) SASU SASU SASU SASU
BOIIN (BLAM)
GWEH!
AAH!!

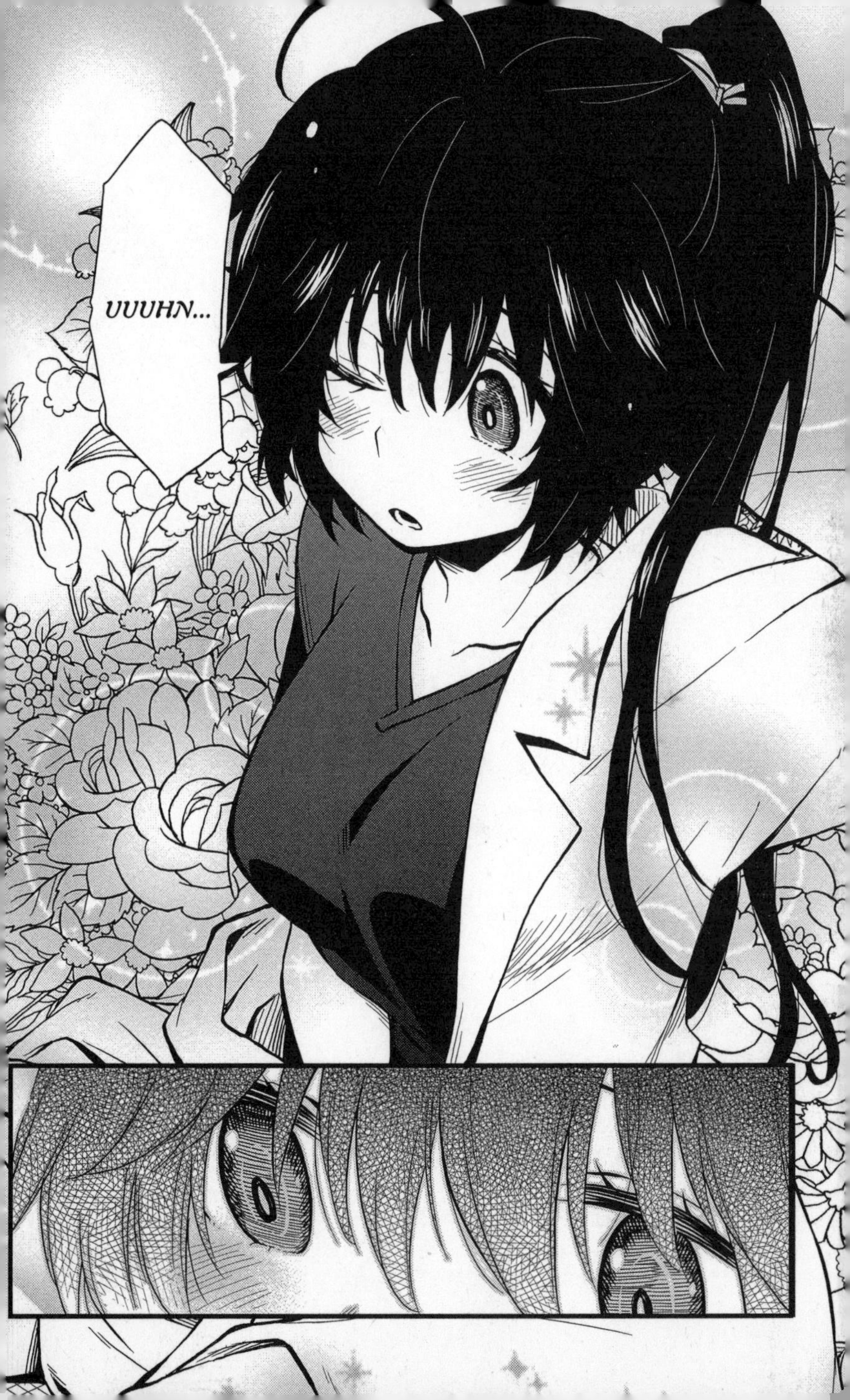
UUUHN...

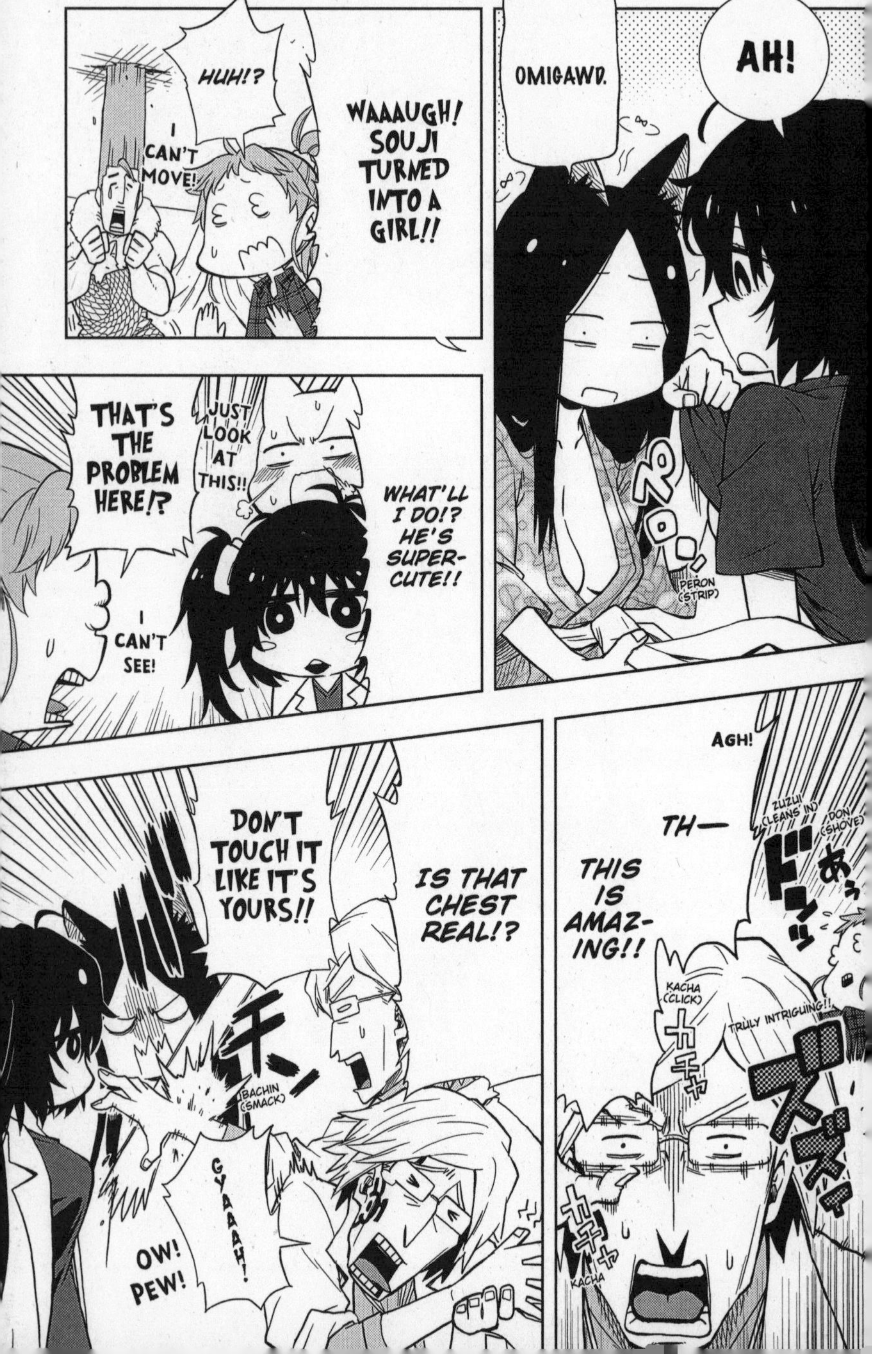
AH!
OMIGAWD.
PERON (STRIP)
WAAAUGH! SOUJI TURNED INTO A GIRL!!
HUH!?
I CAN'T MOVE!
WHAT'LL I DO!? HE'S SUPER-CUTE!!
JUST LOOK AT THIS!!
THAT'S THE PROBLEM HERE!?
I CAN'T SEE!
AGH!
ZUZUI (LEANS IN)
DON (SHOVE)
TH—
THIS IS AMAZ-ING!!
KACHA (CLICK)
TRULY INTRIGUING!!
KACHA
IS THAT CHEST REAL!?
DON'T TOUCH IT LIKE IT'S YOURS!!
BACHIN (SMACK)
GYAAAH!
OW! PEW!

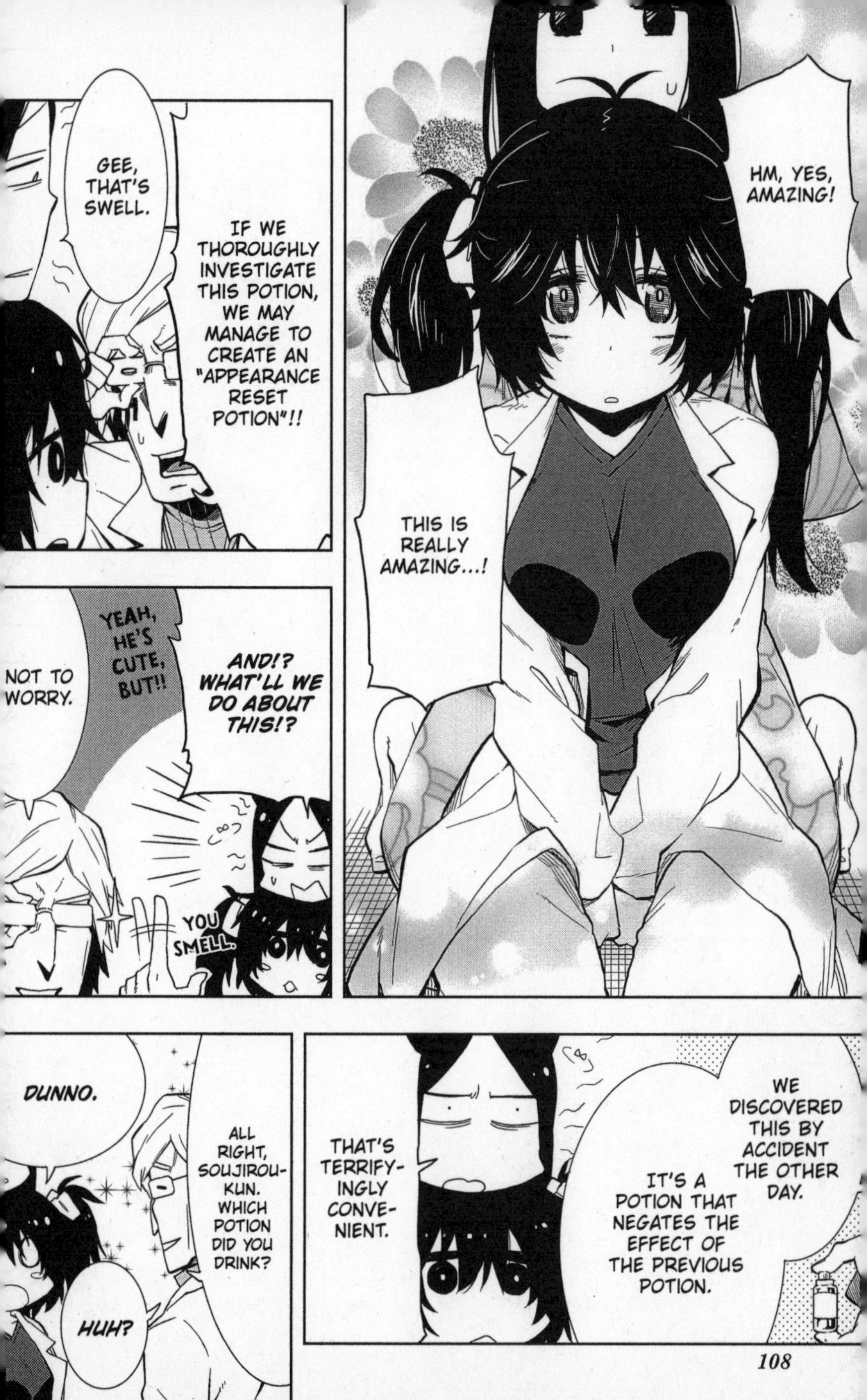
HM, YES, AMAZING!
THIS IS REALLY AMAZING...!
IF WE THOROUGHLY INVESTIGATE THIS POTION, WE MAY MANAGE TO CREATE AN "APPEARANCE RESET POTION"!!
GEE, THAT'S SWELL.
AND!? WHAT'LL WE DO ABOUT THIS!?
YEAH, HE'S CUTE, BUT!!
NOT TO WORRY.
YOU SMELL.
WE DISCOVERED THIS BY ACCIDENT THE OTHER DAY.
IT'S A POTION THAT NEGATES THE EFFECT OF THE PREVIOUS POTION.
THAT'S TERRIFYINGLY CONVENIENT.
ALL RIGHT, SOUJIROU-KUN. WHICH POTION DID YOU DRINK?
DUNNO.
HUH?

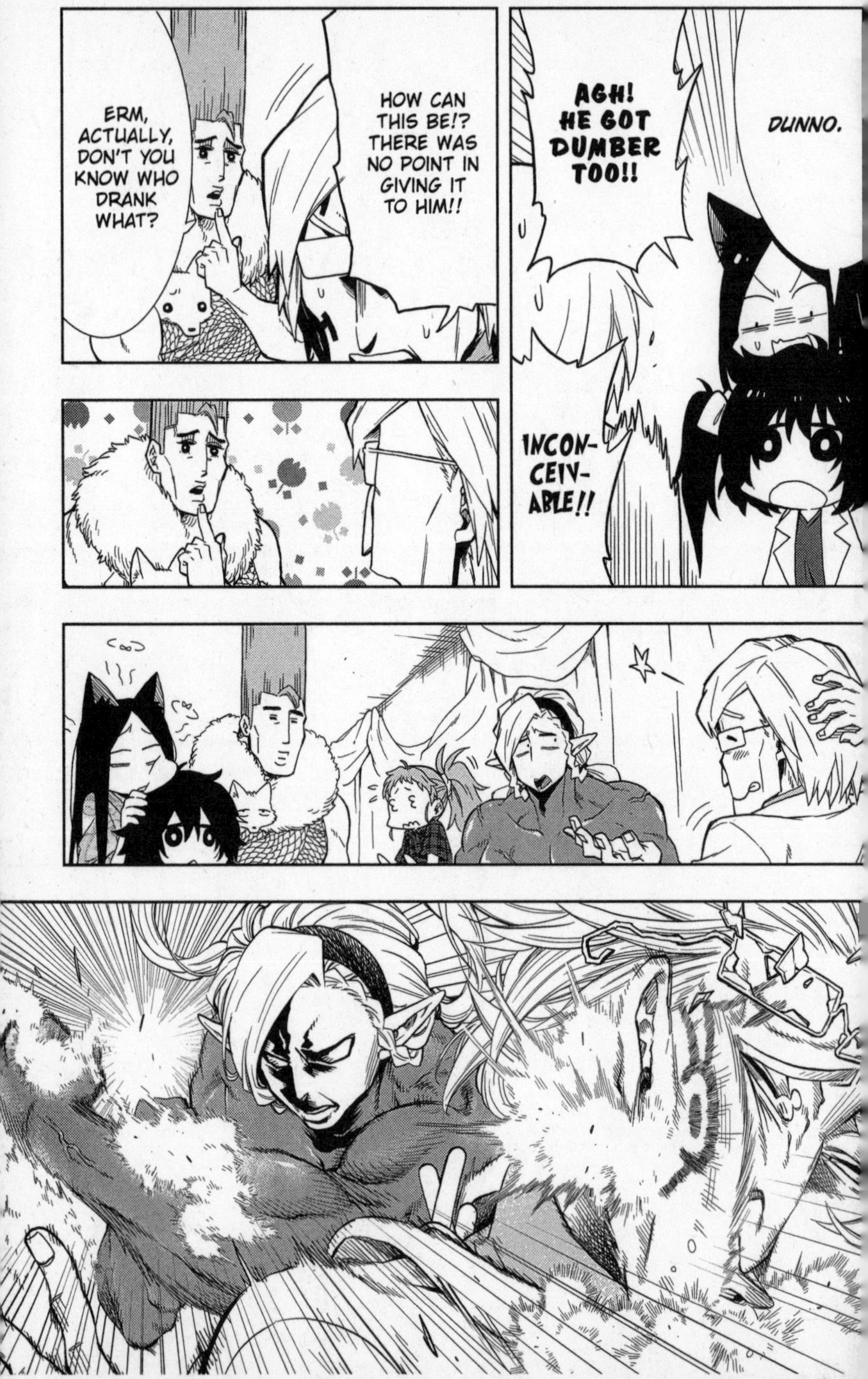
DUNNO.
AGH! HE GOT DUMBER TOO!!
INCON-CEIV-ABLE!!
HOW CAN THIS BE!? THERE WAS NO POINT IN GIVING IT TO HIM!!
ERM, ACTUALLY, DON'T YOU KNOW WHO DRANK WHAT?

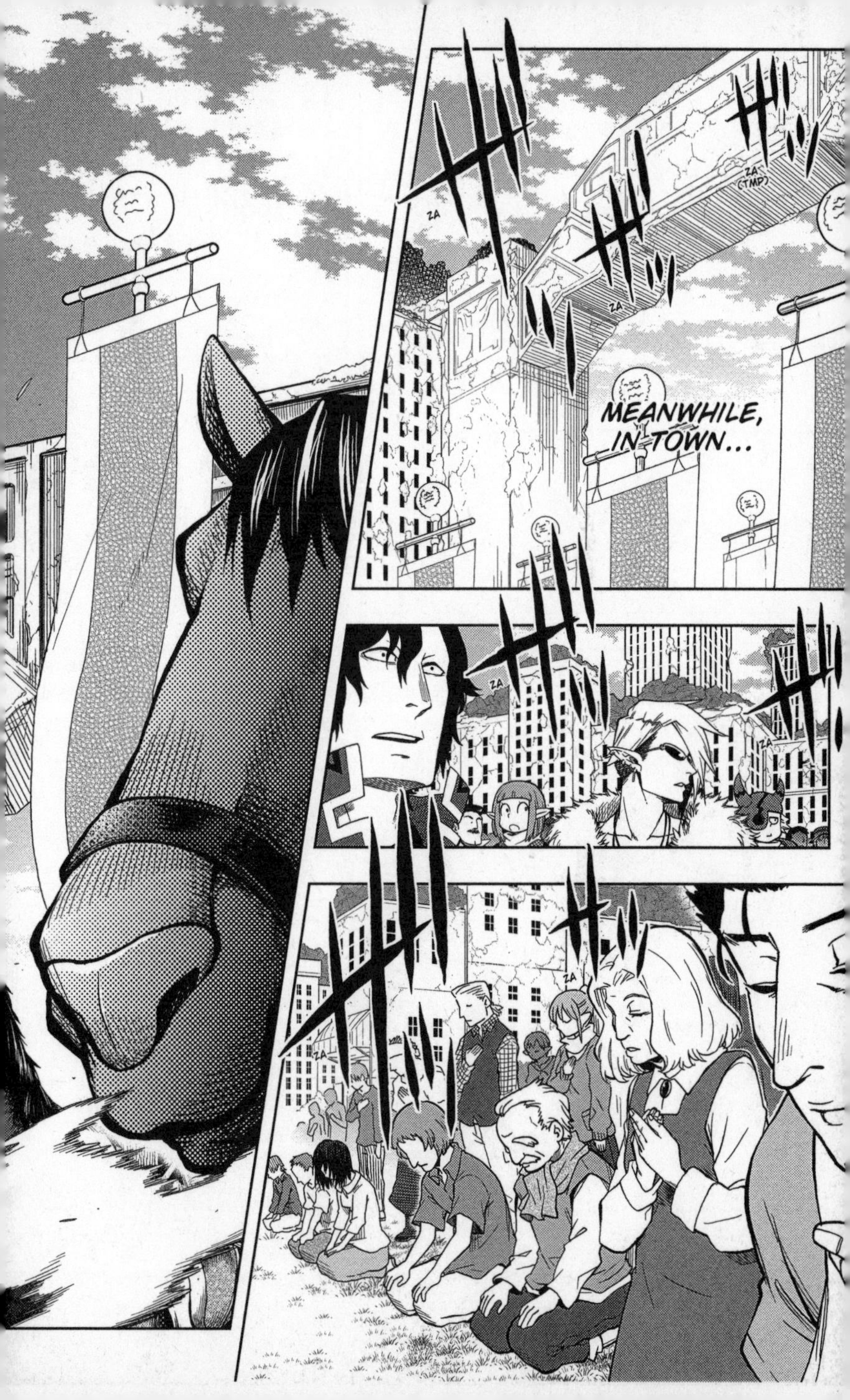
ZA
(TMP)
ZA
ZA
MEANWHILE, IN TOWN...
ZA
ZA
ZA
ZA

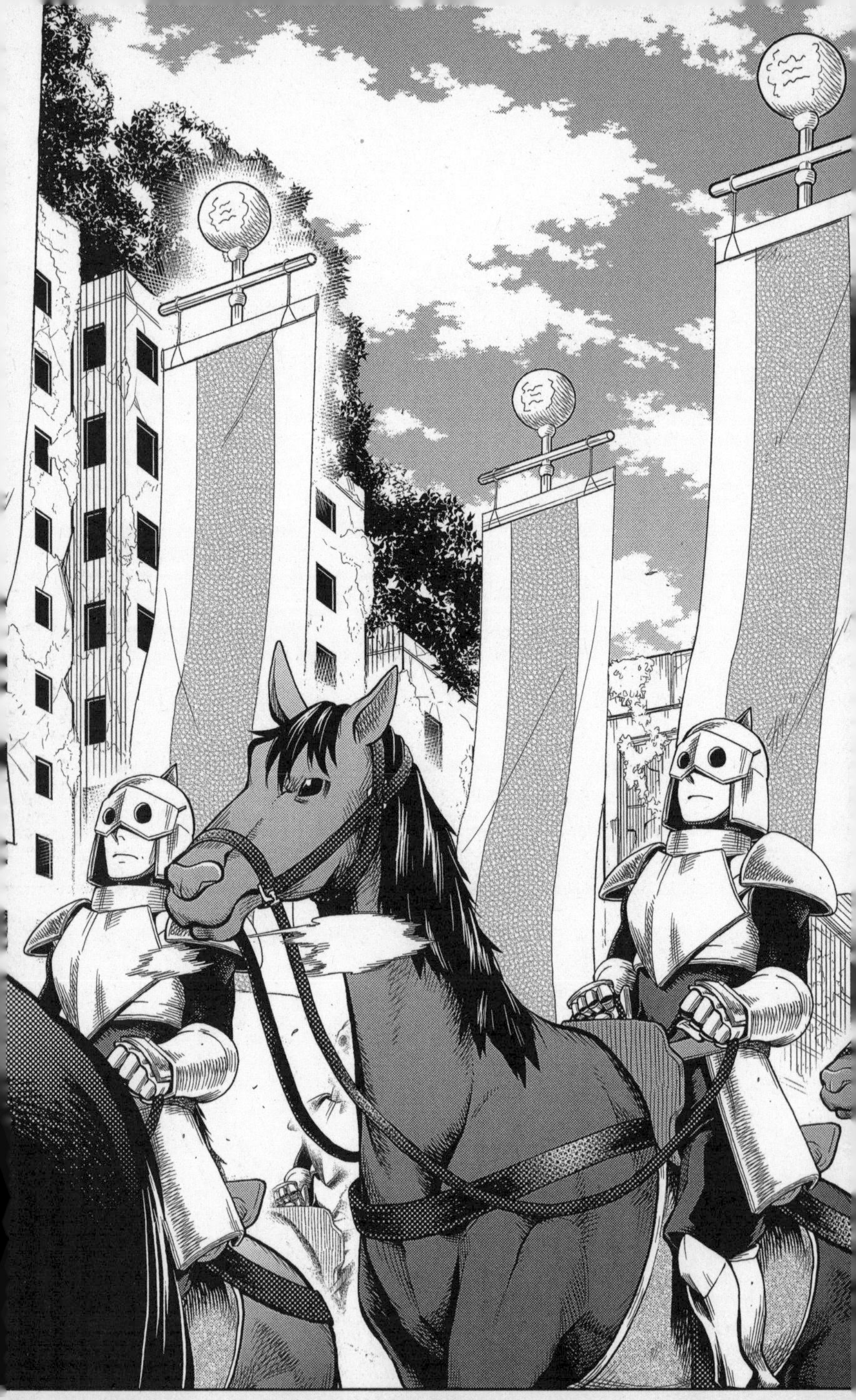

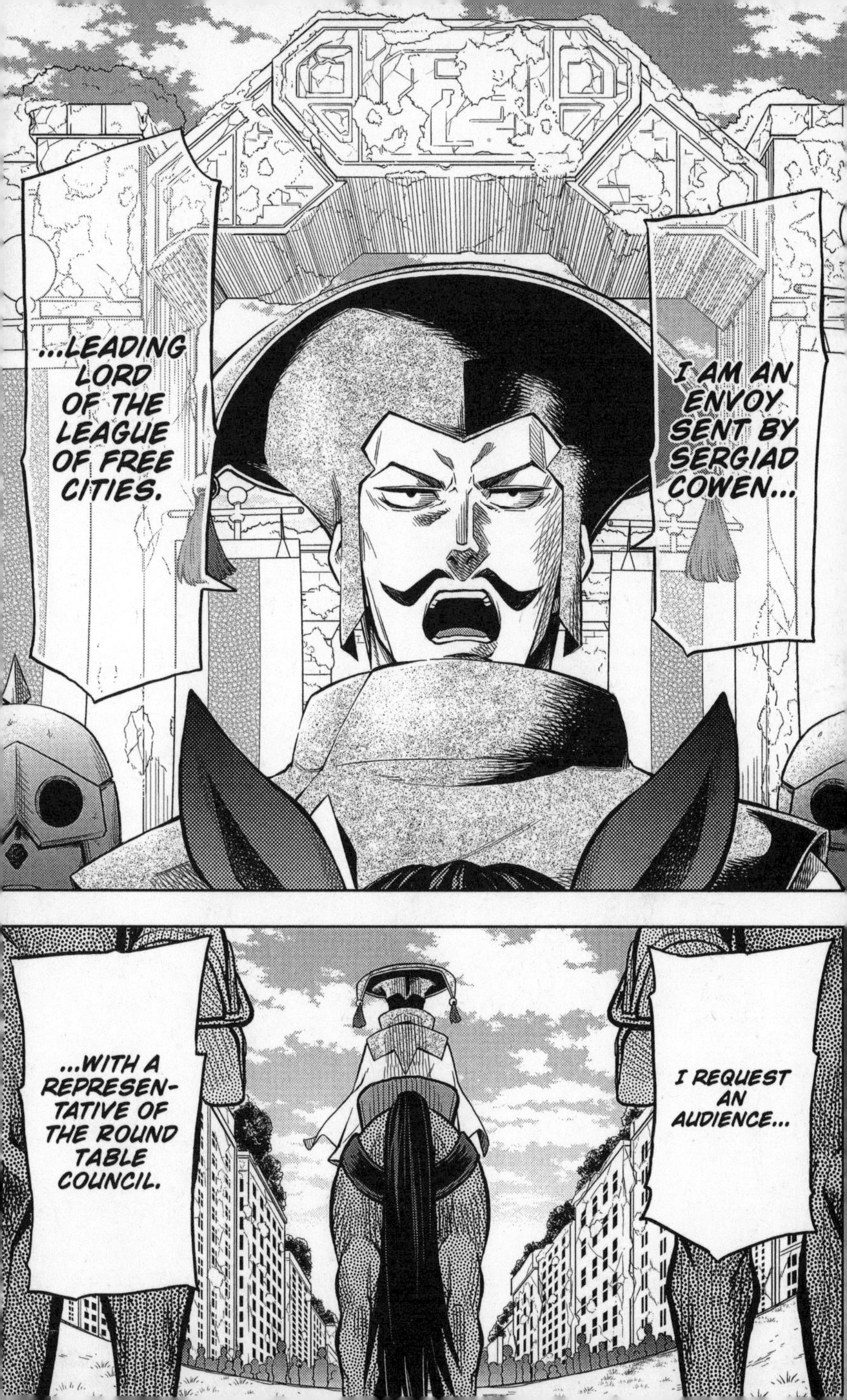
I AM AN ENVOY SENT BY SERGIAD COWEN...
...LEADING LORD OF THE LEAGUE OF FREE CITIES.
I REQUEST AN AUDIENCE...
...WITH A REPRESENTATIVE OF THE ROUND TABLE COUNCIL.

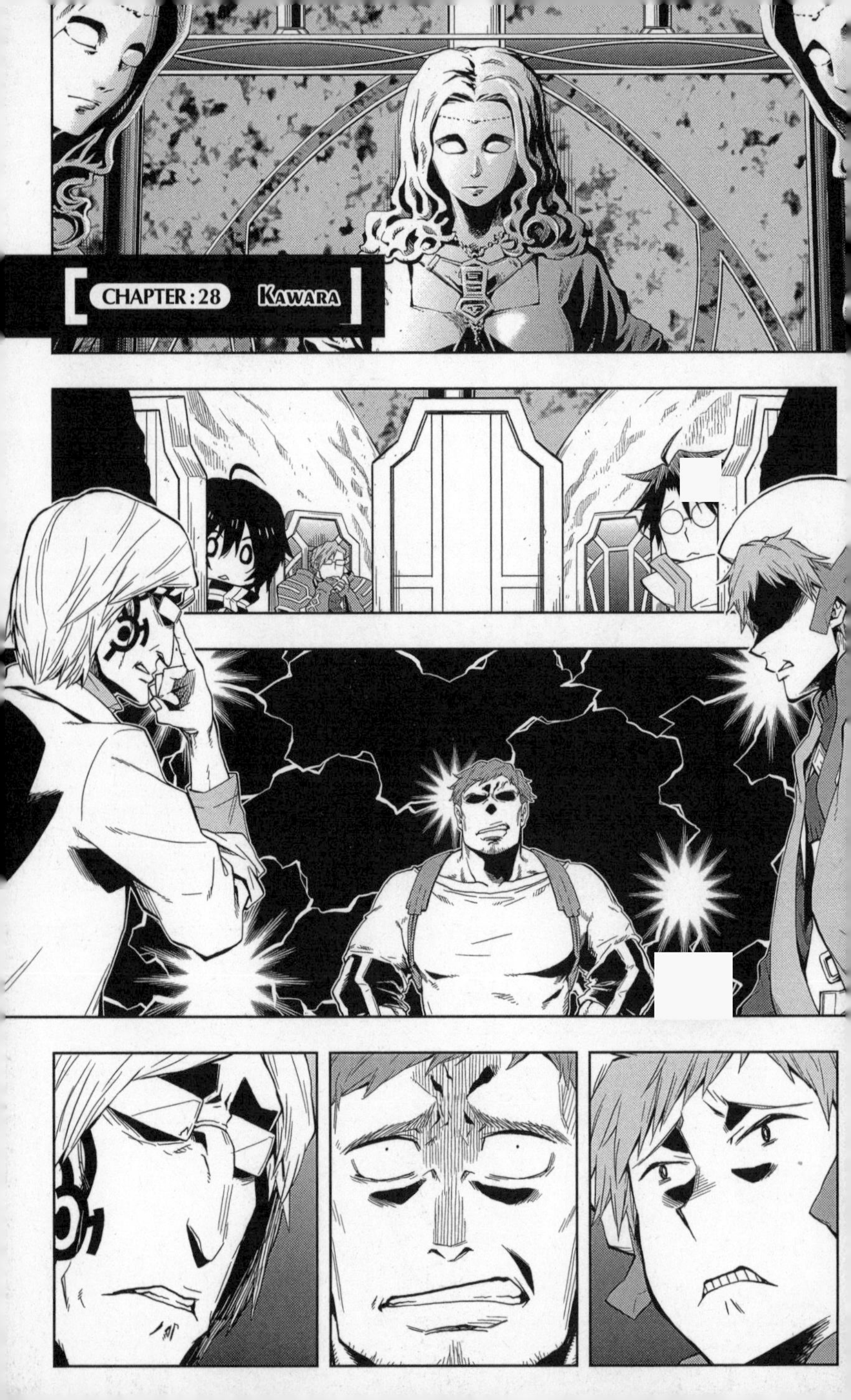
CHAPTER : 28
KAWARA

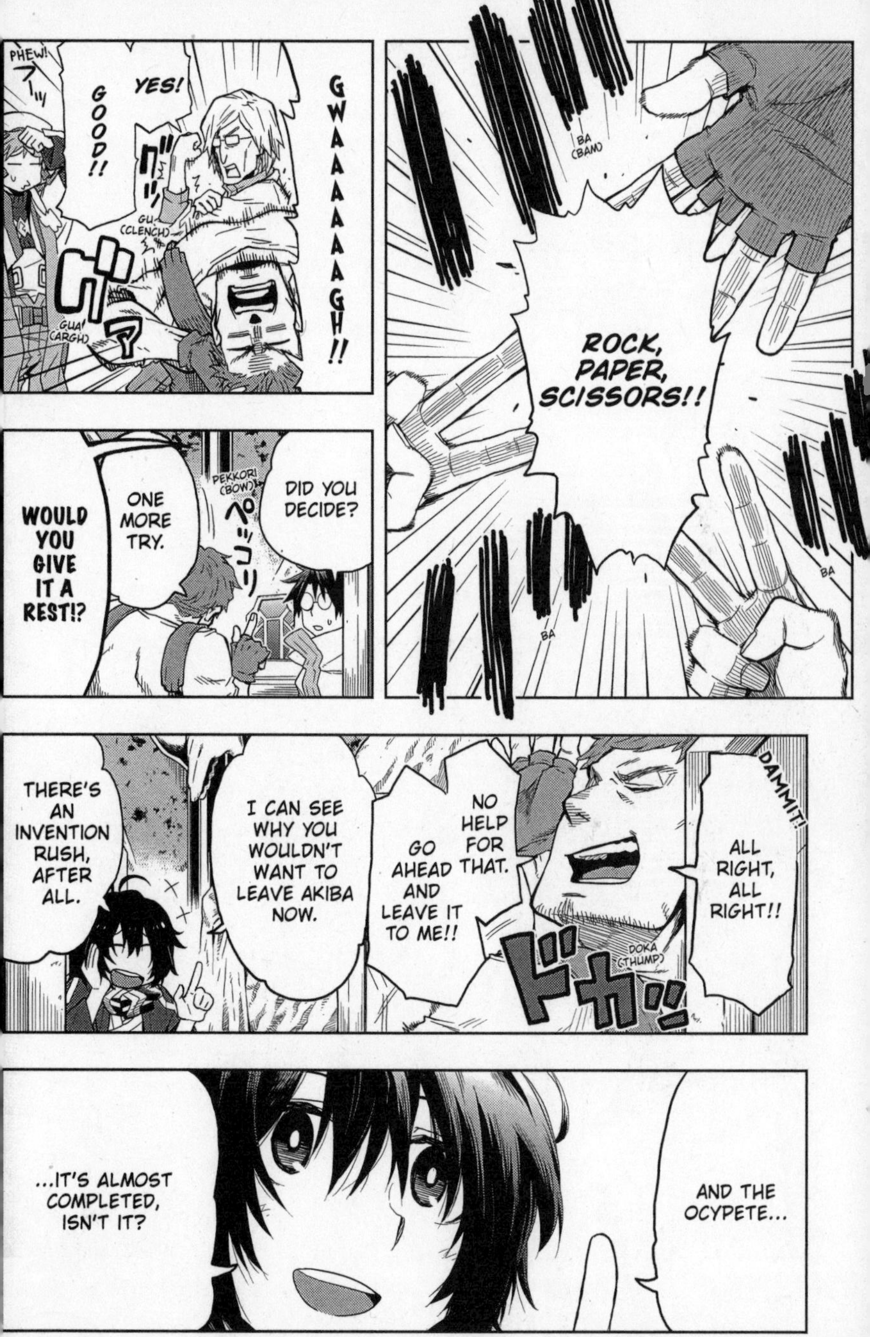
BA (BAM)
ROCK, PAPER, SCISSORS!!
BA
BA
GWAAAAAAAGH!!
YES!
GU (CLENCH)
GOOOD!!
GUA (ARGH)
PHEW!
DID YOU DECIDE?
PEKKORI (BOW)
ONE MORE TRY.
WOULD YOU GIVE IT A REST!?
DAMMIT!
ALL RIGHT, ALL RIGHT!!
DOKA (THUMP)
NO HELP FOR THAT.
GO AHEAD AND LEAVE IT TO ME!!
I CAN SEE WHY YOU WOULDN'T WANT TO LEAVE AKIBA NOW.
THERE'S AN INVENTION RUSH, AFTER ALL.
AND THE OCYPETE...
...IT'S ALMOST COMPLETED, ISN'T IT?

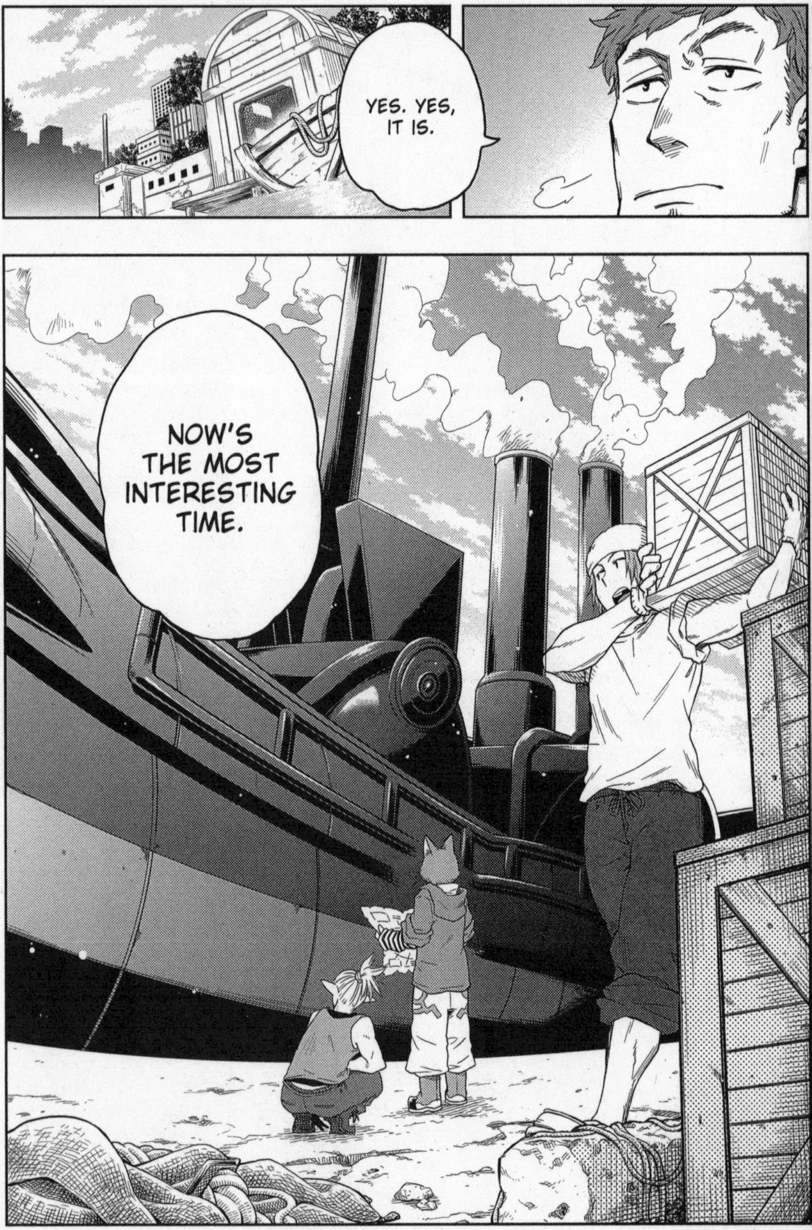
YES. YES, IT IS.
NOW'S THE MOST INTERESTING TIME.

CHAPTER : 28 Kawara

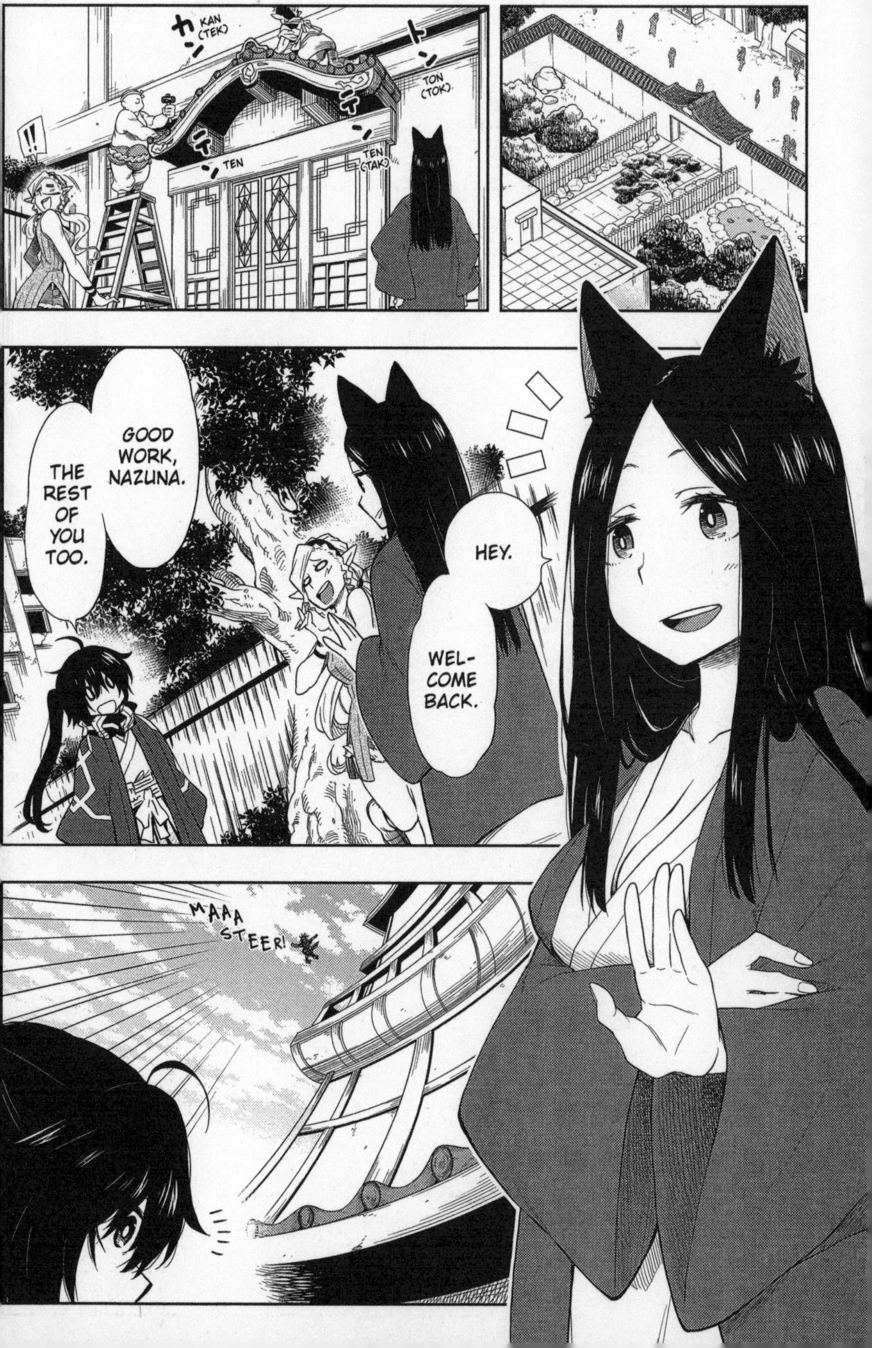
KAN (TEK)
TON (TOK)
TEN (TAK)
TEN
!!
HEY.
WEL-COME BACK.
GOOD WORK, NAZUNA.
THE REST OF YOU TOO.
MAAA STEER!

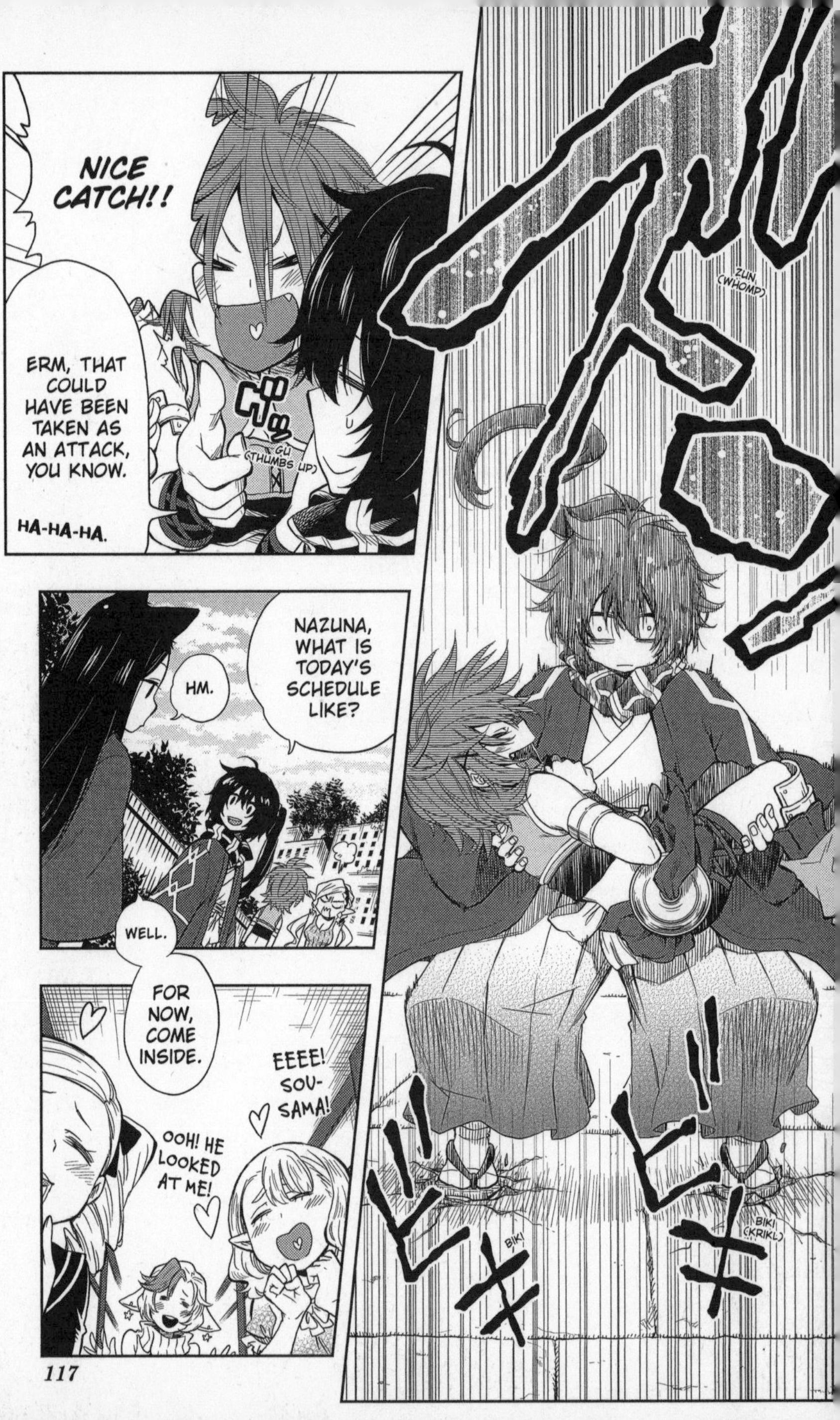
ZUN (WHOMP)
BIKI (KRIKL)
BIKI!
NICE CATCH!!
GU (THUMBS UP)
ERM, THAT COULD HAVE BEEN TAKEN AS AN ATTACK, YOU KNOW.
HA-HA-HA.
NAZUNA, WHAT IS TODAY'S SCHEDULE LIKE?
HM.
WELL.
FOR NOW, COME INSIDE.
EEEE! SOU-SAMA!
OOH! HE LOOKED AT ME!

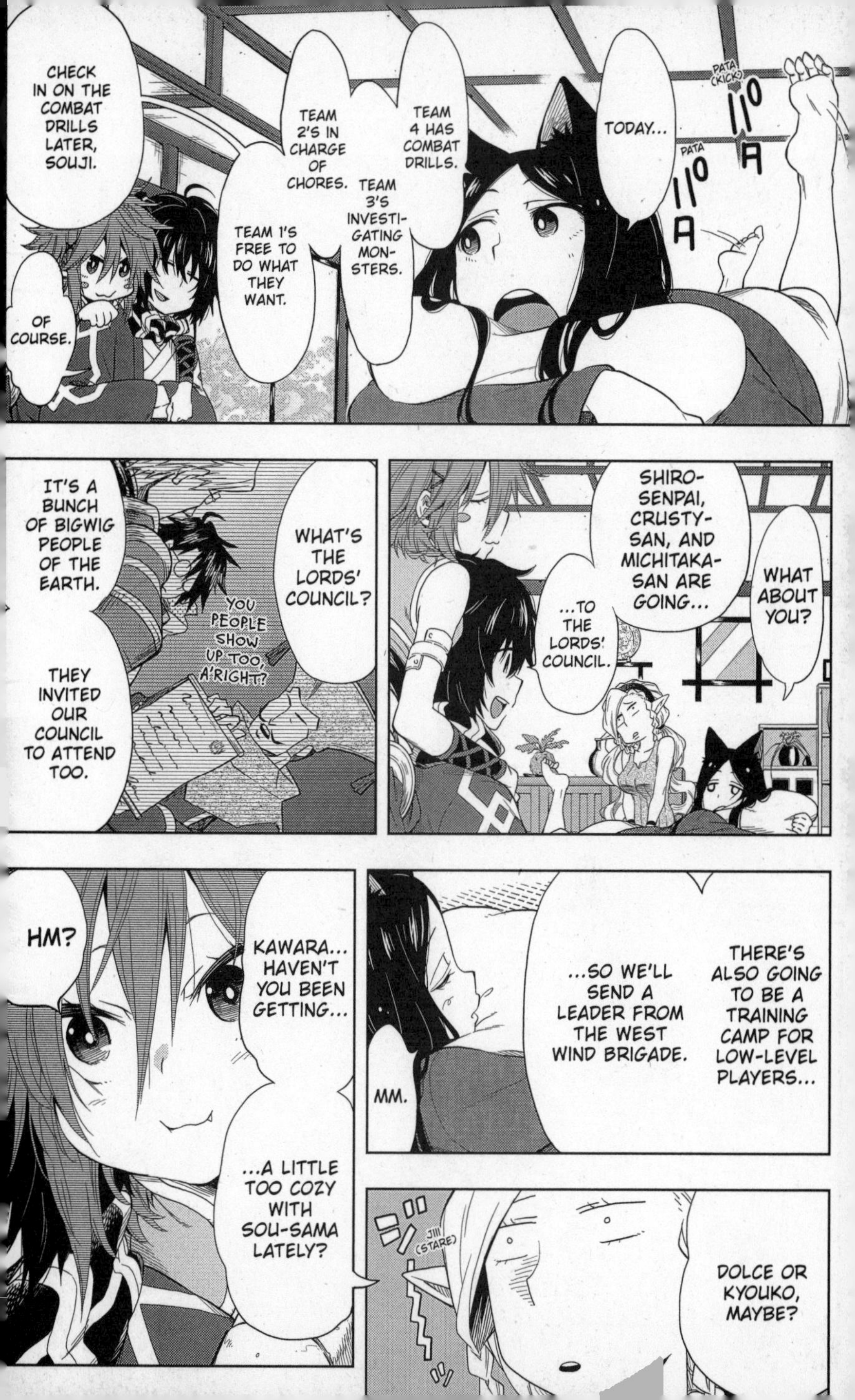
PATA (KICK)
PATA
TODAY...
TEAM 4 HAS COMBAT DRILLS.
TEAM 3'S INVESTIGATING MONSTERS.
TEAM 2'S IN CHARGE OF CHORES.
TEAM 1'S FREE TO DO WHAT THEY WANT.
CHECK IN ON THE COMBAT DRILLS LATER, SOUJI.
OF COURSE.
WHAT ABOUT YOU?
SHIRO-SENPAI, CRUSTY-SAN, AND MICHITAKA-SAN ARE GOING...
...TO THE LORDS' COUNCIL.
WHAT'S THE LORDS' COUNCIL?
IT'S A BUNCH OF BIGWIG PEOPLE OF THE EARTH.
YOU PEOPLE SHOW UP TOO, A'RIGHT?
THEY INVITED OUR COUNCIL TO ATTEND TOO.
THERE'S ALSO GOING TO BE A TRAINING CAMP FOR LOW-LEVEL PLAYERS...
...SO WE'LL SEND A LEADER FROM THE WEST WIND BRIGADE.
MM.
DOLCE OR KYOUKO, MAYBE?
JIII (STARE)
KAWARA... HAVEN'T YOU BEEN GETTING...
HM?
...A LITTLE TOO COZY WITH SOU-SAMA LATELY?

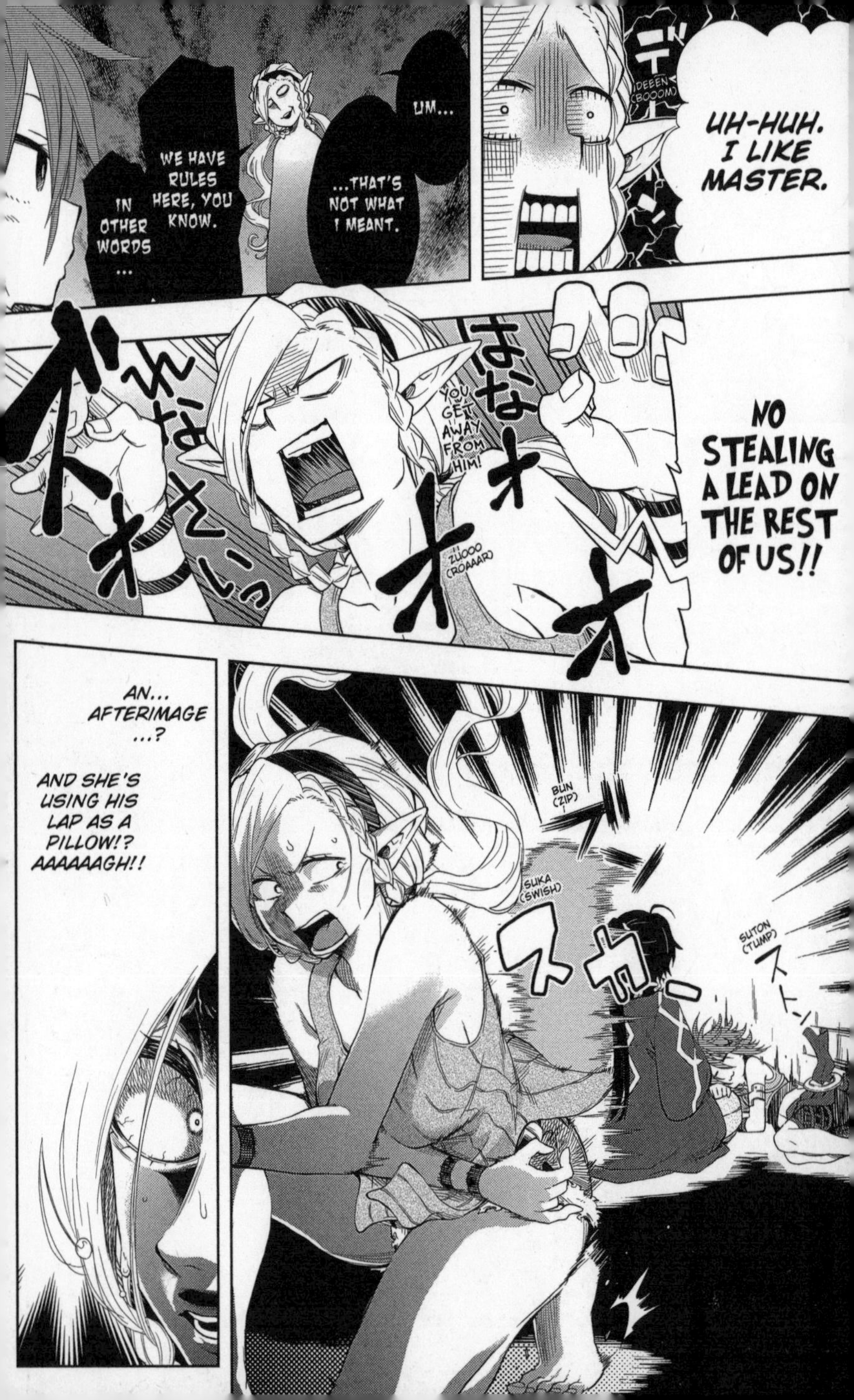
DEEEN (BOOOM)
UH-HUH. I LIKE MASTER.
UM...
...THAT'S NOT WHAT I MEANT.
WE HAVE RULES HERE, YOU KNOW.
IN OTHER WORDS...
NO STEALING A LEAD ON THE REST OF US!!
YOU GET AWAY FROM HIM!
ZUOOO (ROAAAR)
BUN (ZIP)
SUKA (SWISH)
SUTON (TUMP)
AN... AFTERIMAGE ...?
AND SHE'S USING HIS LAP AS A PILLOW!? AAAAAAGH!!

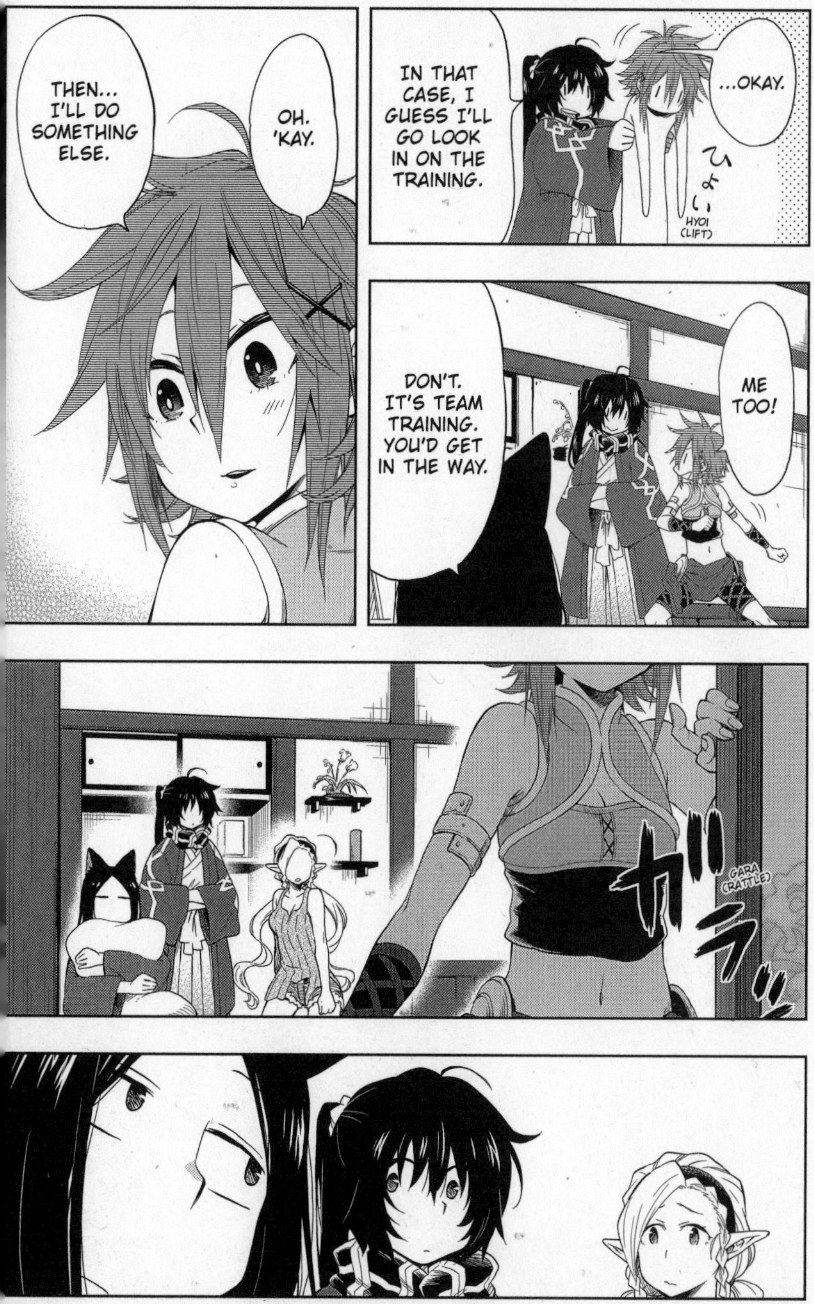
IN THAT CASE, I GUESS I'LL GO LOOK IN ON THE TRAINING.
...OKAY.
ひょい
HYOI (LIFT)
ME TOO!
DON'T. IT'S TEAM TRAINING. YOU'D GET IN THE WAY.
OH. 'KAY.
THEN... I'LL DO SOMETHING ELSE.
ガラッ
GARA (RATTLE)

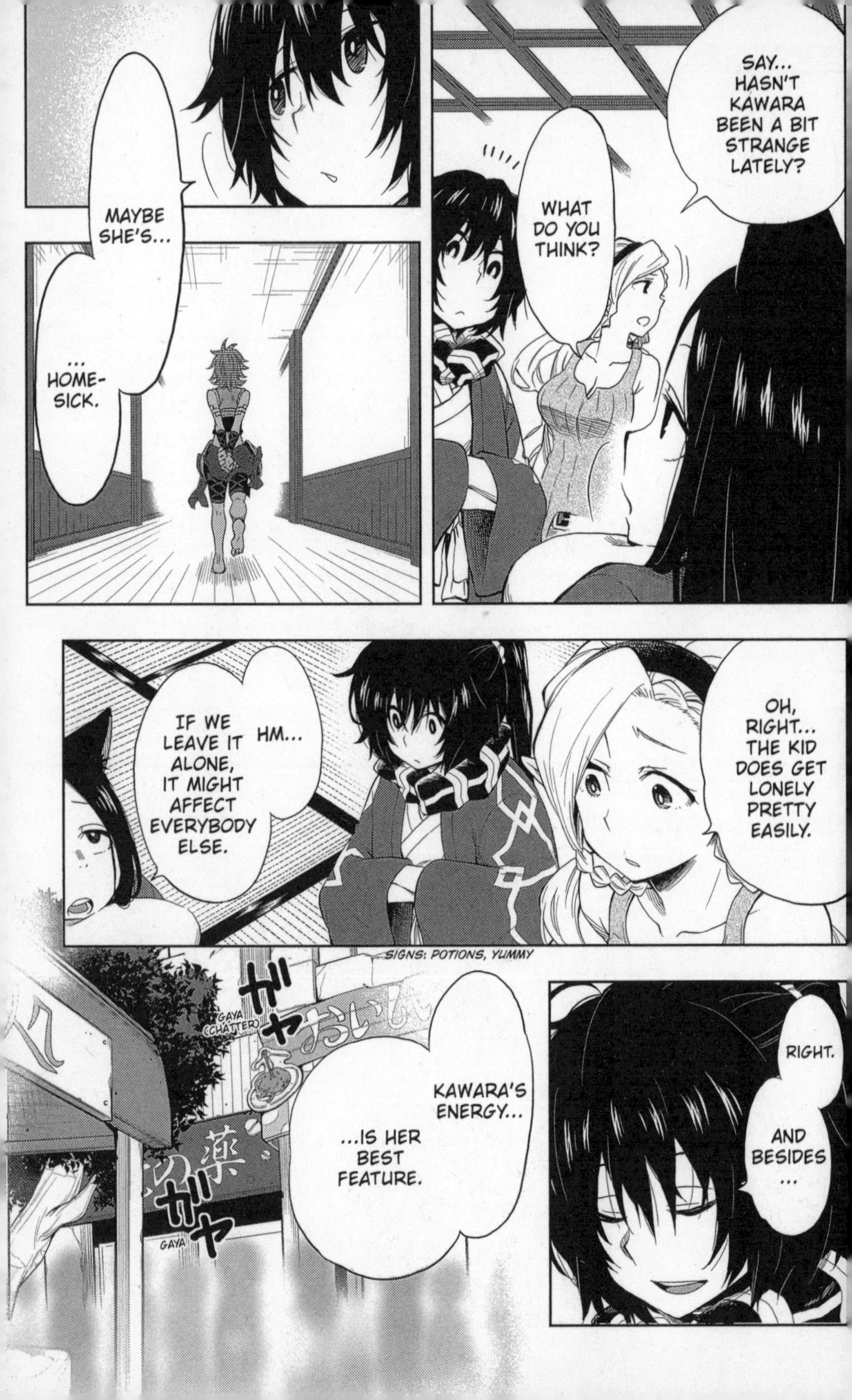
SAY... HASN'T KAWARA BEEN A BIT STRANGE LATELY?
WHAT DO YOU THINK?
MAYBE SHE'S...
...HOME-SICK.
OH, RIGHT... THE KID DOES GET LONELY PRETTY EASILY.
HM...
IF WE LEAVE IT ALONE, IT MIGHT AFFECT EVERYBODY ELSE.
RIGHT.
AND BESIDES...
KAWARA'S ENERGY...
...IS HER BEST FEATURE.
SIGNS: POTIONS, YUMMY
GAYA (CHATTER)
GAYA

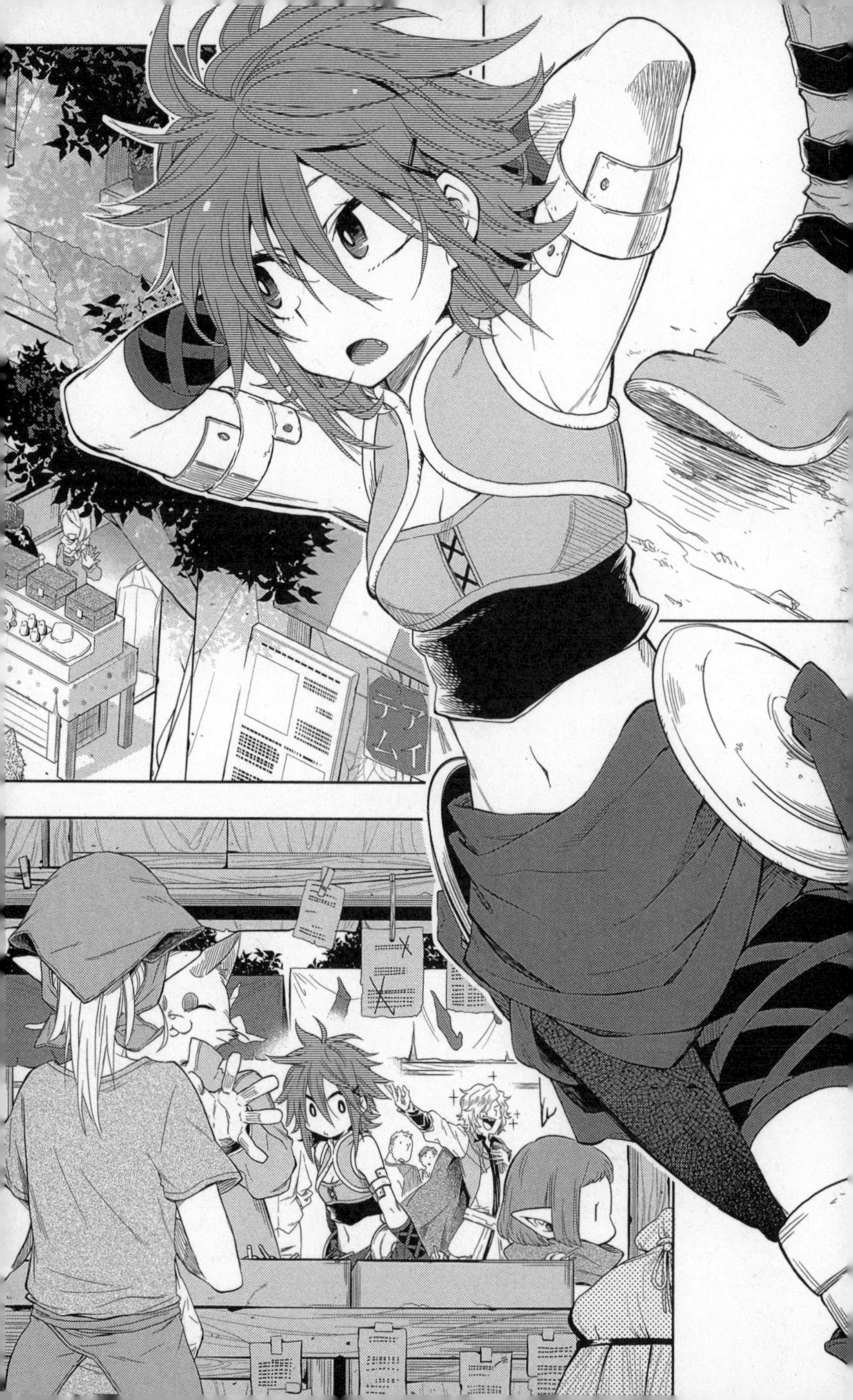
アイテム

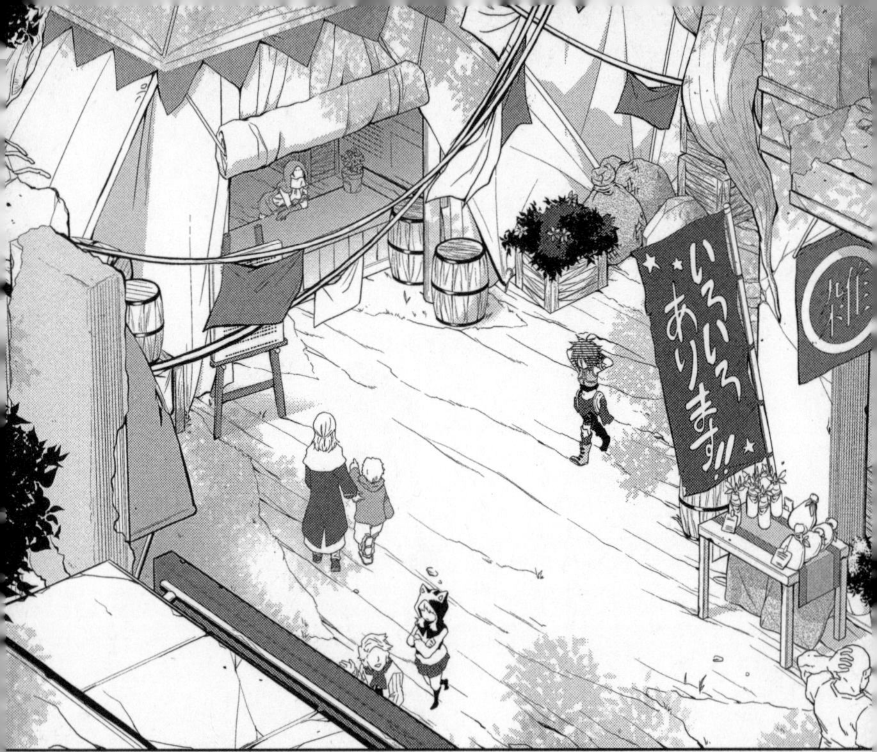
いろいろあります!!

SIGNS: ITEMS, SUNDRIES, FIND IT ALL HERE!!

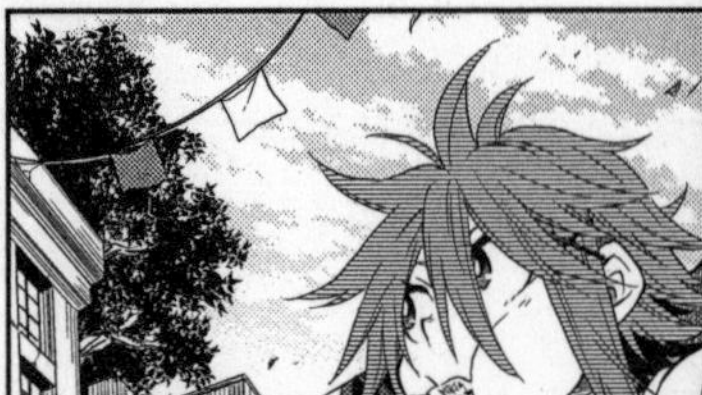

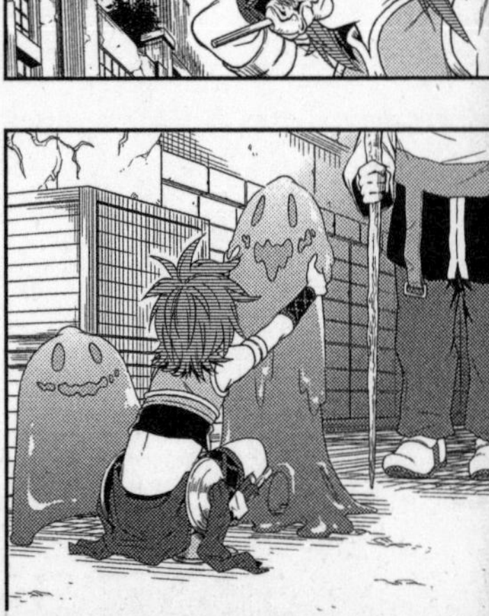

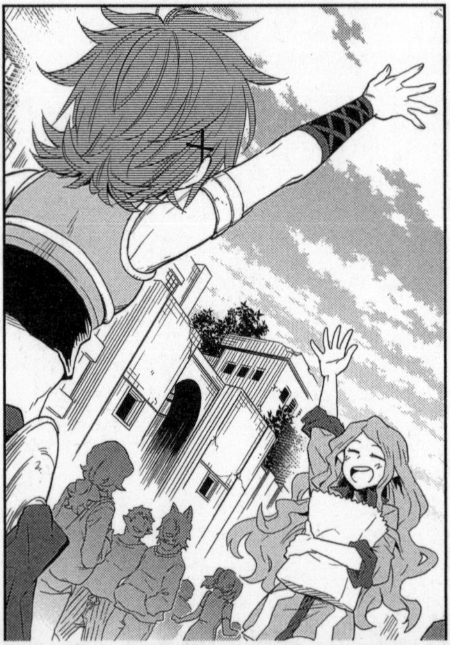

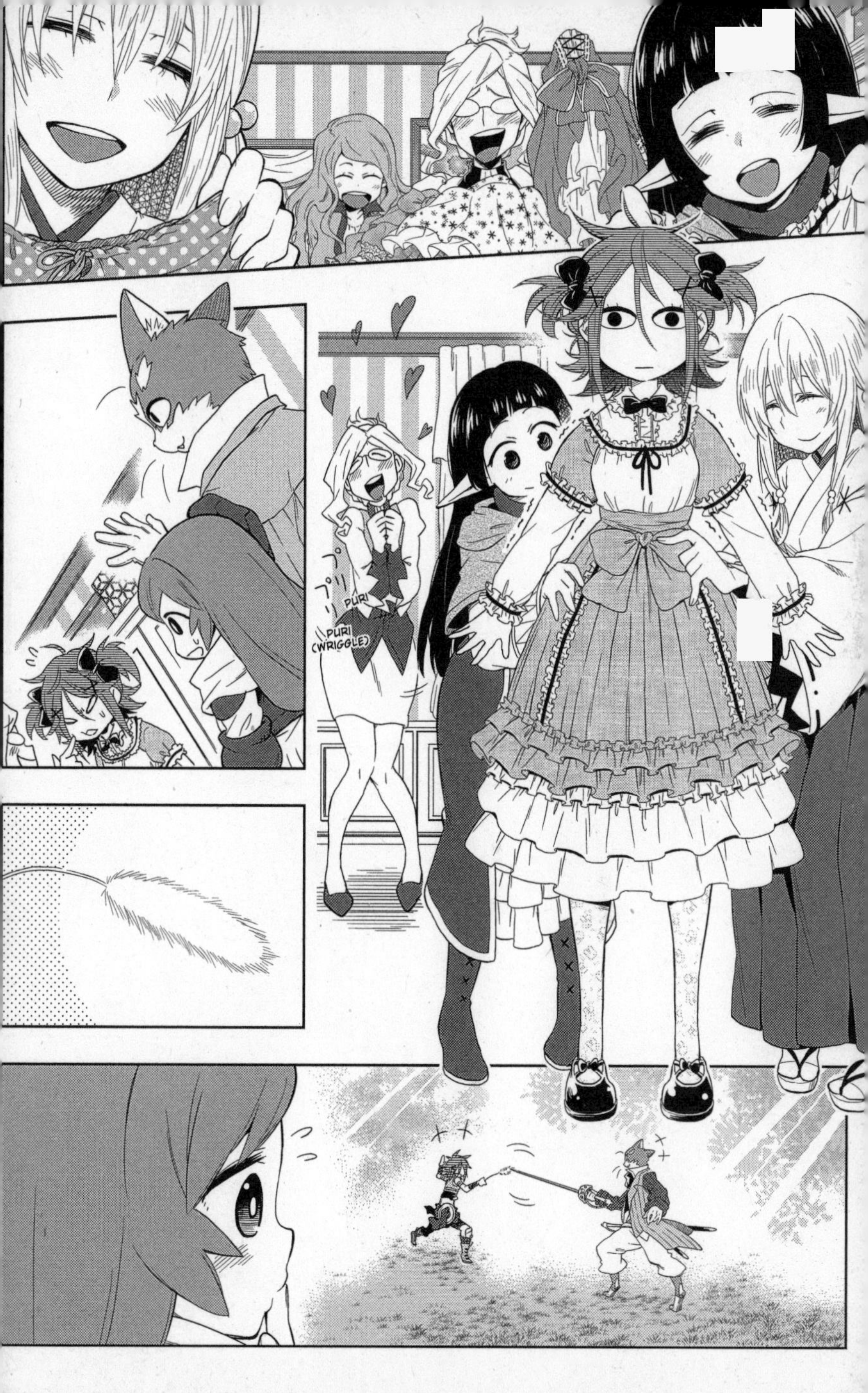
プリ
PURI
プリ
PURI (WRIGGLE)

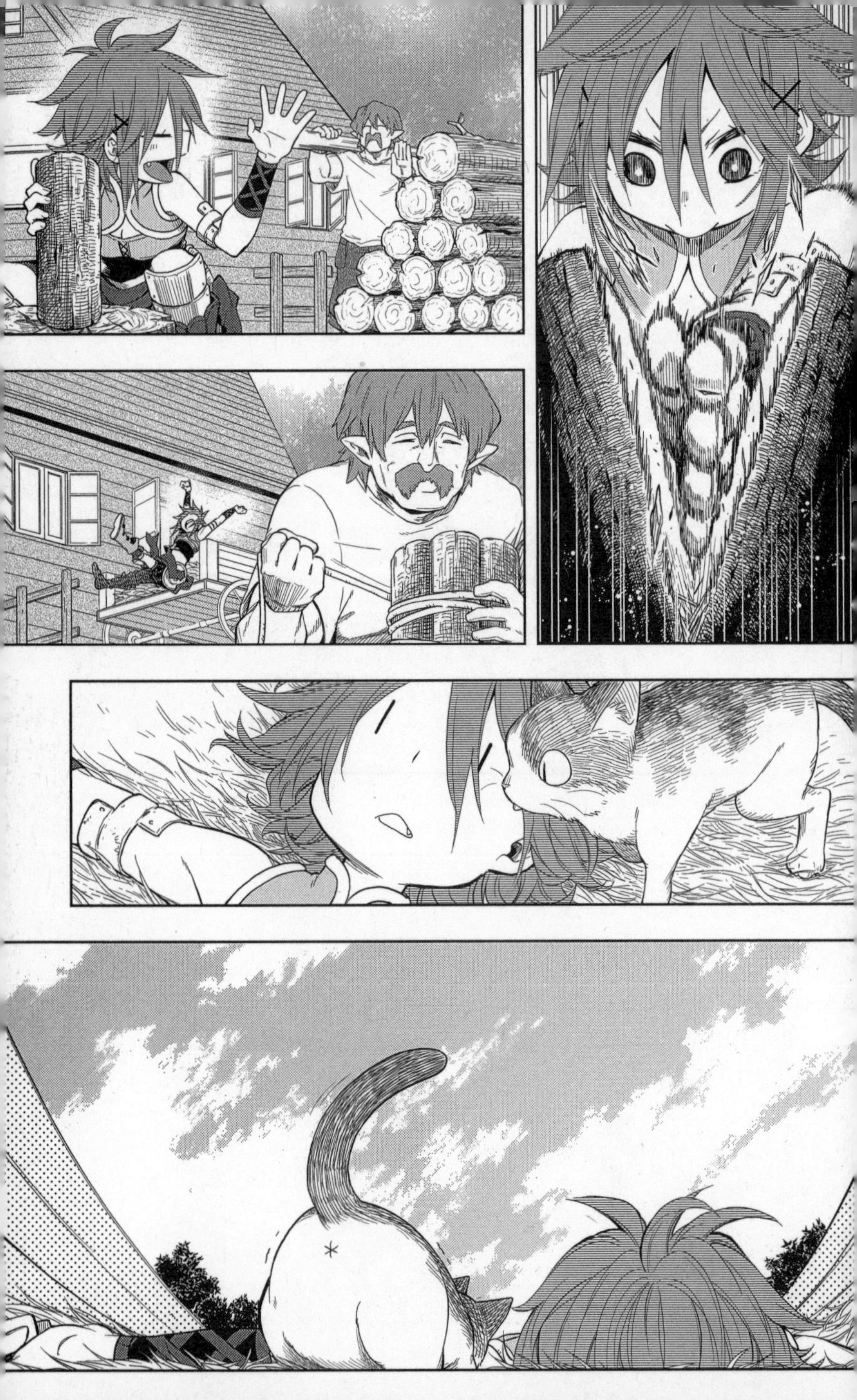

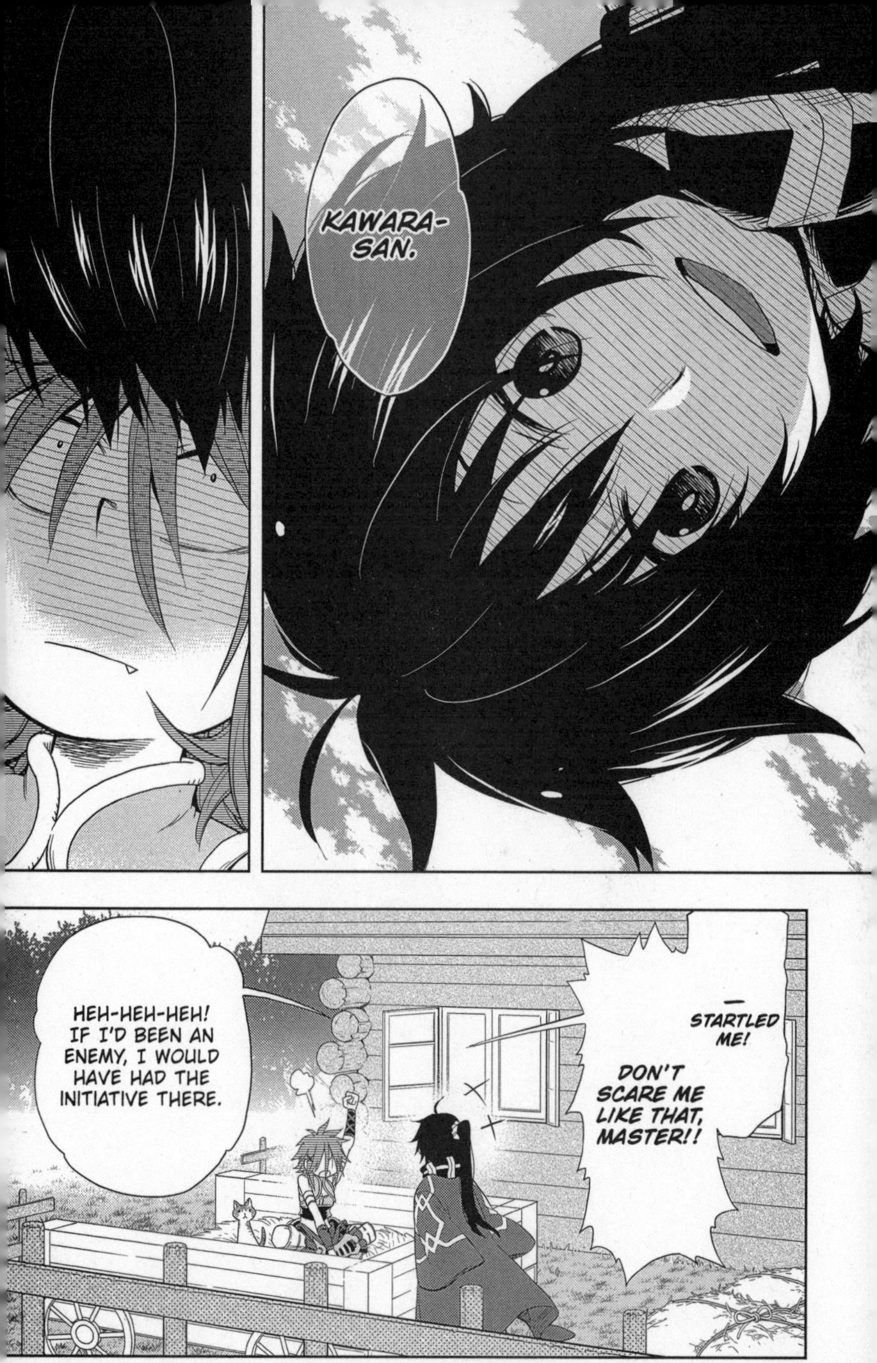
KAWARA-SAN.
—STARTLED ME!
DON'T SCARE ME LIKE THAT, MASTER!!
HEH-HEH-HEH! IF I'D BEEN AN ENEMY, I WOULD HAVE HAD THE INITIATIVE THERE.

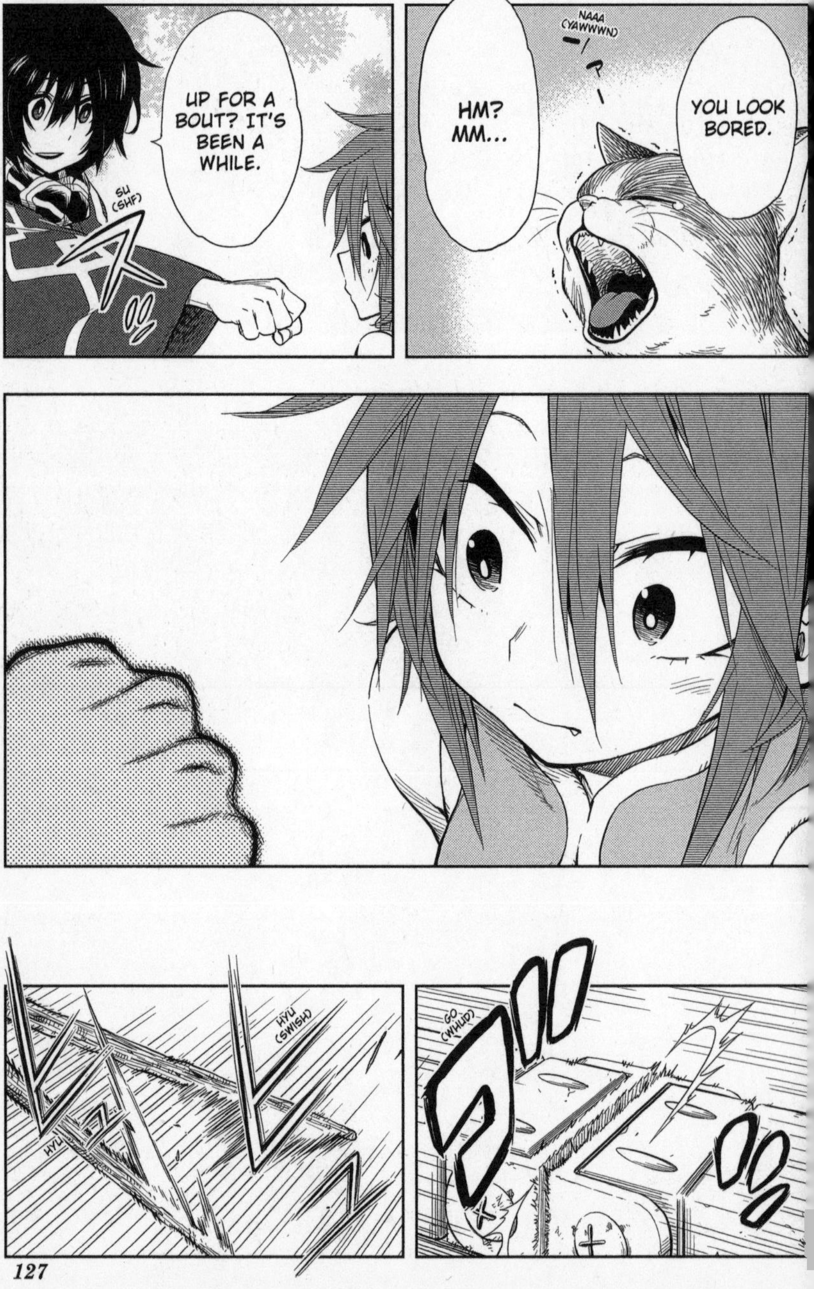
YOU LOOK BORED.
NAAA (YAWWWN)
HM? MM...
UP FOR A BOUT? IT'S BEEN A WHILE.
SU (SHF)
GO (WHUD)
HYU (SWISH)
HYU

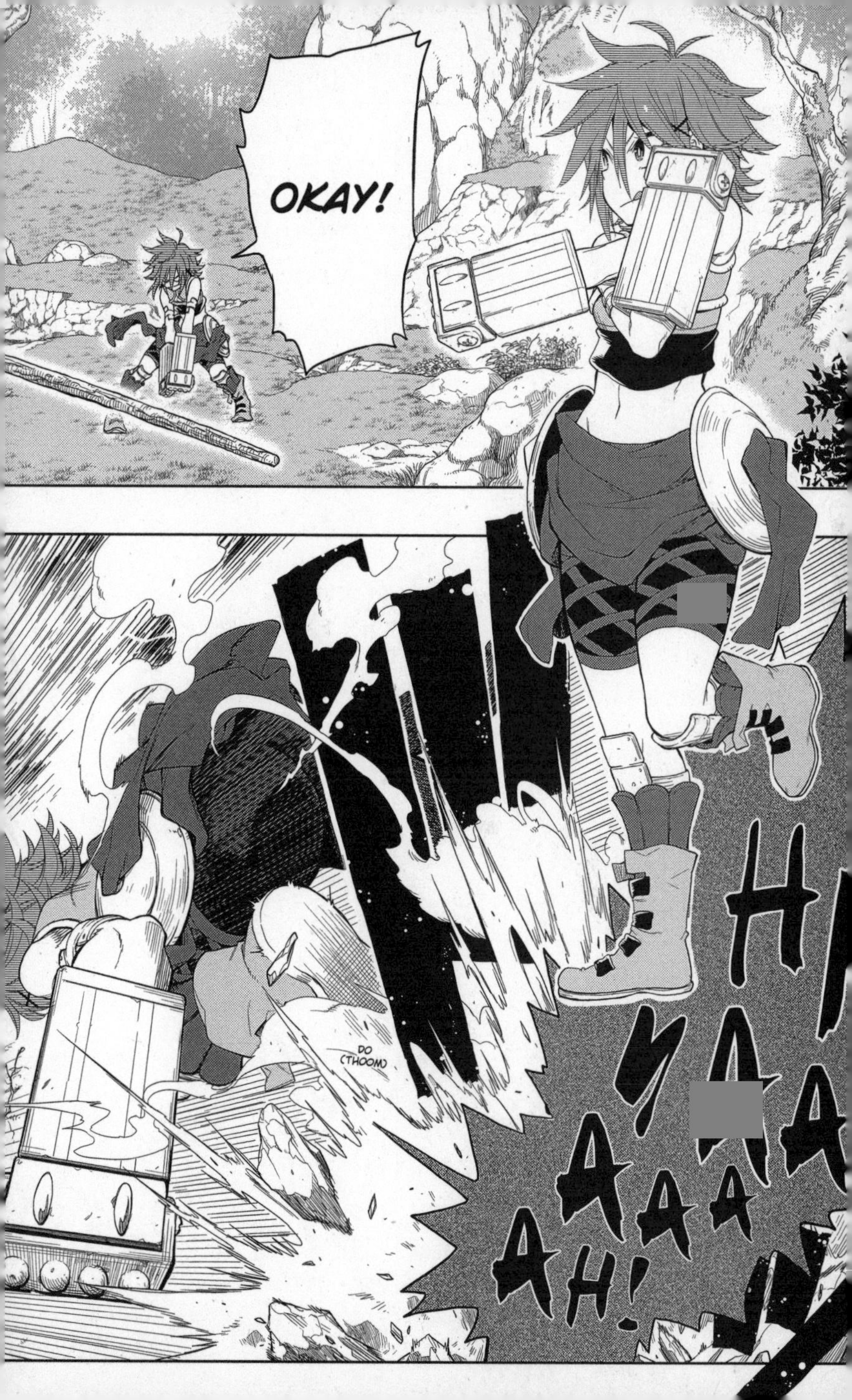
OKAY!
HIYAAAAAAAAAH!
DO
(THOOM)

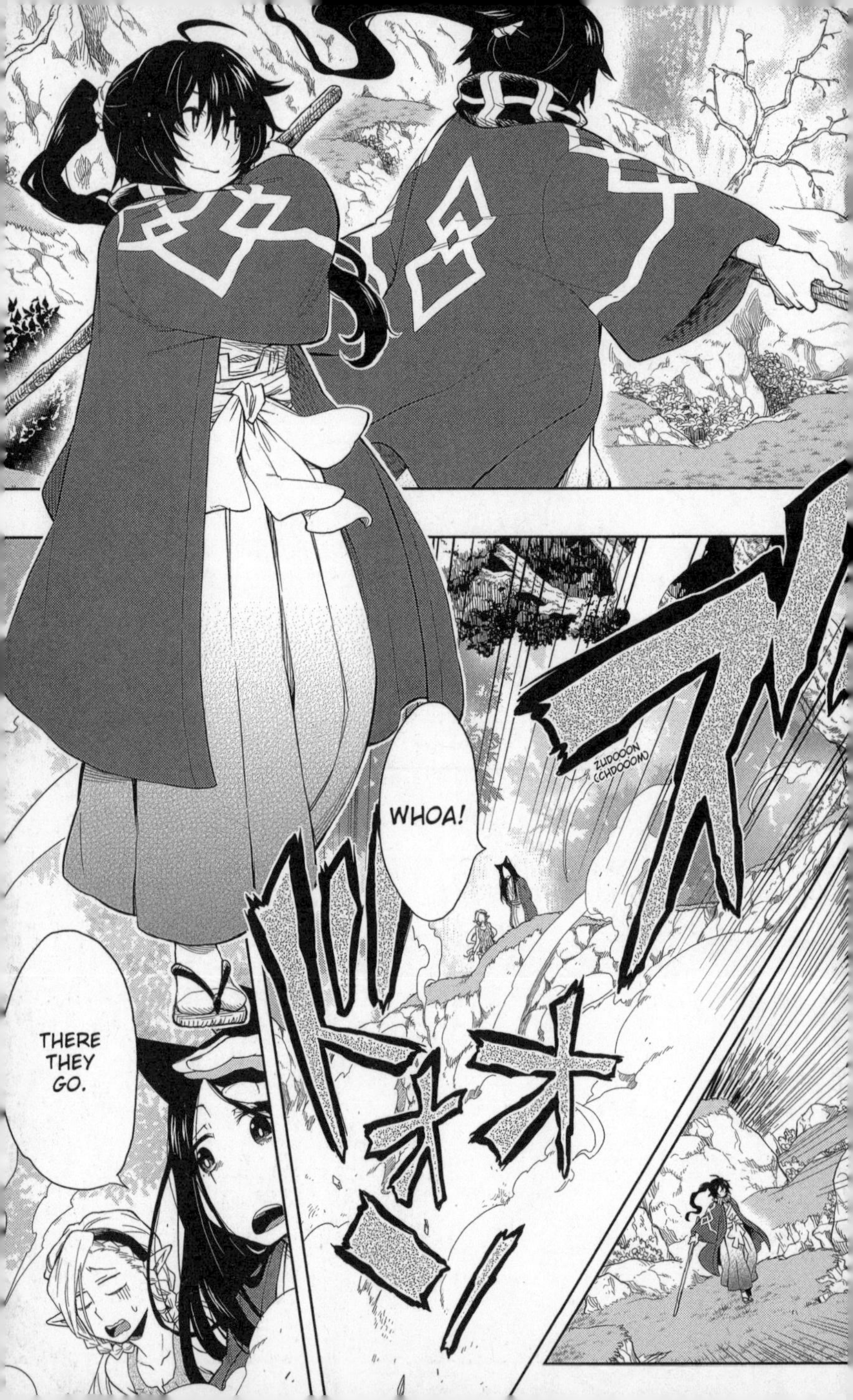

ZUDOOON (CHDOOOM)
WHOA!
THERE THEY GO.

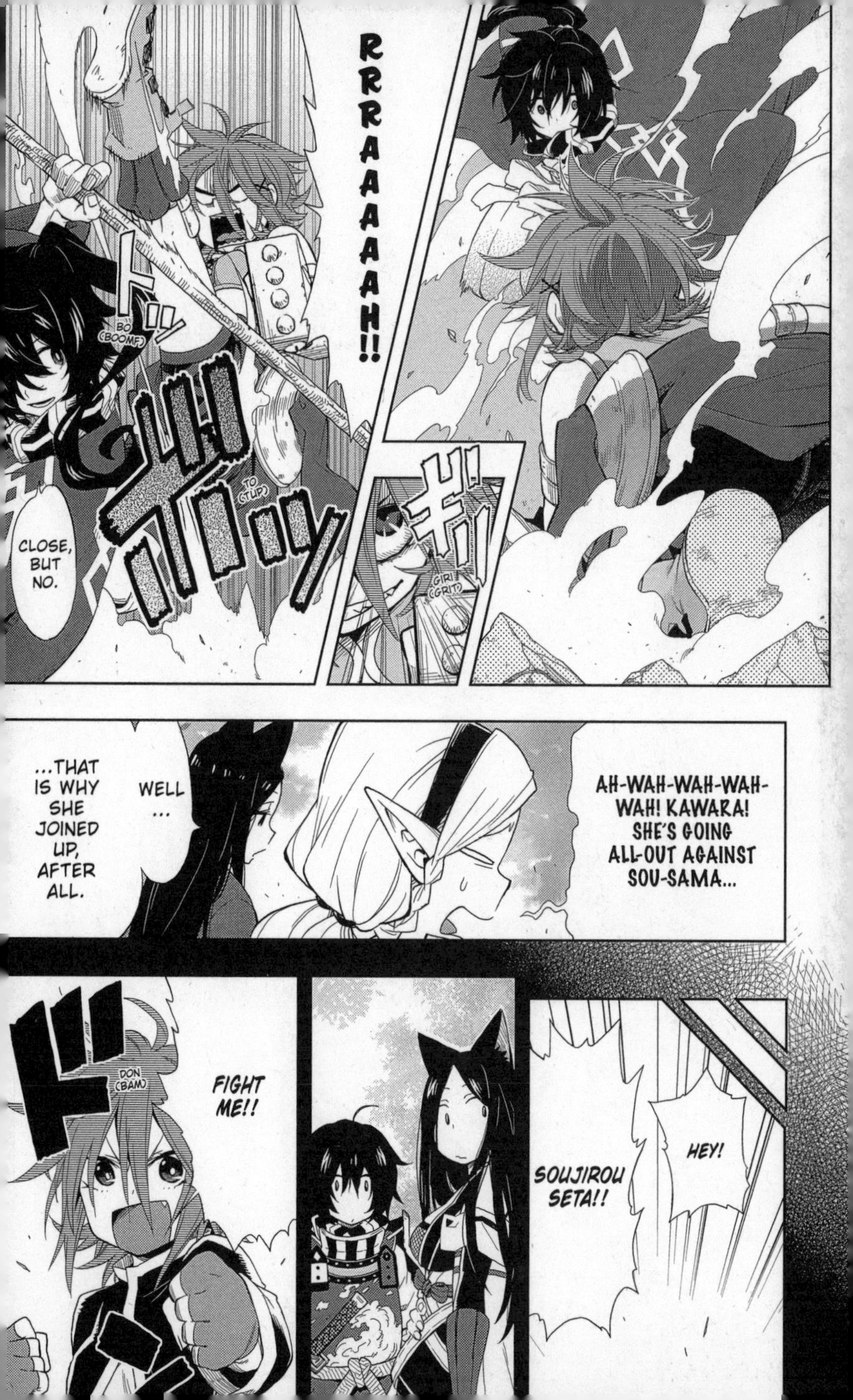
GIRI (GRIT)
RRRAAAAAAAH!!
BO (BOOMF)
TO (TUP)
CLOSE, BUT NO.
AH-WAH-WAH-WAH-WAH! KAWARA! SHE'S GOING ALL-OUT AGAINST SOU-SAMA...
WELL ...
...THAT IS WHY SHE JOINED UP, AFTER ALL.
HEY!
SOUJIROU SETA!!
DON (BAM)
FIGHT ME!!

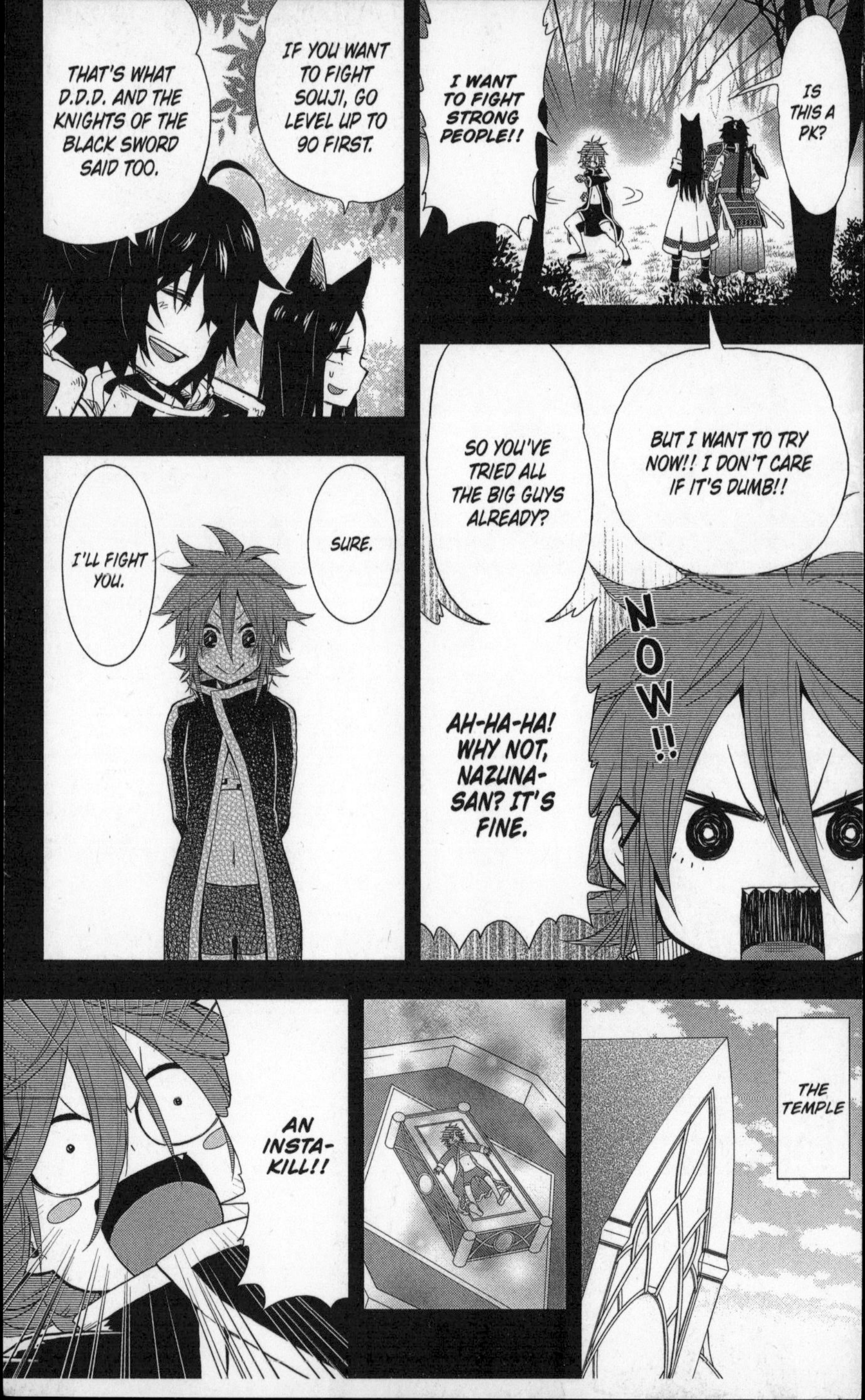
IS THIS A PK?
I WANT TO FIGHT STRONG PEOPLE!!
IF YOU WANT TO FIGHT SOUJI, GO LEVEL UP TO 90 FIRST.
THAT'S WHAT D.D.D. AND THE KNIGHTS OF THE BLACK SWORD SAID TOO.
BUT I WANT TO TRY NOW!! I DON'T CARE IF IT'S DUMB!!
NOW!!
SO YOU'VE TRIED ALL THE BIG GUYS ALREADY?
AH-HA-HA! WHY NOT, NAZUNA-SAN? IT'S FINE.
SURE.
I'LL FIGHT YOU.
THE TEMPLE
AN INSTA-KILL!!

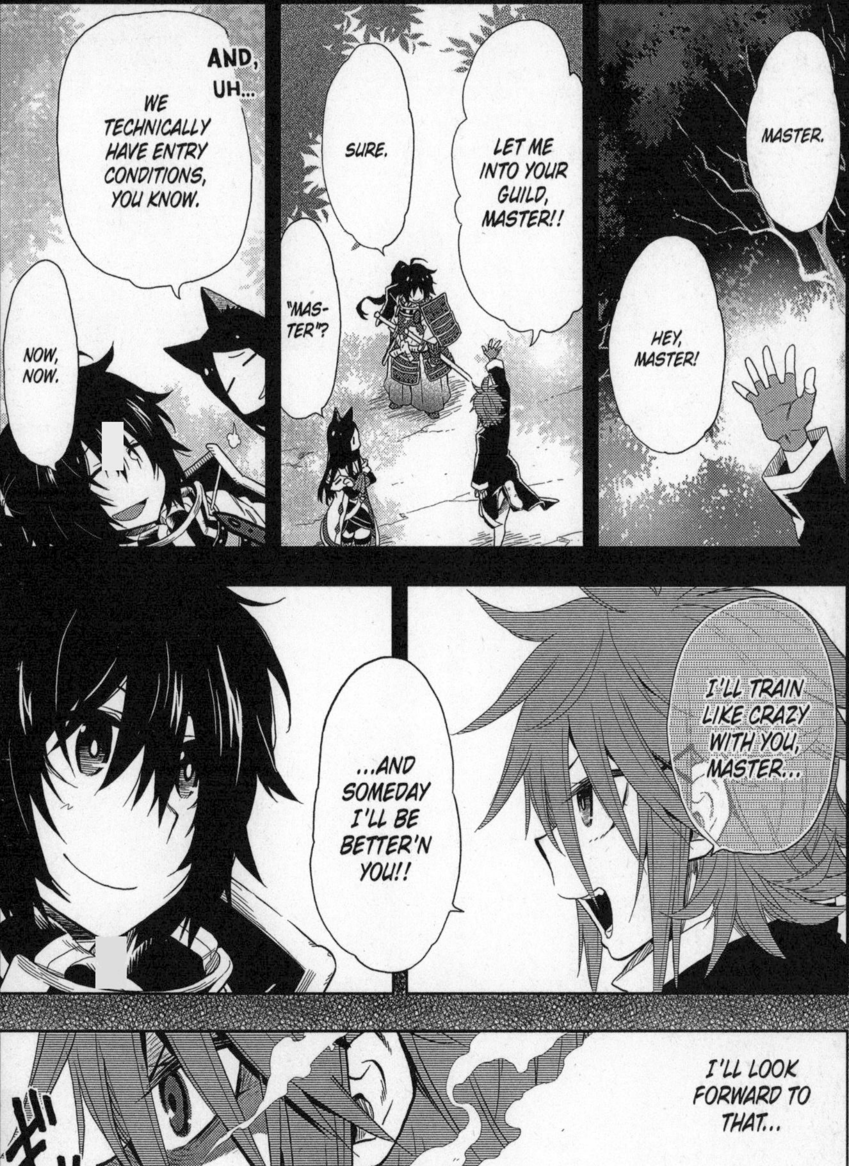
MASTER.
HEY, MASTER!
LET ME INTO YOUR GUILD, MASTER!!
SURE.
"MAS-TER"?
AND, UH...
WE TECHNICALLY HAVE ENTRY CONDITIONS, YOU KNOW.
NOW, NOW.
I'LL TRAIN LIKE CRAZY WITH YOU, MASTER...
...AND SOMEDAY I'LL BE BETTER'N YOU!!
I'LL LOOK FORWARD TO THAT...
ギッ
GI (GLARE)

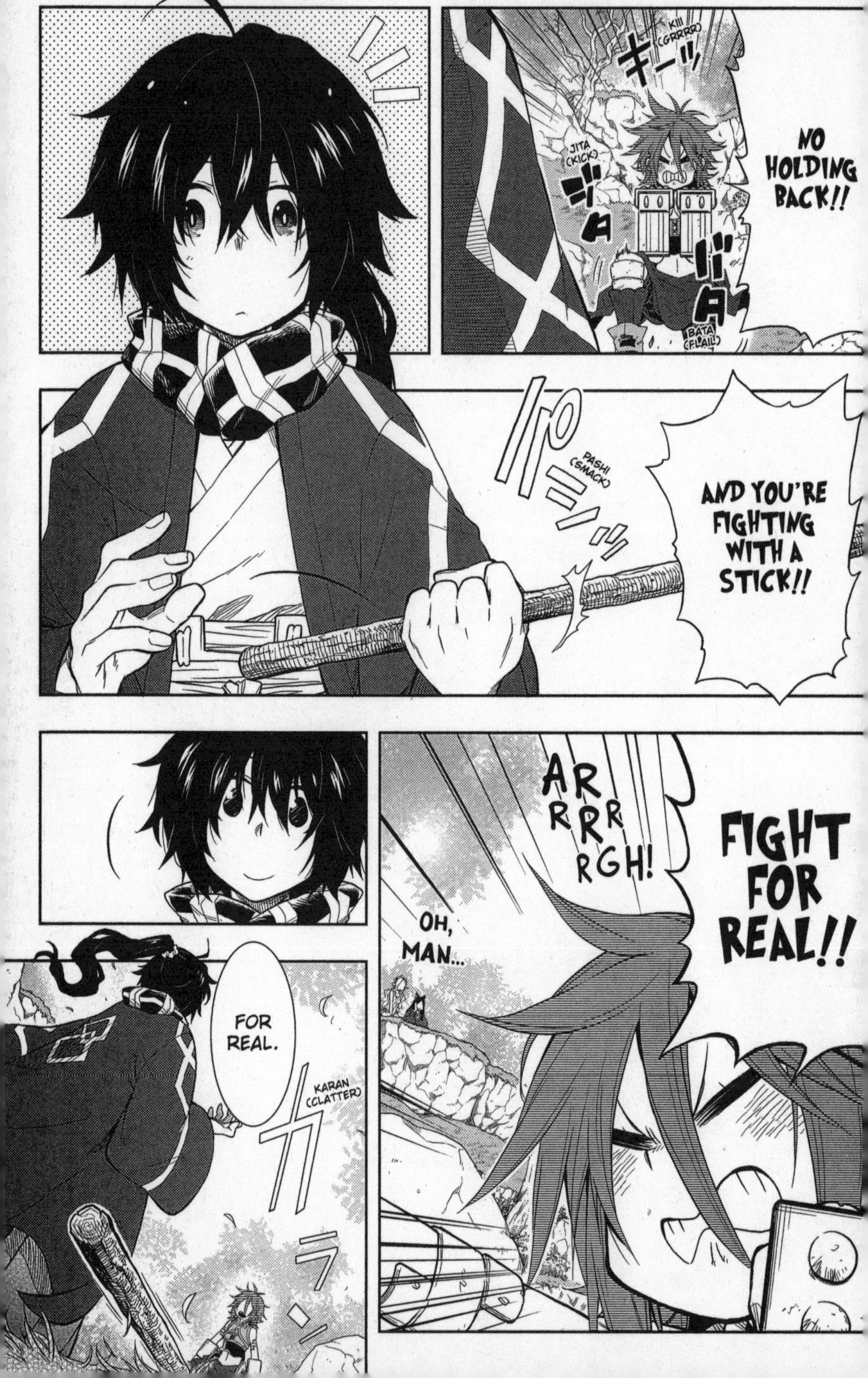
KIII (GRRRR)
NO HOLDING BACK!!
JITA (KICK)
BATA (FLAIL)
PASHI (SMACK)
AND YOU'RE FIGHTING WITH A STICK!!
FIGHT FOR REAL!!
ARRRRRRGH!
OH, MAN...
FOR REAL.
KARAN (CLATTER)

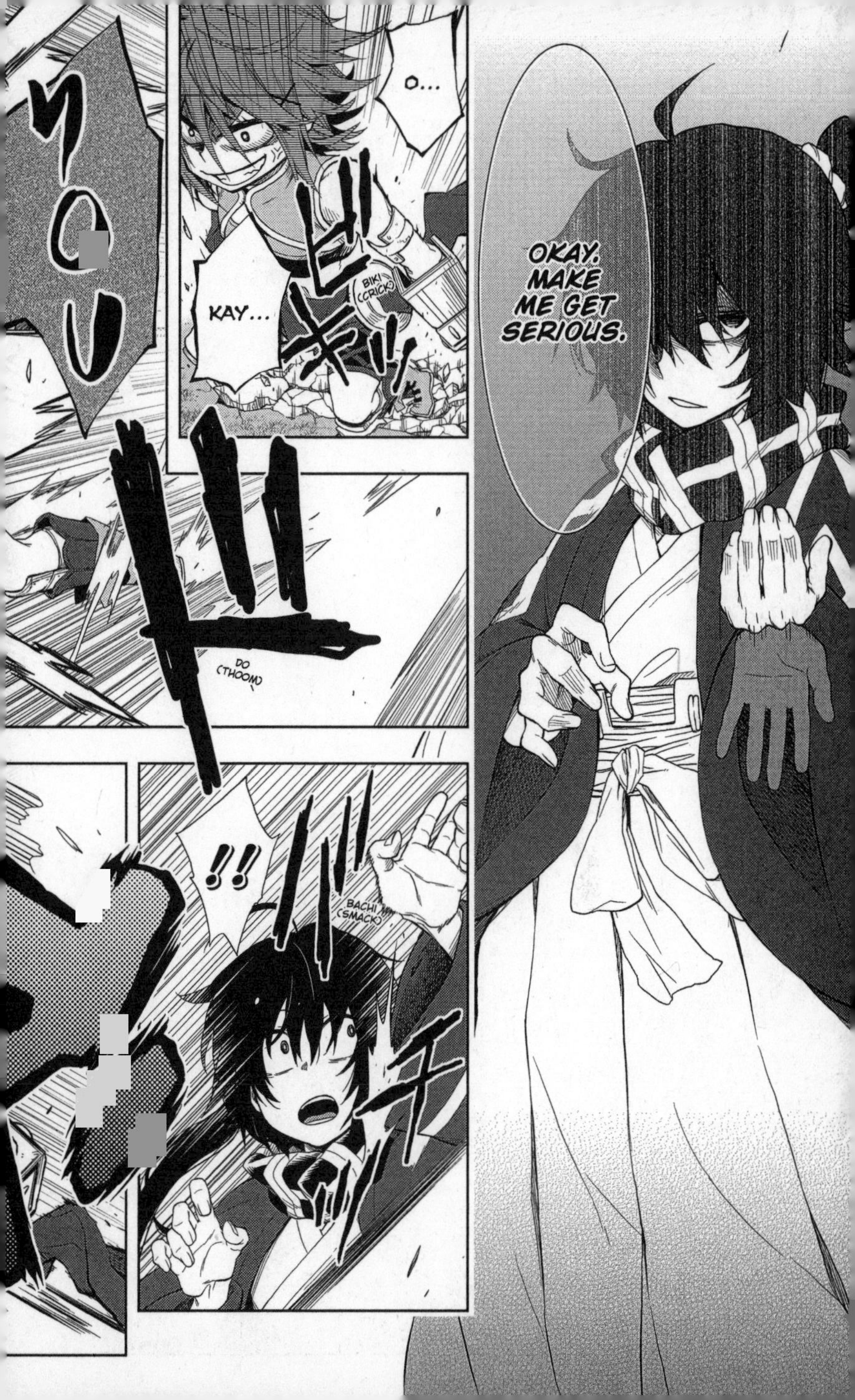
OKAY. MAKE ME GET SERIOUS.
O...
KAY...
BIKI (CRICK)
DO (THOOM)
!!
BACHI (SMACK)

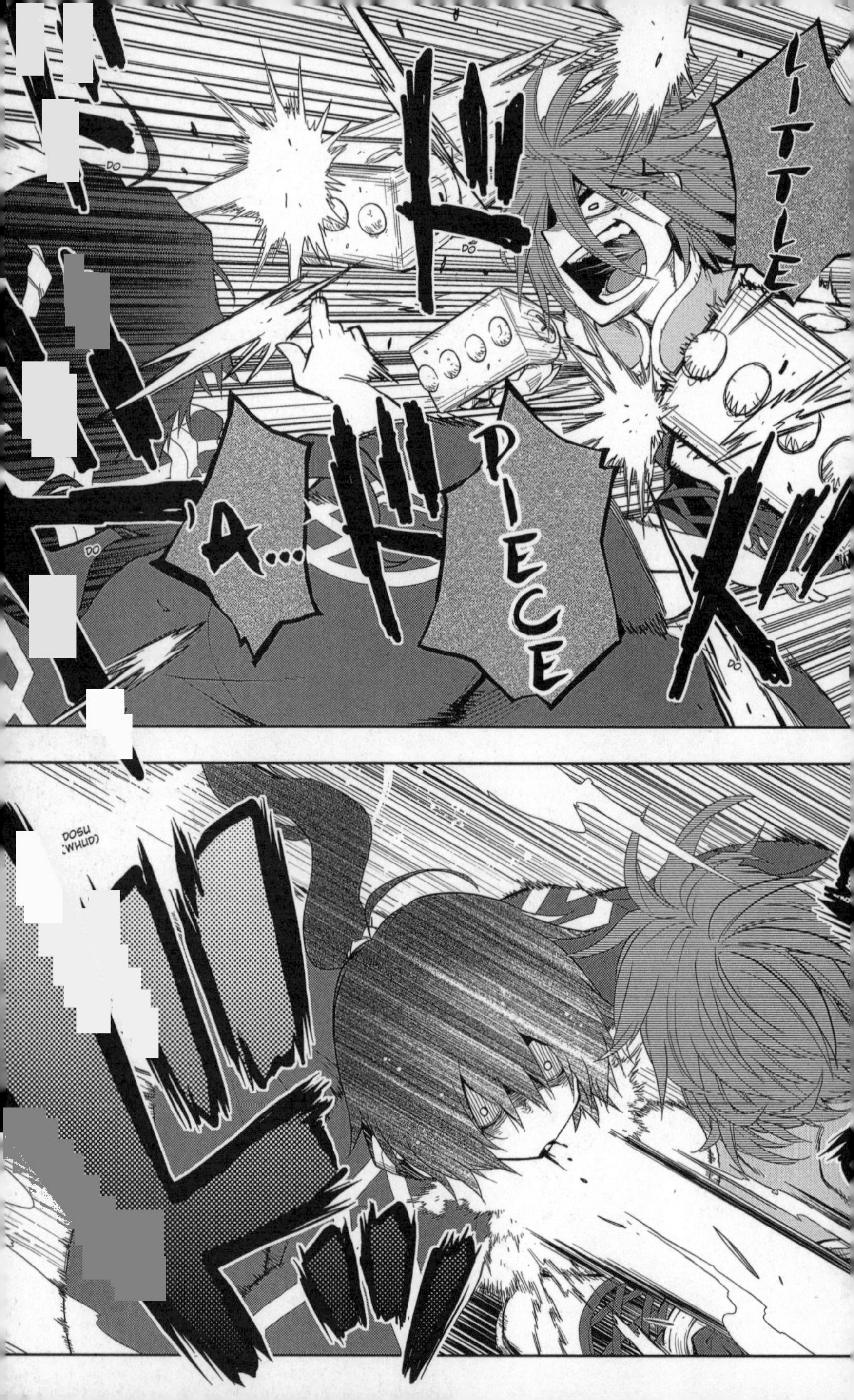
LITTLE
DÔ
DO
PIECE
'A...
DO
DO
DOSU (WHUD)

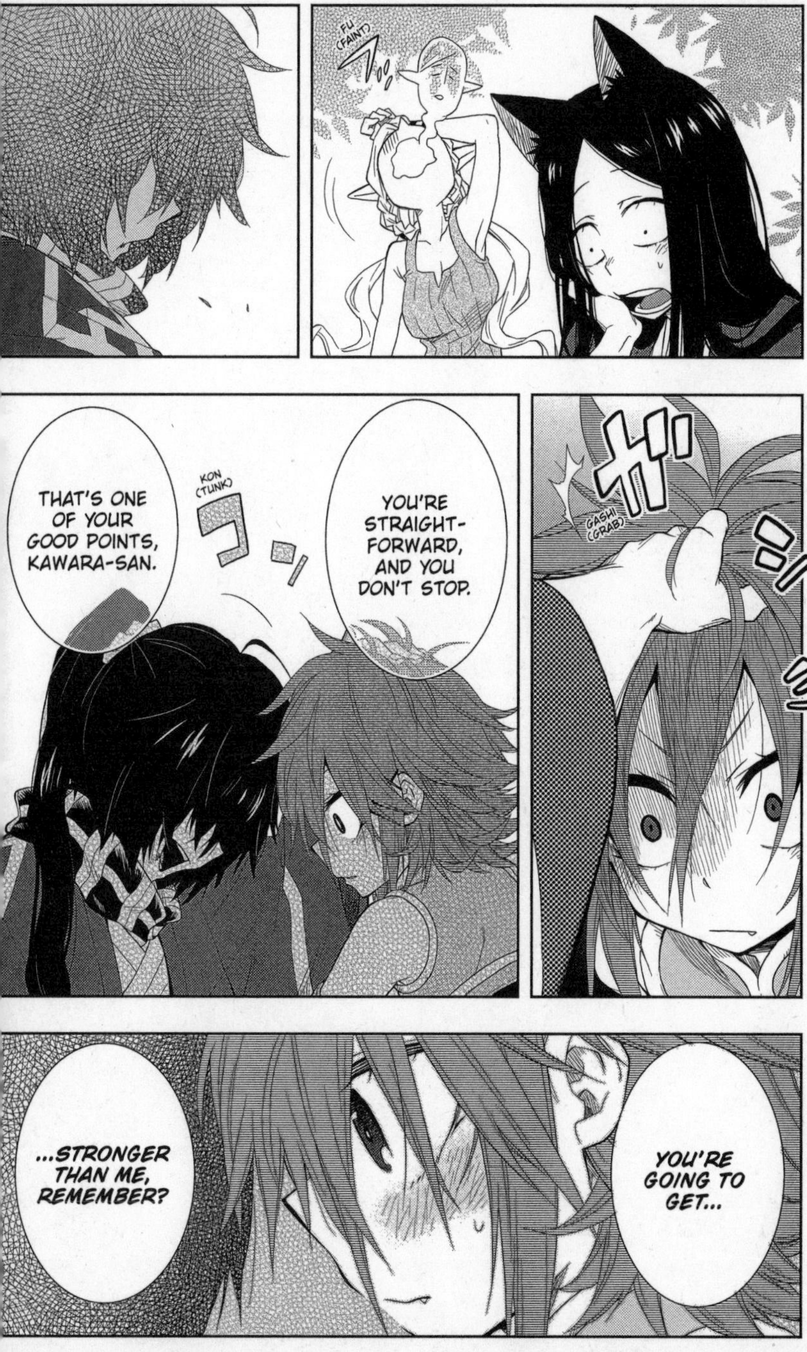
FU (FAINT)
GASHI (GRAB)
YOU'RE STRAIGHT-FORWARD, AND YOU DON'T STOP.
KON (TUNK)
THAT'S ONE OF YOUR GOOD POINTS, KAWARA-SAN.
YOU'RE GOING TO GET...
...STRONGER THAN ME, REMEMBER?

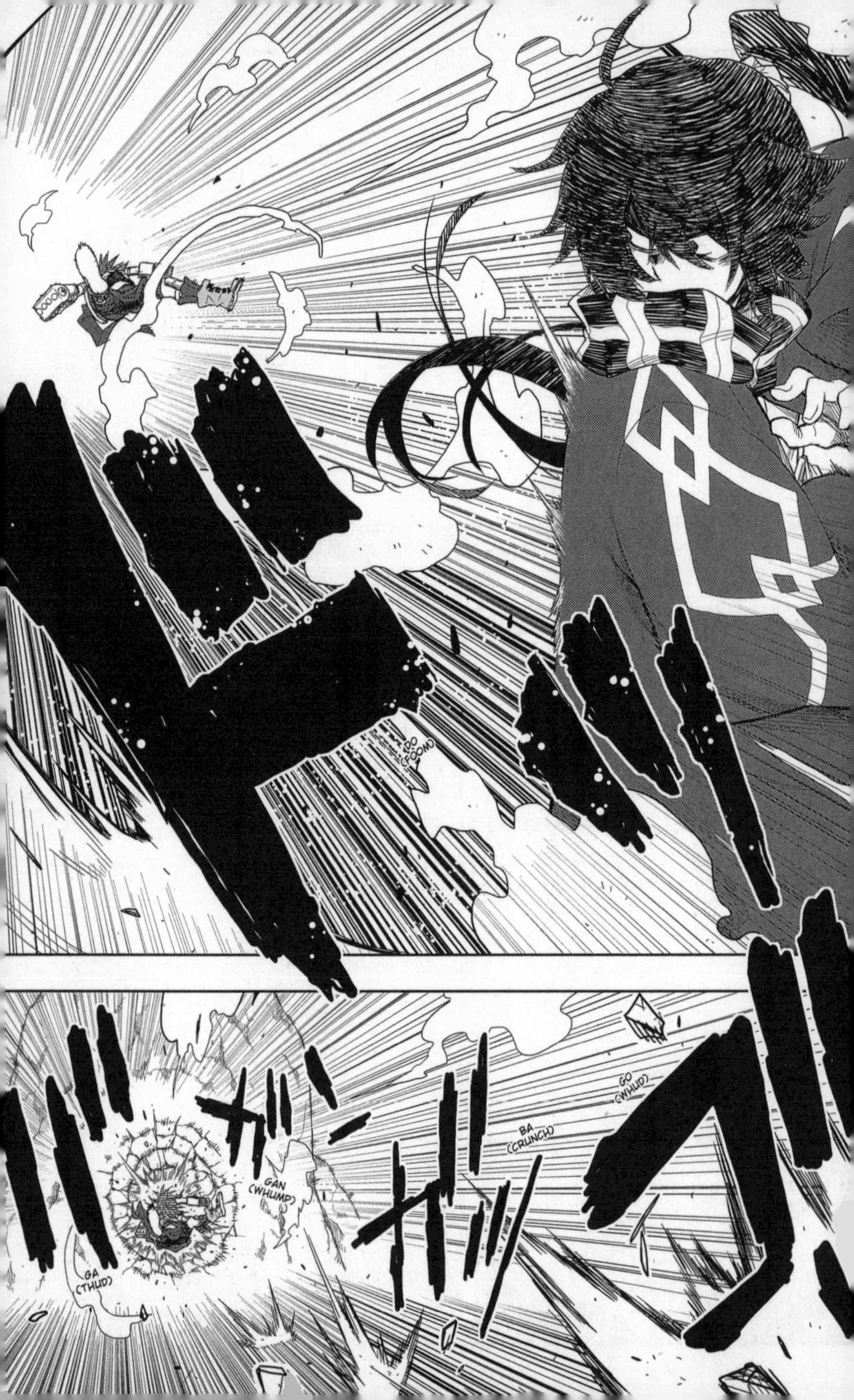
DO (FOOM)
GO (WHUD)
BA (CRUNCH)
GAN (WHUMP)
GA (THUD)

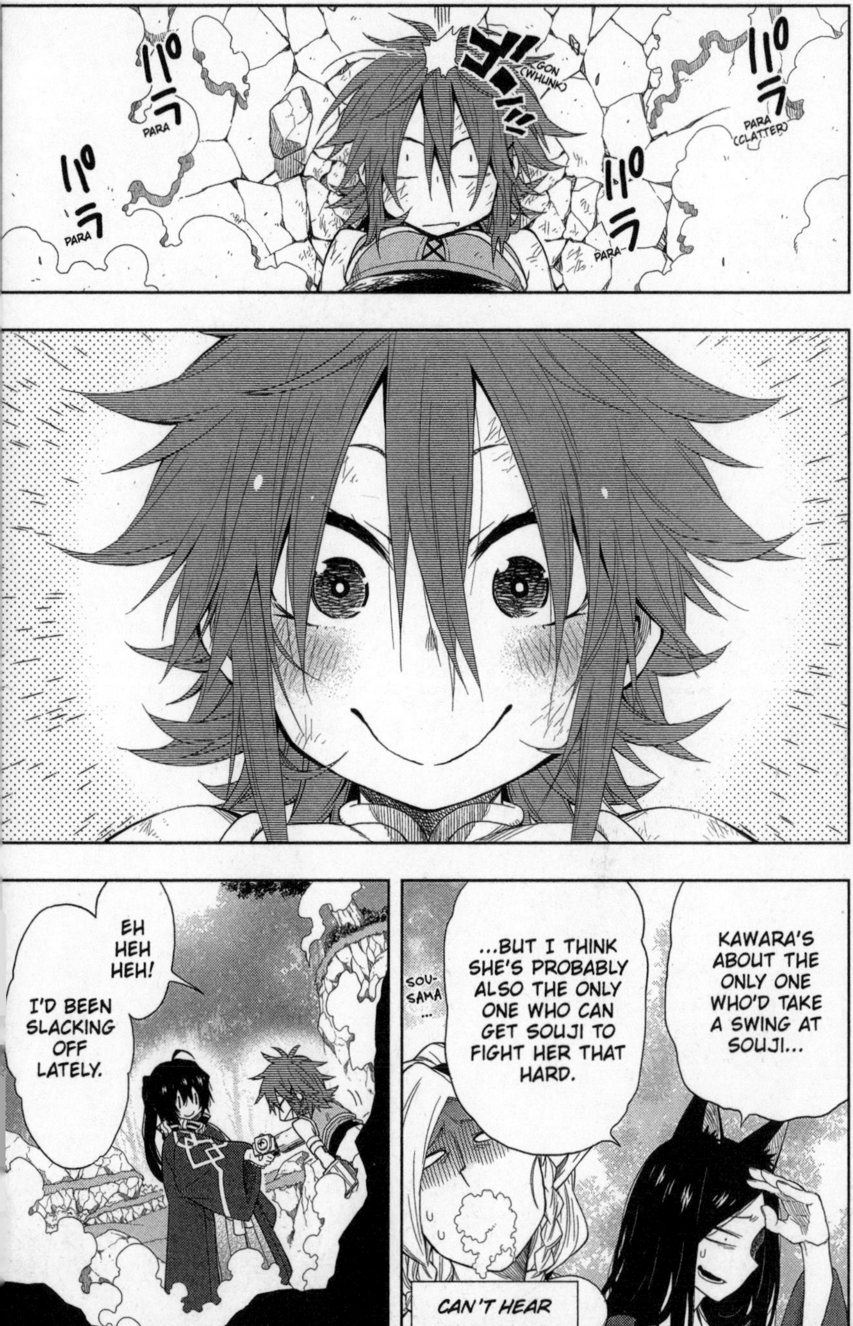
パラ
PARA (CLATTER)
ゴン
GON (WHUNK)
パラ
PARA-
パラ
PARA
パラ
PARA
KAWARA'S ABOUT THE ONLY ONE WHO'D TAKE A SWING AT SOUJI...
...BUT I THINK SHE'S PROBABLY ALSO THE ONLY ONE WHO CAN GET SOUJI TO FIGHT HER THAT HARD.
SOU-SAMA...
CAN'T HEAR
EH HEH HEH!
I'D BEEN SLACKING OFF LATELY.

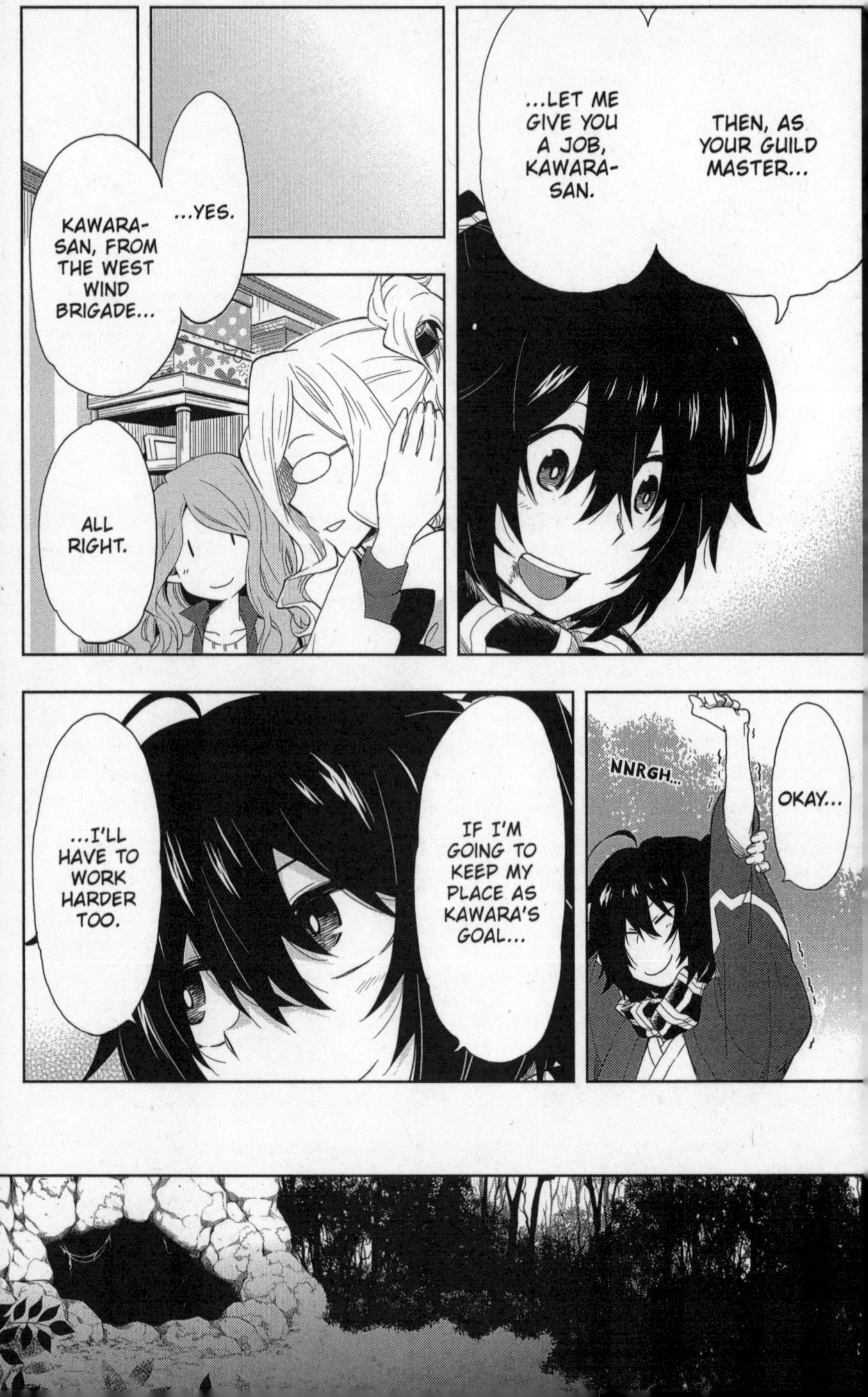
THEN, AS YOUR GUILD MASTER...
...LET ME GIVE YOU A JOB, KAWARA-SAN.
...YES.
KAWARA-SAN, FROM THE WEST WIND BRIGADE...
ALL RIGHT.
OKAY...
NNRGH...
IF I'M GOING TO KEEP MY PLACE AS KAWARA'S GOAL...
...I'LL HAVE TO WORK HARDER TOO.

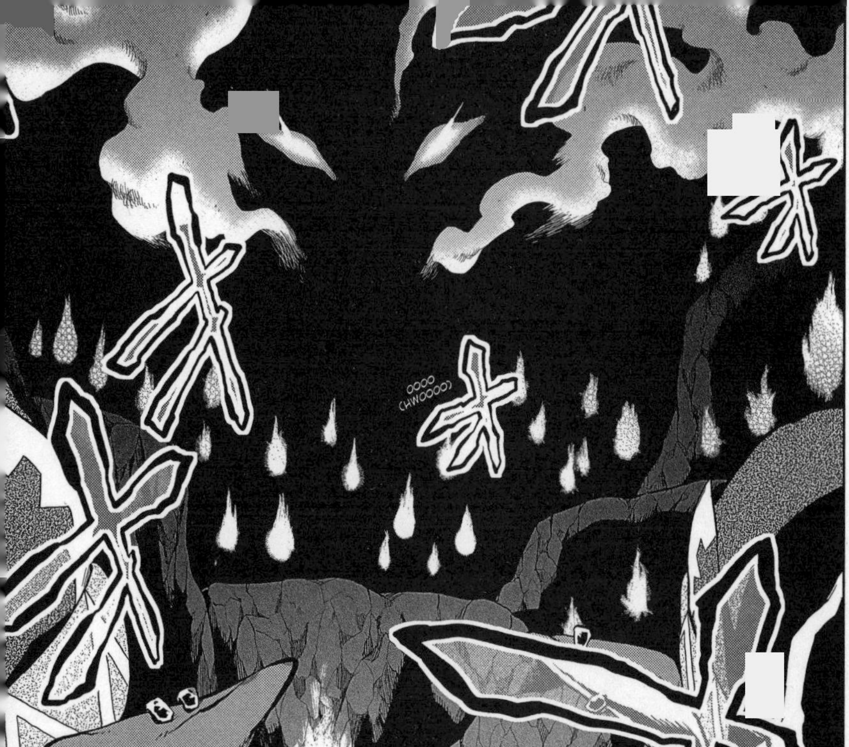
OOOO
(HWOOOOO)
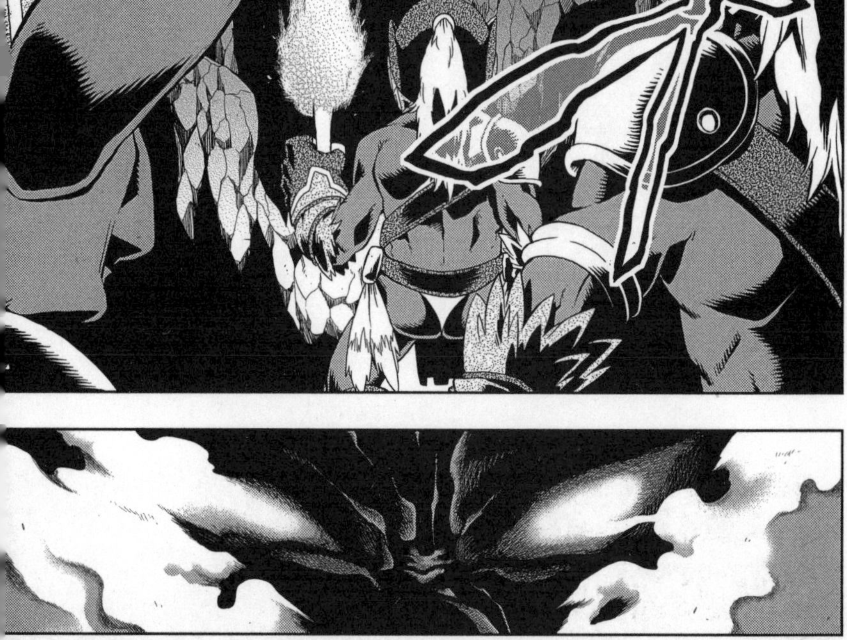

LOG HORIZON

THE WEST WIND BRIGADE

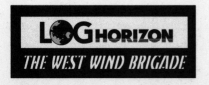

LOG HORIZON
THE WEST WIND BRIGADE

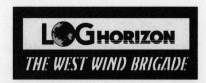

CHAPTER: 29 Departure

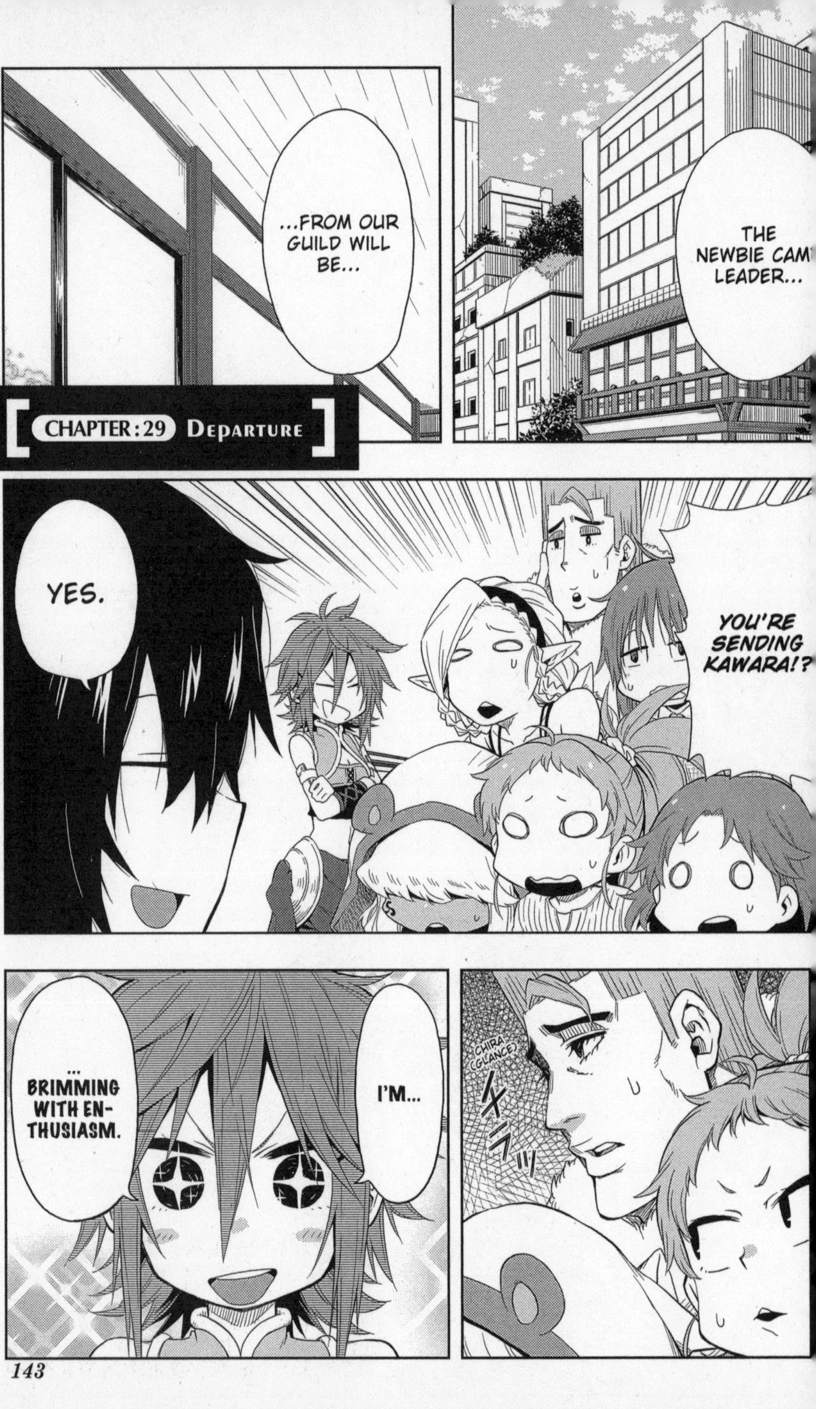

THE NEWBIE CAM LEADER...
...FROM OUR GUILD WILL BE...
YOU'RE SENDING KAWARA!?
YES.
CHIRA (GLANCE)
I'M...
... BRIMMING WITH EN-THUSIASM.

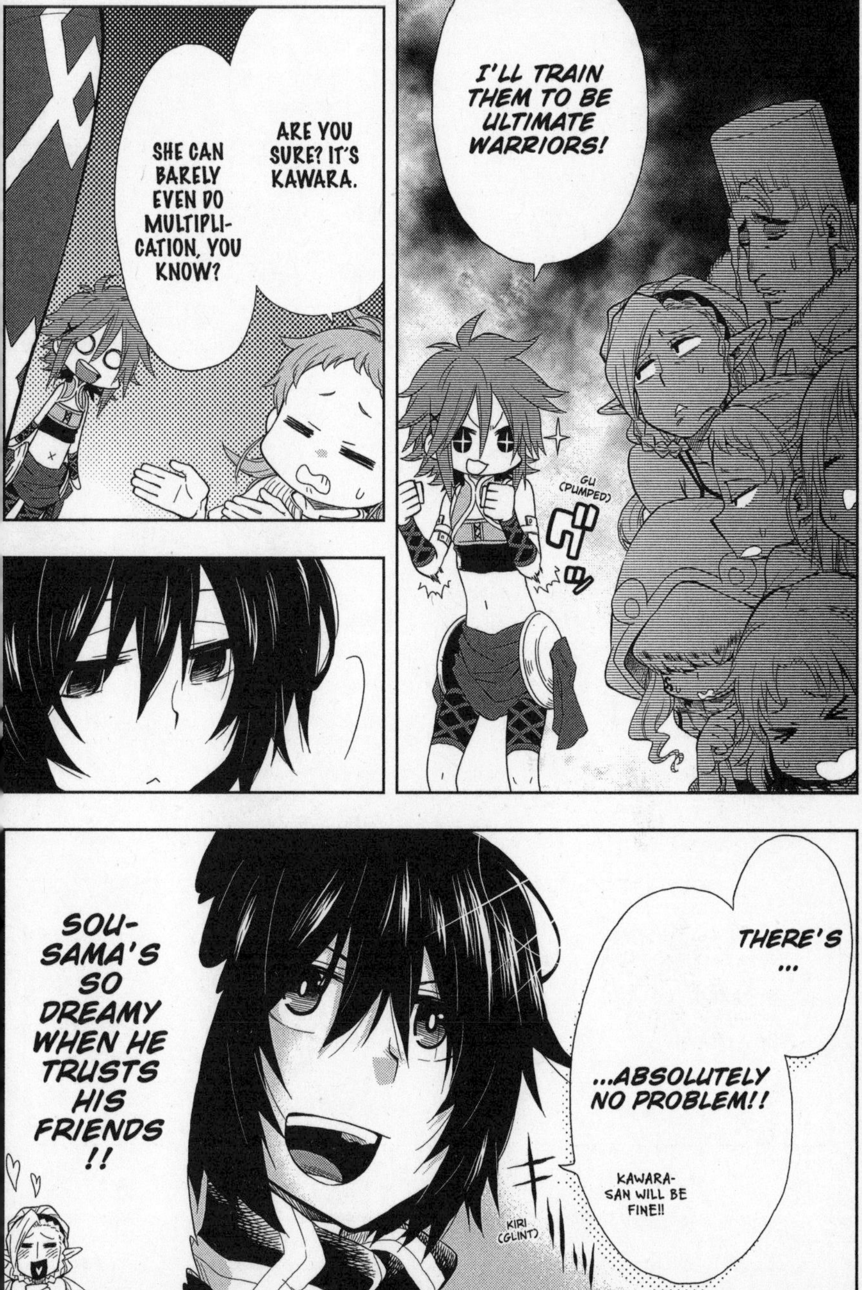
I'LL TRAIN THEM TO BE ULTIMATE WARRIORS!
GU (PUMPED)
ARE YOU SURE? IT'S KAWARA.
SHE CAN BARELY EVEN DO MULTIPLI-CATION, YOU KNOW?
THERE'S ...
...ABSOLUTELY NO PROBLEM!!
KAWARA-SAN WILL BE FINE!!
KIRI (GLINT)
SOU-SAMA'S SO DREAMY WHEN HE TRUSTS HIS FRIENDS !!

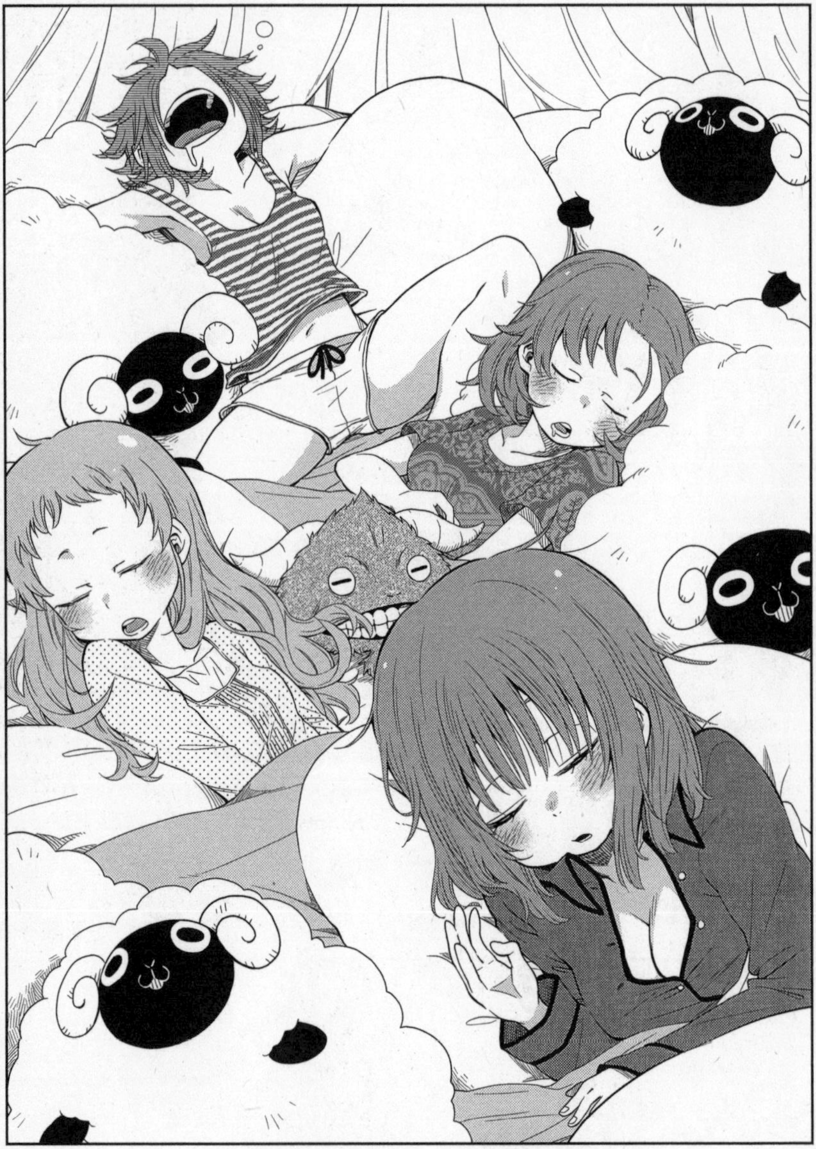

CHAPTER : 29 Departure

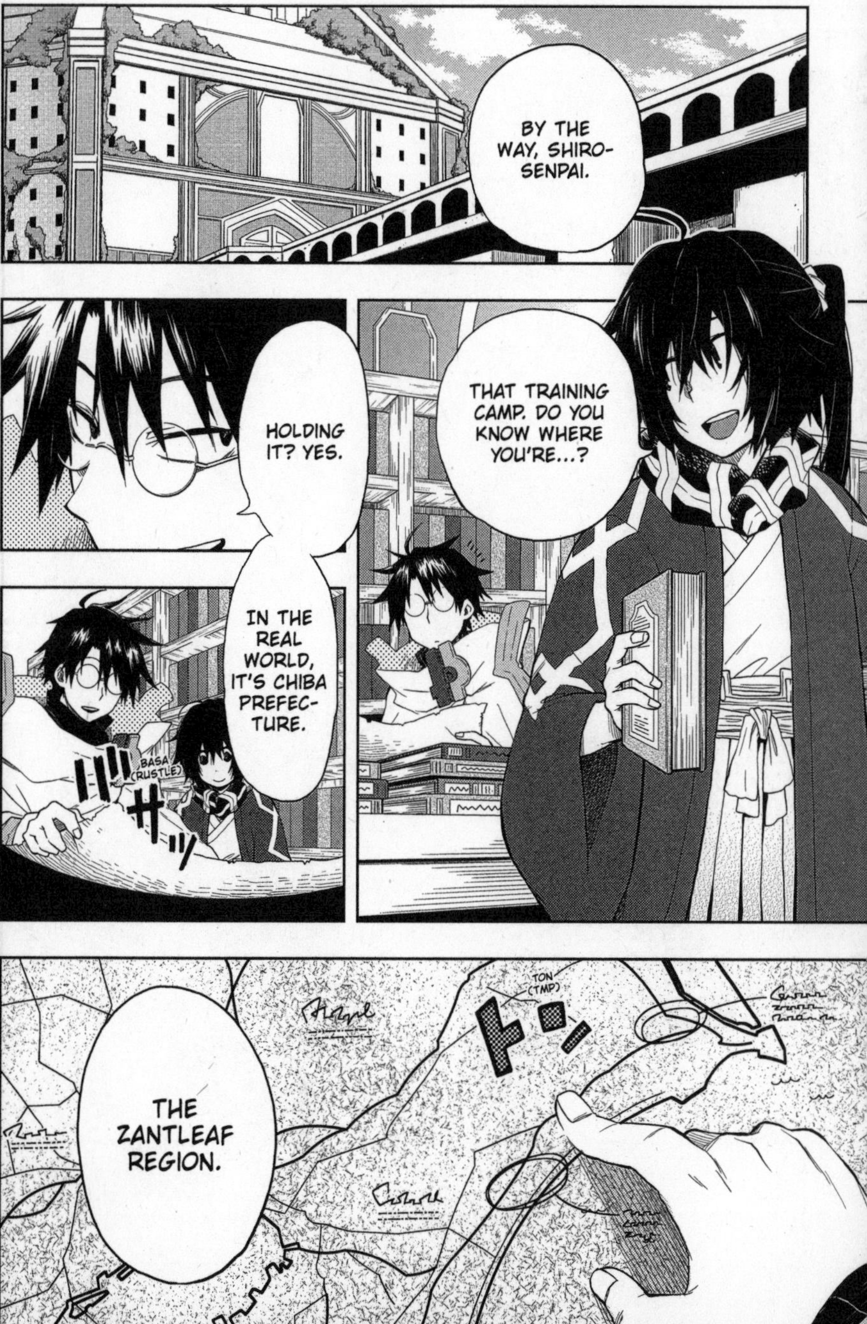
BY THE WAY, SHIRO-SENPAI.
THAT TRAINING CAMP. DO YOU KNOW WHERE YOU'RE...?
HOLDING IT? YES.
IN THE REAL WORLD, IT'S CHIBA PREFECTURE.
BASA (RUSTLE)
TON (TMP)
THE ZANTLEAF REGION.

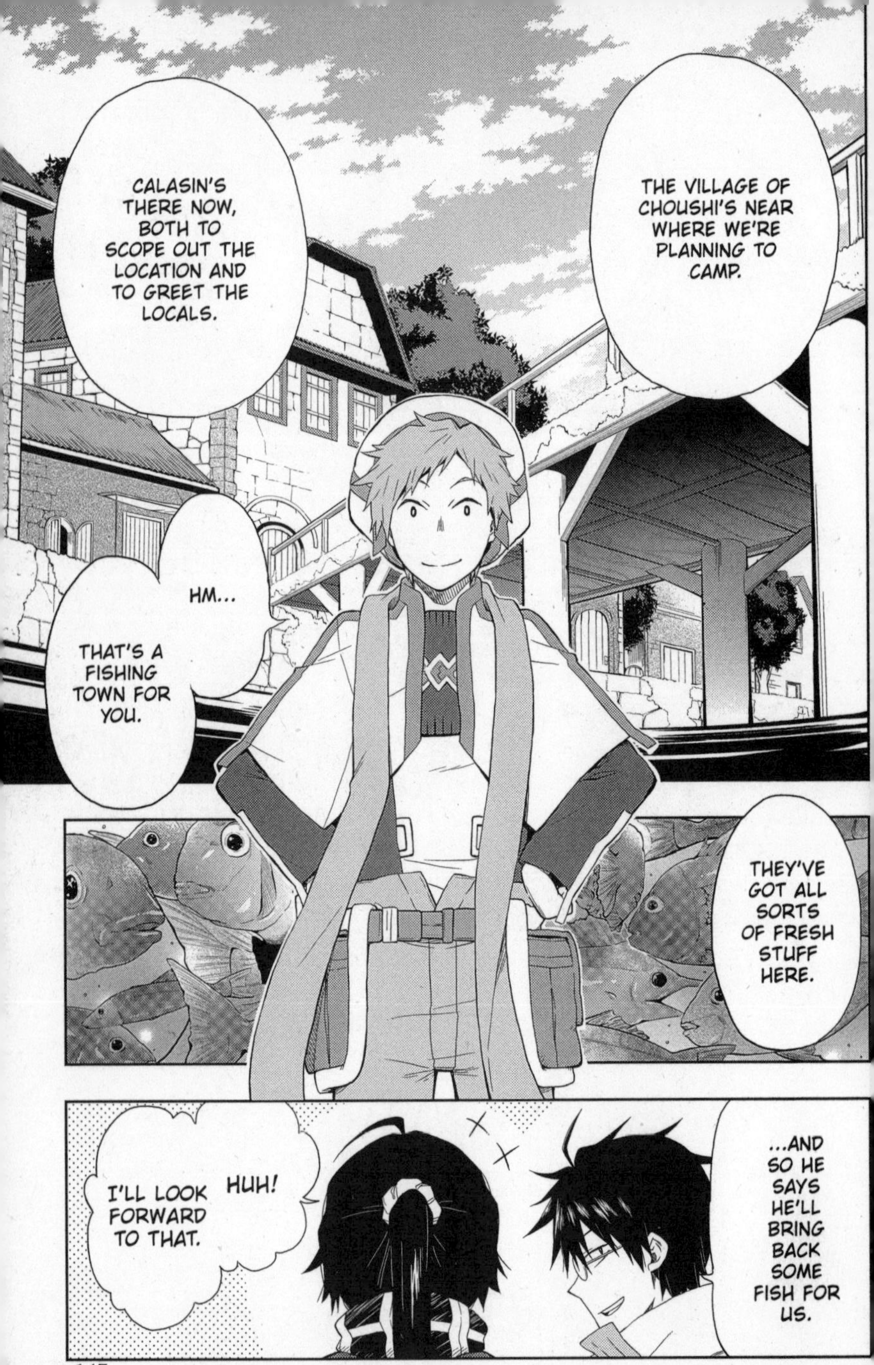
THE VILLAGE OF CHOUSHI'S NEAR WHERE WE'RE PLANNING TO CAMP.
CALASIN'S THERE NOW, BOTH TO SCOPE OUT THE LOCATION AND TO GREET THE LOCALS.
HM...
THAT'S A FISHING TOWN FOR YOU.
THEY'VE GOT ALL SORTS OF FRESH STUFF HERE.
...AND SO HE SAYS HE'LL BRING BACK SOME FISH FOR US.
HUH!
I'LL LOOK FORWARD TO THAT.

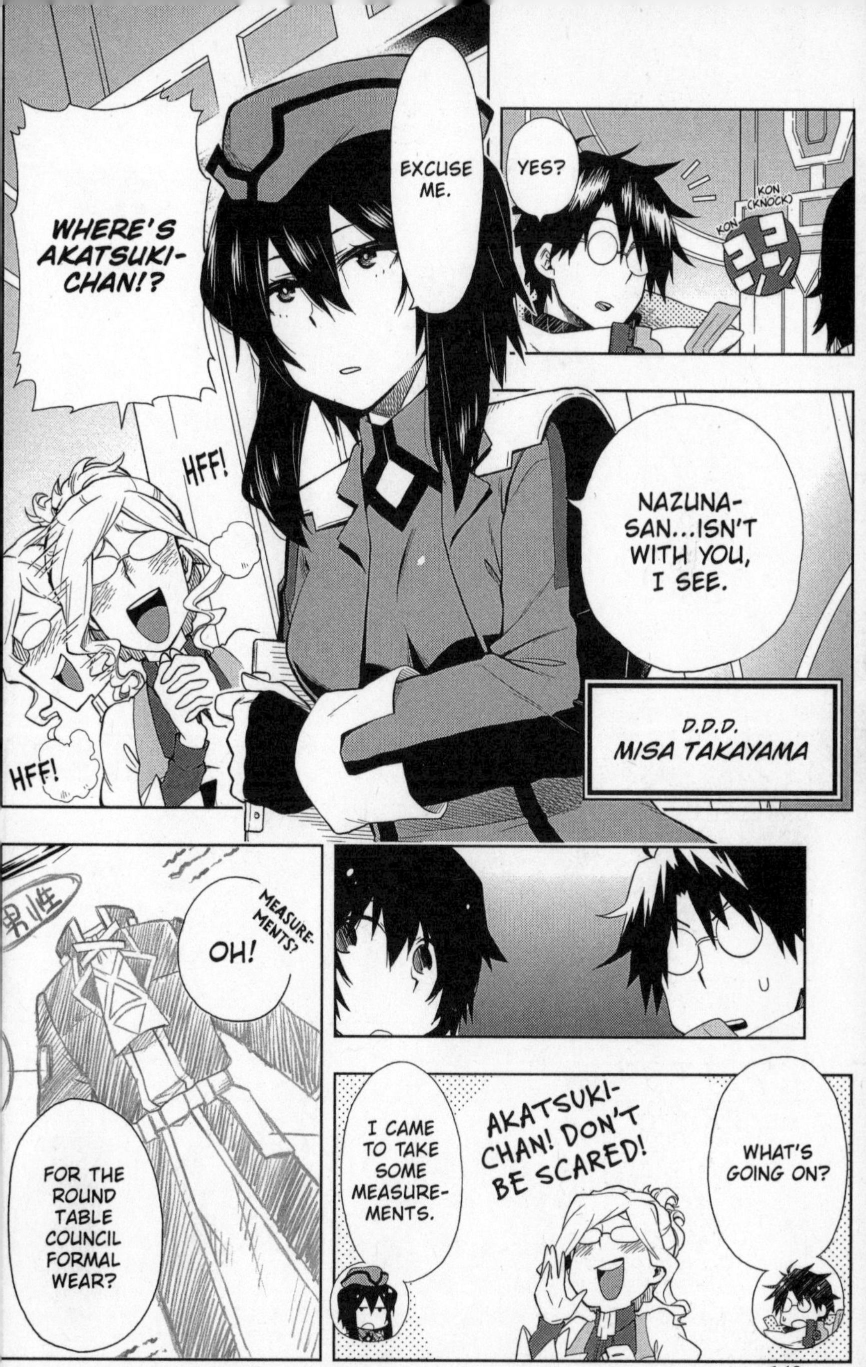
KON KON (KNOCK)
YES?
EXCUSE ME.
NAZUNA-SAN...ISN'T WITH YOU, I SEE.
D.D.D.
MISA TAKAYAMA
WHERE'S AKATSUKI-CHAN!?
HFF!
HFF!
WHAT'S GOING ON?
AKATSUKI-CHAN! DON'T BE SCARED!
I CAME TO TAKE SOME MEASUREMENTS.
MEASUREMENTS?
OH!
FOR THE ROUND TABLE COUNCIL FORMAL WEAR?

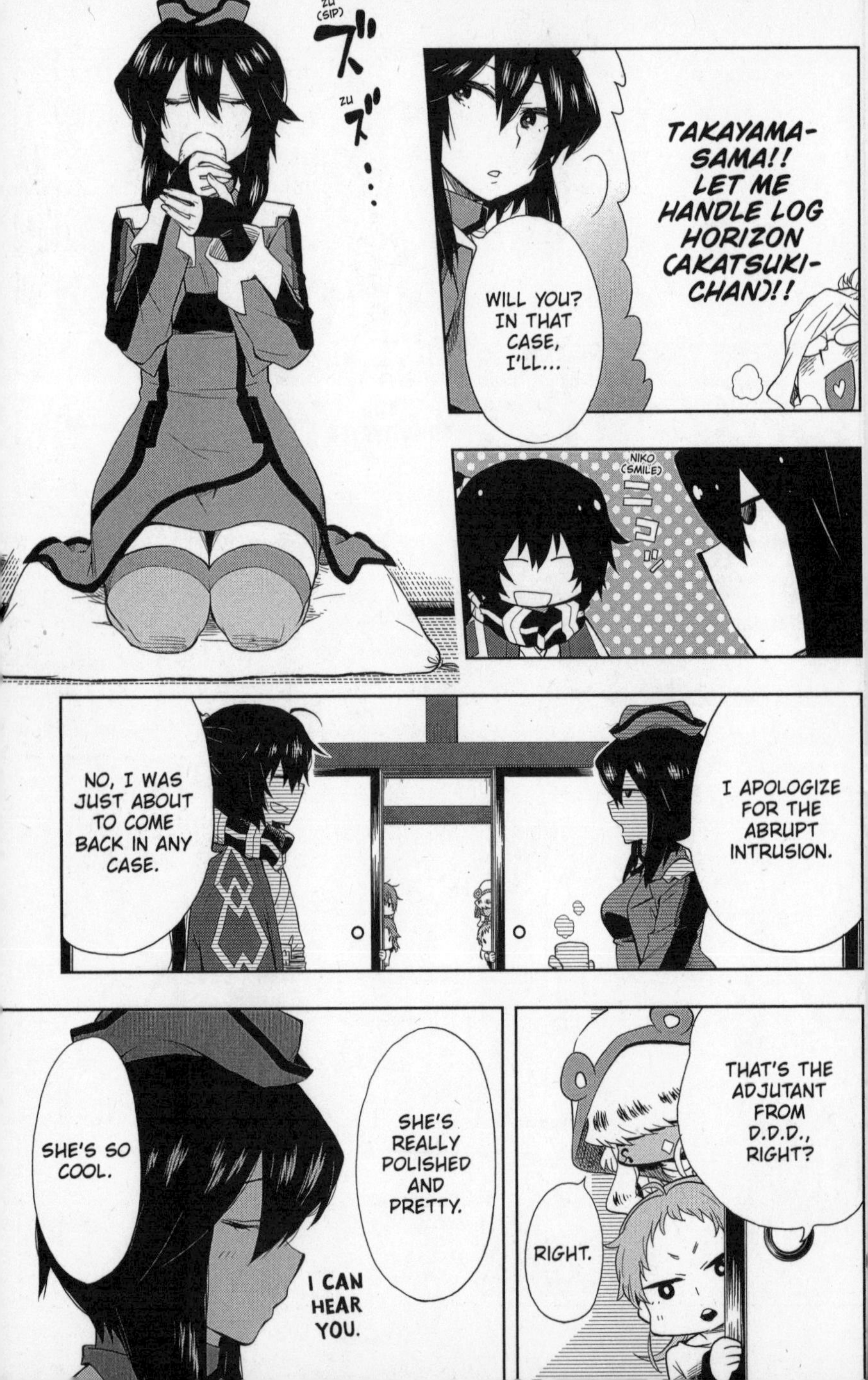
TAKAYAMA-SAMA!! LET ME HANDLE LOG HORIZON (AKATSUKI-CHAN)!!
WILL YOU? IN THAT CASE, I'LL...
NIKO (SMILE)
ZU (SIP)
ZU
I APOLOGIZE FOR THE ABRUPT INTRUSION.
NO, I WAS JUST ABOUT TO COME BACK IN ANY CASE.
THAT'S THE ADJUTANT FROM D.D.D., RIGHT?
RIGHT.
SHE'S REALLY POLISHED AND PRETTY.
SHE'S SO COOL.
I CAN HEAR YOU.

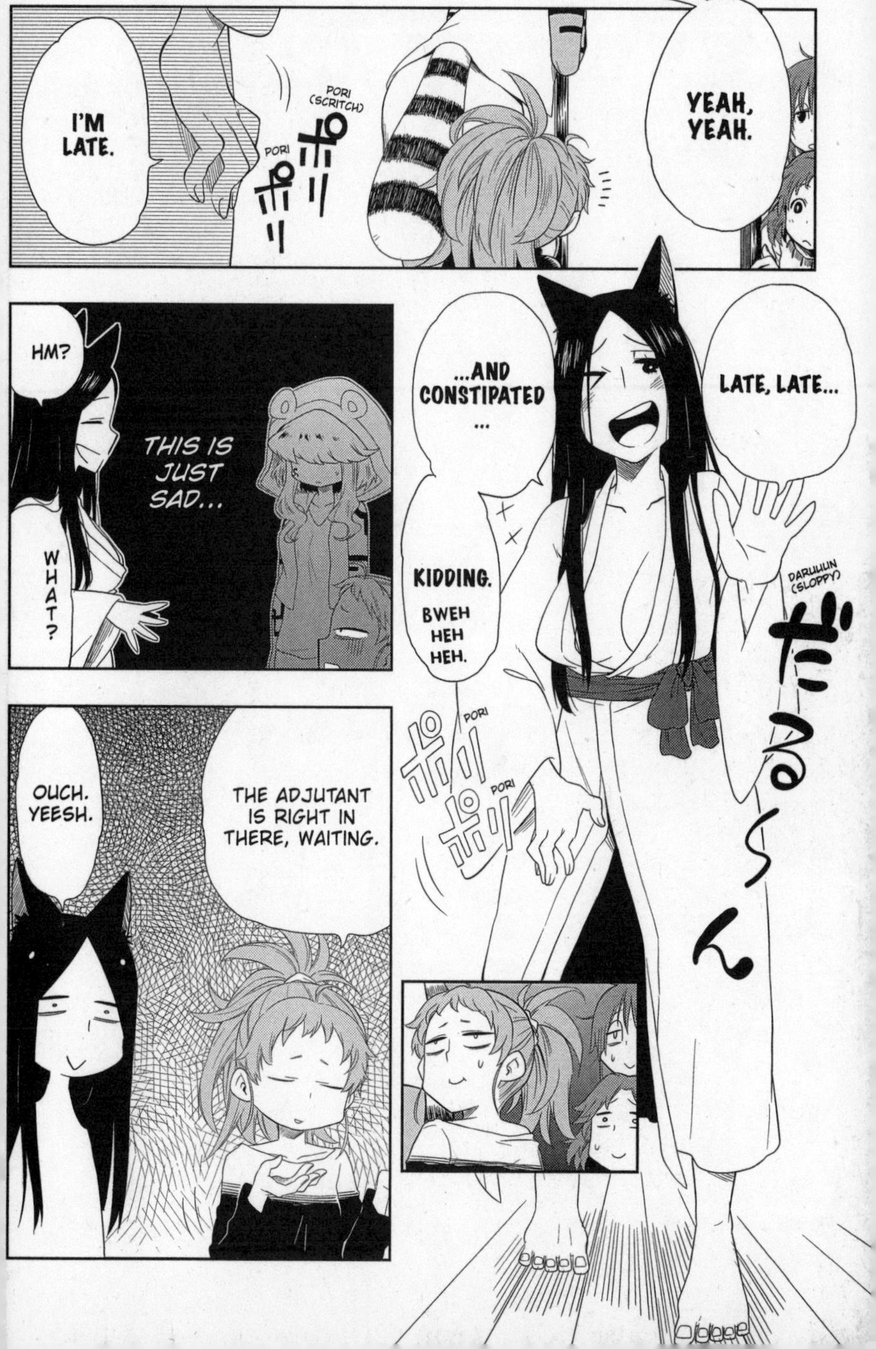
YEAH, YEAH.
PORI (SCRITCH)
ポリ
PORI
ポリ
I'M LATE.
LATE, LATE...
...AND CONSTIPATED ...
DARUUUN (SLOPPY)
だる〜ん
KIDDING.
BWEH HEH HEH.
PORI
ポリ
PORI
ポリ
HM?
THIS IS JUST SAD...
WHAT?
THE ADJUTANT IS RIGHT IN THERE, WAITING.
OUCH. YEESH.

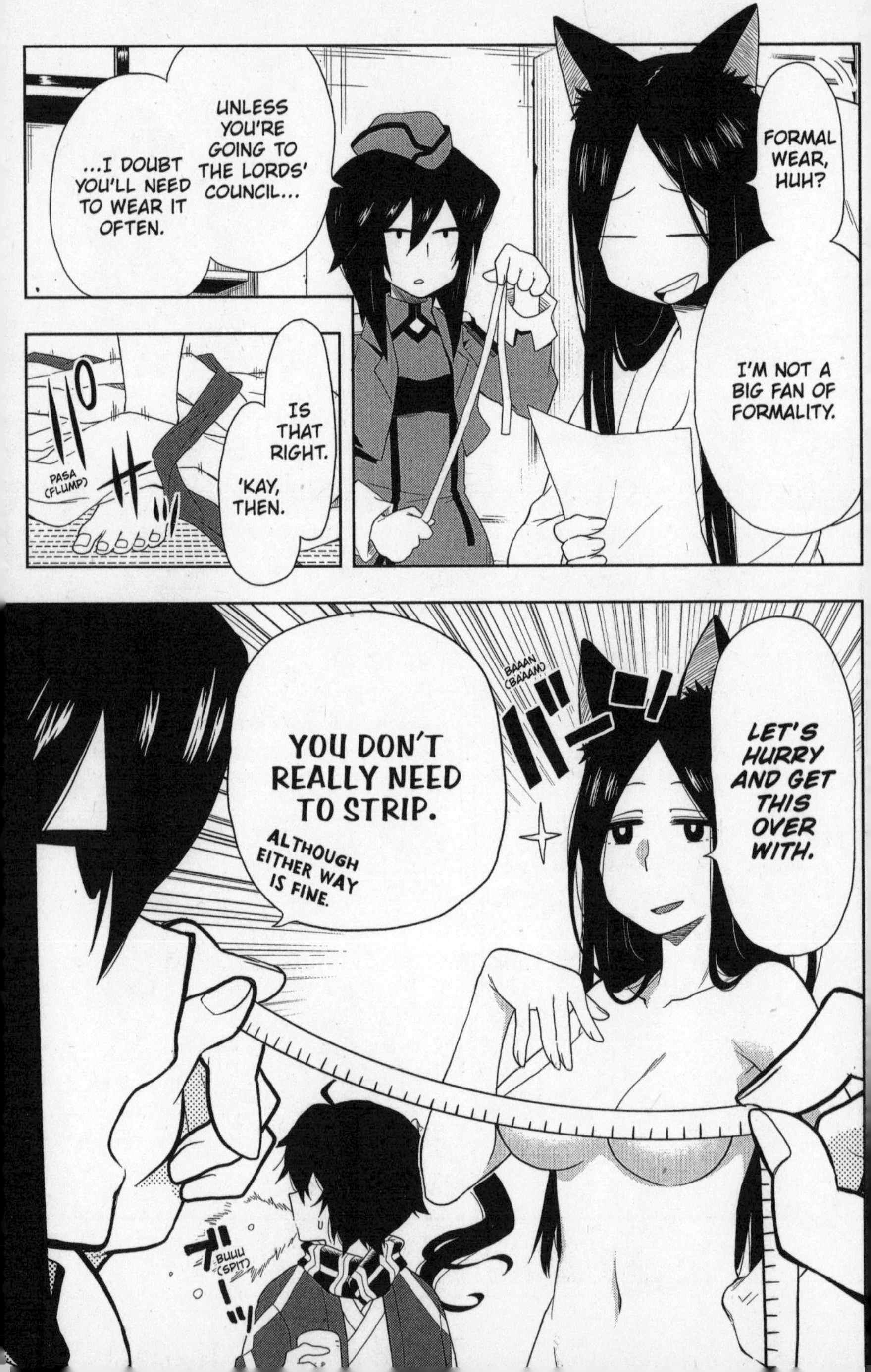
FORMAL WEAR, HUH?
I'M NOT A BIG FAN OF FORMALITY.
UNLESS YOU'RE GOING TO THE LORDS' COUNCIL...
...I DOUBT YOU'LL NEED TO WEAR IT OFTEN.
IS THAT RIGHT.
'KAY, THEN.
PASA (FLUMP)
LET'S HURRY AND GET THIS OVER WITH.
BAAAN (BAAAM)
YOU DON'T REALLY NEED TO STRIP.
ALTHOUGH EITHER WAY IS FINE.
BUUU (SPIT)

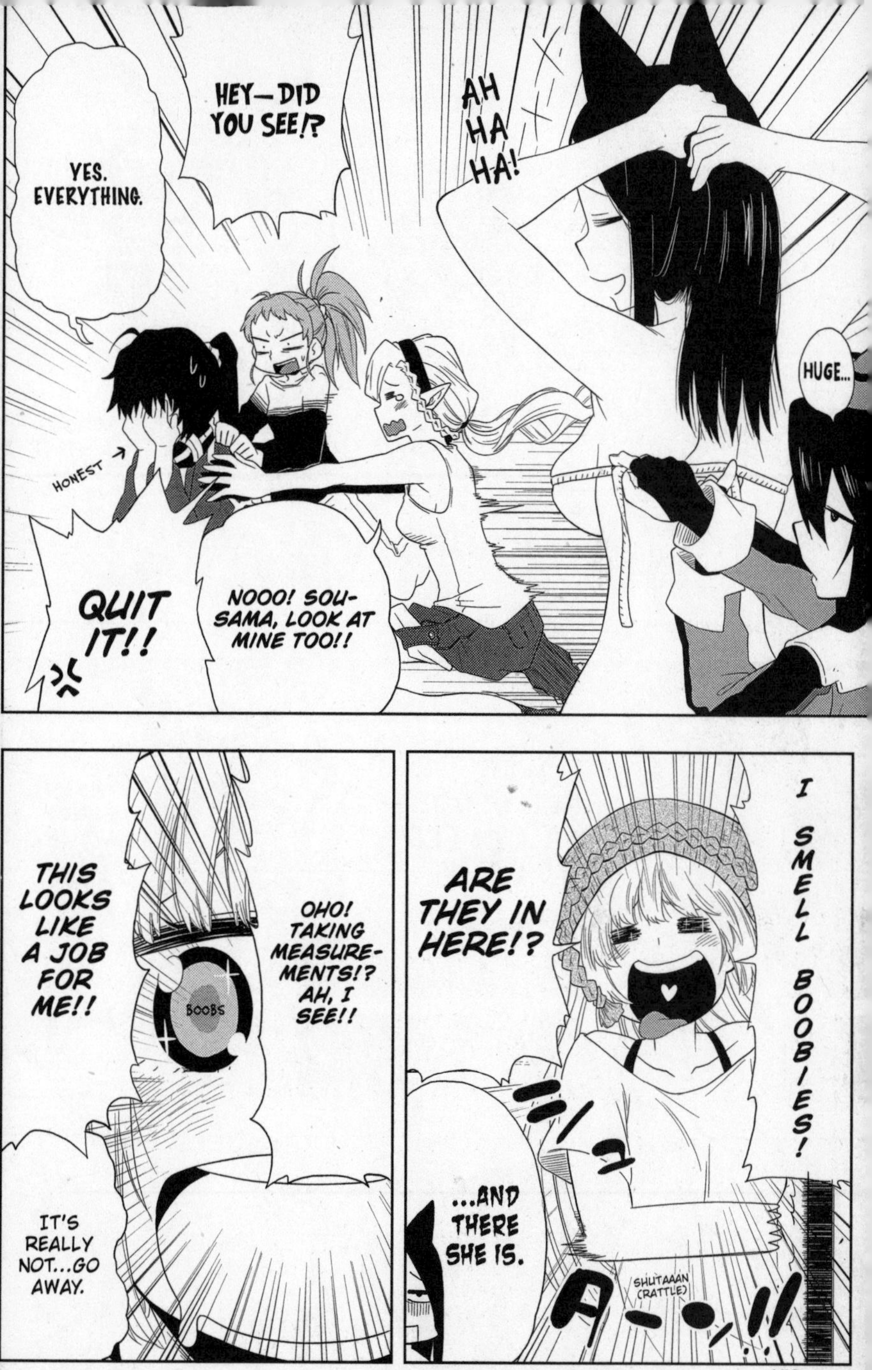
AH HA HA!
HEY—DID YOU SEE!?
YES. EVERYTHING.
HUGE...
HONEST
NOOO! SOU-SAMA, LOOK AT MINE TOO!!
QUIT IT!!
I SMELL BOOBIES!
ARE THEY IN HERE!?
SHUTAAAN (RATTLE)
...AND THERE SHE IS.
OHO! TAKING MEASUREMENTS!? AH, I SEE!!
THIS LOOKS LIKE A JOB FOR ME!!
BOOBS
IT'S REALLY NOT...GO AWAY.

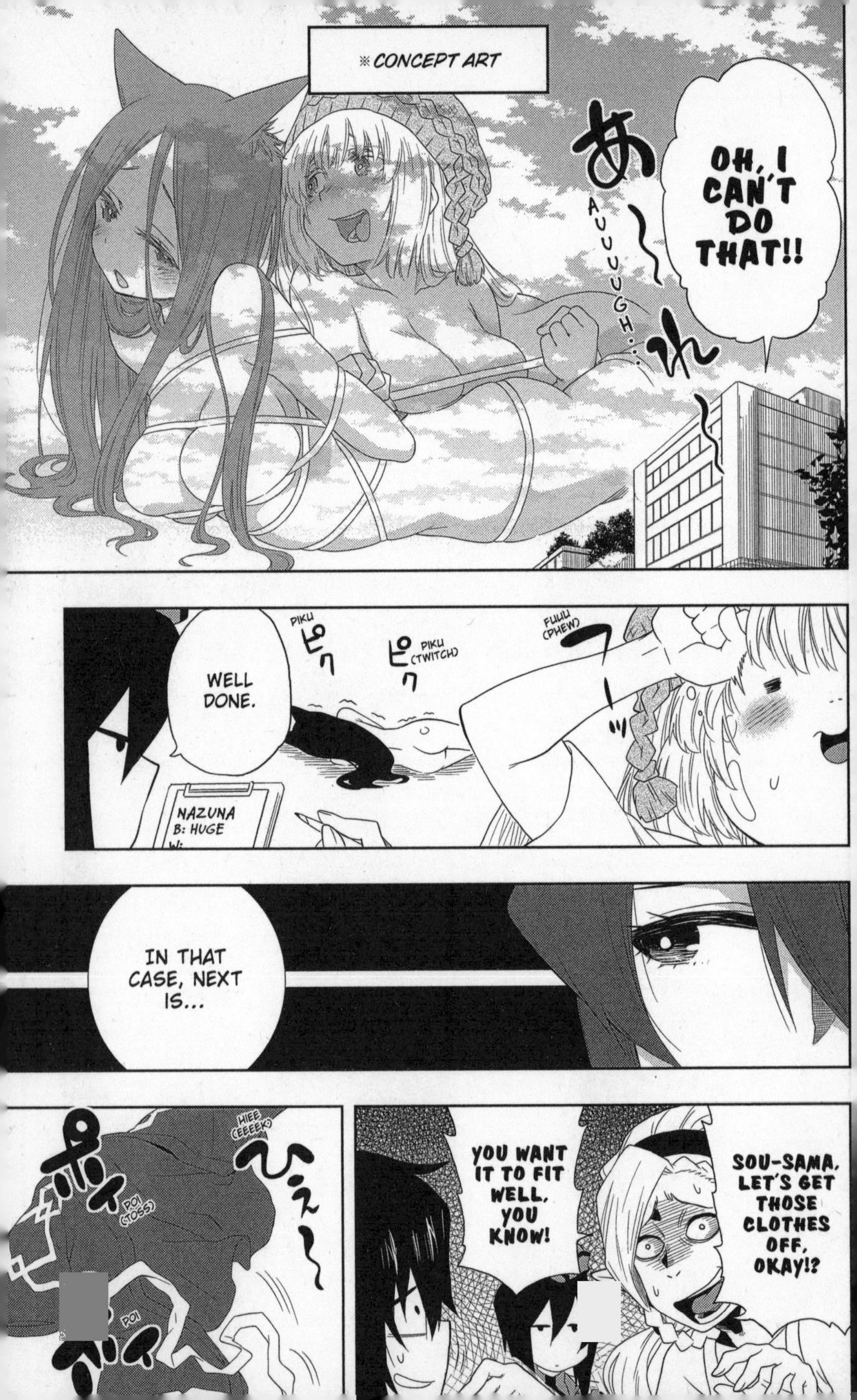
※CONCEPT ART
OH, I CAN'T DO THAT!!
あ～れ～
AUUUUUGH...
FUUU (PHEW)
フーッ
PIKU (TWITCH)
ピク
PIKU
ピク
WELL DONE.
NAZUNA
B: HUGE
W:
IN THAT CASE, NEXT IS...
SOU-SAMA, LET'S GET THOSE CLOTHES OFF, OKAY!?
YOU WANT IT TO FIT WELL, YOU KNOW!
HIEE (EEEEEK)
ひぇ～
POI (TOSS)
ポイ
POI
ポイ

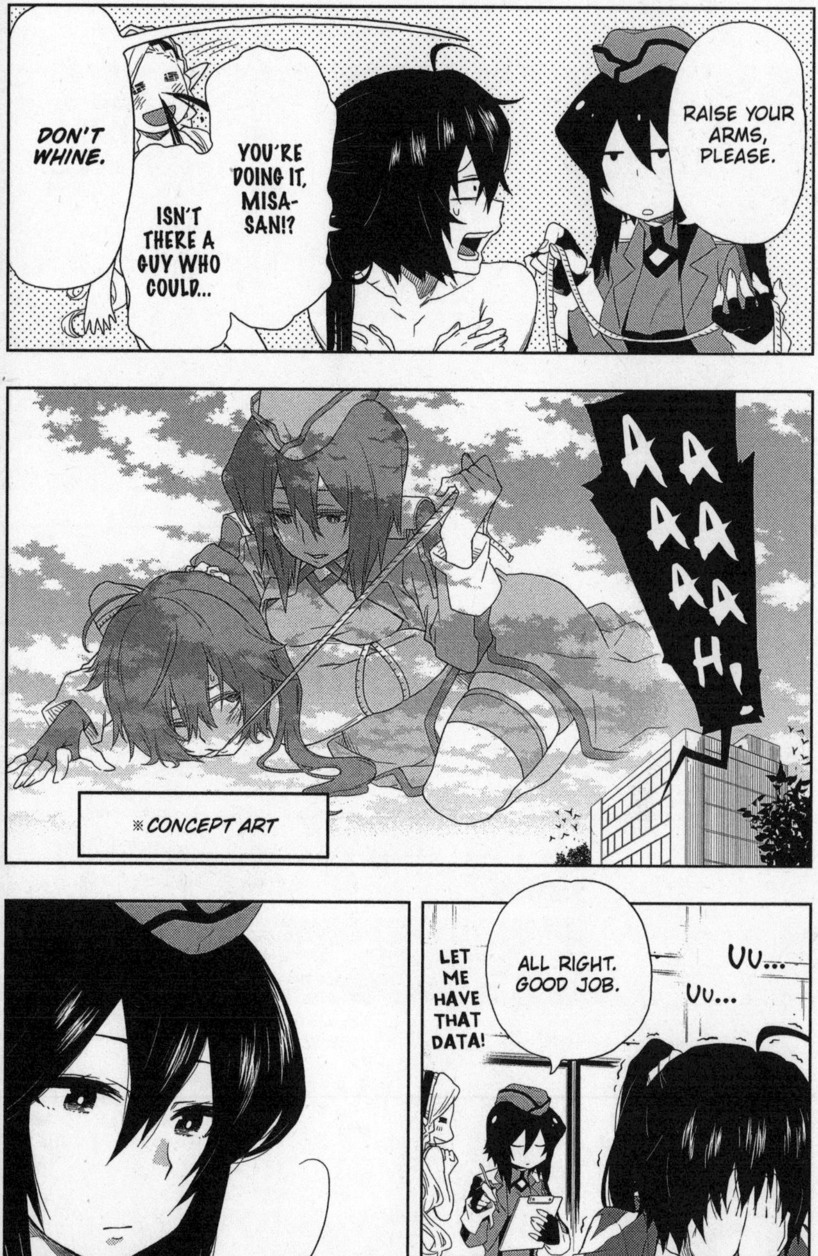
RAISE YOUR ARMS, PLEASE.
YOU'RE DOING IT, MISA-SAN!?
ISN'T THERE A GUY WHO COULD...
DON'T WHINE.
AAAAAAH!
※CONCEPT ART
UU... UU...
ALL RIGHT. GOOD JOB.
LET ME HAVE THAT DATA!

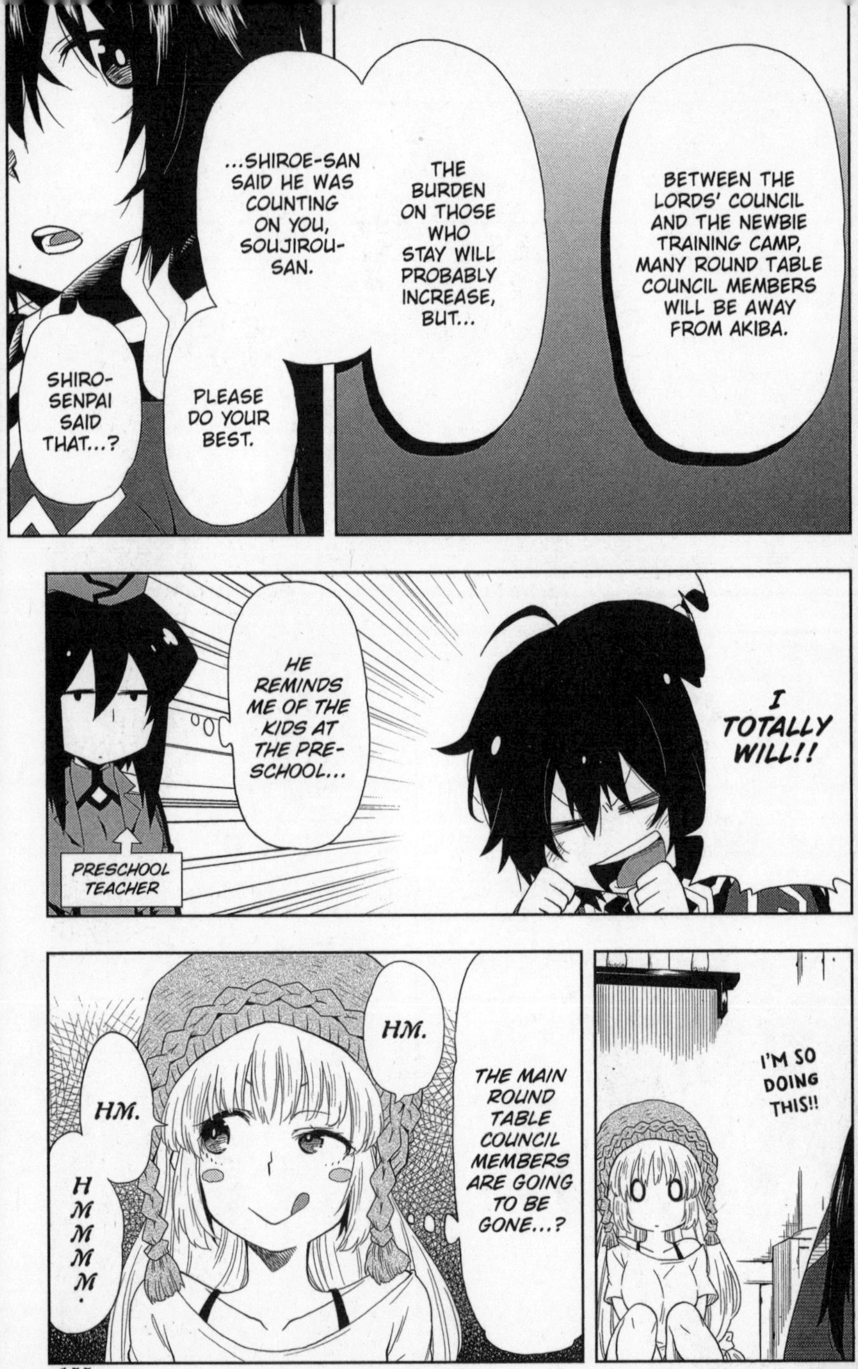
BETWEEN THE LORDS' COUNCIL AND THE NEWBIE TRAINING CAMP, MANY ROUND TABLE COUNCIL MEMBERS WILL BE AWAY FROM AKIBA.
THE BURDEN ON THOSE WHO STAY WILL PROBABLY INCREASE, BUT...
...SHIROE-SAN SAID HE WAS COUNTING ON YOU, SOUJIROU-SAN.
PLEASE DO YOUR BEST.
SHIRO-SENPAI SAID THAT...?
I TOTALLY WILL!!
HE REMINDS ME OF THE KIDS AT THE PRE-SCHOOL...
PRESCHOOL TEACHER
I'M SO DOING THIS!!
THE MAIN ROUND TABLE COUNCIL MEMBERS ARE GOING TO BE GONE...?
HM.
HM.
HMMMMM.

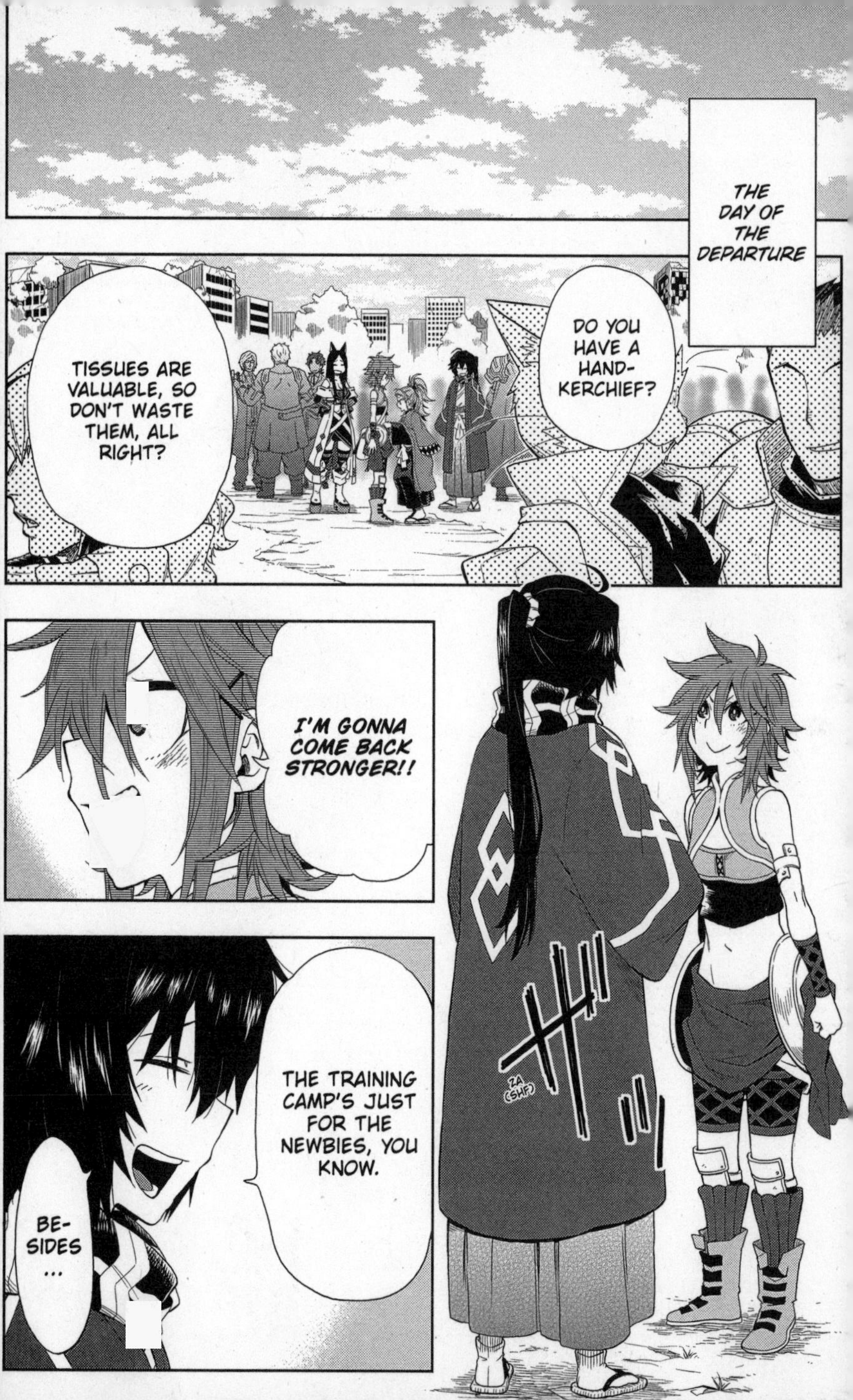
THE DAY OF THE DEPARTURE
DO YOU HAVE A HAND-KERCHIEF?
TISSUES ARE VALUABLE, SO DON'T WASTE THEM, ALL RIGHT?
ZA (SHF)
I'M GONNA COME BACK STRONGER!!
THE TRAINING CAMP'S JUST FOR THE NEWBIES, YOU KNOW.
BE-SIDES...

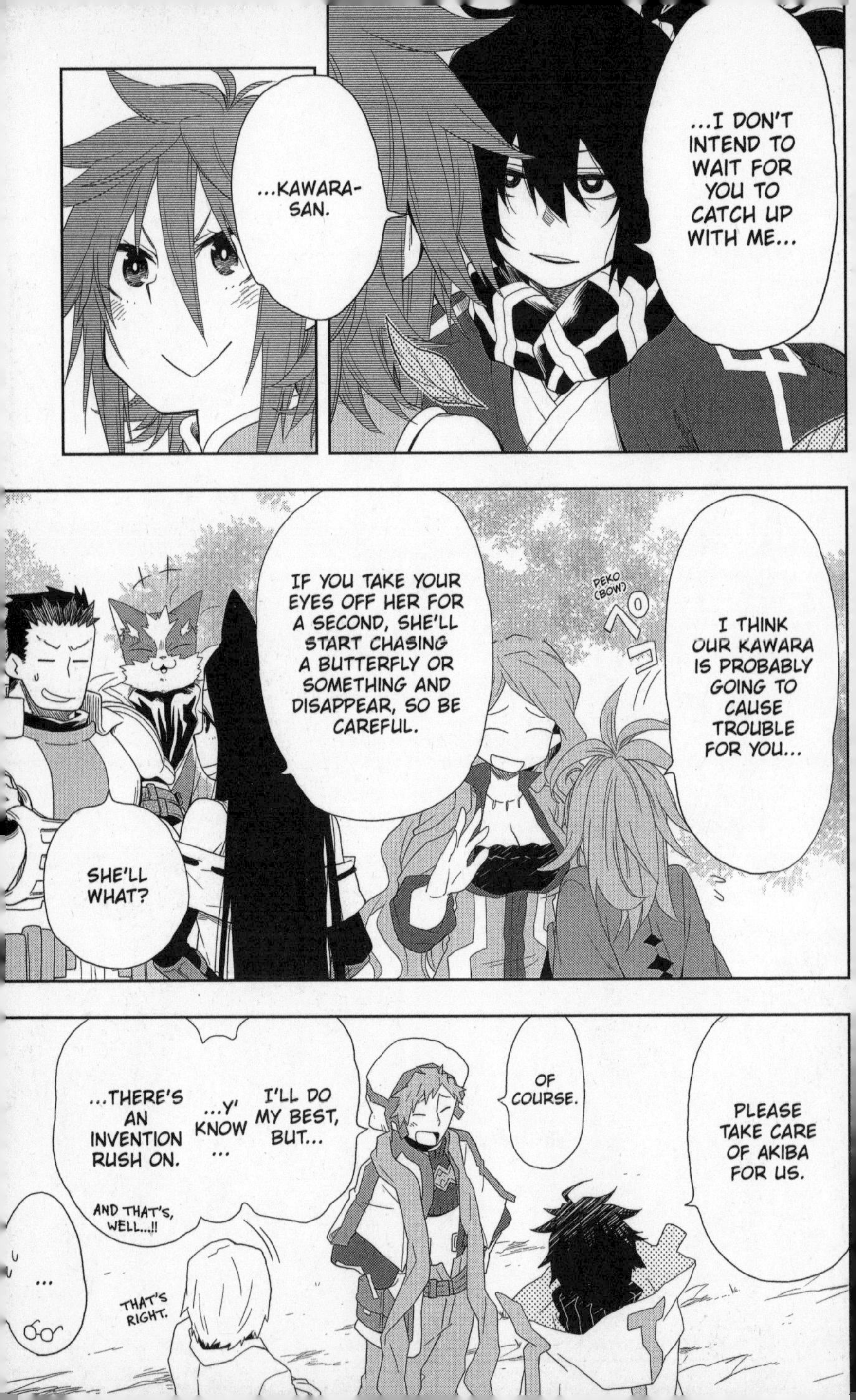
...I DON'T INTEND TO WAIT FOR YOU TO CATCH UP WITH ME...
...KAWARA-SAN.
I THINK OUR KAWARA IS PROBABLY GOING TO CAUSE TROUBLE FOR YOU...
PEKO (BOW)
IF YOU TAKE YOUR EYES OFF HER FOR A SECOND, SHE'LL START CHASING A BUTTERFLY OR SOMETHING AND DISAPPEAR, SO BE CAREFUL.
SHE'LL WHAT?
PLEASE TAKE CARE OF AKIBA FOR US.
OF COURSE.
I'LL DO MY BEST, BUT...
...Y' KNOW ...
...THERE'S AN INVENTION RUSH ON.
AND THAT'S, WELL...!!
THAT'S RIGHT.
...

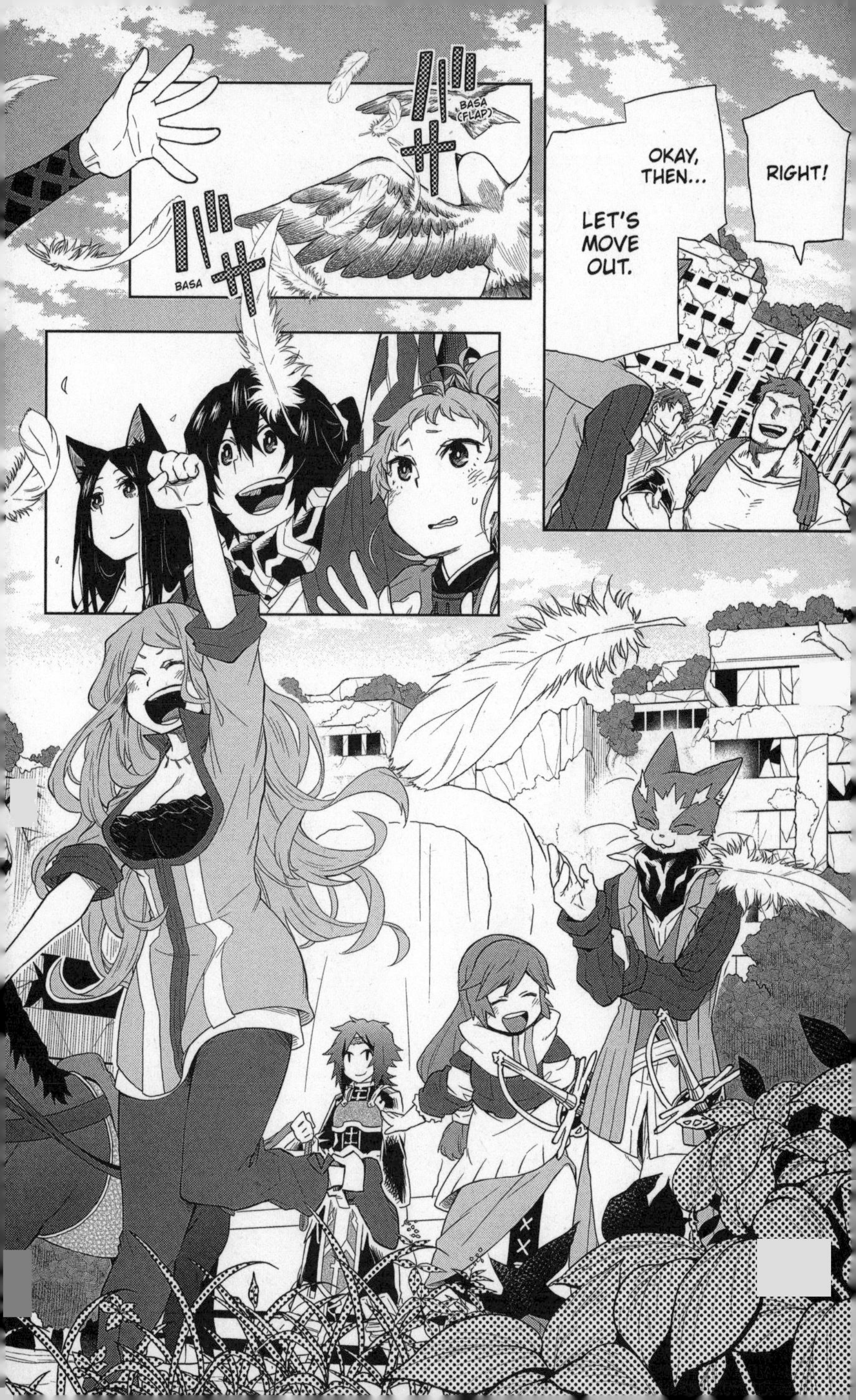
RIGHT!
OKAY, THEN...
LET'S MOVE OUT.
BASA (FLAP)
BASA

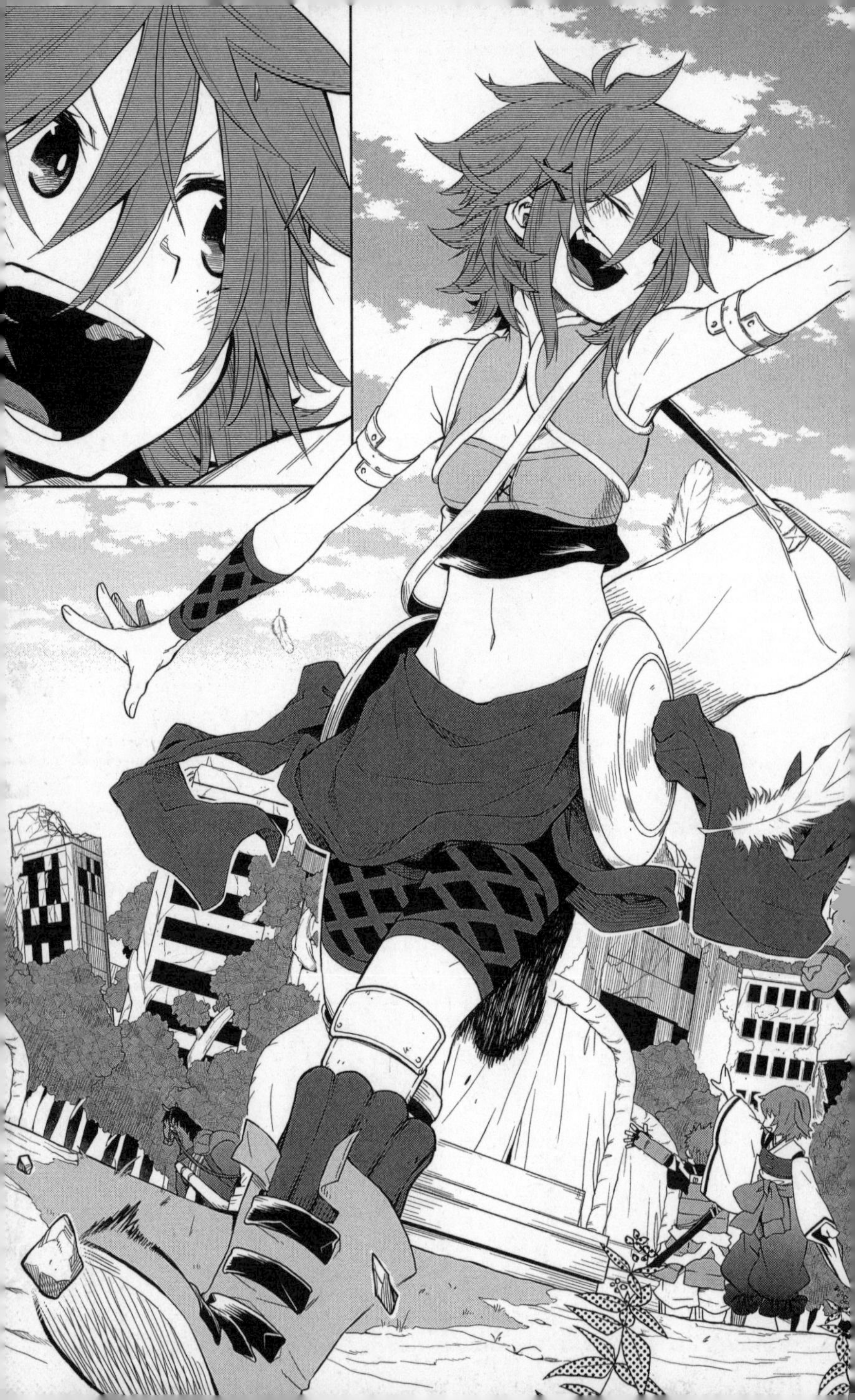

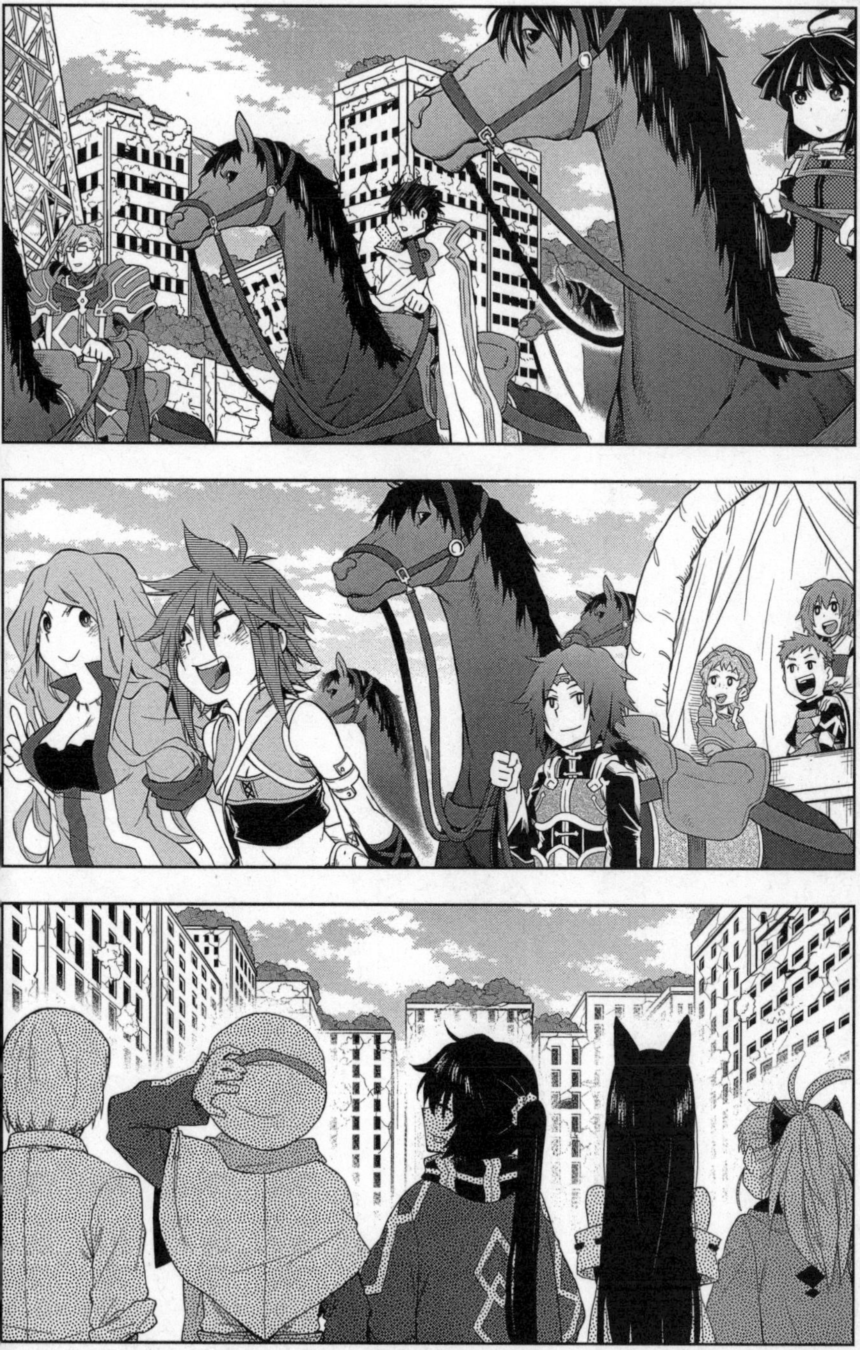

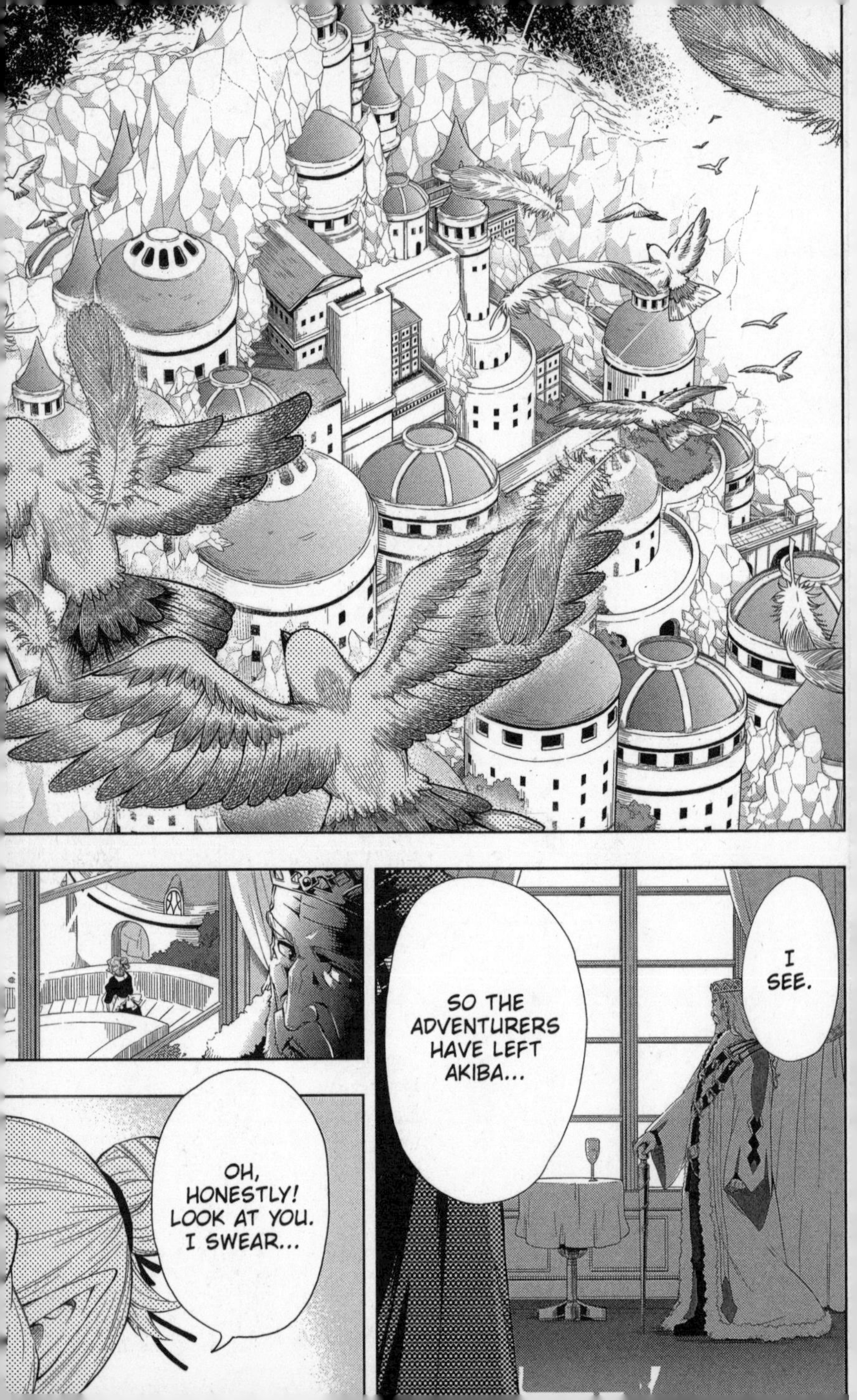
I SEE.
SO THE ADVENTURERS HAVE LEFT AKIBA...
OH, HONESTLY! LOOK AT YOU. I SWEAR...

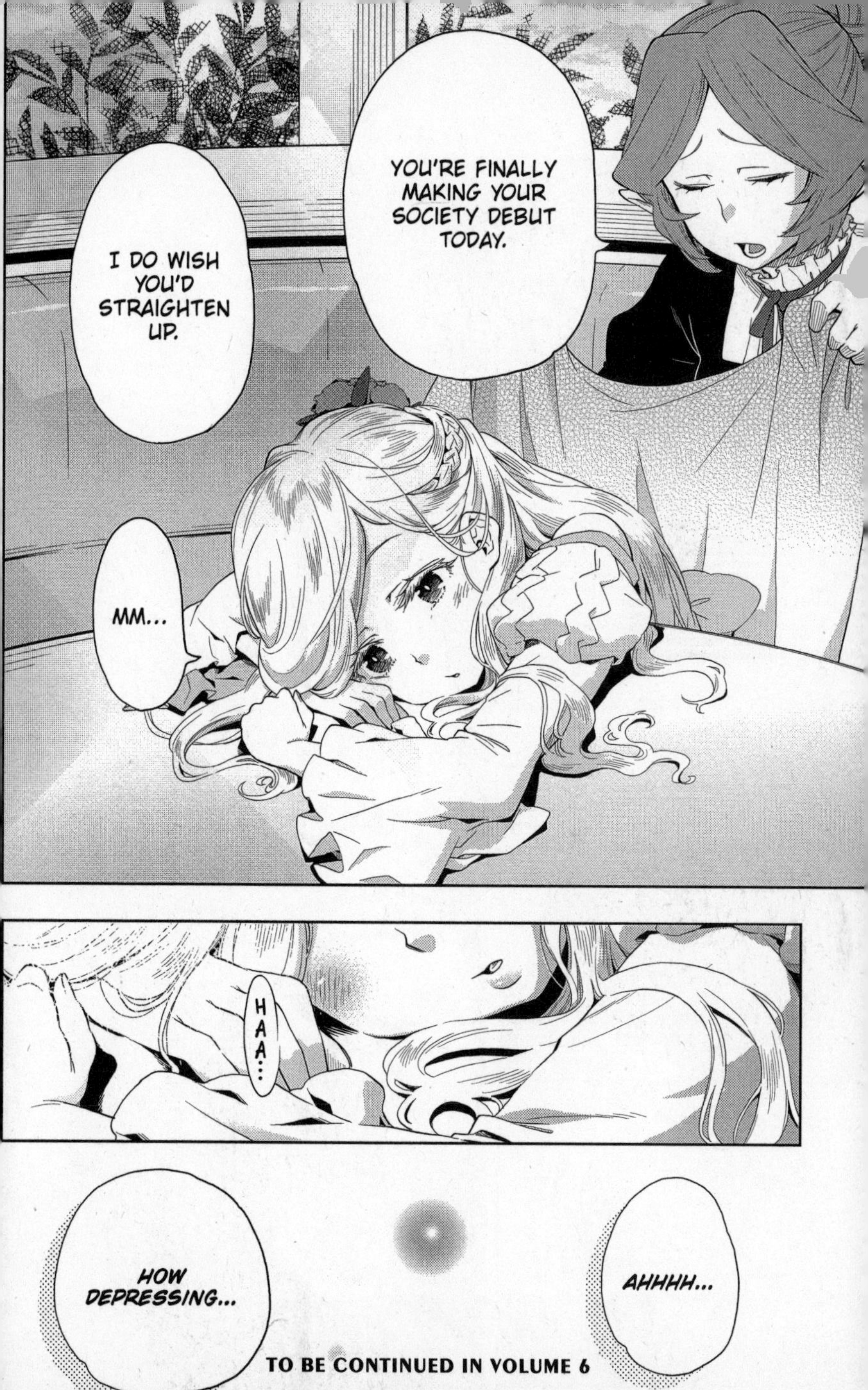
YOU'RE FINALLY MAKING YOUR SOCIETY DEBUT TODAY.
I DO WISH YOU'D STRAIGHTEN UP.
MM...
HAA...
AHHHH...
HOW DEPRESSING...

TO BE CONTINUED IN VOLUME 6

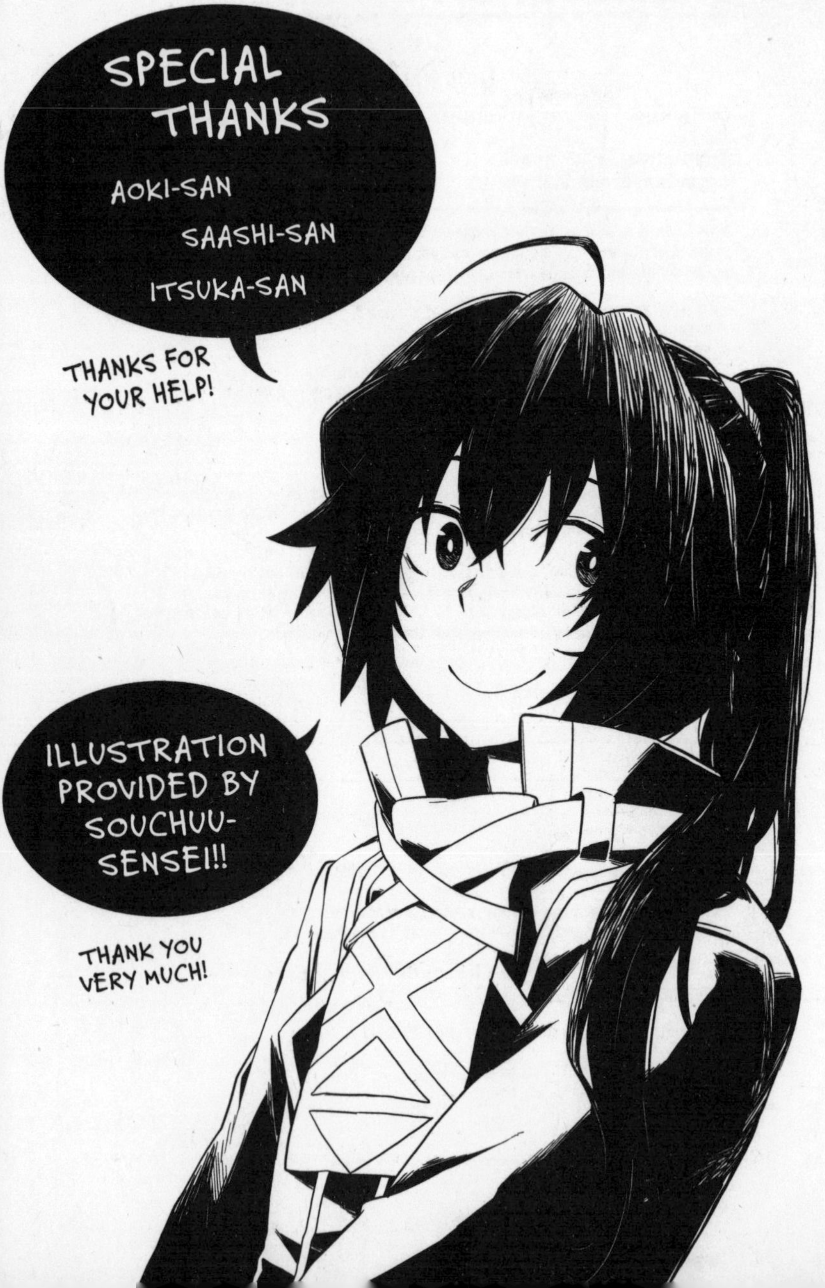
SPECIAL THANKS
AOKI-SAN
SAASHI-SAN
ITSUKA-SAN
THANKS FOR YOUR HELP!
ILLUSTRATION PROVIDED BY SOUCHUU-SENSEI!!
THANK YOU VERY MUCH!

LOG HORIZON
THE WEST WIND BRIGADE ❺

ART: KOYUKI
ORIGINAL STORY: MAMARE TOUNO
CHARACTER DESIGN: KAZUHIRO HARA

Translation: Taylor Engel
Lettering: Brndn Blakeslee

LOG HORIZON NISHIKAZE NO RYODAN volume 5
© KOYUKI 2015
© TOUNO MAMARE, KAZUHIRO HARA 2015
First published in Japan in 2015 by KADOKAWA CORPORATION, Tokyo.
English translation rights arranged with KADOKAWA CORPORATION,
Tokyo, through Tuttle-Mori Agency, Inc., Tokyo.

English translation © 2017 by Yen Press, LLC

Yen Press
1290 Avenue of the Americas
New York, NY 10104

Visit us at yenpress.com
facebook.com/yenpress
twitter.com/yenpress
yenpress.tumblr.com
instagram.com/yenpress

First Yen Press Edition: May 2017

Yen Press is an imprint of Yen Press, LLC.
The Yen Press name and logo are trademarks of Yen Press, LLC.

The publisher is not responsible for websites (or their content) that are not owned by the publisher.

Library of Congress Control Number: 2015952586

ISBNs: 978-0-316-55315-5 (paperback)
        978-0-316-47453-5 (ebook)

10 9 8 7 6 5 4 3 2 1

BVG

Printed in the United States of America